Handbook of
Nonverbal Assessment

Handbook of Nonverbal Assessment

Edited by

R. Steve McCallum

University of Tennessee
Knoxville, Tennessee

Kluwer Academic/Plenum Publishers
New York • Boston • Dordrecht • London • Moscow

Library of Congress Cataloging-in-Publication Data

Handbook of nonverbal assessment/edited by R. Steve McCallum.
   p.   cm.
   Includes bibliographical references and indexes.
   ISBN 0-306-47715-7
    1. Intelligence tests for preliterates.   I. McCallum, R. Steve.

BF432.5.I55H36 2003
153.9′324—dc21

2002043452

ISBN: 0-306-47715-7

©2003 Kluwer Academic / Plenum Publishers, New York
233 Spring Street, New York, New York 10013

http://www.wkap.nl

10 9 8 7 6 5 4 3 2 1

A C.I.P. record for this book is available from the Library of Congress

Permissions for books published in Europe: *permissions@wkap.nl*
Permissions for books published in the United States of America: *permissions@wkap.com*

Printed in the United States of America

Contributors

Achilles N. Bardos, Division of Professional Psychology, University of Northern Colorado, Greeley, Colorado 80633

Linda Brown, 1142 Limit Street, Leavenworth, Kansas 66048

Ruth A. Ervin, Department of Psychology, Western Michigan University, Kalamazoo, Michigan 49008

Craig L. Frisby, Department of Educational, School, and Counseling Psychology, Unviersity of Missouri, Columbia, Missouri 65211

Robin M. Lawhorn, Center for Cognitive Development, Department of Psychology, George Mason University, Fairfax, Virginia 22303

Susan J. Maller, Department of Educational Studies, Purdue University, West Lafayette, Indiana 47907

R. Steve McCallum, Department of Educational Psychology and Counseling, University of Tennessee, Knoxville, Tennessee 37996

Mary McLellan, Department of Educational Psychology, Northern Arizona University, Flagstaff, Arizona

Jack A. Naglieri, Department of Psychology, George Mason University, Fairfax, Virginia 22030

Leah Nellis, Educational and Counseling Psychology, College of Education, University of Kentucky, Lexington, Kentucky 40506

Nils Pearson, 403 W. 35th Street, Austin, Texas 78705

Jean Raven, 30 Great King Street, Edinburgh, Scotland EH3 6QH, United Kingdom

John Raven, 30 Great King Street, Edinburgh, Scotland EH3 6QH, United Kingdom

Gail Roid, Department of Psychology, Peabody College of Vanderbilt University, Nashville, Tennessee 37325

Christopher H. Skinner, Department of Educational Psychology and Counseling, University of Tennessee, Knoxville, Tennessee 37996

John D. Wasserman, Center for Cognitive Development, Department of Psychology, George Mason University, Fairfax, Virginia 22030

Bruce E. Wilhoit, Cherokee Health Systems, Talbott, Tennessee 37877

Preface

Psychologists, educators, and related health care professionals spend an enormous amount of time and energy evaluating the abilities of children and adults they serve. Assessment may be tailored to determine cognitive strengths and weaknesses, academic progress, the effects of central nervous system trauma, personality, and so on. For many children and adults, traditional verbally laden instruments cannot be used. For example, individuals who have speech and/or language deficits, hearing impairments, emotional problems, and those from other cultures, cannot be evaluated with tests that rely on standard English. Our culture is becoming increasingly diverse; as a result, schools and mental-health professionals are required to serve an increasingly large community of nontraditional learners. Because many of these individuals cannot be evaluated fairly by language-loaded tests, there is a need to use techniques and tools that are language free or can be adapted or modified to minimize the effect of language. For these individuals, language is a barrier to assessment rather than a vehicle. The primary goal for the contributors to the *Handbook of Nonverbal Assessment* is to describe the most current assessment strategies and related best practices to professionals who serve individuals from diverse cultures or those who have difficulty using the English language; such professionals include school psychologists, special educators, speech and hearing specialists, rehabilitation counselors, and so on. In general, the intent of this volume is to provide broad, yet detailed coverage of the most relevant information, including the psychological, sociological, and biological context for assessment, best practices in developing fair(er) tests, descriptions of the best and most commonly used individual and group tests of cognition, and strategies for nonverbal assessment of related constructs, including achievement, personality, and neuropsychological functioning.

The *Handbook of Nonverbal Assessment* is organized into three major parts. In Part I, the four chapters provide relevant context for nonverbal assessment. In Chapter 1, McCallum describes briefly the history of nonverbal assessment and the current need for it. In Chapter 2, Maller presents the best practices for detecting bias in nonverbal tests. In Chapter 3, McCallum discusses psychological, sociological, and biological influences on test behaviors. Finally, in Chapter 4, Wilhoit and McCallum provide guidelines for application of cross-battery approaches to nonverbal assessment. Part II (Chapters 5–11) includes descriptions of the best currently available nonverbal cognitive tests, characterized by the experts who know the tests best, their authors. They describe the model or philosophy used to guide development of each test, the test characteristics including administration and scoring procedures, psychmetric properties, and strengths and weaknesses; the instruments, described in order, include the Universal Nonverbal Intelligence Test (UNIT; Bracken & McCallum, 1998) in Chapter 5, the Leiter International Performance Scale (Roid & Miller, 1997) in Chapter 6, the Comprehensive-Test of Nonverbal Intelligence (C-TONI; Hammill, Pearson, & Wiederholt, 1996) in Chapter 7, the General Ability Measure for Adults (Naglieri & Bardos, 1997) in Chapter 8, the Naglieri Nonverbal Intelligence Test (Naglieri, 1996) in Chapter 9, the Test of Nonverbal Intelligence-III (TONI III; Brown, Sherbenou, & Johnsen, 1997) in Chapter 10, and the Raven's Progressive Matrices (Raven, Raven, & Court, 1998) in Chapter 11. In Part III, the chapters describe the nonverbal assessment of related abilities. In Chapter 12, Frisby describes nonverbal assessment of academic achievement with special populations. In Chapter 13, Skinner describes nonverbal assessment of functional behaviors; this chapter elaborates on the use of traditional and updated behavioral strategies adapted for nonverbal assessment. Wasserman describes nonverbal assessment of personality in Chapter 14 and nonverbal assessment of neurological functioning in Chapter 15. Both chapters focus on traditional and innovative strategies for nonverbal assessment. Several sections in these chapters focus on the use of nonverbal techniques for assessment in areas never before addressed.

R. STEVE MCCALLUM

Contents

PART II: SELECTED NONVERBAL TESTS
AND COGNITIVE STRATEGIES

I

Nonverbal Assessment

1

Context for Nonverbal Assessment of Intelligence and Related Abilities

R. Steve McCallum

Typically, verbal responses are assumed to provide a window on the intellect, personality, and related functioning of individuals. However, in some cases, verbal interactions are considered inappropriate as an index of cognitive and interpersonal sophistication. For example, some individuals cannot be assessed via verbal interactions (e.g., those with speech and language impairments and/or hearing deficits, culturally different backgrounds, neurological trauma, emotional problems such as selective mutism). For those individuals, language is a confound and nonverbal tests provide a more rigorous and less biased assessment.

Currently, the terms used to characterize nonverbal assessment are somewhat confusing (e.g., "nonverbal assessment," "nonverbal intellectual assessment," "nonverbal scales," and "nonverbal testing"). The term "nonverbal assessment" may be used to describe a test administration process in which no receptive or expressive language demands are placed on either the examinee or the examiner (Bracken & McCallum, 1998). However, some test manuals for extant "nonverbal tests" claim that the tests are administered in a nonverbal manner, even though these tests are administered using verbal directions. In fact, most "nonverbal tests" are best described as language-reduced instruments with verbal directions—sometimes with lengthy and complex verbal directions. For example,

R. Steve McCallum, Department of Educational Psychology and Counseling, University of Tennessee, Knoxville, Tennessee 37996.

Handbook of Nonverbal Assessment, edited by R. Steve McCallum. Kluwer Academic/Plenum Publishers, 2003.

consider, the *Wechsler Performance Scale*, the nonverbal scales of the *Kaufman Assessment Battery for Children* (K-ABC; Kaufman & Kaufman, 1983), and the *Differential Ability Scales* (DAS; Elliott, 1990)—all are presented with verbal directions. There are very few intelligence tests that are truly nonverbal. The *Test of Nonverbal Intelligence* (TONI-3; Brown, Sherbenou, & Johnsen, 1990, 1997), the *Comprehensive Test of Nonverbal Intelligence* (CTONI; Hammill, Pearson, & Wiederholt, 1996), and the *Universal Nonverbal Intelligence Test* (UNIT; Bracken & McCallum, 1998) are administered in a 100% nonverbal fashion. The *Leiter International Performance Test—Revised* (Leiter; Roid & Miller, 1997) is administered in a nonverbal manner, with the exception of a few subtests.

The term "nonverbal intellectual assessment" may be used to describe the process of assessing the construct of intelligence in a nonverbal fashion. Although other test authors use this term to describe the assessment of a construct called "nonverbal intelligence," "nonverbal reasoning," or "nonverbal abilities" (Brown, Sherbenou, & Johnsen, 2001, 1990, 1997; Hammill, Pearson, & Wiederholt, 1997; Naglieri, 1985a, 1985b), Bracken and McCallum (2001) suggest that the central construct assessed by most "nonverbal intelligence tests" is in fact general intelligence. This distinction in terminology is important because it has implications for how instruments are used with diverse populations. For example, if those intelligence tests that purportedly assess nonverbal intelligence (e.g., TONI-III, CTONI) do in fact assess a construct that is theoretically different from the construct assessed on traditional intelligence tests (i.e., general intelligence), then the inferences drawn from these tests may be different than the inferences drawn from tests purporting to assess general intelligence (e.g., inferences about eligibility for special educational services).

The use of the term "nonverbal assessment" is equally confusing as it relates to assessment of related constructs (e.g., personality, academic achievement). Not all examiners use the term in the same way. Practitioners should describe clearly the techniques and strategies employed in every case; that is, they should operationalize the term "nonverbal assessment" in their particular context so readers will understand and can replicate the assessment session if necessary.

BRIEF HISTORICAL CONTEXT

Jean Itard was among the first to assess the nonverbal cognitive (and related) abilities. He attempted to determine the capabilities of the so-called "Wild Boy of Aveyron," a feral youth discovered wandering in the countryside in the 1800s. He tried to determine whether the youth could acquire functional language skills and attempted to elicit both verbal and nonverbal responses (Carrey, 1995). By 1832, Itard had concluded that the boy could not produce meaningful speech; he was relegated to exploring the nonverbal domain. Similarly, other 18th-century clinicians pursued the problem of assessing the intellectual abilities of children who did not speak, such as Seguin (1907), who is known for the development of unique instrumentation to aid in nonverbal assessment of children's abilities. He developed a "form board" test, which required placement of common geometric shapes into inserts of the same shape; the Sequin Form Board has since been modified and has been adapted for use in many cultures.

Nonverbal assessment became especially important in the United States during the early part of the 20th century. During World War I, the armed forces needed methods to assess abilities of foreign born and illiterate military recruits. The Committee on the Psychological Examination of Recruits was formed to collect/design assessment strategies (Thorndike & Lohman, 1990). According to the Examiner's Guide for the Army Psychological Examination (Government Printing Office, 1918), military testing was used to classify soldiers according to mental ability, identify potential problem soldiers, identify potential officers, and discover soldiers with special talents. The Army Mental Tests included both the Alpha and Beta forms. The Group Examination Alpha (Army Alpha) was administered to recruits who could read and respond to the written English version of the scale; the Group Examination Beta portion of the Mental Tests (Army Beta) was developed as a nonverbal supplement to Army Alpha. In addition, the army also developed the Army Performance Scale Examination, an individually administered test to use for those who could not be tested effectively in group form using the Alpha and Beta tests. Together, the Army Performance Scale Examination and the Army Beta served an important need in a country with a diverse population. These instruments included a variety of performance tasks, many of which were to appear later on the David Wechsler Scales (e.g., puzzles, cube constructions, digit symbols, mazes, picture completions, picture arrangements).

Nonverbal assessment continued after the war. In 1924, Arthur developed the Arthur Point Scale of Performance Tests (Arthur, 1943, 1947). The Point Scale combined and modified a variety of existing performance tests, including a revision of the Knox Cube Test (Knox, 1914), Sequin Form Board, Arthur Stencil Design Test, Porteus Maze Test (Porteus, 1915), and an adaptation of the Healy Picture Completion Test (Healy, 1914, 1918, 1921) into a battery. This scale was made for examinees who were deaf or otherwise hard of hearing, and was designed by Arthur to provide a "multidimensional" IQ.

Development of these language reduced tests continued, and several were widely used when language was a confound (e.g., *Leiter International Performance Scale*; Leiter, 1929, 1948; *Columbia Mental Maturity Scale*; Burgemeister, Blum, & Lorge, 1972; Draw a Person; Goodenough, 1926). However, during the 1960s and 1970s, these tests eventually fell into disfavor because their norms, stimulus materials, or procedures became outdated. Consequently, many psychologists began to rely on tests with language-reduced "performance" tasks from standard batteries in an effort to provide fairer assessments (e.g., the Wechsler Performance Scale of the *Wechsler Intelligence Scale for Children* (WISC; Wechsler, 1949)) and its later editions. These became popular as "nonverbal" tests and were regularly used whenever children's hearing or language skills were considered a confound, even though each of the Wechsler Performance subtests has test directions that are heavily laden with wordy verbal instructions and basic language concepts (Bracken, 1986; Kaufman, 1990, 1994). Other "nonverbal measures" were being developed by those studying cognitive development during the 1950s, 1960s, and 1970s, but these measures did not become part of the mainstream intelligence testing movement (e.g., see the tests of conservation by Jean Piaget, 1963 and the processing tasks of Guilford, 1967). These measures are highly dependent on understanding naturally occurring phenomenon depicted via (nonverbal) abstractions, but they are difficult to administer and score in a standardized format, and most require at least some language.

By the early 1990s, psychologists began to provide updated alternatives to language-based tests to assess the intellectual ability of those with language difficulties. Consequently, several nonverbal intelligence tests were developed during the 1990s. Currently, practitioners have more and better nonverbal intelligence tests available than ever before (see McCallum, Bracken, & Wasserman, 2001).

Even though there are several good nonverbal intelligence tests currently available, nonverbal assessment of related areas such as academics, personality, and neuropsychological functioning is still in its infancy. Some behavioral strategies seem particularly well suited for nonverbal assessment. As Skinner and Ervin note in Chapter 13 of this volume, core functional assessment procedures do not require clients to produce verbal or written reports of their behavior, making functional behavioral assessment (FBA) readily adaptable for assessment of many nonverbal behaviors. FBA relies on direct application of basic principles from the behavioral learning literature (i.e., operant conditioning primarily) and aims to identify the current environmental contingencies that serves to maintain or reinforce behaviors of interest (e.g., hand-flapping, fighting). Once antecedent conditions, target behaviors, and consequent events that are contingent upon target behaviors have been specified, assessment and intervention follow naturally. Nonverbal behaviors are no more difficult to assess and track than verbal behaviors; both rely on tight operationalizations.

When more traditional assessment of nonverbal academic skills is needed, the task is more difficult, primarily because academic content in nearly all content areas is delivered orally or in writing, and students are expected to communicate in kind. Typically, individual or group administered tests are used, and in many cases, these tests are standardized. As Frisby notes in Chapter 12, nonverbal assessment of academic achievement appears to be an oxymoron, given these realities. However, he notes that nonverbal assessment of behaviors is possible using limited means of responding (e.g., pointing, gestures) or adaptive education practices first used for certain disabled populations (e.g., use of American Sign Language, augmentative and alternative communication devices, adapted computer access).

Traditionally, assessment of personality has relied on the use of pencil and paper, just like the assessment of academics, and nonverbal assessment of personality is just as difficult as nonverbal assessment of academic functioning, perhaps more so. Nonverbal assessment of academics has been perceived by certain educational personnel as very important (e.g., special educators); consequently, adaptive techniques have been developed for those with severe impairments, and such techniques can be adapted for nonverbal assessment in some cases. No similar technology exists for personality assessment. As Wasserman notes in Chapter 14, modification and adaptations are possible, however, and some assessment techniques already available can be implemented with little or no change. For example, human figure drawings may be completed without use of verbal directions, and they are sometimes used as measures of personality.

Unlike nonverbal assessment of personality, nonverbal assessment of neuropsychological functioning has a "history." That is, neuropsychological assessment has long relied on certain nonverbal strategies as part of an overall general assessment of verbal and nonverbal functioning. This tradition arises in part because of the need to assess functions assumed to controlled by different central nervous system localization sites, some of which are presumed to be primarily nonverbal (e.g., right hemisphere for most left-handed people, Wernicke's area of the left hemisphere, cite of receptive language skills). And research from the neuropsychological literature has identified a subset of learning difficulties sometimes referred to as "nonverbal learning disabilties" (see Rourke, 1995). In addition, certain "neurological" measures can be (and have been) adapted already for nonverbal assessment (e.g., mazes tasks, presumed to assess prefrontal lobe planning abilities). However, until now, there has been no single source that describes the state of the art/science of nonverbal neuropsychological assessment. In Chapter 15, Wasserman summarizes the current status of nonverbal assessment of neuropsychological functioning.

Sociopolitical Context

Assessment does not exist in isolation; it is embedded in a social context. In fact, assessment operates in the service of social goals, in the broad sense. As George Orwell (1946) humorously conveys in his classic book *Animal farm*, societies seem to select some traits to value over others, even in those cultures that espouse equality. Societies develop informal and formal methods to measure prized abilities, then to sort and reward them. For example, in most societies, intelligence, by whatever name, is highly valued; and in many societies, formal tests have been developed to quantify intelligence and to use these measures to predict and/or improve performance.

One of the early documented uses of formal ability tests occurred over 2,000 years ago in China, where test results were used to select civil service workers. The use of exams to select government employees communicates considerable information about that culture. For example, the practice suggests that jobs were given based on merit, rather than family connections, money or favors, birthright, etc. Apparently, the principles underlying a meritocracy prevailed, at least to some degree, and served to guide the social and cultural Zeitgeist; in turn, this thinking facilitated the development and use of the tests.

Of course, the qualities of intelligence, achievement, and personality valued by a particular society are variously defined within cultures (Dasen, 1984). For example, even though all cultures use a term like "intelligence," the operationalization varies considerably. In the Baoulé culture of Africa, Dasen found a term with roughly the same meaning as intelligence, *n'glouélê*, meaning the ability and motivation to complete activities, which enhance family and community life. Some of the descriptive terms and phrases used by Baoulé community members to illustrate the concept of n'glouélê include: responsibility, politeness, story telling ability, writing and drawing ability, academic ability, memory, obedience, and maturity. Dasen notes that the social skills are prized above the academic; in fact, academic skills are considered practically useless unless they are applied directly to improving the quality of community life. The correlations among Piagetian concrete operational tasks for the n'glouélê typically were very small or even negative. In this culture, intelligence is related closely to the ability to further social and cultural needs, and really cannot be considered in the abstract. So, the effects of culture on the way intelligence, achievement, and personality are conceptualized are significant.

The effects of culture may be subtle but may still impact the way members of society think about intelligence and the way experts measure the construct. For example, Valencia and Rankin (1985) discuss the difficulties inherent in developing equivalent forms of a test of intelligence in two relatively similar cultures. They administered the standard English version of the McCarthy Scales of Children's Abilities and a Spanish translation of that test to over 300 children; 142 were judged to be primarily English language dominant, and the standard English version was administered to them; 162 were judged to be Spanish language dominant, and they were administered the Spanish version. Using an item × group partial correlational analysis, 6 of 16 subtests showed some evidence of bias, as indicated by a significant partial correlation between language and subtest score. Twenty-three of 157 McCarthy items were biased; six were biased against the English-dominant children and 17 against the Spanish-dominant group. The six items showing bias against the English-dominant group came from a variety of subtests and did not appear to reflect a systematic bias. However, most of the items biased against the Spanish-dominant group came from subtests measuring verbal and numerical memory. The authors claim that the biasing effect can be attributed to language differences.

Valencia and Rankin (1985) identified two effects they referred to as "word length effect" and "acoustic similarity effect." That is, because Spanish words of the same meaning are often longer (word-length effect) and because Spanish contains fewer vowel sounds (Spanish, 5 and English, 11), similar sounding words are subject to greater misunderstanding (by the Spanish-dominant children), placing the Spanish-speaking children at a disadvantage.

Language differences can be powerful across cultures, even though the cultures may be similar in many ways. Thus, assessment of individuals in one culture with a language-loaded test developed in another culture and in another language, even when the test has been translated by experts, is a questionable practice. Experts suggest that tests developed in one culture are not typically useful in another unless massive changes are made, including adding items designed specifically for the target culture and restandardization in the target culture.

Of interest, McCallum, Bracken, and Wasserman (2001) describe a relatively efficient procedure to adapt/adopt a nonverbal test designed in one culture for use in another. This procedure requires collection of data in the target population from a small representative sample (e.g., 200 cases) and using those cases in a statistical weighting process to link with the original standardization sample. Such a procedure is more defensible for adaptation of a nonverbal test but even then is not without its problems.

Assessment, educational, rehabilitation, and psychotherapeutic goals are determined in part by broad societal goals and by cultural consensus regarding the importance of education and mental-health treatment. In some societies, the educationally disadvantaged are not prioritized; in this country, the bulk of special education money is spent on children who have educational and cognitive limitations, rather than on improving the opportunities of the brightest portion of the population. Additionally, during the last quarter of the 20th century, considerable attention focused on providing optimal instructional opportunities for culturally or racially different children with learning problems and mental retardation. Of course, these children are identified primarily by using intelligence tests; the use of tests for this purpose has been the subject of considerable litigation.

Social (Re)Action to Assessment

In the United States, the influence of increasingly larger minority populations is growing; consequently, there is heightened sensitivity about the use of ability tests (e.g., intelligence and achievement tests) designed primarily for the majority culture to evaluate ethnic minority children. Back in 1988, Sattler identified ethnic minority children as those who belong to a recognized ethnic group and whose values, customs, patterns of thought, and/or language are significantly different from those of the majority of the society in which they live. In this country, such ethnic groups include African Americans, Mexican Americans, American Indians, Puerto Ricans, Asian Americans, and many others. Using this definition, the United States is very diverse indeed. The diversity is apparent in the four largest school systems in the nations. It has been reported that more than 200 languages are spoken by the children who attend the Chicago City Schools (Pasko, 1994). Statistics from other areas of the United States are just as informative. More than 140 languages are spoken across the state of California (Puente, 1998; Unz, 1997), 67 by the students in the Tempe, Arizona school system (Ulik, 1997), more than 60 in the schools of Plano, Texas (Power, 1996), more than 80 in Palm Beach County Schools (Fast Fact, 1996), 54 in Broward County (Florida) schools (Donzelli, 1996), 50 in Prince William County, Maryland schools

(O'Hanlon, 1997), 45 in Cobb County, Georgia (Stepp, 1997), and 61 in Knox County, Tennessee (S. Forrester, personal communication, March 13, 2000).

Sattler suggests that health-service providers adopt a multifactor, pluralistic approach, to appreciate cultural values and coping patterns, and to guard against inappropriate generalizations when working with minority-group children. He notes that the issues involved in the assessment of ethnic-minority children are complex, partly because they are part and parcel of the greater woes and injustices of society. Experts have criticized the use of tests for minority children; others have argued that such tests are necessary to prevent injustices which may occur when other less objective methods are used to make educational decisions, particularly placement decisions. In some cases, identification of minority children for special education increases when only teacher recommendations are used, as opposed to traditional assessment measures. The use (and misuse) of intelligence tests for ethnic minority children has become an intensely debated topic in recent years. Obviously, if use of such instruments is detrimental, they must be improved.

For years, proponents of discontinuing the use of intelligence tests claim that the tests have a cultural bias against ethnic-minority-group children—that the national norms are inappropriate for minority children; that minority children are handicapped in test-taking skills because they fail to appreciate the achievement aspects of the test situation, lack motivation, and have limited exposure to the culture of the test builders; that most examiners are white, which tends to depress the scores of minority children; and that test results lead to inferior educational opportunities. These and related complaints have been addressed in the courts, in the professional literature, and in the popular press. In particular, concern about the role of intelligence tests in identifying children in need of special education came under strong scrutiny when that practice resulted in overrepresentation of minority group children in special education classes in the early 1970s, primarily because minority-group children tended to earn lower overall IQs.

One of the first cases was brought in California—*Diana v. State Board of Education*, in 1970. Others followed (e.g., in 1979 *Larry P. v. Riles*; in 1980, *PACE v. Hannon*; in 1984, *Marshall v. Georgia*, etc.). The outcomes have varied from case to case, but the overall result has been to encourage test authors to develop better means to assess culturally different children. In addition, these cases have positively influenced statutory innovations, as included in the Education for All Handicapped Children Act (PL 94–142) and the Disabilities Education Act Amendment of 1995.

In summarizing the findings from case and statutory law, Gopaul-McNicol and Armour-Thomas (2001) and Padilla (2001) describe some of the guidelines and safeguards now provided to protect the rights of linguistically and culturally diverse students. In essence, these guidelines require that: students be assessed in their native language, whenever possible; tests evaluate what they were intended to evaluate; examiners be appropriately trained; tests results not be confounded by sensory, manual, or speaking impairments; special educational placement decisions be made by a team of professional educators and not on the basis of any single test; students be evaluated in all areas of suspected disability; special education students be reevaluated every 3 years; and initial evaluations (for special education eligibility) focus on instructionally relevant information in addition to information necessary to make an eligibility decision.

Further, Gopaul-McNicol and Thomas-Presswood (1998) describe some of the competencies that assessment psychologists should possess, including the ability to recognize the limits of their skills, training and expertise in working with culturally/linguistically diverse students, and willingness to ask for appropriate guidance and training when needed. In addition, psychologists must understand the technical and practical limits of the assessment instruments they use, particularly as those limitations relate to particular diverse groups. For example, if a student is bilingual or limited english proficient (LEP), the psychologist should be able to appreciate the culturally determined nonverbal messages of the student *and* interact in the dominant language of the student, or find someone who can. The psychologist is expected to document the cultural, sociological, and sociopolitical factors, which may impact on the assessment process. In fact, Prifitera, Weiss, and Saklofske (1998) note that the minority versus majority group differences typically cited (e.g., 7–15 IQ points) would be reduced drastically or disappear with a more refined match on socioeconomic status (SES) and related variables (e.g., use of household income, accounting for home environment, time parents spend with children, medical history). Finally, as discussed in the next section, the assessment of many culturally and linguistically diverse students may be enhanced by using nonverbal assessment instruments. Psychologists should be appropriately trained to use those instruments and should use instruments that have been developed to promote fair assessment using state-of-the-art techniques (see McCallum, 1999).

Some Promising Remedies

Overall, the results of litigation and social consciousness raising have been positive, that is, the assessment of diverse students is better informed and "fairer" than before the cases were brought. Also, clarifications in the assessment process have resulted. For example, it has become apparent that many of the problems associated with using major individualized intelligence tests have resulted from abuse of the tests, rather than psychometric flaws in the instruments themselves. Data have shown that most of the major individual intelligence tests are not systematically biased in a psychometric sense (see Reynolds, Lowe, & Saenz, 1999). But the tests are not without problems, and they often have been misapplied, overinterpreted, and misused. Because of the heightened sensitivity to the bias issue, most test authors now are careful to address this issue in the test development phase, which is an important change in the way publishers and authors do business. Also, as a result of court action and changes in the law (and the related consciousness raising), the number of students in classes for Educable Mentally Retarded (EMR) children has declined dramatically from the late 1960s. Many children who would have been labeled EMR in the late 1960s and before are now helped in regular classrooms or in classes for learning-disabled children. Another benefit is the emphasis on finding more sensitive means of evaluating minority and culturally different children (e.g., inclusion of adaptive behavior measures).

One of the first assessment strategies designed to promote fairer testing was the System of Multicultural Pluralistic Assessment (SOMPA; Mercer, 1976). This system took into account socioeconomic status and related cultural variables and made adjustments accordingly. The SOMPA produced an overall score, the Estimated Learning Potential (ELP). A somewhat similar system produces a projected IQ (PROIQ) and takes into account low SES levels and other environmental factors, as described by Thorndike and Hagen (1986); these factors are presumed to reduce IQ scores and may include a home language other than standard English, home values which do not appreciate academic success, and/or undereducated parents. The PROIQ was actually developed by Van Denberg (1986), who believed that the PROIQ could be used as a reasonable estimate of the IQ for a deprived child, given intensive long-term remediation, including upgrading the environment. The efficacy of using the SOMPA or the van den Berg technique has not been demonstrated in practice, and they are studied today primarily for historical purposes.

Another promising procedure designed to address the limitations associated with assessing deprived, low SES, LEP children with conventional individual intelligence tests includes the assessment paradigm favored by Feuerstein and colleagues, which has produced the Learning Potential Assessment Device (LPAD) and related instruments. The rationale for the development of the LPAD is based on the work of Vygotsky (1978), who believed strongly in the social influences of intellectual development. According to Vygotsky, children learn from interacting with competent models, particularly adults. As they mature and become more sophisticated from previous interactions, they become more intellectually sophisticated. The process is summarized by Vygotsky's notion of the zone of proximal development (ZPD). The ZPD is conceptualized by the difference between the child's current level of development, as determined by history and maturation, and the level of development possible when the child is aided by a competent model.

The ZPD has implications for teaching and seems conceptually similar to the notion of "readiness." Feuerstein, Rand, and Hoffman (1979) and others (e.g., Budoff, 1987; Lidz, 2001) have developed strategies to assess the ZPD and have conceptualized these strategies as a way of determining the malleability of intelligence via a test–teach–test model. The teaching phase relies on "mediated learning," implementation of effective strategies and prompts conveyed to the child by a competent model. Budoff's (1975) version of the paradigm requires the use of nonverbal intelligence test items. Presumably, these items are less influenced by cultural diversity (e.g., Kohs Block Design Test, Raven's Progressive Matrices). During the mediated learning (teaching) phase, the model provides problem-solving strategies (e.g., avoidance of impulsive responding, active planning, checking progress). These problem-solving strategies are applied to tasks similar to the pretest items. Finally, the pretest items are readministered, and the gain scores are determined. This gain score becomes an operationalization of the ZPD.

According to Braden (1984), results from this kind of dynamic assessment are often different from the results of traditional assessment strategies, and the interactions between examiner and examinee are more fluid. They also report that children who perform competently following dynamic assessment do better in other learning and social situations. In addition, dynamic assessment yields results, which are more directly relevant for educational interventions, are more growth oriented (as opposed to being categorical), and are more descriptive of the student's behavior. But these authors cite some of the problems associated with dynamic assessment also.

Because the test–teach–test paradigm is complicated and characterized by nonstandardized administration, and because the assessment and mediation is multifaceted, it is difficult to develop rigorous tests of the effectiveness of dynamic assessment. Owing to the complexity of the technique, Braden (1984) concludes that the LPAD requires extensive training and much social interaction. Consequently, the procedure may be difficult to implement for handicapped children or for the culturally different (e.g., new immigrants). Glutting and McDermott (1990) criticize the methodology of the LPAD and Budoff's techniques; they conclude that Budoff's technique identifies gainers, those making strong pre- to posttest gains, twice as often as do diagnostic techniques that control statistical artifacts better. Further, they conclude that gainer diagnoses are incorrect over 50% of the time. In summary, in spite of the promise of dynamic assessment techniques, much more research is needed to verify its long-term utility.

Of course, one very positive outcome of the consciousness raising produced by the litigation is the emphasis of development of psychometrically sound nonverbal tests of intelligence. Results of court cases made educators and psychologists more aware of the need to assess minority and culturally different children carefully, without bias, and made them more aware that good nonverbal tests of intelligence are rare. And the use of nonverbal tests has been mandated under certain circumstances. In a letter dated May 26, 1998, The director of special education for the state of Tennessee identified several "protected categories" of schoolchildren in Tennessee who need special assessment procedures if they did not qualify for services for gifted education using traditional procedures. Children from low SES homes and members of certain minority groups (e.g., African American, Mexican American) were included; school-system personnel were instructed to provide additional assessment, including nonverbal tests of intelligence, if these children scored above 110 on conventional language loaded tests such as the Wechsler scales but failed to earn scores high enough to qualify them. These requirements have been modified and elaborated to include even broader criteria using rating scales and performance measures. Similarly, state-department criteria in other states encourage the use of nontraditional measures. In some states, such as Tennessee and more recently Alabama, the Office of Civil Rights (OCR) noted nonrepresentative placement of minority students in certain special education programs and, through policy statements and legal action, have encouraged the use of broader criteria and the use of nontraditional measures, including nonverbal measures of intelligence. In Alabama, the OCR discovered underrepresentation of African American students in classes for gifted education and overrepresentation of African American students in classes for learning-disabled children. Educators in Alabama are working diligently to provide more comprehensive assessment, as documented in their detailed special education guidelines. One strategy requires increased use of nonverbal cognitive measures for children considered for special education when language is assumed to confound the assessment process.

According to Coleman, Scribner, Johnsen, and Evans (1993), tests that measure intelligence nonverbally should possess three essential characteristics. First, the test must not require the examinee to demonstrate another knowledge base (e.g., a particular language); second, the test must require complex reasoning; third, the test must require flexibility in the application of reasoning strategies. According to Coleman et al., many traditional measures of intelligence have relied too heavily on language for limited English-proficient children; they note that such students are best assessed using tests which are untimed, require no listening, speaking, reading or writing skills, and use a test–teach–test model of assessment. Many of the innovations designed to aid in the assessment of culturally different children also benefit assessment of deaf or hearing-impaired children (see Braden, 1984; Braden, Kostrubala, & Reed, 1994; Kamphaus, 2001). Jensen (1993) recommends the use of highly "g"-loaded nonverbal tests to assess those who are deaf or hard of hearing. Good nonverbal tests are only recently becoming available, and six of the best are described in Chapters 5 through 11 of this volume. Two of these, specifically the Leiter International Performance Scale-Revised (Leiter-R; Roid & Miller, 1997) and the Universal Nonverbal Intelligence Test (UNIT; Bracken & McCallum, 1998), are multidimensional batteries and rival the traditional verbal tests in complexity, sophistication, use of manipulatives, and ability to predict relevant real-world performance.

In lieu of using nonverbal tests solely to assess culturally different individuals, Gopaul-McNicol and Thomas-Presswood (1998) describe a comprehensive approach, one that takes into account some of the techniques mentioned above and could include nonverbal assessment as one component. They refer to their approach as "bio-ecological" and describe it in a four-tier system to include Psychometric Assessment, Psychometric Potential Assessment, Ecological Assessment, and Other Intelligences. Each tier is assumed to contribute 25% to an individual's overall intellectual functioning, and taken together, the four tiers address three interrelated and dynamic dimensions of intelligence: biological cognitive processes, culturally coded experiences, and cultural contexts.

Each of the four tiers is multifaceted. The Psychometric Assessment strategy allows the use of traditional standardized measures of intelligence. The Psychometric Potential Assessment measure consists of procedures to be used in conjunction with the psychometric measure; these procedures provide supplementary information and include Suspending Time (tabulation of scores without penalties associated with speeded performance), Contextualizing Vocabulary (allowing the examinee to define words by using them in sentences), Paper and Pencil (e.g., allowing examinees to use pencil and paper for WISC-III Arithmetic problems), and Test–Teach–Retest (allowing the examinee who is unfamiliar with certain tasks such as WISC-III puzzles to be taught those tasks and then assessed). This procedure is similar to the dynamic assessment strategies described in the previous section. Finally, the examiner is instructed to answer relevant questions designed to determine how much the student gained.

Ecological Assessment consists of several components: Family/Community Support Assessment, and Observation Assessment in the three settings of School, Home, and Community to determine item equivalence. These components are based on Armour-Thomas and Gopaul-McNicol's attempts to assess context relevant content, as described in their Ecological Taxonomy of Intellectual Assessment (1997), and relies heavily on observation and questionnaires. The observations in cultural context allow examiners to substitute culture-relevant items for those items typically found on conventional IQ tests (e.g., rather than ask "In what ways are an apple and a banana alike?," a child from a tropical climate might be asked "In what ways are a mango and a banana alike?")

Other Intelligences assess four components including Musical intelligence, Bodily Kinesthetic intelligence, Interpersonal intelligence, and Intrapersonal intelligence. These intelligences have been described by Gardner (1993) and are not assessed well by conventional psychometric measures; they can be assessed in this model using interviews and observation. Many of the techniques described in this section (and particularly those from the four-tier model) are consistent with the suggestions provided by the American Psychological Association (APA, 1993) for examiners who work with culturally and linguistically diverse populations.

Like APA, the American Association of Colleges for Teacher Education (AACTE) endorses cultural pluralism in testing. For example, AACTE encourages teachers to consider the learning styles of their students (e.g., familiarity of immigrants with multiple-choice tests, computers, an independent versus cooperative work format). In addition, many of the educational achievement tests have been criticized, based on the lack of content validity (Shapiro, 1987). This may be particularly problematic for students from diverse backgrounds who are new to U.S. classrooms. Curriculum-based assessment may be helpful because it is tied to the student's curriculum, which should be made relevant by teachers. In turn, teachers can then make even more relevant instructional materials based on their assessment (Hargis, 1987). Additionally, consistent with the need to make assessment more relevant for all children, authentic or "real world" assessment techniques should be particularly helpful for diverse students. For example, teachers should include culturally relevant problems in their testing and the instructional goals. Finally, assessment of achievement should include personalized content for diverse students, who may feel marginalized already. Portfolios are particularly useful for this purpose and may include a picture of the student and examples of work over time (Wiggins, 1990).

IMPETUS FOR NONVERBAL ASSESSMENT

Several factors have contributed to the recent interest in developing and/or adapting technologies for nonverbal assessment. In addition to litigation and related governmental action, there is an increasing need for accountability in education, making assessment data necessary for documenting student progress. In addition, the advent of computers and computer technology makes testing adaptations more "user friendly"; that is, the adaptations are increasingly easier for clients to use and for educators and health professionals to adapt. For many students, assessment with heavily verbally laden tests is not optimal and may even be unethical. In some cases, language is not a window on the intellect, but a barrier, as is true for many minority students. The rapidly shifting world population and rapid influx of immigrants into communities of all sizes and all regions of the United States has produced multicultural, multilingual, multiethnic, and multiracial environments.

Although quality test translations are both possible and available for some, (e.g., Bracken, 1998; Bracken et al., 1990; Bracken & Fouad, 1987), test translations and subsequent norming and validation efforts are costly and time consuming for a single dominant language (e.g., Spanish), let alone 200 or more low-incidence languages. In addition, subtle dialect differences, even within the same language, present translation problems. And, given the relative lack of bilingual school psychologists, the primary alternative to testing children in their native languages is to remove language as a variable and employ nonverbal tests (Frisby, 1999).

DISTINCTION BETWEEN NONVERBAL UNIDIMENSIONAL AND MULTIDIMENSIONAL NONVERBAL TESTS

Of the various nonverbal tests, there are two basic types. There are nonverbal tests that assess a narrow aspect of constructs like intelligence, achievement, or personality through the use of one operationalization (e.g., use of progressive matrices for intelligence and reading for achievement); there are also comprehensive tests of intelligence that assess multiple facets of children's intelligence (e.g., memory, reasoning, attention) just as there are more comprehensive tests of achievement (e.g., reading, arithmetic, writing). The distinction between unidimensional and multidimensional testing is clear in the area of nonverbal assessment of intelligence. For example, there are a plethora of unidimensional progressive matrix tests available; however, there are only two comprehensive nonverbal tests of intelligence (i.e., the UNIT and the Leiter-R). Tests of the matrix solution type include the C-TONI, TONI-3, *Matrix Analogies Test* (MAT; Naglieri, 1985a, 1985b), *Naglieri Nonverbal Ability Test* (N-NAT; Naglieri, 1996), *General Ability Measure for Adults* (GAMA; Naglieri & Bardos, 1997), and Raven's Progressive Matrices (Raven, Raven, & Court, 1998). Given the more narrow focus of the matrix analogy type tests and the fact that many of these tests employ verbal directions, these instruments are best suited for "low stakes" screening applications or, in some cases, large-scale group assessments (i.e., NNAT). When psychoeducational assessments are conducted for "high stakes" placement, eligibility, or diagnostic decision-making reasons, broader, more comprehensive measures of intelligence are more appropriate (i.e., Leiter-R; UNIT).

In any areas of noncognitive assessment (e.g., achievement, personality), the distinction between unidimensional and multidimensional testing is less salient. For example, most tests of achievement, even screening tests, assess more than one facet of performance. Similarly, personality tests are typically multifaceted also, assessing various aspects (e.g., paranoia, inattentiveness, depression). Importantly, nonverbal assessment of achievement, personality, and neurological functioning is not nearly as well defined and developed as nonverbal assessment of intelligence. Thus, the content devoted to nonverbal assessment of achievement, personality, and neuropsychological functioning in the *Handbook of Nonverbal Assessment* represents seminal treatments of these topics.

SUMMARY

Chapter 1 provides context for nonverbal assessment of intelligence and related abilities. The goal is to present the rationale and brief history of nonverbal assessment along with the sociopolitical context, focusing particularly on the developments since the early 20th century. One of the strongest early initiatives for the development of nonverbal measures emerged because of the practical needs associated with illiterate personnel selection in wartime. Similar needs were being expressed in the private sector during the first half of the 20th century. In addition, psychologists and related health-care specialists began to demand more sophisticated measures of language impaired individuals, such as those with central nervous system trauma, psychiatric diagnoses, and so on. Nonverbal tests were developed to meet these needs. Most recently, two major types of nonverbal tests have been developed: unidimensional or "low stakes" tests and more comprehensive "high stakes" multidimensional tests. Importantly, the nonverbal assessment of intelligence is relatively sophisticated; the nonverbal assessment of related constructs is ill defined and/or in its infancy, depending on the particular ability in question. In fact, the content devoted to the nonverbal assessment of achievement, personality, and neurological functioning in the *Handbook of nonverbal assessment* represents the first systematic treatment of those areas.

In general, the assessment strategies mentioned in this chapter and discussed in detail in later chapters are very relevant for assessing individuals who have language-related limitations when expected to perform in mainstream English-speaking environments, that is, those who are often described as culturally and linguistically diverse. Even so, the most defensible assessment should be multifaceted and should consist of a nonverbal *and* a verbal component when possible. Of course, not all children are verbal, and in those cases, a nonverbal assessment is the only option.

REFERENCES

American Psychological Association (1993). Guidelines for providers of psychological services to ethnic, linguistic and culturally diverse populations. *American psychologist, 48,* 45–48.

Armour-Thomas, E., & Gopaul-McNicol, S. (1997). A bio-ecological approach to intellectual assessment. *Cultural diversity and mental health, 3*(2), 25–39.

Arthur, G. (1943). *A point scale of performance tests: Clinical manual.* New York: The Commonwealth Fund.

Arthur, G. (1947). *A point scale of performance tests: Clinical manual.* New York: The Commonwealth Fund.

Bracken, B. A. (1986). Incidence of basic concepts in the directions of five commonly used American tests of intelligence. *School Psychology International, 7,* 1–10.

Bracken, B. A. (1998). *Bracken basic concept scale: Spanish form.* San Antonio, TX: The Psychological Corporation.

Bracken, B. A., Barona, A., Bauermeister, J. J., Howell, K. K., Paggioli, L., & Puente, A. (1990). Multinational validation of the Spanish Bracken basic concept scale for cross-cultural assessments. *Journal of School Psychology, 28,* 325–341.

Bracken, B. A., & Fouad, N. (1987). Spanish translation and validation of the Bracken basic concept scale. *School Psychology Review, 16,* 94–102.

Bracken, B. A., & McCallum, R. S. (1998). *Universal nonverbal intelligence test.* Itasca, IL: Riverside.

Bracken, B. A., & McCallum, R. S. (2001). Assessing intelligence in a population that speaks more than two hundred languages: A nonverbal solution. In L. A. Suzuki, J. G. Ponterotto, & P. J. Meller (Eds.), *Handbook of multicultural assessment: clinical, psychological, and educational applications* (2nd ed., pp. 405–431). San Francisco: Jossey-Bass.

Braden, J. P. (1984). LPAD applications to deaf populations. In D. S. Martin (Ed.), *International symposium on cognition, education, and deafness: Working papers.* Washington, DC: Gallaudet College Press.

Braden, J. P., Kostrubala, C. E., & Reed, J. (1994). Why do deaf children score differently on performance vs. motor-reduced nonverbal intelligence tests? *Journal of psychoeducational assessment, 12*(4), 357–363.

Brown, L., Sherbenou, R. J., & Johnsen, S. K. (1990). *Test of nonverbal intelligence* (2nd ed.). Austin, TX: PRO-ED.

Brown, L., Sherbenou, R. J., & Johnsen, S. K. (1997). *Test of nonverbal intelligence* (3rd ed.). Austin, TX: PRO-ED.

Budoff, M. (1975). *Learning potential test using Raven Progressive Matrices.* Cambridge, MA: Research Institute for Educational Problems.

Budoff, M. (1987). Measures for assessing learning. In C. S. Lidz (Ed.), *Dynamic assessment: An interactive approach to evaluation of learning potential* (pp. 173–195). New York: Guilford Press.

Burgemeister, B. B., Blum, L. H., & Lorge, I. (1972). *Columbia mental maturity scale* (3rd ed.). San Antonio, TX: The Psychological Corporation.

Carrey, N. J. (1995). Itard's 1828 memoire on 'mutism caused by a lesion of the intellectual functions': A historical analysis. *Journal of the American Academy of Child and Adolescent Psychiatry, 341,* 655–661.

Coleman, M., Scribner, A. P., Johnsen, S., & Evans, M. (1993). A comparison between the Wechsler Intelligence Scale for Adults – Revised and the Test of Nonverbal Intelligence – 2 with Mexican American secondary students. *Journal of psychoeducational assessment, 11*(3), 250–258.

Dasen, P. R. (1984). The cross-cultural study of intelligence – Piaget and the Baoule. *International journal of psychology, 19*(4–5), 407–434.

Diana v. State Board of Education (1970). Clearing House Review, 3(10).

Donzelli, J. (1996, September 11). How do you say "milk" in 54 different ways? *Sun sentinel* (Fort Lauderdale) (p. 11). East Broward Edition, Community Closeup section.

Elliot, C. D. (1990). *Differential ability scales: Administration and scoring manual.* San Antonio, TX: The Psychological Corporation.

Fast Fact (1996, December 5). *Sun sentinel* (Fort Lauderdale) (p. 1B). Palm Beach Edition, Local section.

Feuerstein, R., Rand, Y., & Hoffman, M. (1979). *Dynamic assessment of retarded performers: The learning potential assessment device, theory, instruments, and techniques.* Baltimore: University Park Press.

Forester, S. (2000, March 13). *Personal communication.*

Frisby, C. L. (1999). Straight talk about cognitive assessment and diversity. *School Psychology Quarterly, 14,* 195–207.

Gardner, H. (1993). *Multiple intelligences: The theory in practice.* New York: Basic Books.

Glutting, J. J., & McDermott, P. A. (1990). Principles and problems in learning potentials. In C. R. Reynolds & R. W. Kamphaus (Eds.), *Handbook of psychological and educational assessment of children's intelligence and achievement* (pp. 296–347). New York: Guilford.

Goodenough, F. L. (1926). *Measurement of intelligence by drawings.* New York: World Book.

Gopaul-McNicol, S., & Armour-Thomas, E. (2002). *Assessment and culture: Psychological tests with minority populations.* San Diego, CA: Academic Press.

Gopaul-McNicol, S. & Thomas-Presswood, T. (1998). *Working with linguistic and culturally different children: Innovative educational and clinical approaches.* Boston, MA: Allyn & Bacon

Government Printing Office (1918). *Examiners' guide for psychological examining in the army.* Washington, DC: Author.

Guilford, J. P. (1967). *The nature of human intelligence.* New York: McGraw-Hill.

Hammill, D. D., Pearson, N. A., & Wiederholt, J. L. (1996). *Comprehensive test of nonverbal intelligence.* Austin, TX: PRO-ED.

Hargis, C. H. (1987). *Curriculum based assessment: A primer.* Springfield, IL: Charles C. Thomas.

Healy, W. L. (1914). A pictorial completion test. *The Psychological Review, xx,* 189–203.

Healy, W. L. (1918). *Pictorial completion test II.* Chicago: C.H. Stoelting.

Healy, W. L. (1921). *Pictorial completion test II. Journal of Applied Psychology, 5,* 232–233.

Itard, J. M. G. (1932). *The wild boy of Aveyron.* New York: Appleton-Century-Crofts.

Jensen, A. R. (1993). Psychometric g and achievement. In B. R. Gifford (Ed.), *Policy perspectives on educational testing* (pp. 117–227), Boston: Kluwer.

Kamphaus, R. W. (2001). *Clinical assessment of child and adolescent intelligence* (2nd ed.). Boston: Allyn and Bacon.

Kaufman, A. S. (1990). *Assessing adolescent and adult intelligence.* Boston: Allyn & Bacon.

Kaufman, A. S. (1994). *Intelligent testing with the WISC-II.* New York: Wiley.

Kaufman, A. S., & Kaufman, N. L. (1983). *Kaufman assessment battery for children: Administration and scoring manual.* Circle Pine, MN: American Guidance Service.

Knox, H. A. (1914). A scale based on the work at Ellis Island for estimating mental defect. *Journal of the American Medical Association, 62,* 741–747.

Larry P. v. Riles, 495 F. Supp. 926 (N.D. Cal. 1979).

Leiter, R. G. (1948). *Leiter international performance scale.* Chicago: Stoeling.

Lidz, C. S. (2001). Multicultural issues and dynamic assessment. In L. A. Suzuki, J. G. Ponterotto, & P. J. Meller (Eds.), *Handbook of multicultural assessment: Clinical, psychological, and educational applications* (2nd ed., pp. 523–540). San Francisco: Jossey-Bass.

Marshall v. Georgia, No. CV 482–233 (S.D. Ga. 1984).

McCallum, R. S. (1999). A bakers dozen criteria for evaluation fairness in nonverbal testing. *The school psychologist*, 40–43.

McCallum, R. S., Bracken, B. A., & Wasserman, J. (2001). *Essentials of nonverbal assessment*. New York: Wiley.

Mercer, J. R. (1976). Pluralistic diagnosis in the evaluation of Black and Chicano children: A procedure for taking sociocultural variables into account in clinical assessment. In C. A. Hemandez, M. J. Haug, & N. N. Wagner (Eds.), *Chicanos: Social and psychological perspectives* (2nd ed., pp. 183–195). St. Louis, MO: Mosby.

Naglieri, J. A. (1985a). *Matrix analogies test—Sort form*. New York: The Psychological Corporation.

Naglieri, J. A. (1985b). *Matrix analogies test—Expanded form*. New York: The Psychological Corporation.

Naglieri, J. A. (1996). *Naglieri nonverbal ability test*. San Antonio, TX: The Psychological Corporation.

Naglieri, J. A., & Bardos, A. N. (1997). *General ability measure for adults*. Minneapolis, MN: National Computer Systems.

O'Hanlon, A. (1997, May 11). Non-English speakers are testing schools. *The Washington Post* (p. V01). Prince William Extra section.

Orwell, G. (1946). *Animal farm*. New York: Harcourt Brace Jovanovich.

PACE v. Hannon, 506 F. Supp. 831 (N.D. Ill. 1980).

Padilla, A. M. (2001). Issues in culturally appropriate assessment. In L. A. Suzuki, J. G. Ponterotto, & P. J. Meller (Eds.), *Handbook of multicultural assessment: Clinical, psychological, and educational applications* (2nd ed., pp. 5–28). San Francisco: Jossey-Bass.

Pasko, J. R. (1994). Chicago—Don't miss it. *Communiqué*, *23*(4), 2.

Piaget, J. (1963). *The origins of intelligence in children*. New York: Norton.

Porteus, S. D. (1915). Mental tests for the feebleminded: A new series. *Journal of Psycho-Asthenics*, *19*, 200–213.

Power, S. (1996, May 9). Panel suggests school clerks learn Spanish: Board takes no action on report. *The Dallas Morning News* (p. 1F). Plano section.

Prifitera, A., Weiss, L. G., & Saklofske, D. H. (1998). The WISC-III in context. In A. Prifitera and D. H. Saklofske (Eds.). *WISC-III clinical use and interpretation: Scientist-practitioner perspectives*, (pp. 1–38). San Diego, CA: Academic Press.

Puente, M. (1998, May 27). Californians likely to end bilingual ed. *USA Today*, News section (p. 4A).

Raven, J., Raven, J. C., & Court, J. H. (1998). *Manual for Raven's progressive matrices and vocabulary scales*. Oxford, UK: Oxford Psychologists Press.

Reynolds, C. R., Lowe, P. A., & Saenz, A. L. (1999). The problem of bias in psychological assessment. In C. R. Reynolds & T. B. Gutidn (Eds.), *Handbook of school psychology* (pp. 549–595). New York: John Wiley & Sons, Inc.

Roid, G. H., & Miller, L. J. (1997). Leiter international performance scale—revised: Examiner's manual. In G. H. Roid & L. J. Miller (Eds.), *Leiter international performance scale revised*. Wood Dale, IL: Stoelting.

Rourke, B. P. (1995). *Syndrome of nonverbal learning disabilities: Neurodevelopmental manifestations*. New York: Guilford Press.

Sattler, J. M. (1988). Assessment of children (3rd ed.). San Diego, CA: Author.

Seguin, E. (1907). *Idiocy and its treatment by the physiological method*. New York: Teachers College, Columbia University.

Shapiro, E. S. (1987). *Behavioral assessment in school psychology*. Hillsdale, NJ: Lawrence Erlbaum Associates.

Stepp, D. (1997, November 20). School watch; as demographics change, language programs grow; transition help: The international welcome center helps non-English-speaking students adjust. *The Atlanta Journal and Constitution* (p. 02g). Extra section.

Thorndike, R. L., & Hagen, E. P. (1986). Measurement in evaluation in psychology and education (4th ed.). New York: Wiley.

Thorndike, R. M., & Lohman, D. F. (1990). *A century of ability testing*. Chicago: Riverside.

Ulik, C. (1997, January 6). Civil rights officials check Tempe schools; limited-English programs studied. *The Arizona Republic/The Phoenix Gazette*, Tempe Community Section, p. 1.

Unz, R. (1997, October 19). Perspective on education; bilingual is a damaging myth; a system that ensures failure is kept alive by the flow of federal dollars. A 1998 initiative would bring change. *Los Angeles Times*, Opinion section, part M, p. 5

Valencia, R. R. & Rankin, R. J. (1985). Evidence of content bias on the McCarthy Scale with Mexican-American Children – Implications for test translation and nonbiased assessment. *Journal of educational psychology, 77*(2), 197–207.

Van den Berg, A. R. (1986). *The problems of measuring intelligence in a heterogeneous society and possible solutions to some of these problems.* Pretoria: Institute for Psychological and Edumetric Research, Human Sciences Research Council.

Vygotsky, L. S. (1978). *Mind in society: The development of higher psychological process.* Cambridge, MA: Harvard University Press.

Wechsler, D. (1949). *Wechsler intelligence scale for children.* San Antonio, TX: The Psychological Corporation.

Wiggins, G. (1990). *Portfolio-based assessment: Considerations and examples.* Paper presented at meeting of Southern Maine Partnership Network of Renewing Schools, Gorham, ME, 1990.

2

Best Practices in Detecting Bias in Nonverbal Tests

Susan J. Maller

Group comparisons of performance on intelligence tests have been advanced as evidence of real similarities or differences in intellectual ability by Jensen (1980) and, more recently, by Herrnstein and Murray (1994). This purported evidence includes the mean intelligence score differences that have been reported for various ethnic groups (e.g., Jensen, 1969, 1980; Loehlin, Lindzey, & Spuhler, 1975; Lynn, 1977; Munford & Munoz, 1980) or gender (e.g., Feingold, 1993; Nelson, Arthur, Lautiger, & Smith, 1994; Smith, Edmonds, & Smith, 1989; Vance, Hankins, & Brown, 1988; Wessel & Potter, 1994; Wilkinson, 1993).

In the 1970s, concerns regarding potential bias of intelligence tests led to several court cases (e.g., *Larry P. v. Wilson Riles*, 1979; *Diana v. the California State Board of Education*, 1970), and studies of item bias, with conflicting findings (cf., Cotter & Berk, 1981; Illia & Willerman, 1989; Jastak & Jastak, 1964; Koh, Abbatiello, & McLoughlin, 1984; Miele, 1979; Ross-Reynolds & Reschly, 1983; Sandoval, 1979; Sandoval, Zimmerman, & Woo-Sam, 1977; Turner & Willerman, 1977). Bryk (1980) found methodological flaws in the above-mentioned mean score difference and item bias studies, noting that the current psychometric methodologies (e.g., latent trait theory) had not even been mentioned by Jensen (1980). Studies using such methods continue to be promoted as evidence of bias (e.g., Braden, 1999; Frisby, 1998).

Bias refers to a differential validity across subgroups (e.g., males vs. females, minority vs. majority). Bias can be investigated empirically at the

Susan J. Maller, Department of Educational Studies, Purdue University, West Lafayette, Indiana 47907.

Handbook of Nonverbal Assessment, edited by R. Steve McCallum. Kluwer Academic/Plenum Publishers, 2003.

item or test score levels. The various methods to investigate bias relate to the source of bias or differential validity (content, construct, criterion-related). All forms of bias eventually lead to a question of construct validity due to the potential influence of unintended constructs. The presence of bias ultimately suggests that scores have different meanings for members of various subgroups.

Fairness refers to the (a) absence of bias, (b) equitable treatment of examinees during the testing process, (c) equitable outcomes for examinees from different subgroups, and (d) equitable opportunities to learn the content of the test (AERA, 1999). Clearly, there is no such thing as a "non-biased test" or a test that "is fair" or "is valid" for all subgroups under all conditions. Furthermore, test developers can go to extensive lengths to create instruments that lack evidence of bias against subgroups; however, test consumers ultimately are responsible for selecting, administering, and interpreting the results of tests with evidence of validity for the purpose in which tests are used.

The *Standards for Educational and Psychological Testing* (AERA, 1999) devotes an entire chapter to "Fairness in Testing and Test Use." Section 7.10 states that mean score differences are insufficient evidence of bias. When mean score differences are found for subgroups, construct irrelevant variance or construct underrepresentation should be investigated as an explanation. Messick (1989) explained that construct irrelevant variance implies the presence of some variable that is unrelated to the intended construct and that contaminates test scores, and he further explained that criterion-related validity evidence may be insufficient and misleading, because the criterion variable may be similarly contaminated, leading to spurious correlations. Construct underrepresentation refers to the inability of a test to sufficiently measure the intended construct, possibly because the content is not broad enough.

The *Code of Professional Responsibilities in Educational Measurement* (National Council on Measurement in Education, 1995) states that those who develop assessments are responsible for making their products "as free as possible from bias due to characteristics irrelevant to the construct being measured, such as gender, ethnicity, race, socioeconomic status, disability, religion, age, or national origin" (Section 1.2a).

The *Code of Fair Testing in Education* (Joint Committee on Testing Practices; JCTP, 1988) Section C states that test developers should try to construct tests that are fair for members of various subgroups (ethnic, gender, or disability groups) and that test users should use tests with evidence of fairness for members of subgroups. Finally, Section 15 states that the differential performance of various subgroups should be investigated for construct-irrelevant influences.

Section 14 of the *Code of Fair Testing in Education* (JCTP, 1988) states that tests should avoid insensitive content. Test publishers routinely enlist the assistance of experts in the test content domain to conduct *sensitivity reviews* or evaluate the items for content unfairness, including offensive language, insensitivity, or other content that may have unintended influences on the performances of members of various subgroups (e.g., ethnic, gender, disability subgroup). Panel reviews of the item contents in several achievement and scholastic aptitude tests have tied differential item performance to differences in opportunities to learn or differences in socialization. For example, items favoring females have been linked to specific topics involving humanities, esthetics, and human relationships, whereas items favoring males have been linked to content about science, sports, and mechanics (Lawrence & Curley, 1989; Lawrence, Curley, & McHale, 1988; Scheuneman & Gerritz, 1990; Wild & McPeek, 1986). Unfortunately, panel reviews of the item content bias have yielded neither consistent nor accurate results (Engelhard, Hansche, & Rutledge, 1990; Plake, 1980; Sandoval & Miille, 1980).

To study whether specific groups may have difficulties with items due to factors specific to their language, culture, gender, or other differences, psychometricians must do more than examine the language content of the items. The psychometric properties of a test can be investigated for *invariance* (equality) across groups. The type of the invariance investigation depends on the suspected nature of bias and can include a variety of methods (a) to detect differential item functioning (DIF), (b) factor structure invariance, and (c) differential prediction. These methods will be described in detail below.

ITEM BIAS AND DIFFERENTIAL ITEM FUNCTIONING

Although the terms *item bias* and *DIF* are often used interchangeably, the term DIF was suggested more recently (Holland & Thayer, 1988) as a somewhat neutral term to refer to differences in the statistical properties of an item between groups of examinees of equal ability. These groups are often referred to as the *reference* (e.g., majority) and *focal* (e.g., minority or studied) groups. The concept of comparing groups of equal ability is a cardinal feature separating DIF from the traditional item bias detection methods. The traditional methods are affected by differences in the examinee group ability distributions. Overall ability differences may explain differential item performance, resulting in an item appearing to be more difficult when the examinees in the focal group are less able overall. *Impact* is a more appropriate term to refer to differences in item performance that can be explained by group ability differences. DIF detection methods "condition on" or control for ability, meaning that examinees are necessarily matched on ability; thus, only examinees of equal ability (e.g., overall test score) in the reference and focal groups are compared.

Items that exhibit DIF threaten the validity of a test and may have serious consequences for groups as well as individuals, because the probabilities of correct responses are determined not only by the trait that the test claims to measure but also by factors specific to group membership, such as differential opportunities to learn or differences in socialization. The most obvious consequence is the potential impact of DIF on the observed score distributions of specific groups. The less obvious consequence of DIF, yet critically important to the construct validity of a test, is its impact on the meaning and interpretation of test scores, even in the absence of mean score differences between groups. DIF items may cancel and result in similar score distributions across groups. However, when scores comprise different items systematically scored as correct, it may be invalid for clinicians who interpret the scores of individuals, or researchers who make conclusions about groups, to infer that "equal" IQs are comparable or have the same meaning.

Traditional Methods of Detecting Item Bias

Traditional item bias detection methods were commonly used before the development of DIF detection methods and are explained at great length elsewhere (cf., Berk, 1982; Camilli & Shepard, 1994). These methods, which will be mentioned only briefly for historical purposes and to point out their flaws, are based on the item p value (proportion of examinees in a specific sample passing an item) and are inherently sample dependent. That is, unlike the newer DIF detection methods, these methods do not control for ability differences across groups. This lack of control for ability is known as Simpson's (1951) paradox, which illustrates the effect of not comparing groups of equal ability. When differences in proportions passing in two groups are examined at score levels, the conclusions may differ from the total proportions passing in for each of the groups.

The p values obtained for two groups can be correlated using the Spearman rank order correlation; a low correlation indicates the presence of biased items (Jensen, 1974, 1976). Angoff and Ford (1973) developed the Transformed Index of Difficulty (TID) method in an effort to convert p values to normal deviates. The p value is transformed to a z score, which is then linearly transformed to a delta scale ($M = 13$, SD $= 4$). The purpose of developing the delta transformation was to avoid negative values and decimals, which were assumed to be more difficult to interpret. The deltas for the two groups are plotted against each other. A Pearson correlation of $r < 0.98$ indicates that the order of difficulty is significantly different for the two groups (Angoff, 1993). Points that deviate most from the regression line are considered to be biased against one of the two groups.

Another traditional item bias detection method is the within-subjects analysis of variance (ANOVA) method. A group $\times$ item difficulty (p value) ANOVA is used to test the interaction of group membership by the repeated factor of items. A significant main effect for group indicates overall ability differences, and the interaction term (group $\times$ item) indicates item bias. The method, however, is still based on item p values and has been found to lack sufficient power (Camilli & Shepard, 1987), because the unique variance explained by the interaction effect is minimal after accounting for the main effect. Furthermore, the method, like the correlational methods described above, uses overall summary statistics, rather than examining individual item functioning.

The traditional methods are limited for several reasons. The p values are sample dependent, as previously mentioned. These methods can be confounded by the item discrimination parameter in that weakly discriminating items may be retained in the test, leading to a less reliable test; highly discriminating items are more difficult for lower scoring examinees and are, therefore, more likely to be identified as biased for a lower scoring group. In addition, because these methods depend on ordinal data, they are problematic in that the order of every aberrant item affects the order of every other item. Finally, correlation coefficients act as a summary statistic that ignores the functioning of individual items. Thus, the difficulty of a specific item may differ greatly across groups, but the overall correlation between the ranks still may be high.

Chi-Square Methods

Chi-square methods can be used to control for ability differences between groups. Item bias is detected if, for two groups, there is a different proportion of correct responses of individuals within similar score ranges of ability, as determined by total observed test score. Scheuneman (1975) first proposed the method, but the statistic did not follow a chi-square distribution. Veale (1977) and Camilli (1979) proposed a similar method that improved the approximation to the chi-square distribution. Although the creation of score groups may increase power at a given score level, the grouping procedure can "degrade the quality of the matching" (Holland & Thayer, 1988, p. 133), because examinees of various ability levels are grouped into a given category.

Holland and Thayer (1988) recommended the Mantel–Haenszel (MH) procedure (Mantel & Haenszel, 1959) for detection of DIF. For each level of ability, the MH procedure arranges two groups, a focal group and a reference group, in a $2 \times 2 \times s$ contingency table (group $\times$ item score $\times$ level of ability):

	1	0	Total
Reference	R_{rs}	W_{rs}	N_{rs}
Focal	R_{fs}	W_{fs}	N_{fs}
	R_{ts}	W_{ts}	N_{ts}

If there is no DIF, the odds of a correct response at s given ability level for the focal group f, is equal to the odds for the reference group r, and can be expressed as:

$$\frac{R_{fs}}{W_{fs}} = \frac{R_{rs}}{W_{rs}}, \tag{1}$$

where R is the number right, and W is the number wrong. Furthermore,

$$\frac{R_{fs}}{W_{fs}} \Big/ \frac{R_{rs}}{W_{rs}} = \alpha. \tag{2}$$

If $\alpha \neq 1$, there is DIF. Furthermore, the MH chi-square statistic used to test the hypothesis that there is no difference in item functioning for the two groups can be expressed as:

$$\chi^2_{\text{MH}} = \frac{\left(\left| \sum_s R_{rs} - \sum_s \frac{N_{rs} R_{ts}}{N_{ts}} \right| - 0.5 \right)^2}{\sum_s \frac{(N_{rs} N_{fs} R_{ts} W_{ts})}{[N_{ts}^2 (N_{ts} - 1)]}}, \tag{3}$$

where R_{rs} and R_{ts} are the number of correct response in the reference and total (reference and focal) groups, respectively, at score level s; N_{rs}, N_{fs}, and N_{ts} is the total number of correct and incorrect responses in the reference, focal and total groups at the score level; W_{ts} is the number of incorrect responses in the total group at the score level; and -0.5 is a continuity correction to improve the approximation to the chi-square distribution. The MH is approximately chi-square with one degree of freedom.

The Breslow–Day (Breslow & Day, 1980) test for homogeneity of log odds ratios can be examined for *nonuniform* DIF (differences in difficulty that reverse directions at different ability levels). However, the statistic generally is rather insensitive, and other methods to be described later are better choices for detection of nonuniform DIF.

An additional statistic can be used with the MH to facilitate interpretation by taking the natural logarithm of α, or $\beta = \ln(\alpha)$. Holland and Thayer (1988) suggested multiplying β by -2.35, resulting in a statistic that is centered at zero and that ranges from $-\infty$ to $+\infty$. ETS guidelines for interpreting $-2.35\,\beta$, or Δ_{mh}, are the following A, B, C classifications (Zeilky, 1993):

Level	Δ_{mh}		MH
A	$\|\Delta_{\text{mh}}\| < 1.0$	or	$p \geq 0.05$
B	$\|\Delta_{\text{mh}}\| < 1.5$	and	$p < 0.05$
C	$\|\Delta_{\text{mh}}\| \geq 1.5$	and	$p < 0.05$

The MH procedure was extended for ordered response categories (Welch & Hoover, 1993; Zwick, Donoghue, & Grima, 1993). The Breslow–Day statistic is not available for the extended MH. Thus, the extended MH procedure lacks any indicator of nonuniform DIF.

Samples of 100 examinees are adequate for the MH DIF procedure (Hills, 1989), and as few as 50 examinees in the reference group and 10 examinees in the focal group have been suggested for MH DIF screening (Kromrey & Parshall, 1991). The MH or extended MH procedures can be run easily and quickly in available statistical analysis packages, such as SAS or SPSS and are, therefore, relatively inexpensive procedures. Furthermore, chi-square methods improve on traditional methods, because DIF is investigated for different levels of ability. To estimate ability, the MH procedure uses observed scores, which may be unreliable indicators of true scores or ability category, and requires sufficient numbers of subjects to be available in order to obtain cell frequencies. Other methods, to be described later, conceptualize ability as a underlying latent trait.

To improve the matching procedure, Holland and Thayer (1988) recommend the use of a *purification* step to refine, or remove DIF items that might contaminate the matching criterion (observed score level). In this procedure, items that exhibit DIF in the initial MH analysis are removed. This initial analysis is referred to as the DIF screening. Only non-DIF items remain to comprise the purified subtest. Next, all other items are referred to as *studied* items and are individually tested for DIF. This is done by including the purified items plus one studied item in separate DIF analyses. In doing so, examinees are matched on the purified subtest and the studied item. Although it may be counterintuitive to include the studied item in the matching criterion, exclusion of the studied item would change the calculation of the MH (Holland & Thayer, 1988). The method of purification is more labor intensive and thus more expensive. Regardless, purification is strongly encouraged for the obvious theoretical reasons. Purification allows examinees in the reference and focal groups to be matched on a criterion without the contamination of DIF items.

Standardization Approach

Dorans (1989) recommended the use of the standardized p difference. Unlike traditional methods of item bias detection, the standardization approach compares examinees of equal ability, as determined by observed test score. The standardization method is based on the following:

$$D_s = P_{fs} - P_{rs},\qquad(4)$$

where P_{fs} is the proportion passing in the focal group, and P_{rs} and is the proportion passing in the reference group.

Two additional statistics are available. First, the standardized p difference:

$$D_{STD} = \sum_{s=1}^{S} K_s(P_{fs} - P_{rs})/\sum_{s=1}^{S} K_s,\qquad(5)$$

where $K_s/\Sigma K_s$ is the proportion of the standardization group at a specific score level. The standardization group is usually the focal group, because it serves as a weighting factor to weight the probability differences by the score levels most frequently observed in the standardization group. A standardized p difference of 0.10 indicates that the item should be flagged for further examination of potential content bias (Dorans, 1989). The standardized p difference is a signed (negative or positive) value and thus provides an indication of the direction of DIF. However, the presence of nonuniform DIF can result in cancellation of negative and positive probabilities. An alternative index to provide an index of the average difference in probabilities across groups, regardless of direction, is the root mean weighted standardized difference (RMWSD; Dorans, 1989), which is expressed as:

$$\text{RMWSD} = \left[\sum_{s=1}^{S} K_s (P_{fs} - P_{rs})^2 / \sum_{s=1}^{S} K_s \right]^{1/2}. \tag{6}$$

Notice that the formula is similar to the D_{STD}, except that the probability values are squared, and the square root is then taken, thus avoiding the problem of cancellation.

Logistic Regression (LR)

DIF detection methods (Rogers & Swaminathan, 1993; Swaminathan & Rogers, 1990) improve on MH DIF methods, because LR methods can be used to test nonuniform DIF directly. In LR DIF, the probability of a correct response is based on Equation (7),

$$P(x = 1) = \frac{e^z}{1 + e^z}, \tag{7}$$

where τ_2 is the g group difference when controlled for θ ability (to test for uniform DIF), and τ_3 is the effect for the interaction between ability and group (to test for nonuniform DIF).

$$z = \tau_0 + \tau_1 \theta + \tau_2 g + \tau_3 (\theta g). \tag{8}$$

As can be seen in the Equation (8), the continuous variable of the total test score is used to control for ability, instead of contingency tables at each score level, as is done in the MH approach. In addition, examinees can be matched on more than one variable, including external matching criteria (Clauser, Nungester, & Swaminathan, 1996). Sample sizes of at least 200 examinees in each group are recommended (Zumbo, 1999).

LR is more labor intensive, and thus expensive, than the MH procedure, because the DIF analysis is conducted in several steps. The first analysis involves the *augmented* model, which is presented in Equation (8) above, and which yields a likelihood ratio chi-square. The next step involves a *compact* model, which includes only the first three terms in Equation (8) (τ_0, τ_1, and τ_2), which also yields a likelihood ratio chi-square. Because chi-squares are additive, the explanatory power of the interaction term is tested by subtracting the likelihood ratio of the less restrictive (augmented) model chi-square from the more restrictive (compact) model chi-square, yielding a difference chi-square with one degree of freedom. If the difference chi-square is significant, the interaction term is necessary, and the item is concluded to exhibit nonuniform DIF. If, however, the difference is not significant, the next step involves a test of a compact model including only the first two terms (τ_0 and τ_1) and an augmented model involving the first three terms (τ_0, τ_1, and τ_2). If the difference chi-square between the compact and augmented models is significant, the item is concluded to exhibit uniform DIF (constant differences in difficulty). The estimates of τ_2 and τ_3 can serve as effect sizes and are interpreted like the β obtained for the MH procedure.

IRT DIF

Item response theory (IRT) methods improve on other methods that condition on observed ability scores, because a model is fitted to the data. The model conceptualizes ability as a latent trait. Formal tests of model-data fit provide greater confidence in the results, because if a model does not fit the data, it makes little sense to compare item difficulties. Of particular interest to the topic of DIF are some of the assumptions of IRT. First, IRT models assume invariance; that is, item parameters do not differ across groups, unless there is DIF. In addition, IRT models generally assume unidimensionality (the test measures one dominant latent trait); however, the presence of DIF could signal multidimensionality in that construct-irrelevant factors related to group membership could influence the probability of a correct response. Unfortunately, IRT DIF detection methods require relatively larger sample sizes (ranging from 100 to about 3,000), depending on the model, than are often available for studies of DIF in clinical tests.

Using DIF methods based on IRT, Figure 2.1 shows what are known as *trace lines*. The lines trace the probability (from zero to perfect probability) of a correct response to an item for persons from low to high ability. The

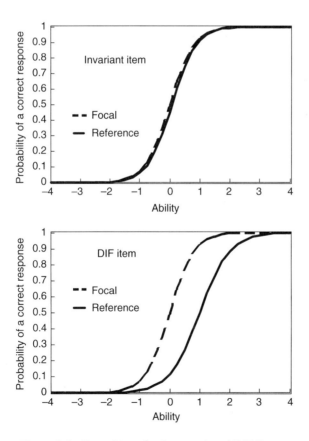

Figure 2.1   Trace Lines for Invariant and DIF Items.

first set of trace lines is for an item that is invariant (does not exhibit DIF), because the trace lines for reference and focal overlap. The second set of trace lines is for an item that does exhibit DIF. Notice that the trace lines are separated, and the probability of a correct response differs for males and females across all levels of ability.

IRT models commonly used to investigate DIF in intelligence tests include the one-, two-, and three-parameter models, as well as Samejima's Graded Response Model. The two-parameter (2 PL) models the probability of a correct response based on both the difficulty (the point on the trace line where there is a 50% probability of correct response) and discrimination (proportional to the slope of the trace line) of an item and the ability of the person. The 2 PL model is expressed as:

$$P(x = 1/\theta) = \frac{1}{1 + e^{-a(\theta - b)}}, \tag{9}$$

where x is an item response, θ is the estimated ability, a is the item discrimination parameter, and b is the item difficulty parameter. The 1 PL (also known as Rasch) model differs from the 2 PL model in that the discrimination parameter is held constant across items. This is a very stringent assumption that rarely can be met in practice. However, examination of fit statistics can indicate whether the assumption is met. Regardless, if sufficient sample sizes are available, the 2 PL model is generally preferable to test the invariance of item discriminations across groups. A 3 PL model is recommended for multiple-choice items, because the model includes a C guessing parameter. This guessing parameter, however, often results in poorly estimated item parameters. Therefore, a modified 3 PL model has been recommended with a prior distribution on the c parameter (Lord, 1980; Thissen, Steinberg, & Wainer, 1993).

When items are scored using necessarily ordered categories, they can be fitted with Samejima's (1969) graded response model. For example, for items that are scored 0, 1, or 2, the graded response model provides two item difficulty estimates (based on the probability of scoring 1 or the probability of scoring 2). The graded response model is as follows (Samejima, 1969):

$$P^*_{kni} = \frac{1}{1 + e^{-a_i(\theta_n - b_{ik})}} \tag{10}$$

where P^*_{kni} is the probability of person n reaching category k or higher on item i, b_{ik} is the difficulty in reaching category k. $P_{0ni} = 1 - P^*_{1ni}$ is the probability of person n scoring 0 on item i and is equal to the probability of person n scoring 0, 1, or 2 (perfect probability) minus the probability of the person scoring 1 or higher. $P_{1ni} = P^*_{1ni} - P_{2ni}$ is the probability of person n scoring 1 on item i and is equal to the probability of person n scoring at or above 1 (1 or 2) minus the probability of person n scoring 2. $P_{2ni} = P^*_{2ni}$ is the probability of person n scoring 2 on item i and is equal to the probability of person n scoring a 2.

IRT LR Method

Following a multistep procedure, items found to be invariant (equally difficult) for reference and focal groups are used as a purified, or anchor, subtest to match examinees of equal ability. First, items in each subtest are screened using the MH DIF or extended MH procedure for ordered response categories. Following the recommendations of Thissen, Steinberg, and Wainer (1988), a set of at least four or five items that do not exhibit MH DIF should be selected for the initial purified subtest to be calibrated in the subsequent IRT analysis. These items should be roughly equally spaced in terms of difficulty. The anchor items are then calibrated using the MULTILOG software (Thissen, 1991), which uses the Marginal Maximum Likelihood estimation procedure via the EM algorithm (Bock & Aitkin, 1981). The fit of the model to the data is evaluated using the likelihood ratio goodness-of-fit statistic, G^2, which is distributed as chi-square and is a test of the model against a general multinomial alternative model, as discussed by Thissen, Steinberg, and Gerrard (1986):

$$G^2 = 2 \sum_{g=1}^{g} \sum_{c=1}^{c} r_g(x) \ln \left[\frac{r_g(x)}{N_g P_g(x)} \right], \tag{11}$$

where g is the group (reference or focal), c represents the cell of a contingency table of response patterns, and r is the count for response pattern x. The degrees of freedom are the number of cells of a contingency table of response patterns minus the number of fitted parameters. Because a graded response item has k^n possible response patterns, the cells in the contingency table of response patterns may contain too few data to conduct a meaningful likelihood ratio test but can still be used for nested model comparisons (Bock, 1997; Thissen & Steinberg, 1997), as is done in the IRT DIF detection procedure (Thissen et al., 1986, 1988, 1993). Therefore, to examine the fit of the model to the data, subsets of two or three items should be evaluated for goodness of fit, as recommended by Maller (2001).

When a model is found to fit the data for a particular set of items (referred to hereafter as the *free* model), the hypothesis that all items in the purified subtest are invariant between groups is tested by imposing equality constraints on all item parameters (referred to hereafter as the *constrained* model). The difference $G^2_{\text{constrained}} - G^2_{\text{free}}$ is used as an omnibus test to determine the invariance of the purified subtest. If $G^2_{\text{constrained}} - G^2_{\text{free}}$ is significant, parameters for individual items are tested for invariance. If an item is found to lack invariance, it is replaced with another item that does not exhibit MH DIF. This iterative procedure is continued until a final set of non-MH DIF items is found to have invariant item parameters.

The items not included in the purified, or anchor, subtest are then individually tested for DIF using the following IRT likelihood ratio DIF detection method, similar to the method proposed by Thissen et al. (1988,

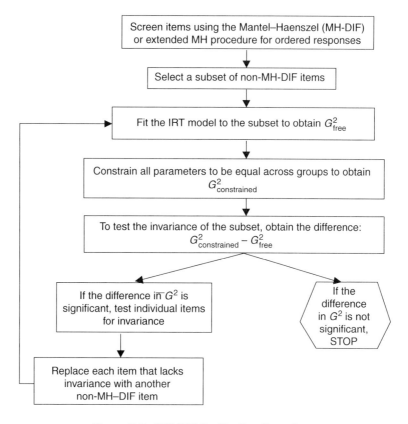

Figure 2.2   IRT DIF Purification Procedure.

1993). The model is fitted for the samples of reference and focal simultaneously, constraining the anchor item parameters to be equal across groups, while allowing for an individual studied item parameter to be estimated separately for each group to obtain a G_{free}^2. Next, the studied item parameter estimate is constrained to be equal across groups to obtain $G_{\text{constrained}}^2$. The difference $G_{\text{constrained}}^2 - G_{\text{free}}^2$ is used to test the hypothesis that a parameter estimate (a discrimination parameter or b difficulty parameter) is invariant across groups. The following hypotheses can be tested: H_0: $a_{\text{reference}} = a_{\text{focal}}$, H_0: $b_{\text{reference}} = b_{\text{focal}}$ ($b1_{\text{reference}} = b1_{\text{focal}}$ to $bk_{\text{reference}} = bk_{\text{focal}}$ in the graded model). In general, one additional constraint is added to each successive model, except when a parameter is found to lack invariance. In such cases, the constrained parameter model is compared with a less restrictive model where other equality constraints are placed only on invariant parameter estimates. Figures 2.2 and 2.3 provides a flow chart for implementing the IRT LR method with the 2 PL model.

To examine the magnitude of the DIF effect, the root mean squared probability difference (RMSD) is computed as follows:

$$\text{RMSD} = \sqrt{\frac{\sum_{(j=1)}^{n} \left[P_{\text{reference}}(\theta_j) - P_{\text{focal}}(\theta_j) \right]^2}{n}} \tag{12}$$

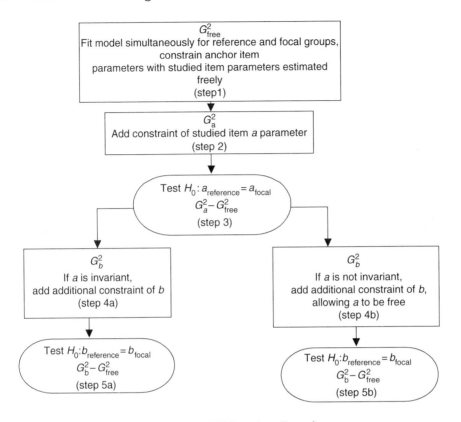

Figure 2.3   IRT DIF Detection Procedure.

where, j is the estimated theta value for a given examinee and n is the total number of estimated theta values or examinees. RMSD statistics are interpreted as the unsigned average difference between groups in their probabilities of a correct response, with a value of 0.05 or greater frequently used by Educational Testing Service to indicate DIF (O'Neill & McPeek, 1993). The unsigned method is recommended, because signed versions of the RMSD can result in smaller DIF magnitudes due to cancellation in the presence of nonuniform DIF. To determine the direction of DIF, the differences in item parameter estimates for each group (e.g., $a_{reference} - a_{focal}$, $b_{reference} - b_{focal}$) can be examined, and item trace lines can be plotted to provide graphical illustration.

In addition to the reporting of effect sizes, exact probability values should be reported along with significance tests, given that numerous significance tests are reported. Cohen, Kim, and Wollack (1996) have reported Type I error rates to be close to the 0.05 nominal level. However, because power calculations are not yet available, it is recommended that a baseline estimate of the number of items that would exhibit DIF due to chance be obtained by dividing the sample in half at random and repeating all DIF analyses (Maller, 2000, 2001). A z test of proportion differences can indicate whether the proportions of DIF items found for the focal/reference group and random groups studies differ significantly.

TEST BIAS

Test bias refers to the differential validity of test scores. Investigations of test bias usually include studies of (a) unequal psychometric properties, (b) unequal factor structures, or (c) differential prediction of performance between groups, such as majority and minority groups. Often, test developers and consumers believe that special *subgroup norms* may be useful for comparing individuals with a more representative peer group. For example, special norms were developed for the *Wechsler Intelligence Scale for Children—Revised Performance Scale for Deaf Children* (Anderson & Sisco, 1977). However, subgroup norms may be a superficial solution to a larger problem concerning content and construct validity. If test items have different meanings for examinees belonging to different subgroups, then subgroup norms result in comparing members with other members on some trait not claimed to be measured by the test (Maller, 1996).

Differences in reliability coefficients also may indicate bias. Reliability coefficients give an indication of how consistently a construct, such as intelligence, is measured across groups. Statistical tests are used to assess differences in the coefficients (Feldt & Brennan, 1989).

Factor Invariance

Construct equivalence suggests that test constructs are conceptualized and measured similarly across groups (Shelley-Sireci & Sireci, 1998; Sireci, Bastar, & Allalouf, 1998). Factor-analytic methods are used to examine the internal structure of a test and to investigate whether a construct is equally indicated for groups. Exploratory (EFA) and confirmatory (CFA) factor analyses are used to examine the similarity of the factor structures. In EFA, the *coefficient of congruence*, a type of correlation, is used to determine the similarity of the factor loadings for groups. Values above 0.90 indicate factor invariance (Cattell, 1978), meaning that factors are equivalently indicated across groups and provide evidence against test bias.

Reynolds (1982) stated, "bias exists in regard to construct validity when a test is shown to measure different hypothetical traits (psychological constructs) for one group than another or to measure the same trait but with different degrees of accuracy" (p. 194). Furthermore, Reynolds added that multisample CFA based on the techniques of Jöreskog is a more promising and sophisticated method in detecting such construct bias than the previously relied upon method of exploratory factor analysis, which examines factorial similarity using the coefficient of congruence.

Multisample CFA has been used to test the invariance of factor structures (Alwin & Jackson, 1981; Bollen, 1989; Jöreskog, 1971; Jöreskog & Sörbom, 1989; McGaw & Jöreskog, 1971) and improves on exploratory methods because it allows for a chi-square test of the fit of the model across two samples. Multisample CFA provides a formal procedure for testing factor structure invariance.

Following the procedures recommended by Bollen (1989) and Jöreskog and Sörbom (1989), the general form (hereafter referred to as the $Model_{form}$) of the theoretical model is tested for invariance across samples to obtain the model χ^2, which equals the sum of the chi-squares for the individual groups analyses, and to obtain fit statistics of the model across groups. To assess the fit of the model, the following fit indices are recommended: GFI, CFI, and RMSEA. The GFI is interpreted as the proportion of the observed variances and covariances that can be accounted for by the model. The CFI is recommended by Bentler (1990, 1992) and Rigdon (1996) to indicate the difference in fit of the null and target models relative to the fit of the null model, with values greater than or equal to 0.90 indicating reasonable fit. The RMSEA is recommended by Browne and Cudeck (1993) and Rigdon (1996) to indicate the fit of the empirical and modeled variance–covariance matrices, with values less than 0.05 indicating excellent fit and values less than 0.08 indicating reasonable fit (Rigdon, 1996). In addition, the Satorra–Bentler scaled chi-square (Satorra & Bentler, 1988) also might be examined, because it has been reported to be reliable for various distributional conditions and sample sizes (Hu, Bentler, & Kano, 1992).

If the general form does not fit across groups, test constructs are measured differently across the groups, and a more exploratory approach might be taken to reveal a model that fits the data. These approaches may include exploratory factor-analytic studies or model-fitting approaches in CFA. Regardless of the different structure revealed for the focal group, scaled scores based on the theoretical model lack evidence of construct equivalence. If, however, the general form of the model adequately fits across groups, progressively more restrictive models are then tested for invariance. Three progressively more restricted models may be tested by adding one additional constrained matrix of: (a) factor loadings or path coefficients, describing the relationships between the latent and observed variables, and interpreted like regression coefficients, (b) error variances, and (c) factor variances and covariances. The chi-squares for each of the restricted models are compared with the chi-square for the $Model_{form}$, using a difference chi-square test, which involves subtracting the $Model_{form}$ chi-square from the chi-square obtained for the restricted model, with degrees of freedom equal to the degrees of freedom for the restricted model minus the degrees of freedom for the $Model_{form}$.

Factor-loading invariance is the most critical concern regarding construct validity, because factor loadings indicate the relationship between the variable (subtest) and factor (construct). If the matrix of factor loadings is not invariant, at least one element of the matrix lacks invariance. Individual elements of the matrix subsequently should be individually tested for invariance to isolate the source(s) of invariance (Maller & Ferron, 1997; Maller, Konold, & Glutting, 1998). The restricted model is the $Model_{form}$ with one equality constraint of the studied parameter. The chi-square difference is obtained by comparing the restricted and $Model_{form}$ chi-squares with one degree of freedom. A lack of factor-loading invariance suggests that factor loadings should not be constrained to be invariant when testing the invariance of error variances and factor variances and covariances. In fact, a lack of factor loading invariance is sufficient to lead to the conclusion of differential validity.

If the factor loadings are invariant, the matrix of error variances should be tested for invariance. If the matrix is not invariant, individual elements subsequently can be tested for invariance, as described above. A lack of error variance invariance suggests that the measurement of the variables (subtests) are differentially affected by extraneous sources of variance.

If the error variances are invariant, the matrix of factor variances and covariances is then tested for invariance. If this matrix lacks invariance, subsequent elements can be tested for invariance.

If factor covariances are found to lack invariance, differential variability in the factors may be the source of invariance, resulting in less or more redundancy in the constructs claimed to be measured by the factors. In other words, the "separate" factors may be measuring overlapping abilities for one of the groups.

If factor variances and covariances are invariant, it makes sense to do a follow-up test of the invariance of means structures to investigate whether the latent means differ across groups. A lack of invariance suggests that, although the measurements of test constructs do not differ, the groups differ in terms of ability.

Prediction Bias

The examination of differential predictive validity is especially important when tests are used for placement and selection decisions. Differential prediction has been used as an indication of test bias (Cleary, 1968). Predictive validity coefficients that differ significantly between groups indicate that the test has different relationships with the criterion across the groups. Another type of differential prediction refers to a systematic under or overestimation of a criterion for a given group (Cleary, 1968; Scheuneman & Oakland, 1998). Specifically, differential prediction occurs when examinees belonging to different subgroups, but with comparable ability based on some predictor test score, tend to obtain different scores on some criterion test. To investigate differential prediction, regression lines for criterion (e.g., achievement) and predictor (e.g., intelligence) test scores are compared for focal and reference groups. Figure 2.4 depicts an example of regression lines with different intercepts. The criterion is underpredicted for the focal group. Suppose the intelligence test in Figure 2.4 is required for admission to a gifted education program. Members of the focal group actually will obtain higher scores on the achievement test than would be expected based on their intelligence scores, when using the regression line for the reference group. Focal group members who would be successful on the criterion may be denied acceptance into the gifted program based on their intelligence-test scores. A test that does not exhibit differential predictive validity still may be biased based

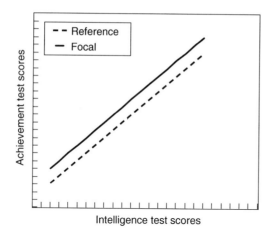

Figure 2.4 Regression Lines for Reference and Focal Groups Where Intelligence Scores Underpredict Achievement Test Scores for the Focal Group.

on other definitions of bias. Furthermore, predictor and criterion tests may be spuriously correlated due to systematic factors, including construct bias. That is, factors specific to group membership that similarly affect scores on both tests actually may inflate predictive validity coefficients. Consistent with Messick's (1989) concerns, this method is not recommended in the absence of other bias investigations related to construct validity.

CURRENT STATUS AND RECOMMENDATIONS

The best practices for detecting bias in nonverbal tests are really no different from the best practices for detecting bias in other psychoeducational tests. Some of the methods used to investigate bias in several nonverbal intelligence tests are summarized in Table 2.1. Until very recently, there were few published studies of invariance at the item or test levels in intelligence tests using state-of-the-art methods. Regardless, these methods have been used for quite some time to study bias in various scholastic aptitude tests (e.g., Dorans & Kulick, 1983; Green, Crone, & Folk, 1989; Holland & Thayer, 1988; Linn, Levine, Hastings, & Waldrop, 1980; Scheuneman, 1987). Most recently, several nonverbal intelligence test manuals or independent researchers have begun to report investigations of invariance under various labels, such as studies of "fairness," "bias," "DIF," etc. For example, the *Comprehensive Test of Nonverbal Intelligence* (CTONI; Hammill, Pearson, & Wiederholt, 1997) reported item bias investigations using two methods: IRT (using a 3 PL model) and the delta approach, depending on the numbers of examinees available for comparison. Very little information was provided concerning the analyses (e.g., sample sizes, model-data fit indices). The manual states that at most 5% of CTONI items were found to be biased against any one minority group.

Table 2.1   Summary of Bias Studies for Several Nonverbal Intelligence Tests

Test	Item bias/DIF	Factor invariance	Differential prediction	Other
CTONI	The IRT 3 PL was used to compare groups (male/female, African American/non-African American, ESL/non-ESL, American Indian/non-American Indian, and Learning Disabled/non-Learning Disabled), although specific details of the analysis were not described. The Delta Approach was also used to show high correlations of item difficulty indices (p values) between groups.	Exploratory factor analysis was conducted on 11 subgroups. One factor was extracted for all subgroups, although the congruence of the factors across groups was not reported.	Evidence of predictive validity is lacking for all groups.	None
LIPS-R	1 PL IRT (Rasch) was used to detect DIF. DIF items were excluded, unless they were critical for starting points or reliability.	None	Predictive validity coefficients (between the Leiter-R and the California Achievement Test) were not significant for samples of 50 Caucasians and 20 African Americans.	The lack of mean score differences was used as evidence of fairness, although a few differences were found between the following: Caucasians/Hispanics, Normative sample members/Navajos, and males/females.

NNAT	The Mantel–Haenszel procedure was used to detect DIF for males/females, Whites/ African Americans, and Whites/ Hispanics. Specific details regarding the analyses were not reported. DIF items were reviewed for possible removal.	None	None	None
UNIT	Mantel–Haenszel DIF detection indicated only two items exhibited DIF in favor of two subgroups. 1 PL IRT-LR for Deaf Examinees (Maller, 2000).	Confirmatory factor analysis for various subgroups, including males, females, African Americans; Hispanics, all showed a good fit to the data, although hypotheses regarding invariance were not tested using simultaneous, multisample CFA.	None — Prediction of achievement, as measured by the WJ-R, was not influenced by race or sex.	Mean score comparisons of several subgroups indicated some differences between groups. Internal consistency reliability coefficients were consistently high across subgroups (males, females, African Americans, Hispanics).

The *Leiter International Performance Scale-R* (LIPS-R; Roid & Miller, 1997) manual devotes three paragraphs to item bias, stating that a Rasch model was used to calibrate item difficulties separately across several groups. Subsequent correlations were used to indicate the uniformity of indices across groups. This method suffers from at least two flaws. First, no mention was made regarding whether item difficulty estimates were placed on a similar scale; this step is not necessary in the IRT LR approach. Second, like traditional methods, this method used a summary statistic, ignoring the functioning of specific items. The *Universal Nonverbal Intelligence Test* (UNIT; Bracken & McCallum, 1998) manual includes probably the most detailed report of fairness studies for a variety of groups (gender, ethnic, bilingual/ESL, hearing impaired), including the results of MH DIF studies, although the manual does not state whether the analyses included purification. Maller (2000) subsequently reported that no items were found to exhibit DIF (using the IRT LR approach) against deaf children compared with a matched (on internal and external criteria) sample of hearing children from the standardization sample.

Using IRT LR DIF detection methods, the WISC-III Picture Completion subtest was reported to contain 14 items that exhibit uniform or nonuniform DIF when boys and girls from the standardization sample were compared (Maller, 2001), 10 of which were more difficult for girls. Items that contained a picture of a male or a female were more difficult for girls or boys, respectively. However, the author states that more research is needed to determine whether the items can be judged, reliably, to be unfair in terms of their content. Certainly, such research is needed to provide developers of clinical tests more insight into what kinds of items are likely to exhibit DIF. An item that exhibits considerable DIF still should be considered for removal, even when judges are unable to determine the nature of the content bias, because the inclusion of DIF items may affect the meaning of test scores.

A test may contain considerable DIF, yet focal and reference groups may have similar score distributions due to cancellation DIF, which occurs when some items favor the reference group and others favor the focal group. Scores may be based in part on different items systematically scored as correct. Although some might believe that DIF cancellation results in a fairer test, the presence of even a one-point systematic raw score difference on individual subtests due to DIF may result in systematic age-based standard score differences at the subtest level and may have cumulative effects at the scale score level for individuals. Furthermore, when ceiling rules are used and numerous adjacent items exhibit DIF against one group, individual examinees may reach a ceiling for reasons related to both group membership and intelligence. It is very likely that different items systematically scored as correct comprise the scores of examinees from different groups with the same test scores.

In addition to DIF studies, studies of factor invariance using multisample CFA are encouraged. Such studies have been reported for the WISC-III (Konold, Maller, & Glutting, 1998; Maller & Ferron, 1997) and the Differential Abilities Scale (Maller, Konold, & McDermott, 2001).

The scores from tests that lack item or test invariance cannot be assumed to have the same meaning across groups. Differential prediction studies are not recommended in the absence of DIF and factor invariance investigations, because tests may be correlated due to construct irrelevant factors. Thus, bias studies should begin with DIF studies, move to factor invariance studies, and conclude with differential prediction studies. The results of bias studies are crucial to the interpretation of test scores. A lack of item and test score invariance can be a function of possible differential opportunities to learn or other differences in socialization. Unfortunately, results of state-of-the-art item and test-structure invariance investigations traditionally have not been reported for individually administered intelligence tests. Thus, conclusions regarding intellectual similarities or differences may be unfounded, and the interpretation of test scores influenced by unintended constructs may have serious consequences for individuals and groups. Although such investigations are labor intensive and expensive, and it is impossible to compare psychometric properties for all possible groups, test developers are encouraged to conduct more invariance investigations for nonverbal and other psychoeducational tests used for high-stakes educational decisions.

Even if a test developer makes a thorough attempt to create a test that lacks evidence of bias against a variety of subgroups, the test cannot be assumed to be fair for all subgroups under all conditions. Ultimately, practitioners must take responsibility for understanding the psychometric properties and potential unintended consequences, as discussed by Messick (1989), of using tests without the necessary validity evidence. Specifically, practitioners should question whether (a) the test should be used for a given purpose, based on the empirical validity evidence, and (b) score interpretation reflects intended test constructs. That is, adverse outcomes for examinees should not be a result of construct-irrelevant variance. Messick (1989) points out that, given the social consequences of test use and value implications of test-score interpretation, testing practices should be based on both scientific evidence and ethical consideration.

REFERENCES

Alwin, D. F., & Jackson, D. J. (1981). Applications of simultaneous factor analysis to issues of factorial invariance. In D. Jackson & E. Borgatta (Eds.), *Factor analysis and measurement in sociological research: A multi-dimensional perspective* (pp. 249–279). Beverly Hills, CA: Sage.

American Educational Research Association, American Psychological Association, & National Council on Measurement in Education. (1999). *Standards for educational and psychological testing.* Washington, DC: American Psychological Association.

Anderson, R. J., & Sisco, F. H. (1977). *Standardization of the WISC-R performance scale for deaf children. (Office of Demographic Studies Publication Series T, No. 1).* Washington, DC: Gallaudet College.

Angoff, W. H. (1993). Perspectives on differential item functioning methodology. In P. W. Holland & H. Wainer (Eds.), *Differential item functioning* (pp. 3–24). Hillsdale, NJ: Erlbaum.

Angoff, W. H., & Ford, S. F. (1973). Item–race interaction on a test of scholastic aptitude. *Journal of Educational Measurement, 10,* 95–105.

Bentler, P. M. (1990). Comparative fit indexes in structural models. *Psychological Bulletin,* *107,* 238–246.

Bentler, P. M. (1992). On the fit of models to covariances and methodology in the Bulletin. *Psychological Bulletin, 112,* 400–404.

Berk, R. A. (Ed). (1982). *Handbook of methods for detecting test bias.* Baltimore: Johns Hopkins University Press.

Bock, R. D. (1997). The nominal categories model. In W. J. van der Linden & R. K. Hambleton (Eds.) *Handbook of modern item response theory* (pp. 33–49). New York: Springer.

Bock, R. D., & Aitkin, M. (1981). Marginal maximum likelihood estimation of item parameters: Application of an EM algorithm. *Psychometrika, 46,* 443–459.

Bollen, K. A. (1989). *Structural equations with latent variables.* New York: Wiley.

Bracken, B. A., & McCallum, R. S. (1998). *Universal Nonverbal Intelligence Test: Examiner's manual.* Itasca, IL: Riverside Publishing.

Braden, J. P. (1999). Straight talk about assessment and diversity: What do we know? *School Psychology Quarterly, 14,* 343–355.

Breslow, N. E., & Day, N. E. (1980). *Statistical methods in cancer research, Volume 1: The analysis of case–control studies.* Lyon: International Agency for Research on Cancer.

Browne, M. W., & Cudeck, R. (1993). Alternative ways of assessing fit. In K. A. Bollen & J. S. Long (Eds.), *Testing structural equations models* (pp. 136–162). Newbury Park, CA: Sage.

Bryk, A. (1980). Review of Bias in mental testing. *Journal of Educational Measurement, 17,* 369–374.

Camilli, G. (1979). *A critique of the chi-square method for assessing item bias.* Unpublished paper, Laboratory of Educational Research, University of Colorado.

Camilli, G., & Shepard, L. A. (1987). The inadequacy of ANOVA for detecting test bias. *Journal of Educational Statistics, 12,* 87–89.

Camilli, G., & Shepard, L. A. (1994). *Methods for identifying biased test items.* Thousand Oaks, CA: Sage.

Cattell, R. B. (1978). *The scientific use of factor analysis in behavioral and life sciences.* New York: Plenum.

Clauser, B. E., Nungester, R. J., & Swaminathan, H. (1996). Improving the matching for DIF analysis by conditioning on both test score and an educational background variable. *Journal of Educational Measurement, 33,* 453–464.

Cleary, T. A. (1968). Test bias: Prediction of grades of Negro and White students in integrated colleges. *Journal of Educational Measurement, 5,* 115–124.

Cohen, A. S., Kim, S., & Wollack, J. A. (1996). An investigation of the likelihood ratio test for detection of differential item functioning. *Applied Psychological Measurement, 20,* 15–26.

Cotter, D. E., & Berk, R. A. (1981, April). *Item bias in the WISC-R using black, white, and hispanic learning disabled children.* Paper presented at the Annual Meeting of the American Educational Research Association, Los Angeles (ERIC Document Reproduction Service ED 206 631).

Diana v. the California State Board of Education. Case No. C-70-37 RFP. (N.D. Cal. 1970).

Dorans, N. J. (1989). Two new approaches to assessing differential item functioning: Standardization and the Mantel–Haenszel method. *Applied Psychological Measurement, 2,* 217–233.

Dorans, N. J., & Kulick, E. (1983). *Assessing unexpected differential item performance of female candidates on SAT and TSWE forms administered in December 1977: An application of the standardization approach* (Research Rep. No. 83-9). Princeton, NJ: Educational Testing Service.

Engelhard, G., Hansche, L., & Rutledge, K. E. (1990). Accuracy of bias review judges in identifying differential item functioning on teacher certification tests. *Applied Psychological Measurement, 3,* 347–360.

Feingold, A. (1993). Cognitive gender differences: A developmental perspective. *Sex Roles, 29,* 91–112.

Feldt, L. S., & Brennan, R. L. (1989). Reliability. In R. L. Linn (Ed.), *Educational measurement* (3rd ed., pp. 105–146). New York: American Council on Education & Macmillan.

Frisby, C. L. (1998). Poverty and socioeconomic status. In J. L. Sandoval, C. L. Frisby, K. F. Geisinger, J. D. Scheuneman, & J. R. Grenier (Eds.), *Test interpretation and diversity: Achieving equity in assessment* (pp. 241–270). Washington, DC: American Psychological Association.

Green, B. F., Crone, C. R., & Folk, V. G. (1989). A method for studying differential distractor functioning. *Journal of educational measurement, 26,* 147–160.

Hammill, D. D., Pearson, N. A., & Wiederholt, J. L. (1997). *Comprehensive test of nonverbal intelligence.* Austin, TX: PRO-ED.

Herrnstein, R. J., & Murray, C. (1994). *The bell curve.* New York: Free Press.

Hills, J. R. (1989). Screening for potentially biased items in testing programs. *Educational Measurement: Issues and Practice, 8*(4), 5–11.

Holland, P. W., & Thayer, D. T. (1988). Differential item functioning and the Mantel–Haenszel procedure. In H. Wainer & H. I. Braun (Eds.), *Test validity* (pp. 129–145). Hillsdale, NJ: Erlbaum.

Hu, L., Bentler, P. M., & Kano, Y. (1992). Can test statistics in covariance structure analysis be trusted? *Psychological Bulletin, 112,* 351–362.

Ilai, D., & Willerman, L. (1989). Sex differences in WAIS-R item performance. *Intelligence, 13,* 225–234.

Jastak, J. E., & Jastak, S. R. (1964). Short forms of the WAIS and WISC vocabulary subtests. *Journal of Clinical Psychology, 20,* 167–199.

Jensen, A. R. (1969). How much can we boost IQ and scholastic achievement? *Harvard Educational Review, 39,* 1–123.

Jensen, A. R. (1974). How biased are culture-loaded tests? *Genetic Psychology Monographs, 90,* 185–224.

Jensen, A. R. (1976). Test bias and construct validity. *Phi Delta Kappan, 58,* 340–346.

Jensen, A. R. (1980). *Bias in mental testing.* New York: Free Press.

Joint Committee on Testing Practices. (1988). *Code of fair testing practices in education.* Washington, DC: National Council on Measurement in Education.

Jöreskog, K. G. (1971). Simultaneous factor analysis in several populations. *Psychometrika, 57,* 409–426.

Jöreskog, K. G., & Sörbom, D. (1989). *LISREL7: A guide to the program and applications* (2nd ed.). Chicago: SPSS.

Koh, T., Abbatiello, A., & McLoughlin, C. S. (1984). Cultural bias in WISC subtest items: A response to Judge Grady's suggestions in relation to the PASE case. *School Psychology Review, 13,* 89–94.

Kromrey, J. D., & Parshall, C. G. (1991, November). *Screening items for bias: An empirical comparison of the performance of three indices in small samples of examinees.* Paper presented at the annual meeting of the Florida Educational Research Association, Clearwater, FL.

Larry P. et al. v. Wilson Riles, Superintendent of Public Instruction for the State of California, et al., Case No. C-71-2270 (N.D. Cal., 1979).

Lawrence, I. M., & Curley, W. E. (1989, March). *Differential item functioning of SAT-Verbal reading subscore items for males and females: follow-up study.* Paper presented at the annual meeting of the American Educational Research Association, San Francisco.

Lawrence, I. M., Curley, W. E., & McHale, F. J. (1988, April). *Differential item functioning of SAT-Verbal reading subscore items for male and female examinees.* Paper presented at the annual meeting of the American Educational Research Association, New Orleans.

Linn, R. L., Levine, M. V., Hastings, C. N., & Waldrop, J. L. (1980). *An investigation of item bias in a test of reading comprehension* (Technical Rep. No. 163). Urbana: Center for the Study of Reading, University of Illinois at Urbana-Champaign.

Loehlin, J. C., Lindzey, G., & Spuhler, J. N. (1975). *Race differences in intelligence.* San Francisco: W. H. Freeman.

Lord, F. M. (1980). *Applications of item response theory to practical testing problems.* Hillsdale, NJ: Lawrence Erlbaum.

Lynn, R. (1977). The intelligence of the Japanese. *Bulletin of the British Psychological Society, 30,* 69–72.

Maller, S. J. (1996). WISC-III Verbal item invariance across samples of deaf and hearing children of similar measured ability. *Journal of Psychoeducational Assessment, 14,* 152–165.

Maller, S. J. (2000). Item invariance in four subtests of the Universal Nonverbal Intelligence Test across groups of deaf and hearing children. *Journal of Psychoeducational Assessment, 18,* 240–254.

Maller, S. J. (2001). Differential item functioning in the WISC-III: Item parameters for boys and girls in the national standardization sample. *Educational and Psychological Measurement, 61*, 793–817.

Maller, S. J., & Ferron, J. (1997). WISC-III factor invariance across deaf and standardization samples. *Educational and Psychological Measurement, 7*, 987–994.

Maller, S. J., Konold, T. R., & Glutting, J. J. (1998). WISC-III Factor invariance across samples of children displaying appropriate and inappropriate test-taking behavior. *Educational and Psychological Measurement, 58*, 467–475.

Mantel, N., & Haenszel, W. (1959). Statistical aspects of the analysis of data from the retrospective studies of disease. *Journal of the National Cancer Institute, 22*, 719–748.

McGaw, B., & Jöreskog, K. G. (1971). Factorial invariance of ability measures in groups differing in intelligence and socio-economic status. *British Journal of Mathematical and Statistical Psychology, 24*, 154–168.

Messick, S. (1989). Validity. In R. L. Linn (Ed.), *Educational measurement* (3rd ed., pp. 13–103). New York: American Council on Education & Macmillan.

Miele, F. (1979). Cultural bias in the WISC. *Intelligence, 3*, 149–164.

Munford, P. R., & Munoz, A. (1980). A comparison of the WISC and WISC-R on Hispanic children. *Journal of Clinical Psychology, 36*, 452–458.

National Council on Measurement in Education (1995). *Code of professional responsibilities in educational measurement*. Washington, DC: NCME.

Nelson, K. M., Arthur, P., Lautiger, J., & Smith, D. K. (1994, March). *Does the use of color on the WISC-III affect student performance?* Paper presented at the annual meeting of the National Association of School Psychologists, Seattle, WA.

O'Neill, K. A., & McPeek, W. M. (1993). Item and test characteristics that are associated with differential item functioning. In H. Wainer & H. I. Braun (Eds.). *Test validity* (pp. 255–276). Hillsdale, NJ: Erlbaum.

Plake, B. S. (1980). A comparison of a statistical and subjective procedure to ascertain item validity: One step in the test validation process. *Educational and Psychological Measurement, 30*, 397–404.

Reynolds, C. R. (1982). The problem of bias in psychological assessment. In C. R. Reynolds & T. B. Gutkin (Eds.), *The handbook of school psychology* (pp. 178–108). New York: John Wiley.

Rigdon, E. E. (1996). CFI versus RMSEA: A comparison of two fit indexes for structural equation modeling. *Structural Equation Modeling, 3*, 369–379.

Roid, G. H., & Miller, L. J. (1997). Leiter *International performance scale-revised: Examiner's manual.* In G. H. Roid and L. J. Miller, Leiter *International performance scale-revised*, Wood Dale, IL: Stoelting.

Rogers, H. J., & Swaminathan, H. (1993). A comparison of logistic regression and the Mantel–Haenszel procedures for detecting differential item functioning. *Applied Measurement in Education, 17*, 105–116.

Ross-Reynolds, J., & Reschly, D. J. (1983). An investigation of item bias on the WISC-R with four sociocultural groups. *Journal of Consulting and Clinical Psychology, 51*, 144–146.

Samejima, F. (1969). Estimation of latent ability using a response pattern of graded scores. *Psychometrika Monograph, 4(2)*, Whole No. 17.

Sandoval, J. (1979). The WISC-R and internal evidence of test bias with minority groups. *Journal of Consulting and Clinical Psychology, 47*, 919–927.

Sandoval, J., & Miille, M. P. W. (1980). Accuracy of judgements of WISC-R item difficulty for minority groups. *Journal of Consulting and Clinical Psychology, 48*, 249–253.

Sandoval, J., Zimmerman, I. L., & Woo-Sam, J. M. (1977). Cultural differences on the WISC-R verbal items. *Journal of School Psychology, 21*, 49–55.

Satorra, A., & Bentler, P. M. (1988). Scaling corrections for chi-square statistics in covariance structure analysis. *Proceedings of the Business and Economic Statistics Section of the American Statistical Association*, 303–313.

Scheuneman, J. (1975, April). A new method of assessing bias in test items. Paper presented at the annual meeting of the American Educational Research Association, Washington, DC.

Scheuneman, J. D., & Gerritz, K. (1990). Using differential item functioning procedures to explore sources of item difficulty and group performance characteristics. *Journal of Educational Measurement, 27*, 109–131.

Scheuneman, J. D., & Oakland, T. (1998). In J. Sandoval, C. L. Frisby, K. F. Geisinger, J. D. Scheuneman, & J. R. Grenirer (Eds.), *Test interpretation and diversity: Achieving equity in assessment* (pp. 77–103). Washington, DC: American Psychological Association.

Shelley-Sireci, & Sireci, S. G. (1998, August). *Controlling for uncontrolled variables in cross-cultural research.* Paper presented at the annual meeting of the American Psychological Association, San Francisco.

Sireci, S. G., Bastari, B., & Allalouf, A. (1998, August). *Evaluating construct equivalence across adapted tests.* Paper presented at the annual meeting of the American Psychological Association, San Francisco.

Simpson, E. H. (1951). Interpretation of interaction contingency tables. *Journal of the Royal Statistical Society, (Series B), 13,* 238–241.

Smith, T. C., Edmonds, J. E., & Smith, B. (1989). The role of sex differences in the referral process as measured by the Peabody Picture Vocabulary Test—Revised and the Wechsler Intelligence Scale for Children—Revised. *Psychology in the Schools, 26,* 354–358.

Swaminathan, H., & Rogers, H. J. (1990). Detecting differential item functioning using logistic regression procedures. *Journal of Educational Measurement, 27,* 361–370.

Thissen, D. (1991). MULTILOG (Version 6.30) [Computer software]. Chicago: Scientific Software.

Thissen, D., & Steinberg, L. (1997). A response model for multiple-choice items. In W. J. van der Linden & R. K. Hambleton (Eds.), *Handbook of modern item response theory* (pp. 51–65). New York: Springer.

Thissen, D., Steinberg, L., & Gerrard, M. (1986). Beyond group mean differences: The concept of item bias. *Psychological Bulletin, 99,* 118–128.

Thissen, D., Steinberg, L., & Wainer, H. (1988). Use of item response theory in the study of group differences in trace lines. In H. Wainer & H. I. Braun (Eds.), *Test validity* (pp. 149–169). Hillsdale, NJ: Erlbaum.

Thissen, D., Steinberg, L., & Wainer, H. (1993). Detection of differential item functioning using the parameters of item response theory. In P. W. Holland & H. Wainer (Eds.), *Differential item functioning* (pp. 67–114). Hillsdale, NJ: Erlbaum.

Turner, R. G., & Willerman, L. (1977). Sex differences in WAIS item performance. *Journal of Clinical Psychology, 33,* 795–798.

Vance, B., Hankins, N. & Brown, W. (1988). Ethnic and sex differences on the Test of Nonverbal Intelligence, Quick Test of Intelligence, and Wechsler Intelligence Scale for Children—Revised. *Journal of Clinical Psychology, 44,* 261–265.

Veale, J. R. (1977). *A note on the use of chi-square with "correct/incorrect" data to detect culturally biased items* (Statistical Research in the Behavioral Sciences, Technical Report No. 4). (Available from J. R. Veale, PO Box 4036, Berkeley, CA 94704.)

Welch, C., & Hoover, H. D. (1993). Procedures for extending item bias techniques to polytomously scored items. *Applied Psychological Measurement, 6,* 1–19.

Wessel, J., & Potter, A. (1994, March). *Analysis of WISC-III data from an urban population of referred children.* Paper presented at the annual meeting of the National Association of School Psychologists, Seattle, WA.

Wild, C. L., & McPeek, W. M. (1986, August). *Performance of the Mantel–Haenszel statistic in identifying differentially functioning items.* Paper presented at the annual meeting of the American Psychological Association, Washington, DC.

Wilkinson, S. C. (1993). WISC-R profiles of children with superior intellectual ability. *Gifted Child Quarterly, 2,* 84–92.

Zeiky, M. (1993). Practical questions in the use of DIF statistics in item development. In P. W. Holland & H. Wainer (Eds.), *Differential item functioning* (pp. 337–364). Hillsdale, NJ: Erlbaum.

Zumbo, B. D. (1999). *A handbook on the theory and methods of differential item functioning (DIF): Logistic regression modeling as a unitary framework for binary and Likert-type (ordinal) item scores.* Ottawa: Directorate of Human Resources Research and Evaluation, Department of National Defense.

Zwick, R., Donoghue, J. R., & Grima, A. (1993). Assessing differential item functioning in performance tasks. *Journal of Educational Measurement, 30,* 233–251.

3

Physiological and Psychological Influences on Multicultural and Nonverbal Assessment

R. Steve McCallum

One of the animals in George Orwell's *Animal Farm* (1946) says, "All animals are equal, but some animals are more equal than others," acknowledging in a humorous way the biological reality that animals, including humans, really are not created equal. Nor are all external environments equal. Some of us are born into affluent families, with all the advantages inherent in that situation; others are born into poverty, and face the associated problems. Similarly, assessment of individual differences is influenced by a variety of (internal and external) factors. For example, examinees are influenced by the biology they bring to the testing setting; also, they bring perceptions of the testing enterprise forged in their particular subcultural milieus. The assessment environment is typically created to increase the motivation of the examinee and to establish the best testing situation. In this chapter, I discuss some assessment influences emanating from an examinee's physiological and psychological environment, and focus primarily on the impact of these variables on nonverbal assessment.

R. Steve McCallum, Department of Educational Psychology and Counseling, University of Tennessee, Knoxville, Tennessee 37996.

Handbook of Nonverbal Assessment, edited by R. Steve McCallum, Kluwer Academic/Plenum Publishers, 2003.

SOME PHYSIOLOGICAL INFLUENCES

A detailed treatment of physiological influences on test performance is beyond the scope of this chapter. However, it is important to sensitize examiners to some of the more salient physiological conditions of examinees. Obviously, examiners need to accommodate to biologically determined conditions such as deafness, cerebral palsy, Down syndrome, etc. These impairments result from physiological anomalies and trauma impact in a mutually reciprocal fashion and both on the external and the internal environments of examinees. In addition, there are other more subtle physiological influences that result primarily from the contribution of multiple-gene pairs (interacting with the environment). In their important article entitled *The Genetic Basis of Complex Human Behaviors*, Plomin, Owen, and McGuffin (1994) discuss the case genetic research has built for the importance of genetic factors in the acquisition of many complex personality and cognitive abilities (and disabilities), including reading disability, autism, affective disorders, schizophrenia, Alzheimer's disease, memory, processing speed, extraversion, verbal and spatial reasoning, and general intelligence. Using twin studies and other sources of data, these researchers discuss the "heritability factor" for these characteristics, noting that heritability can be estimated roughly by doubling the differences between the intraclass correlations obtained from monozygotic and dizygotic twins. This statistic is considered to represent the proportion of phenotypic variance in a population that can be attributed to genetic influence. According to the calculations reported by Plomin, Owen, and McGuffin, heritabilities for personality, scholastic achievement, verbal and spatial reasoning, and general intelligence range from 40% to 50%. Others (e.g., Pool, 1997) discuss how genes contribute to very specific individual personality differences such as optimism, risk-taking, gregariousness, even homosexuality. It is increasingly apparent that many behavioral scientists have shifted dramatically from "nurture" to "nature" as an explanation of the origin of behavior. In fact, environmentalism peaked in the 1950s and 1960s, and has been on the decline since, due in part to the increasing sophisticated knowledge base now available via innovative medical technologies. These medical advances are capable of showing the power of biology to explain behaviors once thought to be almost totally environmentally determined (e.g., autism).

Many of the physiological influences are so powerful that they restrict assessment totally to nonverbal means (e.g., severe cerebral palsy, deafness). In fact, most of this book is devoted to describing nonverbal strategies to assess intelligence and related constructs. However, as mentioned above, many physiological influences on the assessment process are subtle, and those less obvious influences are the primary focus of this chapter.

Examiners are becoming increasingly aware that even the subtle physiological contributions to the testing session can create significant impact. How does this information help in the evaluation of nonverbal behavior? This awareness can sensitize examiners to be alert to these sources of behavioral variation. One important line of research that is helping to define the link between the influence of physiology and test behavior focuses on behavior constellations or traits referred to as temperaments; temperaments are assumed to be the building blocks of personality and produce individual differences in problem-solving abilities in general and influence the manner in which intelligence is displayed in testing situations in particular.

Although a number of child development experts have discussed the origin and typology of temperaments (e.g., Kagan, 1994), perhaps the most comprehensive description has been offered by Thomas, Chess, and Birch (1968) and colleagues. Chess and Thomas (1996) describe temperament as akin to a "behavioral style" and note that it may be best viewed as referring to the how of behavior. They note that two children may dress themselves alike and may have similar interests and even similar success in meeting life's challenges. However, they may differ significantly with regard to the quickness with which they move, the ease with which they approach a new task or physical environment, the intensity of their mood, the effort they display, the activity level, and so on. Thomas et al. note that temperaments are forged by biology via interactions with the environment; however, biology seems to be a strong determinant because variation in temperaments can be distinguished very early in an infant's life.

Thomas et al. (1968) identified nine temperaments by observing (and following over time) the behavior of very young infants. They identified nine basic temperaments along continua, as follows: activity level, rhythmicity (regularity of habits), distractibility, tendency to approach or avoid new situations, adaptability, attention span and task persistence, quality of mood, intensity of reaction, and threshold of responsiveness. In a longitudinal study (the New York Longitudinal Study), children were followed for years, from infancy through the toddler stage, and even into adolescence. Using these nine categories, Thomas et al. found that most children could be identified as "easy," "difficult," or "slow to warm up." Easy children were those positive in mood, adaptable, regular in feeding, eating, sleeping habits, able to attend and persevere, etc. The difficult children exhibited very irregular habits, responded impulsively, were labile in mood, unable to maintain task persistence, etc. The "slow to warm up" group exhibited behaviors somewhere in between, for example, showing a reluctance to engage the environment until they were sure it held no surprises, somewhat irregular in habits and mood, somewhat persistent, etc. A few of the children were not easy to categorize and did not fit well into the three groups.

Obviously, it is possible to see how temperaments can impact the testing situation. For example, examinees who are highly distractible, show little task persistence, or are highly active, impulsive, or extremely shy will present significant challenges to the examiner. Of course, these characteristics may interact with other influences, such as medications, lack of sleep, hunger, etc. Examiners should be aware of and report whether the examinee was on or off medications. Of course, examiners may request that parents refrain from administering behavior-altering medications on the day of the evaluation if the intent is to assess the child's natural state.

Examiners should become aware of the power of certain commonly administered medications to affect testing behavior. There are several resources available to examiners that describe behavioral effects of medications (e.g., Wilens, 1999), and many children take either over-the-counter or prescribed medicines currently. Some of the more commonly used medications include methylphenidate, pemoline, or dextroamphetamine for attention deficits and hyperactivity; diazepam, or clorazepate for anxiety; haloperidol, thioridazine, or clorzapine for psychoses; imipramine, amitriptyline, desipramine, bupropion, or trazodone for affective disorders and/or obsessive-compulsive disorders and/or enuresis; albuterol for asthma; diphenhydramine, hydroxyzine, promethazine, or cyproheptadine for congestion; and phenobarbitol for seizures. All of these medications can cause side effects, including impulsivity, excitability, drowsiness, agitations, etc. (See the Appendix for some of the more common medications, generic and trade names of those medications, and side effects, taken primarily from Wilens's (1999) book *Straight Talk about Psychiatric Medications for Children*.)

Examiners who are knowledgeable regarding physiological influences will be alert to how these influences can affect the examinee in the testing session, realizing that many of these behaviors will be present also in the classroom and home settings, and will impact the success of the child in social and academic situations. Examiners who possess this knowledge can help parents and teachers modify the environment to facilitate behavior change, but they can also help parents and teachers understand the relative influences of physiology and environment. Thus, they can help target environmentally based behavior change efforts toward those behaviors more amenable to environmental impact.

Obviously, the physiological environment of the examinee significantly contributes to the quality of the testing session and, by inference, to the quality of the child's life in general. The experienced examiner will be alert to these influences and note those that are salient, in either a positive or negative manner. Because these influences will also contribute to the examinee's success outside the testing session, the experienced examiner will help teachers and parents identify and link appropriate treatments to problem behaviors, treatments that take into account the extent to which particular problem behaviors are amenable to environmental influences (vs. those which might be more resistant to environmentally focused treatments but more amenable to biological treatments, such as medication).

PSYCHOLOGICAL INFLUENCES

Psychological influences on the assessment process could be considered from a variety of perspectives (e.g., within-the-child characteristics such as personality, as well as outside-the-child variables such as reinforcement history). For the purposes of this chapter, discussion will focus on specific psychological influences produced by certain unique characteristics of the examinee, by the environment of the test session, and by the examiner. The unique characteristics of the examinee that make nonverbal assessment necessary are of particular interest.

Examinee Characteristics

Nonverbal assessment is appropriate in a number of situations (e.g., for deaf children, those with language deficits, and those from other cultures). Examinees from cultures other than the mainstream culture may possess shared characteristics, that is, behaviors associated with membership in their particular culture. These shared characteristics allow for some generalizations about the problem-solving strategies and general test-taking strategies, attitudes, etc. of examinees from that culture (e.g., the reflective styles of some Asian cultures), though examiners must guard against making stereotypical judgments that would negatively impact performance (see Sattler, 2001). Seasoned examiners will want to explore the subculture of examinees before the testing session. For example, speeded performance, wearing high-status clothes, and glibness are prized in the United States, but are not emphasized in some cultures. As Bracken and Barona (1991) note, "The specific individual experiences of nonmajority culture individuals will greatly influence their educational, emotional, and language development" (p. 129). Examinees from nonmainstream cultures (as well as those who are deaf and/or from other language-deficit populations) may have unique styles of problem-solving. For example, they may not prize an independent problem-solving milieu, but may be much more comfortable working in a cooperative arrangement. They may not value speeded performance, or appreciate the "logic" inherent in western-style categorization and classification (Sternberg & Grigorenko, 2001). And, for those examinees whose first language is not English, an interpreter or bilingual psychologist or teacher may be needed to interact successfully with the examinee and/or family members. Importantly, examiners must not assume that the primary instrument used for *bilingual* examinees should be an English language instrument; often, bilingual students are not sufficiently proficient for a valid assessment in English and would be better served by administration of a nonverbal measure. The successful examiner will be alert to these types of population differences and know in advance how best to address them.

Examiners should be aware that a parent's perceptions of their child's social skills, cognitive sophistication, academic motivation and integration into the U.S. culture may be helpful in interpreting test behavior and results. Parent interviews are often extremely helpful to establish a more meaningful context (e.g., the extent to which education is valued, the extent to which the examinee's nonverbal behavior is encouraged/discouraged). Takushi and Uomoto (2001) describe the components of a successful multicultural clinical interview, and many of their suggestions are relevant for interviewing parents of referred children as well as the children themselves.

As previously noted, examinees who have special needs (e.g., speech and language problems, difficulty hearing, very limited cognitive ability, as in Down's syndrome, serious emotional or psychiatric disorders) require unique expertise. But, unlike culturally different examinees who have a history of adequate communication in a language other than English, these examinees sometimes have a long history of frustration associated with their inability to hear and/or express themselves effectively in any language. In some cases, there is an emotional overlay associated with this frustration that negatively impacts assessment. For example, these individuals may exhibit less persistence when they are not understood. Examiners should bring to bear all their behavior-management skills to establish rapport, gently but firmly maintain control of the session, and implement assessment in a timely and efficient manner. Usually, the best strategy for the examiner is to spend a short amount of time establishing a productive relationship, then relatively quickly engage the examinee in the test process. Remember, the goal of the examiner is not to provide treatment, but to obtain optimal test performance in a timely manner.

Examinees who have physical disabilities, such as cerebral palsy, present particular challenges. The examiner must observe the examinee beforehand to determine the level of proficiency available relative to the test demands. Some modifications may be necessary, such as altering the height of the testing table, providing smaller or larger chairs than the room initially provides, obtaining unusually bright lighting for those with limited vision, etc. Recent innovations in technology make certain aspects of existing tests available to physically limited individuals via menu-driven computer programs and laser-guided "pointers," guided only by head movement. Examiners must report the extent to which a particular test administration differs from standardized administration and estimate the effects on the obtained scores.

Finally, examinees with limited verbal skills due to emotional problems are particularly challenging. For example, selective/elective mutes will not talk to the examiner in all likelihood; in addition, they may be very shy and noncompliant in other ways. Also, examinees with certain emotional problems and poor reality testing, such as autism, or Asperger's disorder may be particularly difficult to motivate, as are those who are socially maladjusted or oppositional. Establishing rapport may be very difficult. These examinees are socially disconnected and may seem distant and uninvolved. Similarly, establishing rapport with examinees who are oppositional or defiant may be difficult, if not impossible. Examiners should know the characteristics of these diagnostic categories and not be surprised or discouraged by examinee behavior. Examinees who have particularly poor reality testing (e.g., those with diagnoses of psychotic conditions, including schizophrenia) may be completely uncooperative.

Time spent in reviewing records to determine characteristics, hobbies, and interests of the examinees may be useful. Seasoned examiners will be aware of the characteristics associated with typical "diagnostic categories" in general and will take the time to become familiar with the particular characteristics of specific examinees before the evaluation begins.

Certainly, it is important to know how diagnostic characteristics may interact with setting and examiner characteristics.

Examiner Characteristics

Examiners who conduct routine individualized assessments should possess the necessary training, and those who provide specialized individualized assessment beyond the traditional strategies should receive even more extensive training. Those who use individualized standardized tests of intelligence, personality, or achievement typically will have been trained to administer those tests in university training programs under close supervision. Standardized tests must be administered using the same procedures created when the test was developed (and normed). If administration procedures are not followed, the obtained scores contain error, more or less, depending on the amount of deviation (Cronbach, 1960). Because nonverbal tests may require use of pantomime, gestures, etc., administration of nonverbal measures require even more extensive training, building on the basic skills.

Even before the assessment actually starts, examiners need to know how to establish rapport, deal with unusual or oppositional examinees (as suggested in the previous section) and obtain extra-test data to provide a context for the obtained scores—skills typically taught in university training programs. In addition to knowing these basic skills, it is the responsibility of each examiner to know particular test instruments extremely well so that the test administration procedures are automatized. As mentioned above, particular tests may use unique administration procedures. For example, the UNIT (Bracken & McCallum, 1998) uses eight specific administration gestures—the examiner should know how to use the gestures well before administering this test. In short, the examiner should not have to devote energy and attention to the mechanics of test administration but should be relatively free to observe the examinee's behavior in the test situation and to establish a good pace, with little or no dead time between activities and subtests.

The examiner should be pleasant, sincere, encouraging, and even cheerful, but should maintain a structured and somewhat business-like attitude. Encouragement for effort is essential, particularly early on in the session, and the examiner should be attuned to the tempo of the examinee and follow suit, allowing those who are more comfortable with a rapid pace to proceed accordingly. Examiners should be sensitive to the needs of the examinees. For example, younger examinees may need restroom breaks more often; examinees who are easily frustrated or give up easily should be given more encouragement; and examinees who become bored easily should be moved along quickly to allow them to engage the more difficult items.

Testing Environment Characteristics

The testing environment should be pleasant, but not distracting. Materials should be accessible to the examinee, which requires furniture of the appropriate height and size. Lighting, temperature, and noise levels should be appropriate. The testing room should be pleasant but not filled with distracting bulletin boards or windows. Test materials should be presented in a manner consistent with standardization but close enough to the examinee to facilitate easy use. Most test-administration manuals describe the juxtaposition of materials, examiner, and examinee. For standardized testing, it is typical for the examinee and the examiner to sit at an angle across the corner of the testing table; the examiner usually sits closest to the examinee's dominant hand to facilitate manipulating the materials more easily and seeing the examinee's responses. The table should be flat and smooth, and cleared of all material except the test stimuli. Typically, the testing room contains only the examiner and examinee, but occasionally, a third person may be necessary, at least initially (e.g., an interpreter, a parent for a very young or frightened child). If a third party is present, the testing guidelines should be explained to prevent spoiling the examinee's responses. For example, parents need to know that the examinee should provide answers to the particular test questions without help.

SUMMARY

This chapter describes some salient physiological and psychological influences on multicultural and nonverbal assessment. Obviously, examinees from culturally diverse settings and those with emotional problems and/or language deficits may behave in ways that are different from mainstream examinees and those who present no language-related problems. Examiners who are sensitive to these differences, the psychological impact of the testing environment, and the impact of biology on test behavior will be more successful in obtaining accurate estimates of intellectual, educational, and emotional functioning. In addition, examiners who can relate the impact of these influences to the success or failure of the child in the testing session and then extrapolate the impact of these influences to the school and home will be more successful in helping teachers and parents help their children.

REFERENCES

Bracken, B. A., & Barona, A. (1991). State of the art procedures for translating, validating, and using psychoeducational tests in cross-cultural education. *School Psychology International*, *12*(1–2), 119–132.

Bracken, B. A., & McCallum, R. S. (1998). *Universal nonverbal intelligence test*. Itasca, IL: Riverside.

Chess, S., & Thomas, A. (1996). *Temperament: Theory and practice*, New York: Brunner/Mazel.

Cronbach, L. J. (1960). *Essentials of psychological testing* (2nd ed.). New York: Harper.

Kagan, J. (1994) Inhibited and uninhibited temperaments. In W. B. Carey & S. C. McDevitt (Eds.), *Prevention and early intervention*. New York: Brunner/Mazel.

Orwell, G. (1946). *Animal farm.* New York: Harcourt Brace Jovanovich.

Plomin, R., Owen, M. J., & McGuffin, P. (1994). The genetic basis of complex human behaviors. *Science, 264,* 1733–1739.

Pool, R. (1997). Portrait of a gene guy. *Discover,* 51–57.

Sattler, J. M. (2001). *Assessment of children* (4th ed.). San Diego, CA: Author.

Sternberg, R. J., & Grigorenko, E. L. (2001). Ability testing across cultures. In L. A. Suzuki, J. G. Ponterotto, & P. J. Meller (Eds.), *Handbook of multicultural assessment: Clinical, psychological, and educational applications* (2nd ed., pp. 335–358). San Francisco: Jossey-Bass.

Takushi, R., & Uomoto, J. M. (2001). The clinical interview from a multicultural perspective. In L. A. Suzuki, J. G. Ponterotto, & P. J. Meller (Eds.), *Handbook of multicultural assessment: Clinical, psychological, and educational applications* (2nd ed., pp. 47–66). San Francisco: Jossey-Bass.

Thomas, A., Chess, S., & Birch, H. G. (1968). *Temperament and behavior disorders in children.* New York: New York University Press.

Wilens, T. E. (1999). *Straight talk about psychiatric medications for kids.* New York: The Guilford Press.

APPENDIX: SOME MEDICATIONS (AND DOSES) USED FOR THE TREATMENT OF CHILDHOOD DISORDERS

Generic name	Brand name	Sizes and preparation	Side effects
Stimulants			
Methylphenidate	Ritalin	5, 10, 20 mg; regular tablets	Weight loss, exacerbates moodiness, anorexia, insomnia, irritability, sadness, agitation, dizziness, "rebound" effect," tics
Dextroamphetamine	Dexedrine	20 mg; sustained-release tablets	
		5, 10 mg; regular tablets	
		5, 10, 15 mg; spansules	
Magnesium pemoline	Cylert	18.75, 37.5, 75 mg; tablets	
		37.5 mg; chewable tablets	
Amphetamine	Biphetamine	5 mg	
Methamphetamine	Desoxyn	5 mg; gradumet tablets	
Amphetamine compounds	Adderall	5, 10, 20, 30 mg; tablets	
Antidepressants (serotonin reuptake inhibitors)			
Fluoxetine	Prozac	10, 20, 60 mg; capsules	Stomach aches, weight gain, headaches, agitation, sedation, diarrhea, irritability, insomnia
		20 mg/tsp: suspension	
Sertraline	Zoloft	50, 100 mg; tablets	
Fluvoxamine	Luvox	50, 100 mg; tablets	
Paroxetine	Paxil	20, 30 mg; tablets	
Citalopram	Celexa	20, 40 mg; tablets	
Antidepressants (tricyclics)			
Desipramine	Norpramin	10, 25, 50, 75, 100, 150 mg; tablets	Stomach aches, vivid dreams, blurred vision, constipation, headaches, dry mouth, sedation, rash
	Pertofrane		
Nortriptyline	Pamelor	10, 25, 50 mg; capsules	
	Vivactyl	10 mg/tsp: oral suspension	
Imipramine	Tofranil	10, 25, 50, 75, 100, 150 mg; tablets and capsules	
Amitriptyline	Elavil	10, 25, 50, 75, 100, 150 mg; tablets	
Protriptyline	Vivactyle	5, 10 mg; capsules	
Maprotiline	Ludiomil	25, 50, 75 mg; tablets	
Clomipramine	Anafranil	25, 50, 100 mg; tablets	

Antidepressants (atypical)			
Venlafaxine	Effexor	25, 37.5, 50, 75 mg; tablets 37.5, 75, 150 mg; extended-release tablets	Nausea, headache, stomach aches, agitation
Trazodone	Desyrel	50, 100, 150, 300 mg; tablets	Dry mouth, sedation, agitation,
Nefazodone	Serzone	50, 100 mg; tablets	confusion, constipation
Bupropion	Wellbutrin	75, 100 mg; tablets 100, 150 mg; sustained-release tablets	Insomnia, irritability, exacerbation of tics, anorexia, seizures
Mirtazapine	Remeron	150 mg; tablets	Sedation, stomach aches
Antidepressants (monoamine oxidase inhibitors)			
Tranylcypromine	Parnate	10 mg; tablets	High blood pressure, drowsiness,
Phenelzine	Nardil	15 mg; tablets	dizziness
Antipsychotics (high strength)			
Haloperidol	Haldol	0.5, 1, 2, 5, 10, 20 mg; tablets 2 mg/ml; suspension	Blurred vision, muscle tightness or spasms, dry mouth, confusion,
Pimozide	Orap	2 mg; tablet	sweating, increased appetite,
Fluphenazine	Prolixin	2.5, 5, 10 mg; tablets 5 mg/ml; suspension	drowsiness
Antipsychotics (middle strength)			
Trifluoperazine	Stelazine	1, 2, 5, 10 mg; tablets	Dizziness, congestion, blurred vision,
Perphenazine	Trilafon	2, 4, 8, 16 mg; tablets	increased appetite, drowsiness
Thiothixene	Navane	2, 5, 10, 20 mg; tablets 5 mg/ml; suspension	
Loxapine	Loxitane	5, 10, 25, 50 mg; tablets 5 mg/tsp; suspension	
Antipsychotics (weaker strength)			
Molindone	Moban	5, 10, 25, 50, 100 mg; tablets 4 mg/tsp; suspension	Blurred vision, increased appetite, drowsiness, dizziness, dry mouth,
Mesoridazine	Serentil	10, 25, 50, 100 mg; tablets 25 mg/tsp; suspension	congestion

Continued

APPENDIX (*Continued*)

Medication			
Generic name	Brand name	Sizes and preparation	Side effects
Thioridazine	Mellaril	10, 15, 25, 50, 100, 200 mg; tablets 5, 6, 20 mg/tsp; suspension	
Chlorpromazin	Thorazine	10, 25, 50, 100, 200 mg; tablets 6, 20 mg/tsp; suspension	Blurred vision, seizures, drowsiness, increased appetite, dry mouth
Antipsychotics (newer generation with fewer side effects)			
Risperidone	Risperidal	1, 2, 3 mg; tablets	
Clozapine	Clozaril	25, 50, 100 mg; tablets	
Quetiapine	Seroque	25, 100, 200 mg; tablets	
Olanzapine	Zyprexa	2.5, 5, 7.5, 10 mg; tablets	
Mood stabilizers			
Lithium salts	Lithobid, Lithonate, Lithotabs, Eskalith, Cibalith	150, 300, 450 mg; tablet 8 meq/tsp (= 300 mg; tablet)	Kidney damage, tremors, nausea, weight gain, sleepiness, thirst hypothyroidism
Carbamazepine	Tegretol	100, 200 mg; tablets 100 mg/tsp; suspension	Drowsiness, nausea, blurred vision, dizziness
Valproic acid	Valproate Depakote, Depakene sprinkles	125, 250, 500 mg; tablets and capsules 250 mg/tsp; suspension	Sedation, nausea, loss of appetite, weight gain
Gabapentin	Neurontin	100, 200, 300, 500 mg; capsules	Tiredness, dizziness
Lamotrigine	Lamictal	25, 100, 150, 200 mg; tablets	Tiredness, dizziness, blurred vision, rash
Topiramate	Topamax	25, 100, 200 mg; tablets	Nervousness, dizziness, tiredness, tingling
Tiagabine	Gabitril	4, 12, 16, 20 mg; tablets	Unstable gait, tiredness
Anxiety-breaking agents (anxiolytics)			
Antihistamines			
Chlorpheniramine	Chlor-Trimeton	2, 4, 8 mg; tablets	
Hydroxyzine	Vistaril, Atarax	25, 50 mg; tablets 2 mg/tsp; suspension	
Diphenhydramine	Benadryl	25, 50 mg; tables 25 mg/tsp; suspension	Sedation, dry mouth, drowsiness

Benzodiazepines			
Clonazepam	Klonopin	0.5, 1, 2 mg; tablets	Decreased mental acuity, agitation, disinhibition, sedation, drowsiness, insomnia
Alprazolam	Xanax	0.25, 0.5, 1 mg; tablets	
Triazolam	Halcion	0.5, 1 mg; tablets	
Lorazepam	Ativan	0.5, 1 mg; tablets	
Oxazepam	Serax	15, 30 mg; tablets	
Diazepam	Valium	2, 5, 10 mg; tablets	
Clorazepate	Tranxene	3.75, 7.5, 15 mg; capsules	
Chlordiazepoxide	Librium	10, 25 mg; capsules	
Buspirone	Buspar	5, 10, 15 mg; tablets	Confusion, sedation, disinhibition

Note: See Wilens (1999) for elaboration, particularly regarding the appropriateness of certain medications for specific disorders and side effects.

4

Cross-Battery Assessment of Nonverbal Cognitive Ability

Brian E. Wilhoit and R. Steve McCallum

The Cattell–Horn–Carroll (CHC) Cross-Battery approach, originally known as the Gf–Gc Cross-Battery model of assessment, has been defined as "a time efficient method of intellectual assessment that allows practitioners to measure validly a wider range (or a more in-depth but selective range) of cognitive abilities than that represented by any one intelligence battery in a way consistent with contemporary psychometric theory and research on the structure of intelligence" (McGrew & Flanagan, 1998, p. 357). The CHC Cross-Battery approach provides at least two unique advantages: (a) data gathered both within and across test batteries can be interpreted theoretically and empirically within meaningful patterns; and (b) cognitive test data lead to examination of empirically validated links between specific cognitive abilities and specific academic areas (Flanagan & Ortiz, 2001). The approach provides practitioners with a classification system of cognitive abilities; existing cognitive tests can be evaluated according to the model, that is, subcomponents/subtests can be described based on their ability to assess cognitive abilities within the CHC model.

According to Flanagan and McGrew (1997), the CHC Cross-Battery Assessment system is based on three pillars. The three pillars provide the theoretical underpinnings of the Cross-Battery approach, and depicts a relatively complete taxonomic framework for describing the structure and nature of intelligence. Pillar one classifies cognitive abilities at three levels, or "strata," that differ on the degree of generality, as described in the next section. Pillar two illustrates the placement of subtests of major

Brian E. Wilhoit, Cherokee Health Systems, Talbott, Tennessee 37877. R. Steve McCallum, Department of Educational Psychology and Counseling, University of Tennessee, Knoxville, Tennessee 37996.

Handbook of Nonverbal Assessment, edited by R. Steve McCallum. Kluwer Academic/Plenum Publishers, 2003

published cognitive batteries along the 10 broad (Stratum II) abilities. Pillar three illustrates the placement of subtests of the major published cognitive batteries according to their ability to assess multiple narrow (Stratum I) abilities described in the CHC theory. The second and third pillars are described in later sections for the major nonverbal cognitive batteries and tests. For a complete description of all traditional intelligence batteries' ability to assess Stratum II and Stratum I abilities, readers are referred to McGrew and Flanagan (1998) and Flanagan and Ortiz (2001).

THE THEORETICAL FOUNDATION OF CHC CROSS-BATTERY ASSESSMENT

The theoretical underpinnings of the Cross-Battery approach lie within an enormous body of literature beginning with only the two basic abilities—fluid (Gf) and crystallized (Gc; Cattell, 1941, 1957, 1963), and later expanding to several abilities (Horn, 1965, 1968, 1976, 1985, 1988, 1991; Woodcock, 1994). Further empirical research conducted by Carroll (1993) clarified a multiple-component intelligence theory, elaborated upon by Flanagan and McGrew (1997). McGrew (1997) proposed a model designed to synthesize Horn, Cattell, and Carroll's work, with refinements following factor analyses by Flanagan and McGrew (1997). Finally, Flanagan and McGrew (1998) outlined a taxonomy of intellectual abilities that came to be known as the Cattell–Horn–Carroll (CHC) Theory of Cognitive Abilities (Flanagan & Ortiz, 2001).

The CHC Theory of Cognitive Abilities, as outlined by Flanagan and McGrew (1998), included 10 broad cognitive abilities and approximately 70 narrow cognitive abilities (Flanagan & Ortiz, 2001). The 10 broad cognitive abilities located at the Stratum II level include: Crystallized Intelligence (Gc), Fluid Intelligence (Gf), Quantitative Knowledge (Gq), Reading and Writing Ability (Grw), Short-Term Memory (Gsm), Visual Processing (Gv), Auditory Processing (Ga), Long-Term Storage and Retrieval (Glr), Processing Speed (Gs), and Decision/Reaction Time or Speed (Gt). These abilities form the cornerstone of interpretation within the CHC model. The broadest, or most general, level is represented by Stratum III and is located at the apex of the hierarchy. Stratum III subsumes both the broad Stratum II and narrow Stratum I abilities and represents a general factor "g" that is presumed to represent complex higher order cognitive processes (Gustafsson & Undheim, 1996); however, McGrew (1997) and McGrew and Flanagan (1998) judge it to have very little practical relevance for assessment and interpretation of cognitive abilities. Below, we describe the 10 Stratum II and the multiple Stratum I abilities (notation as outlined by McGrew & Flanagan, 1998, follows).

Gc—Crystallized Intelligence

Crystallized Intelligence is the breadth and depth of cultural information that is acquired and applied. There are 12 Stratum I narrow abilities within Gc. These include: Language Development (LD), Lexical Knowledge

(VL), Listening Ability (LS), General Information (KO), Information about Culture (K2), General Science Information (K1), Communication Ability (CM), Oral Production and Fluency (OP), Grammatical Sensitivity (MY), Foreign Language Proficiency (KL), and Foreign Language Aptitude (LA).

Gf—Fluid Intelligence

Fluid Intelligence can be characterized as the ability to solve novel tasks. Gf comprises five component narrow abilities. These narrow abilities include: General Sequential Reasoning (RG), Induction (I), Quantitative Reasoning (RQ), Piagetian Reasoning (RP), and Speed of Reasoning (RE).

Gq—Quantitative Knowledge

Quantitative Knowledge is the acquired factual and conceptual knowledge possessed by an individual. Gq comprises two component narrow abilities: Mathematical Knowledge (KM) and Mathematical Achievement (A3).

Grw—Reading and Writing Ability

Reading and Writing Ability is the acquired basic reading and writing skills necessary to comprehend and express ideas in written language. Grw comprises eight component narrow abilities: Reading Decoding (RD), Reading Comprehension (RC), Verbal Language Comprehension (V), Cloze Ability (CZ), Spelling Ability (SG), Writing Ability (WA), English Usage Knowledge (EU), and Reading Speed (RS). Grw is not typically assessed via intellience tests.

Gsm—Short-Term Memory

Short-Term Memory can be characterized as the ability to apprehend, hold, and use information within a few seconds. Gsm comprises two narrow abilities: Memory Span (MS) and Learning Abilities (L1).

Gv—Visual Processing

Visual Processing is "the ability to generate, perceive, analyze, synthesize, manipulate, transform, and think with visual patterns and stimuli" (p. 23). Gv comprises eleven component narrow abilities. These narrow abilities include: Visualization (VZ), Spatial Relations (SR), Visual Memory (MV), Closure Speed (CS), Flexibility of Closure (CF), Spatial Scanning (SS), Serial Perceptual Integration (PI), Length Estimation (LE), Perceptual Illusions (IL), Perceptual Alternations (PN), and Imagery (IM).

Ga—Auditory Processing

Auditory Processing is the ability to "perceive, analyze, and synthesize patterns among auditory stimuli, especially the ability to perceive and discriminate subtle nuances of patterns of sound ... and speech that may be presented under distorted conditions" (p. 23). Ga comprises 13 component narrow abilities: Phonetic Coding (PC), Speech Sound Discrimination (US), Resistance to Auditory Stimulus Distortion (UR), Memory for Sound Patterns (UM), General Sound Discrimination (U3), Temporal Tracking (UK), Musical Discrimination and Judgment (U1,U9), Maintaining and Judging Rhythm (U8), Sound-Intensity/Duration Discrimination (U6), Sound-Frequency Discrimination (U5), Hearing and Speech Threshold Factors (UA, UT, UU), Absolute Pitch (UP), and Sound Localization (UL). Ga is not currently assessed via nonverbal intelligence tests.

Glr—Long-Term Storage and Retrieval

Long-Term Storage and Retrieval is the ability to store and retrieve information for more than a few minutes. Glr comprises 13 component narrow abilities: Associative Memory (MA), Meaningful Memory (MM), Free Recall Memory (M6), Ideational Fluency (FI), Associational Fluency (FA), Expressional Fluency (FE), Naming Facility (NA), Word Fluency (FW), Figural Fluency (FF), Figural Flexibility (FX), Sensitivity to Problems (SP), Originality/Creativity (FO), and Learning Abilities (L1).

Gs—Processing Speed

Processing Speed is the ability to "fluently perform cognitive tasks ... when under pressure to maintain focused attention and concentration" (p. 24) and may last for minutes. Gs comprises three narrow abilities: Perceptual Speed (P), Rate-of-Test-Taking (R9), and Number Facility (N).

Gt—Decision/Reaction Time or Speed

Decision/Reaction Time or Speed can be characterized as quickness in reacting and/or making decisions and is described as a latency to respond. Gt comprises four component narrow abilities: Simple Reaction Time (R1), Choice Reaction Time (R2), Semantic Processing Speed (R4), and Mental Comparison Speed (R7). Gt is not typically assessed by currently available intelligence tests.

APPLICATION OF CHC CROSS-BATTERY ASSESSMENT TO NONVERBAL ASSESSMENT

The use of CHC Cross-Battery Assessment procedures, while comprehensive in scope, carries an implied assumption that the examinee presents with language faculties intact. There are many cases; however, when the examinee presents with language deficits so severe that traditional language-laden instruments cannot be utilized to obtain a measure of cognitive abilities, nonverbal measures of cognitive abilities may be more appropriate. Use of the CHC Cross-Battery Assessment procedures is possible even for those with limited English proficiency; the procedures simply require nonverbal assessment techniques and instruments. Unfortunately, there are fewer measures that are appropriate for nonverbal assessment, and of those measures, there are salient differences that practitioners must consider when making assessment choices.

Some nonverbal instruments such as the Universal Nonverbal Intelligence Test (UNIT; Bracken & McCallum, 1998) require the use of pantomime and gestures and can be administered completely nonverbally; however, the majority of "nonverbal" instruments include some verbal communication of either expression or reception. Additional training may be necessary before practitioners can administer some instruments requiring nonverbal presentations. Most of the nonverbal instruments are individually administered, but a few may allow group administration. Administration characteristics may limit a practitioner's choices of instruments depending on the individual needs of the clients (e.g., motor requirements). So, practitioners need to acquaint themselves with the unique characteristics of each instrument and be aware of the task demands during interpretation of the results.

Another consideration that practitioners must consider when selecting an instrument is whether the standardization sample included verbally limited individuals in proportion to the general population, or whether there were less than proportional numbers of verbally limited individuals included. Obviously, when available, an instrument that most closely and inclusively resembles the general population would be more appropriate for normative comparisons; even so, instruments with less proportionate standardization samples may provide adequate measures of narrow abilities in some cases.

Several nonverbal instruments are considered unidimensional; that is, they measure only one aspect or narrow sliver of intelligence. For a comprehensive assessment of intelligence, a unidimensional instrument will not be appropriate, unless combined with other measures. Multidimensional nonverbal instruments provide a better coverage of broad abilities than unidimensional tests and are generally appropriate for high-stakes assessment (e.g., placement decisions); however these tests may not be inclusive enough to measure the total range of broad cognitive abilities that have been identified. Use of the CHC Cross-Battery Assessment approach helps address this limitation.

The primary principle of CHC Cross-Battery Assessment and Nonverbal Assessment is the same: to obtain the most accurate measure of cognitive abilities available. It is through the combination of these procedures that a more comprehensive evaluation can be completed for verbally limited individuals.

NONVERBAL CHC CROSS-BATTERY ASSESSMENT

Seven Steps of the Nonverbal Cross-Battery Assessment Approach

The steps in a cross-battery assessment are adapted from McGrew and Flanagan (1998) and rely heavily on the processes they describe and on their categorizations of existing nonverbal instruments according to their ability to assess Stratum II and Stratum I cognitive components. These steps are appropriate for verbal and nonverbal assessment and are presented below, along with elaboration and specific directions.

1. *Choose the most appropriate core intelligence battery.* The evaluator should select a core intelligence battery that is multidimensional. A multidimensional battery provides more coverage of Gf–Gc abilities. Thus, the examiner reduces the need to supplement the battery with a large number of subtests selected from other batteries. Generally, a battery is also selected to meet respective States' requirements for a Full-Scale IQ score. For individualized nonverbal assessment, examiners will probably choose one of two multidimensional batteries currently—the Leiter International Performance Scale (Roid & Miller, 1997) and the Universal Nonverbal Intelligence Test (UNIT; Bracken & McCallum, 1998).

2. *Decide which Gf–Gc abilities are adequately represented in core intelligence battery.* Once a comprehensive intelligence battery has been selected, the examiner needs to attend to the scope of Gf–Gc broad and narrow ability coverage. The examiner can accomplish this by simply reviewing the worksheets found in Appendix A or in tables found in McGrew and Flanagan (1998) and Flanagan and Ortiz (2001) to determine those abilities assessment by particular subtests. In order for a broad Stratum II ability to be adequately represented, it must consist of at least two qualitatively different narrow Stratum I abilities that measure the broad ability of interest. For example, if fluid reasoning is the broad ability of interest, two qualitatively different narrow abilities, such as induction and general sequential reasoning, would suffice to adequately measure the broad ability characterized as fluid reasoning. However, two measures of the same narrow ability would be insufficient coverage of a broad ability. It is important to use the fewest number of batteries necessary to provide adequate coverage (McGrew & Flanagan, 1998) to avoid confounds associated with the use of multiple standardization samples.

3. *Decide which Gf–Gc abilities are un- or underrepresented.* Deciding which Gf–Gc abilities are un- or underrepresented is accomplished by examining the worksheets in Appendix A or those worksheets and tables provided by McGrew and Flanagan (1998) and Flanagan and Ortiz (2001). There are no currently published intelligence batteries that provide adequate coverage of all broad and narrow abilities (Flanagan & Ortiz, 2001). Some batteries provide two or more narrow abilities within a broad ability; however, in may cases, these narrow abilities do not differ qualitatively within the respective broad abilities (McGrew & Flanagan, 1998).

4. *Determine which supplemental subtests are needed to assess those un- or underrepresented abilities.* Nonverbal cognitive batteries provide a good source for Gf–Gc ability measures for visual processing, fluid reasoning, processing speed, and long-term retrieval. In addition, selective subtests of another nonverbal battery, or other nonverbal tests (e.g., Test of Nonverbal Intelligence—Third Edition; TONI-III; Brown,

Sherbenou, & Johnson, 1997) provide further narrow abilities of interest that may be used in conjunction with subtests already present on the core cognitive battery. Importantly, nonverbal assessment is necessarily limited due to constraints associated with the examinee. For example, nonverbal assessment is usually indicated when examinees are deaf, culturally different, have language impairments, etc.; consequently, the choice of measures will be limited due, in part, to the level of reliance upon language related skills. In some cases, receptive language can be assessed using instruments such as the Peabody Picture Vocabulary Test—Third Edition (PPVT-III; Dunn, Dunn, & Williams, 1997).

5. *Administer core battery and supplemental subtests.* The core battery is administered to obtain the required Full-Scale IQ using the standardized procedures specified by the respective test publishers. The supplemental subtests that are necessary to complete the cross-battery assessment are also administered as specified by the test publishers. Standardized procedures should be followed unless there are extenuating circumstances, and documentation of breaking standardization would be necessary in those circumstances.

6. *Complete cross-battery worksheets.* Cross-battery worksheets are given in Appendix B for the nonverbal intelligence tests discussed in this chapter. Broad Stratum II Abilities can be calculated for visual processing, fluid reasoning, processing speed, short-term memory, and crystallized intelligence. A Narrow Stratum I Ability score can be calculated for associative memory, a measure of long-term retrieval. All standard scores must be converted to the most common metric, which uses a mean of 100 and a standard deviation of 15. Once the scores obtained are entered into the worksheets, all the necessary computations are entered within the worksheets to compute Broad or Narrow abilities. (Importantly, some Broad Stratum II abilities are operationalized by only one Narrow Stratum I measure.) If considered helpful, examiners may transfer the Gf–Gc narrow ability standard scores and broad ability averages from the worksheets to a Gf–Gc profile. The profile provides a visual graphic depicting strengths and weaknesses at a glance. An example of a typical Gf–Gc profile worksheet can be found in either McGrew and Flanagan (1998) or Flanagan and Ortiz (2001).

7. *Interpret the results.* Interpreting test results is itself a multistep process. Results can be interpreted using the guidelines provided by McGrew and Flanagan (1998) and Flanagan and Ortiz (2001). In general, the goal of interpretation is to determine cognitive strengths and weaknesses, which are assumed to underlie real-world performance in school and in the workplace. "Best Practice" interpretation of abilities at the Stratum II level requires at least one measure of two different Stratum I abilities; these measures operationalize the broader Stratum II ability. The two scores are averaged to provide a particular Stratum II score. (If the two narrow Stratum I abilities are significantly different from each other, each of the two Stratum I abilities should be assessed with an additional measure, and the four subtests averaged—significance is defined for our purposes as a difference greater than 15 points, or one standard deviation.)

In order to interpret cognitive strengths and weaknesses at the Stratum II level, Stratum II ability scores are averaged, and each measure is compared with the overall Stratum II average (to determine whether there are any outliers). If so, these outliers are assumed to be strengths and weaknesses. Again, outliers are defined as those (Stratum II) abilities that deviate more than 15 points from the overall mean. As Flanagan and McGrew note, Stratum II abilities have been empirically linked to, and are assumed to underlie, certain real-world skills. For example, processing speed is assumed to relate to reading because it influences the ability to rapidly identify words (Bowers & Wolf, 1993). See Flanagan and McGrew (1998) and Mather (1991) for other important relationships between CHC Stratum II abilities and academic areas (e.g., visual processing and math). The astute examiner will be able to relate these abilities to referral problems. Parents and teachers can use this information to plan curricular changes. Following our example above, a child who exhibits slow processing may be given more time to identify words and may be instructed using a particular strategy designed to enhance word-identification speed, such as "reading previewing"; reading previewing requires that a model gradually increase oral reading speed as a student reads along silently.

STRENGTHS AND WEAKNESSES OF CHC CROSS-BATTERY ASSESSMENT

Use of the Cross-Battery strategy provides some advantages over traditional assessment. For example, it is theory-based, it allows targeted assessment of specific cognitive abilities, and it provides a framework for assessing a wide range of abilities based on extensive factor analytic data (Floyd, 2002). However, Cross-Battery assessment is not without its critics. In a series of articles featured in the NASP *Communique*, a number of assessment experts expressed pros and cons. After Floyd's positive article appeared, Watkins and Youngstrom (2002) described a number of limitations, including (a) lack of comparability of scores from different tests; (b) uncertainty of the effect of administering subtests out of order, i.e., in an order different from standardization; (c) overreliance on rational analysis of abilities measured by subtests across batteries; and (d) questionable efficiency and economy of the method. Ortiz and Flanagan (2002a,b) addressed those criticisms (and more) in a subsequent article. Examiners who read these articles must decide whether the arguments mounted in favor of Cross-Battery assessment outweigh those against its use. Obviously, we believe the strategy has merit, despite some salient limitations. Although use of Cross-Battery assessment requires time to master and a fairly sophisticated knowledge base to implement, it can provide a wealth of information efficiently.

SUMMARY

The purpose of cross-battery assessment is to provide psychological assessment specialists/examiners with an overall cognitive assessment strategy. More specifically, it is designed to make examiners aware of the subconstructs of intelligence, as defined by the Cattell–Horn–Carroll Model of Intelligence, and to make them aware of how these constructs can be assessed, using the best available operationalizations (of the constructs). Cross-battery assessment principles can be used by examiners to determine cognitive strengths and weaknesses and are generally considered to provide the steps necessary to complete a very comprehensive evaluation of cognitive abilities. We have adapted the guidelines and principles from McGrew and Flannagan (1998) for those examiners who engage in nonverbal assessment of cognitive abilities and intelligence. In addition, we provide a listing of the best nonverbal assessment instruments (Appendix A) and a set of worksheets to guide interpretation of scores obtained from nonverbal cross-battery assessment (Appendix B). Finally, we provide a case for illustrative purposes in Appendix C. As is apparent from reading the case, the basic principles and strategies are the same for both verbal and nonverbal assessment, but the number of instruments available for nonverbal assessment is lower than for verbal assessment.

REFERENCES

Bowers, P., & Wolf, M. (1993). Theoretical links among naming speed, precise timing mechanisms, and orthographic skill in dyslexia. *Reading and Writing, 5,* 69–86.

Bracken, B. A., & McCallum, R. S. (1998). *Universal nonverbal intelligence test.* Itasca, IL: Riverside.

Brown, L., Sherbenou, R. J., & Johnson, S. K. (1997). *Test of nonverbal intelligence* (3rd ed.). Austin, TX: Pro-Ed.

Carroll, J. B. (1993). *Human cognitive abilities: A survey of factor-analytic studies.* Cambridge: Cambridge University Press.

Cattell, R. B. (1941). Some theoretical issues in adult intelligence testing. *Psychological Bulletin, 38,* 592.

Cattell, R. B. (1957). *Personality and motivation structure and measurement.* New York: World Book.

Cattell, R. B. (1963). Theory of crystallized and fluid intelligence. *Journal of Educational Psychology, 54,* 1–22.

Dunn, L. M., Dunn, L. M., & Williams, K. T. (1997). *Peabody picture vocabulary test—third edition.* Circle Pines, MN: American Guidance Services.

Fell Greene, J. (2001) *Language!* Longmont, CO: Sopris West.

Flanagan, D. P., & McGrew, K. S. (1997). A cross-battery approach to assessing and interpreting cognitive abilities: Narrowing the gap between practice and cognitive science. In D. P. Flanagan, J. L. Genshaft, & P. L. Harrison (Eds.), *Contemporary intellectual assessment: Theories, tests, and issues* (pp. 314–325). New York: Guilford.

Flanagan, D. P., & Ortiz, S. (2001). *Essentials of cross-battery assessment.* New York: Wiley.

Floyd, R. G. (2002). The Cattell-Horn-Carroll (CHC) cross-battery approach: Recommendations for school psychologists. *Communique, 30*(5), 10–14.

Gustafsson, J. E., & Undheim, J. O. (1996). Individual differences in cognitive functions. In C. D. Berliner & R. D. Cabfee (Eds.), *Handbook of educational psychology.* New York: Macmillan.

Hammill, D. D., Pearson, N. A., & Wiederholt, J. L. (1996). *Comprehensive test of nonverbal intelligence.* Austin, TX: Pro-Ed.

Horn, J. L. (1965). *Fluid and crystallized intelligence: A factor analytic and developmental study of the structure among primary mental abilities.* Unpublished doctoral dissertation, University of Illinois, Champaign.

Horn, J. L. (1968). Organization of abilities and the development of intelligence. *Psychological Review, 75*, 242–259.

Horn, J. L. (1976). Human abilities: A review of research and theory in the early 1970s. *Annual Review of Psychology, 27*, 437–485.

Horn, J. L. (1985). Remodeling old theories of intelligence: Gf–Gc theory. In B. B. Wolman (Ed.), *Handook of intelligence* (pp. 267–300). New York: Wiley.

Horn, J. L. (1988). Thinking about human abilities. In J. R. Nesselroade & R. B. Cattell (Eds.), *Handbook of multivariate psychology* (rev. ed., pp. 645–685). New York: Wiley.

Horn, J. L. (1991). Measurement of intellectual capabilities: A review of theory. In K. S. McGrew, J. K. Werder, & R. W. Woodcock (Eds.), *Woodcock–Johnson technical manual* (pp. 197–232). Chicago: Riverside.

Kellogg, C. E., & Morton, N. W. (1999). *Beta III manual*. San Antonio, TX: Psychological Corporation.

Mather, N. (1991). *An instructional guide to the Woodcock–Johnson psychoeducational battery—revised*. Brandon, VT: Clinical Psychology.

McGrew, K. S. (1997). Analysis of the major intelligence batteries according to a proposed comprehensive Gf-Gc framework. In D. P. Flanagan, J. L. Genshaft, & P. L. Harrison (Eds.), *Contemporary intellectual assessment: Theories, tests, and issues* (pp.151–180). New York: Guilford.

McGrew, K. S., & Flanagan, D. P. (1998). *The intelligence test desk reference (ITDR): Gf–Gc cross-battery assessment*. Boston: Allyn & Bacon.

Naglieri, J. A. (1985a). *Matrix analogies test—expanded form*. San Antonio, TX: Psychological Corporation.

Naglieri, J. A. (1985b). *Matrix analogies test—short form*. San Antonio, TX: Psychological Corporation.

Naglieri, J. A. (1996a). *Naglieri nonverbal ability test*. San Antonio, TX: Psychological Corporation.

Naglieri, J. A. (1996b). *NNAT multilevel technical manual*. San Antonio, TX: Harcourt Brace Educational Measurement.

Naglieri, J. A. (1997). *General ability measure for adults*. Minneapolis, MN: NCS Assessments.

Ortiz, S. O., & Flanagan, D. P. (2002a). Cross-battery assessment revisited: Some cautions concerning "some cautions" part I. *Communique, 30*(7), 32–34.

Ortiz, S. O., & Flanagan, D. P. (2002b). Some cautions concerning "some cautions concerning cross-battery assessment" part II. *Communique, 30*(8), 36–38.

Raven, J. C. (1938). *Progressive matrices: A perceptual test of intelligence*. San Antonio, TX: Psychological Corporation.

Roid, G. H., & Miller, L. J. (1997). *The Leiter International Performance Scale—Revised edition*. Wood Dale, IL: Stoelting.

Slingerland, B. H. (1971). A multisensory approach to language arts for specific language disability children. Cambridge, MA: Educator's Publishing Services, Inc.

Watkins, M. W., Youngstrom, E. A., & Glutting, J. J. (2002). Some cautions concerning cross-battery assessment. *Communique, 30*(5), 16–20.

Woodcock, R. W. (1994). Measures of fluid and crystallized intelligence. In R. J. Sternberg (Ed.), *The encyclopedia of intelligence* (pp. 452–456). New York: Macmillan.

APPENDIX A: BROAD AND NARROW ABILITIES MEASURED BY NONVERBAL INTELLIGENCE BATTERIES AND TESTS

Battery/test	Test/subtest	Broad ability	Narrow ability
UNIT	Object memory Spatial memory Symbolic memory	Visual processing	Visual memory
	Cube design	Fluid intelligence	General sequential reasoning
		Visual processing	Spatial relations
	Mazes	Visual processing	Spatial scanning
	Analogic reasoning	Fluid intelligence	Induction
Raven's	Raven's progressive matrices	Fluid intelligence	Induction
Leiter-R	Classification Design analogies Repeated patterns Sequential order	Fluid intelligence	Induction
	Picture context Visual coding	Fluid intelligence	General sequential reasoning
	Figure rotation	Visual processing	Spatial relations
	Matching Form completion Paper folding	Visual processing	Visualization
	Immediate recognition Forward memory	Visual processing	Visual memory
	Figure ground	Visual processing	Flex of closure
	Delayed recognition Associated pairs Delayed pairs	Long-term retrieval	Associative memory
	Attention sustained	Processing speed	Perceptual speed
MAT	Matrix analogies	Fluid intelligence	Induction
Beta III	Coding	Processing speed	Rate of test taking
	Picture completion	Visual processing	Closure speed
	Clerical checking	Processing speed	Perceptual speed
	Picture absurdities	Crystallized intelligence	Language development
	Matrix reasoning	Fluid intelligence	Induction
CTONI	Pictorial analogies Geometric analogies	Fluid intelligence	Induction
	Pictorial categories Geometric categories Pictorial sequences Geometric sequences	Fluid intelligence	Induction
GAMA	Matching	Visual processing	Visualization
	Sequences	Fluid intelligence	General sequential reasoning
	Analogies	Fluid intelligence	Induction
	Construction	Visual processing	Spatial relations

NNAT	Pattern completion	Visual processing	Visualization
	Reasoning by analogy	Fluid intelligence	Induction
	Serial reasoning	Fluid intelligence	General sequential reasoning
	Spatial visualization	Visual processing	Spatial relations
TONI-III	TONI-III	Fluid intelligence	Induction
PPVT-III	PPVT-III	Crystallized intelligence	Lexical knowledge

Notes: UNIT = Universal Nonverbal Intelligence Test; Raven's = Raven's Progressive Matrices (Raven, 1938); Leiter-R = Leiter International Performance Scale—Revised; MAT = Matrix Analogies Test; Beta III = Beta III (Kellogg & Morton, 1999); CTONI = Comprehensive Test of Nonverbal Intelligence; GAMA = General Ability Measure for Adults (Naglieri, 1985a, 1985b, 1986a, 1986b, 1997); NNAT = Naglieri Nonverbal Ability Test; TONI-III = Test of Nonverbal Intelligence—Third Edition.

APPENDIX B: CROSS-BATTERY WORKSHEETS FOR USE WITH NONVERBAL INTELLIGENCE TESTS

Table B1   Visual Processing (Gv)

Spatial relations		
Battery/test	Test/subtest	Standard score ($M = 100$, $SD = 15$)
UNIT	Cube design	
Leiter-R	Figure rotation	
NNAT	Spatial visualization	
	Sum of subtests	
	Number of subtests	
	Sum of subtests ÷ Number of subtests	
	Spatial relations standard score	
Spatial scanning		
Battery/test	Test/subtest	Standard score ($M = 100$, $SD = 15$)
UNIT	Mazes	
	Spatial scanning standard score	
Visualization		
Battery/test	Test/subtest	Standard score ($M = 100$, $SD = 15$)
Leiter-R	Matching	
	Form completion	
	Paper folding	
GAMA	Matching	
NNAT	Pattern completion	
	Sum of subtests	
	Number of subtests	
	Sum of subtests ÷ Number of subtests	
	Visualization standard score	
Flexibility of closure		
Battery/test	Test/subtest	Standard score ($M = 100$, $SD = 15$)
Leiter-R	Figure ground	
	Flexibility of closure standard score	

Closure speed		
Battery/test	Test/subtest	Standard score ($M = 100$, $SD = 15$)
Beta-III	Picture completion	
	Closure speed standard score	

Visual memory		
Battery/test	Test/subtest	Standard score ($M = 100$, $SD = 15$)
UNIT	Object memory	
	Spatial memory	
	Symbolic memory	
	Visual processing	
Leiter-R	Immediate recognition	
	Forward memory	
	Sum of subtests	
	Number of subtests	
	Sum of subtests ÷ Number of subtests	
	Visual memory standard score	

Visual processing broad ability score conversion	
Spatial relations narrow ability score	
Spatial scanning narrow ability score	
Visualization narrow ability score	
Flexibility of closure narrow ability score	
Closure speed narrow ability score	
Visual memory narrow ability score	
Sum of narrow ability scores	
Number of narrow ability scores	
Sum of narrow ability scores ÷ Number of narrow ability scores	

Visual processing broad ability score (Gv)

Table B2 Fluid Reasoning (Gf)

Induction		
Battery/test	Test/subtest	Standard score ($M = 100$, $SD = 15$)
UNIT	Analogic reasoning	
Raven's	Raven's progressive Matrices	
Leiter-R	Classification	
	Design analogies	
	Repeated patterns	
	Sequential order	
Matrix analogies	Matrix analogies	
Beta-III	Matrix reasoning	
CTONI	Pictorial analogies	
	Geometric analogies	
	Pictorial categories	
	Geometric categories	
	Pictorial sequences	
	Geometric sequences	
GAMA	Analogies	
NNAT	Reasoning by analogy	
TONI-III	TONI-III	
	Sum of subtests	
	Number of subtests	
	Sum of subtests ÷ Number of subtests	
	Induction standard score	

General sequential reasoning

Battery/test	Test/subtest	Standard score ($M = 100$, $SD = 15$)
UNIT	Cube design	
GAMA	Sequences	
NNAT	Serial reasoning	
Leiter-R	Picture context	
	Visual coding	
	Sum of subtests	
	Number of Subtests	
Sum of Subtests ÷ Number of Subtests		
General Sequential Reasoning Standard Score		

Fluid reasoning broad ability score conversion

Induction narrow ability score	
General sequential reasoning narrow ability score	
Sum of narrow ability scores	
Number of narrow ability scores	
Sum of narrow ability scores ÷ Number of narrow ability scores	
Fluid reasoning broad ability score (Gf)	

Table B3   Long-Term Retrieval (Glr)

Associative memory

Battery/test	Test/subtest	Standard score ($M = 100$, $SD = 15$)
Leiter-R	Delayed recognition	
	Associated pairs	
	Delayed pairs	
	Sum of subtests	
	Number of subtests	
	Sum of subtests ÷ Number of subtests	
	Associative memory standard score	

Table B4   Processing Speed (Gs)

Perceptual speed

Battery/test	Test/subtest	Standard score ($M = 100$, $SD = 15$)
Leiter-R	Attention sustained	
Beta-III	Clerical checking	
	Sum of subtests	
	Number of subtests	
	Sum of subtests ÷ Number of subtests	
	Perceptual speed standard score	

Rate of test taking

Battery/test	Test/subtest	Standard score ($M = 100$, $SD = 15$)
Beta-III	Coding	
Rate of test taking standard score		

Processing speed broad ability score conversion

Induction narrow ability score	
General sequential reasoning narrow ability score	
Sum of narrow ability scores	
Number of narrow ability scores	
Sum of narrow ability scores ÷ Number of narrow ability scores	
Processing speed broad ability score (Gs)	

Table B5   Crystallized Intelligence (Gc)

Language development

Battery/test	Test/subtest	Standard score (M = 100, SD = 15)
Beta-III	Picture absurdities	
	Language development standard score	

Lexical knowledge

Battery/test	Test/subtest	Standard score (M = 100, SD = 15)
PPVT-III	PPVT-III	
	Lexical knowledge standard score	

Crystallized intelligence broad ability score conversion

Induction narrow ability score	
General sequential reasoning narrow ability score	
Sum of narrow ability scores	
Number of narrow ability scores	
Sum of narrow ability scores ÷ Number of narrow ability scores	
Crystallized intelligence broad ability score (Gc)	

Table B6   Short-Term Memory (Gsm)

Visual memory

Battery/test	Test/subtest	Standard score (M = 100, SD = 15)
UNIT	Object memory	
	Spatial memory	
	Symbolic memory	
	Visual processing	
Leiter-R	Immediate recognition	
	Forward memory	
	Sum of subtests	
	Number of subtests	
	Sum of subtests ÷ Number of subtests	
	Visual memory standard score	

APPENDIX C: CONFIDENTIAL PSYCHOLOGICAL REPORT

Miguel D.

Examiner: Jamie L. Yarbrough   **Test Dates**: 03/16/2002,
                                                         03/27/2002
Grade Placement: 2nd grade
School: Green Valley
               Elementary School   **Birth Date**: 01/21/1994
Sex: Male   **Age**: 8 years 1 month, 20 days

Referral Question

Miguel was referred for testing by his teacher because of reading difficulty, particularly reading comprehension. According to his teacher, Miguel can decode words, but this skill is not automatic, and his reading lacks fluency. His general academic progress has been much slower than the other students in his classroom and is marked by poor grades. His teacher requested a psychological evaluation to determine whether this problem is a function of mental retardation, a learning disability, or a language-related limitation.

Background Information

Miguel is an 8-year-old boy who is in the second grade at Green Valley Elementary School. He is of Hispanic origin and moved with his family from Venezuela 1 year ago. Miguel's parents are migrant workers and work on a local farm. He has two older brothers and a younger sister. Spanish is the dominant language within Miguel's household. His current academic functioning has been described as low by both his teacher and parents, though they say that his English is average when compared with other Hispanic children his age. Miguel's mother states that he works diligently on his homework every day but struggles to find the right answers. An interview with Miguel's mother revealed that he has had no significant health, medical, or emotional problems. He is not currently taking any medications. Miguel interacts well with his peers and is well liked by the other children in his classroom. Miguel is right-handed and does not wear glasses. A recent vision/hearing exam revealed no visual or auditory acuity problems.

Tests Administered

- Beta-III (3/16/02)
- Leiter International Performance Scale-Revised (Leiter-R) (3/16/02)
- Woodcock—Johnson—III Tests of Achievement (WJ-ACH-III) (3/16/02)

- Universal Nonverbal Intelligence Test (UNIT) (3/27/02)
- Peabody Picture Vocabulary Test, Third Edition, Spanish Version (PPVT-III) (3/27/02).

Clinical and Behavioral Observations

Miguel was tested on a couple of occasions in the school psychology clinic. Typically, he was dressed casually and appeared somewhat reserved. Rapport was easily established and maintained. During the testing sessions, he was quiet yet cooperative. He maintained eye contact easily but took several minutes to respond to many questions. Miguel's language skills seemed below average for his age, and his activity level was generally low during testing. He took longer than usual to answer questions and seemed to have trouble selecting the word that he wanted to use. At times, Miguel had difficultly articulating his thoughts and needed to be queried to facilitate a response. He became frustrated when the items became more difficult (e.g., he bit his nails, frowned). He would not voluntarily admit that he did not know the answer to the more difficult items, but rather, would wait until prompted by the examiner to say that he did not know. Miguel's concentration level was extremely high during all of the tests. He did not display any unusual habits or mannerisms, and conveyed a sense of respect towards the examiner. Overall, the testing conditions were deemed adequate to obtain valid responses from this child.

Referral Question Determination

Table C1   Universal Nonverbal Intelligence Test

Global scale	Standard score	Percentile rank
Full Scale IQ	82	12th
Memory quotient	91	27th
Reasoning quotient	77	6th
Symbolic quotient	79	8th
Non-symbolic quotient	91	27th

State regulations and guidelines require the use of standard scores to diagnose mental retardation and a discrepancy score to diagnose learning disabilities. The UNIT was administered to obtain a Full-Scale IQ, from which a discrepancy score could be calculated. Miguel obtained a Full-Scale IQ of 82, which is ranked at the 12th percentile nationally and is classified as Low Average. We can be 90% certain that Miguel's true score falls somewhere between 77 and 89. This score rules out mental retardation, because it falls in the low average range and is considerably above the cutoff score necessary to help establish a diagnosis of mental retardation (two standard deviations below the mean). In addition, the similarity between Miguel's IQ score and achievement scores (discussed later) rules out the possibility of a learning disability, as defined by a discrepancy score. Strengths and weaknesses from the UNIT are discussed as part of the cross-battery assessment.

Assessment of Cognitive Strengths and Weaknesses

Certain subtests from the Leiter-R (3/16/02), Beta-III (3/16/02), UNIT (3/27/02), and PPVT-III (3/27/02) were combined by CHC Cross-Battery principles and procedures. These scores yielded six broad cognitive ability clusters, which include Fluid Intelligence (Gf), Crystallized Intelligence (Gc), Visual Processing (Gv), Short-Term Memory (Gsm), Long Term Retrieval (Glr), and Processing Speed (Gs). A summary of Miguel's performance across these domains is provided below.

Cross-Battery Assessment of Gf

Fluid intelligence applies to mental operations that are used when one is faced with a novel task that cannot be performed automatically. It includes forming concepts, identifying relationships, problem-solving, drawing inferences, and reorganizing information. Miguel's Gf ability was assessed through tasks that required him complete conceptual or geometrical analogies presented in matrix format (Analogic Reasoning, SS = 75 ± 7, *Low*). In addition, Gf was assessed by tasks requiring him to construct abstract, geometrical designs with cubes while viewing a picture of the design (Cube Design, 75 ± 7, *Low*). Miguel's Fluid Intelligence cluster score of 75 ± 5 is ranked at the 5th percentile and is classified as *Low*. The variation of scores Miguel earned in this area was not statistically significant, suggesting uniform ability within this domain. Overall, Miguel's ability to reason and form concepts is low, compared with his peers.

Cross-Battery Assessment of Gc

Crystallized intelligence is defined as the breadth and depth of a person's acquired knowledge. Included in this category is verbal communication, cultural knowledge, and reasoning with abilities that have already been developed. Miguel's Gc ability was assessed through tasks that required him to place an "X" on one picture out of four that illustrated an object that is wrong or foolish (Picture Absurdities, 74 ± 7, *Low*) and to identify pictures which corresponded to words that are presented orally (PPVT-III, 76 ± 7, *Low*). The variation in scores Miguel earned in this area was not statistically significant, suggesting uniform ability within this domain. Miguel's Crystallized Intelligence cluster score of 75 ± 5 is ranked at the 5th percentile nationally and is classified as *Low*. Overall, Miguel's ability to use his acquired knowledge and accumulated experiences to solve everyday problems is low.

Cross-Battery Assessment of Gv

Visual processing refers to the ability to perceive, generate, synthesize, analyze, and think with visual patterns and stimuli. Miguel's Gv ability was assessed by constructing abstract, geometrical designs while viewing a picture of the design (Cube Design, 75 ± 7, *Low*). In addition, Miguel was asked to identify a random array of pictures after being exposed to the stimulus for 5 second(s) (Object Memory, 80 ± 7, *Low*). Because there is little variance, Miguel's obtained scores on these Gv subtests combined to yield a cluster score of 78 ± 5, which is ranked at the 8th percentile nationally. This score suggests Miguel's Visual Processing is low.

Cross-Battery Assessment of G*sm*

Short-term memory describes the ability to apprehend and hold information in immediate awareness and then use it within a few seconds. Miguel's G*sm* was assessed through tasks that required him to recreate a random pattern of dots after viewing the stimulus for 5 s (Spatial Memory, 105 ± 7, *Average*) and by asking him to reproduce sequences of symbols after being exposed to the stimulus for 5 s (Symbolic Memory, 95 ± 7, *Average*). Because there was little variation in Miguel's scores, a Short-Term Memory cluster score of 100 ± 5 was obtained. This score is ranked at the 50th percentile nationally and falls in the Average Classification.

Cross-Battery Assessment of G*lr*

Long-term retrieval refers to the ability to store information and concepts in long-term memory and retrieve it later through association. Miguel's G*lr* was assessed through tasks that required him to recall objects depicted on the Associated Pairs subtest after approximately 30 min (Delayed Pairs, 93 ± 7, *Average*). More specifically, this subtest measured Miguel's Associate Memory, which is a narrow cluster included in the G*lr* factor. Because this was the only subtest that Mackenzie was administered in this factor, the narrow cluster of Associative Memory is the only representation of long-term retrieval.

Cross-Battery Assessment of G*s*

Processing speed is defined as the ability to perform cognitive tasks automatically, particularly when under pressure to concentrate. Miguel's G*s* ability was assessed through tasks that required him to identify and cross out target stimuli embedded within rows of stimuli on a page that included both target stimuli and several foils (Attention Sustained, 70 ± 7, *Low*), and to write numbers that corresponded to symbols, based upon a number-symbol key provided at the top of the page (Coding, 75 ± 7, *Low*). Miguel's cluster score was 73 ± 5, which is ranked at the 3rd percentile and is classified as *Low*. Because there was no variation of scores in this area, Miguel's processing speed can be considered uniform.

Assessment of Academic Achievement

Miguel's achievement scores are consistent with his scores on the various tests of cognitive functioning. On the Woodcock–Johnson III Tests of Achievement (3/16/02), Miguel earned scores that ranged from *Very Low* to *Low Average*.

Reading

The Letter–Word Identification subtest measures the child's word identification and basic reading skills, including sight vocabulary, phonics, and structural analysis. Miguel's score of 68 (66–71, *Very Low*) on this test is equivalent to the average score of a child aged 6 years, 6 months. This score is low for Miguel's age and is ranked at the 2nd percentile nationally.

The Reading Fluency subtest provides a measure of the child's ability to quickly read and comprehend simple sentences. This test is part of the Broad Reading Cluster, which measures reading decoding, reading speed, and the ability to comprehend connected discourse while reading. Miguel's score of 73 (69–77, *Very Low*) on this subtest is equivalent to the average score of a child aged 6 years, 6 months. This score is ranked at the 4th percentile.

The Passage Comprehension subtest measures reading comprehension and lexical knowledge using the modified cloze procedure. Miguel's score of 69 (65–72, *Very Low*) on this test is equivalent to the average score of a child aged 6 years, 2 months. This score is low for Miguel's age and is at the 2nd percentile.

The Reading Vocabulary subtest measures word comprehension skills. Miguel's score of 75 (70–79, *Low*) is equivalent to the average score of a child aged 6 years, 1 months, and is at the 4th percentile rank.

Math

The Calculation subtest falls in the Broad Math and Math Calculation Clusters, which provide a measure of math achievement including problem-solving, number facility, automaticity, and reasoning. The Calculation subtest requires the child to perform mathematical computations. Miguel's score of 83 (78–89, *Low Average*) on this subtest is equivalent to the average score of a child aged 7 years, 0 months. This score falls at the 13th percentile nationally.

Finally, the Applied Problems subtest is included in the Broad Math and Math Reasoning subtests and provides a measure of problem-solving, analysis, reasoning, and vocabulary. Miguel's score of 88 (84–91, *Low Average*) on this subtest is equivalent to the score of a child aged 6 years, 11 months. This score is ranked at the 20th percentile.

Data Integration and Interpretation

Data derived from the administration of selected cognitive and achievement tests suggest that Miguel demonstrates low to average functioning across the various cognitive and academic domains. According to the Cross-Battery analyses, Miguel exhibits an intrapersonal strength in short- and long-term memory. However, in general, Miguel's pattern of cognitive weaknesses helps to explain the referral concerns and appears to underlie his reported difficulties in reading. For example, his low processing speed, fluid reasoning, crystallized intelligence, and visual processing all fall within the borderline to low average range. A pattern of scores such as Miguel's often predict limited academic functioning, particularly as the content becomes more complex and relies less on rote memorization. The shift in task demands from a high dependence on memory to a stronger emphasis on understanding patterns and relationships is particularly salient at the third-grade level.

Because Miguel's specific cognitive weaknesses appear to underlie his academic difficulties, his poor academic skills do not appear to be solely or even primarily the result of factors such as limited English proficiency, nonsupportive educational environment, or cultural differences, although these variables may reduce academic skill acquisition to some degree.

Summary and Recommendations

Miguel is an 8-year-old boy who was administered selected cognitive and achievement tests. Data from these tests indicate that his cognitive functioning is low average, and his academic achievement is considerably below average in Reading. Other academic areas are slightly below average also. He has several cognitive weaknesses. Miguel's memory scores were average when compared with other children his age, suggesting that his abilities in this area are not impaired. However, as the academic content becomes more sophisticated and less memory dependent, he will experience increasing difficulty unless instructional strategies are developed to take advantage of his relatively good memory. The integration of data from the various tests and teacher reports has provided the basis for the following recommendations:

1. Reading skills will be enhanced via exposure to a strong code-emphasis approach (e.g., *Lanugage!* authored by J. Fell Greene in 2001 and published by Sopris West, and Slingerland's (1971) multisensory approach).

2. In order to address Miguel's reading comprehension difficulties, he should be provided with organizational strategies and worksheets to use when reading a passage or story. And in general, he will be aided by the use of advance organizers and other structural devices to facilitate awareness of relationships and structure inherent in to-be-learned content.

3. Miguel will profit from the use of mnemonics and other strategies designed to take advantage of his relatively strong memory. He will benefit from exposure to concrete, factual information, using memory aids, rather than through discovery learning instructional techniques. Instruction requiring higher-order comprehension should rely on well-learned rules, principles and laws (e.g., "A pint is a pound the world round.")

Jamie L. Yarbrough, M.S.
Examiner in School Psychology

II

Selected Nonverbal Tests and Cognitive Strategies

5

The Universal Nonverbal Intelligence Test

R. Steve McCallum

The *Universal Nonverbal Intelligence Test* (UNIT) can be conceptualized as a measure of intelligence, obtained nonverbally. The UNIT is designed to provide a unique measure of cognitive organization (i.e., symbolic and nonsymbolic content) and function (memory and reasoning); even so, it is first and foremost a strong measure of *g*, primarily because of the complex nature of its six subtests.

TEST MODEL AND PHILOSOPHY

Three of the six subtests included on the UNIT require memory, primarily; these subtests are Object Memory (OM), Spatial Memory (Spa M), and Symbolic Memory (Sym M). Similarly, three subjects were developed to assess reasoning, primarily; these subjects are Cube Design (CD), Mazes (M), and Analogic Reasoning (AR). Five of the subjects require minor motoric manipulation (i.e., CD, OM, M, Sym M, Spa M), and one requires only a pointing response (AR). With two exceptions (CD, M), the subjects that require motoric manipulation can be adapted to allow for a pointing response only, as needed.

UNIT symbolic subtests require the use of concrete and abstract symbols to conceptualize the environment; these symbols are typically language related (e.g., words), although symbols may take on any form (e.g., numbers, Rebus characters). Cognitive development enables individuals to

R. Steve McCallum, Department of Educational Psychology and Counseling, University of Tennessee, Knoxville, Tennessee 37996

Handbook of Nonverbal Assessment, edited by R. Steve McCallum. Kluwer Academic/Plenum Publishers, 2003.

internalize symbols increasingly as they label, mediate, etc. Nonsymbolic strategies require the ability to perceive and make meaningful judgments about the physical relationships within the environment; this ability is symbol-free, or relatively so, and is closer to fluid-like intellectual abilities.

Thus, the UNIT assesses four basic cognitive abilities, as seen below.

Conceptual model for the UNIT

	Memory subtests	Reasoning subtests
Symbolic subtests	Symbolic memory	Analogic reasoning
	Object memory	
Nonsymbolic subtests	Spatial memory	Cube design
		Mazes

The UNIT model is based on several lines of theory and research. In 1939, Wechsler emphasized the importance of distinguishing between highly symbolic (verbal) and nonsymbolic performance. Jensen (1980) provides rationale for a two-tiered hierarchical conceptualization of intelligence consisting of the two subconstructs of memory (Level I) and reasoning (Level II). Also, the theoretical organization of the UNIT can be conceptualized within the Gf–Gc Model of fluid and crystallized abilities, as described by Cattell (1963), Horn (1968), and others (e.g., Woodcock, 1990). According to an analysis presented by McGrew and Flannagan (1998) in their Intelligence Test Desk Reference, UNIT subtests assess a number of the Gf–Gc stratum II and III abilities. For example, Symbolic Memory assesses visual memory (MV) from Stratum I and visual processing (Gv) from Stratum II; Spatial Memory assesses MV and spatial relations (SR) from Stratum I and Gv from Stratum II; Object Memory assesses MV (Stratum I) and Gv (Stratum II); Cube Design assess quantitative reasoning (RG; Stratum I) and fluid intelligence (Gf; Stratum II); Analogic Reasoning assess induction (I; Stratum I) and Gf (Stratum II); and Mazes assess SS from Stratum I and Gv from Stratum II. Noted experts have characterized the psychometric qualities of the UNIT as "acceptable," "well standardized" with "support for two factors—Reasoning and Memory ... and a strong g factor" (Sattler, 2001, p. 568). Kamphaus (2001) called the UNIT "... a promising addition to the armamentarium of psychologists ..." (p. 449). He notes that the FSIQ appears to have enough evidence to be used routinely for interpretation, characterizes the other global scores as "intuitively appealing," and calls for more research to support their routine clinical use.

Goals for UNIT Development

Ten goals guided the development of the UNIT (Bracken & McCallum, 1998). The overarching goal was to ensure a fair assessment of intelligence for those children and adolescents whose cognitive and intellectual abilities cannot be fairly assessed with language-loaded measures or with existing unidimensional nonverbal measures. These individual include those who are deaf or have hearing impairments, those from different cultural backgrounds, individuals who have learning/language disabilities, those with speech impairments, and those with serious emotional or intellectual limitations. The UNIT was designed to be administered in a 100% nonverbal format and was standardized accordingly (the only nonverbal test so developed). Test authors designed the test to possess psychometric rigor and to be appropriate for cross-cultural assessment. They included tasks that maximize existing examiner knowledge and experience. Efficient administration is achieved by allowing the examiner three assessment options using examinee-friendly tasks.

Description of the UNIT

Several scores can be calculated for the UNIT total test, including a Full-Scale score (FSIQ), Memory Quotient (MQ), Reasoning Quotient (RQ), Symbolic Quotient (SQ), and Nonsymbolic Quotient (NSQ). Individual subtest scores can be derived for each of the six subtests for further analysis of examinee's performance. UNIT subtests are described below.

- Symbolic memory: The examinee recalls and recreates sequences of visually presented universal symbols (e.g., green boy, black woman)
- Spatial memory: The examinee must remember and recreate the placement of black and/or green chips on a 3×3 or 4×4 cell grid
- Object memory: The examinee is shown a visual array of common objects (e.g., shoe, telephone, tree) for 5 s, after which the examinee identifies the pictured objects from a larger array of pictured objects
- Cube design: The examinee completes a three-dimensional block design task using between one and nine green and white blocks
- Analogic reasoning: The examinee completes a matrix analogies task using common objects (e.g., hand : glove : foot :___?) and novel geometric figures
- Mazes: The examinee completes a maze task by tracing a path through each maze from the center starting point to an exit.

STANDARDIZATION AND PSYCHOMETRIC PROPERTIES

Standardization of the UNIT was based on data from 2,100 children from ages 5 years 0 months through 17 years 11 months 30 days. The data were closely representative of the U.S. population. Stratification variables included: sex, race, Hispanic origin, geographic region, community setting, classroom placement, special education status, and parent education attainment. There were 175 children in each of 12 age groups. An additional 1,765 children and adolescents participated in related reliability, validity, and fairness studies.

Reliability

Average internal consistency reliability estimates were computed by subtests and global scores. The median of the average subtest reliability coefficients across ages is 0.83 for the Standard Battery and 0.80 for the Extended Battery, with average subtest reliability coefficients across age groups ranging from 0.64 (Mazes) to 0.91 (Cube Design). Coefficients for a Clinical/Exceptional sample are uniformly higher, ranging from 0.82 (Mazes) to 0.96 (Cube Design). The average reliability coefficients for the global scores from the Standard Battery range from 0.87 (Symbolic) to 0.91 (Nonsymbolic) for the standardization sample, and from the Extended Battery, the coefficients range from 0.86 (Reasoning) to 0.90 (Memory) for the standardization sample. Coefficients for the Full-Scale (FS) IQ ranged from 0.91 to 0.98 across all Batteries and the two samples. The FSIQ is well above 0.90, the minimum for scores used for making selection/placement decisions (see Bracken, 1987; Bracken & McCallum, 1998).

To help ensure fairness, internal reliability estimates are reported in the UNIT Manual for special populations (e.g., children with Learning Disabilities, Speech and Language Impairments) and for the important decision-making points (i.e., FSIQ of 70, ±10; 130, ±10). Obtained coefficients and those corrected for restriction and expansion in range are reported. In general, these coefficients are impressive, and are comparable with those reported for the standardization sample.

Test–retest stability was assessed using a sample of 197 participants who took the UNIT twice over an interval of approximately 3 weeks. The average test–retest practice effects are 7.2 points for the Abbreviated Battery, 5.0 points for the Standard Battery, and 4.8 points for the Extended Battery. Obtained coefficients and those corrected for restriction and expansion in range are reported in the Manual. Corrected subtest coefficients range from 0.58 (Mazes) to 0.85 (Cube Design), and corrected global coefficients from 0.78 to 0.88. Coefficients for Full-Scale IQs across the three batteries range from 0.83 (Abbreviated Battery) to 0.88 (Standard Battery).

Validity

The UNIT Manual presents results from several validity studies. Support for construct validity is provided using results from both exploratory and confirmatory factor analytic results, as well as model-testing statistics. For example, "g" loadings from five of the six subtests are above 0.70, the value Kaufman (1979) describes as "good," and additional factor analytic results provide support for the Reasoning and Memory factors as well as the Symbolic and Nonsymbolic components (Bracken & McCallum, 1998).

Coefficients showing the relationship between other tests of intelligence and the UNIT also provide construct validity support. For example, coefficients between Wechsler Intelligence Scale for Children—III (WISC-III; Wechsler, 1991) and UNIT Standard Battery FSIQs across four populations (e.g., children with Learning Disabilities, Mental Retardation) ranged from 0.81 to 0.84. The corrected correlations between the UNIT FSIQs and the Woodcock–Johnson—Revised (WJ-R; Woodcock & Johnson, 1989/1990) Broad Cognitive Ability score are 0.80, 0.83, and 0.82, respectively, for the Abbreviated, Standard, and Extended batteries for a sample of 88 examinees in regular education classes. The correlation between the Kaufman Brief Intelligence Test (K-BIT; Kaufman & Kaufman, 1990) FSIQ and the

UNIT Abbreviated Battery, both screening tests, is 0.71 for a sample of 31 examinees. Coefficients between the UNIT Standard Battery FSIQ and three matrices-based tests are 0.50 (Raven's Standard Progressive Matrices; Raven, 1960), 0.68 (Test of Nonverbal Intelligence II; TONI-II; Brown, Sherbenou, & Johnsen, 1990) and 0.79 (Matrix Analogies Test Total Test Standard Score; MAT; Naglieri, 1985). Additional validity studies are reported in the Manual showing relationships between the UNIT and various achievement test scores across several populations; most of these coefficients range from 0.25 to 0.50, with a few exceptions below and above this range.

Fairness

The UNIT is the only intelligence test that devotes an entire chapter to describing efforts of the authors to reduce bias (e.g., description of expert bias panels to eliminate faulty items; presentation of reliability and internal and external validity data for several populations of interest such as African Americans, Hispanic Americans, Native Americans, Asian Americans, individuals with hearing impairments). Reliability coefficients for all global scale scores are in the 0.90s across four different populations. Of interest to many users of nonverbal tests are mean difference analyses showing average FSIQ differences between minority populations and matched nonminority samples. For example, the Standard Battery FSIQ average for a sample of 352 African Americans is 90.68; Table 6.4 in the UNIT Manual compares that score with the mean obtained from a matched sample of White examinees drawn from the standardization sample (99.31), a difference of 8.63. The difference between a sample of Hispanic examinees and matched controls is 2.13. A more refined matching procedure results in a greater reaction of the minority-majority group mean difference—less than 3 points for the FSIQ difference between African Americans and White examiners for the Standard Battery and less than 1 point between Hispanic Americans and Whites (Bracken, McCallum, & Upson, 2002).

As is apparent, considerable effort was expended to establish fairness for the populations of interest to users of nonverbal tests. McCallum (1999) describes some 13 criteria that the authors of the UNIT used to establish fairness for the test.

ADMINISTRATION AND SCORING

UNIT authors encourage examiners to consider three elements: the examinee, the examiner, and the environment. The UNIT Manual describes in considerable detail considerations associated with these three elements (Bracken & McCallum, 1998). Because the UNIT was developed to be sensitive to *examinees* from different cultures and with various disabilities, the UNIT Manual devotes several pages to the unique needs associated with these populations. *Examiners*' characteristics are also very important. A well-trained and sensitive examiner is essential for a valid assessment. Examiners must be able to establish rapport, be aware of the need to follow standardization directions carefully, be aware of the unique administration demands of the UNIT (e.g., administration gestures, use of pantomime, time constraints), and be aware of the physical demands (e.g., juxtaposition of the examiner/examinee depending on the handedness of the examinee). The UNIT Manual provides graphics showing the placement of test materials and the examinee/examiner relative to those materials. Of course, good examiners are aware of the need to use the language of the child or UNIT gestures to maintain motivation (e.g., gesturing "thumbs up" for effort, saying "good job"). Importantly, examiners have considerable latitude in communicating the nature of the task demands to the examinee, with the use of gestures and pantomime, as well as demonstration, sample, and checkpoint items. Each subtest uses a simple point–wave–shrug sequence. That is, the examiner points to the stimulus materials, uses the hand wave to highlight the response materials, and uses the open-handed shrug to communicate to the examiner the need to respond. Finally, *environmental* characteristics are also important. As mentioned above, the examiner should be aware of the particular needs/requirements of certain subtests, such as the use of a stop watch, and placement on the tables of certain blocks during particular items of the Cube Design subtest. General directions are provided below.

Starting and Discontinuing Subtests

UNIT subtests have two starting points, one for 5-year 0-month-old to 7-year 11-month-old children, and a second for examinees 8 and older. Starting points for each subtest are indicated on the UNIT Record Booklet, as are the discontinue rules.

Test Booklets

Examinees will find critical administration information on the UNIT Test Booklets. For example, the booklets show correct responses for all subtests, as well as indications of start points, designation of item type (i.e., demonstration, sample, checkpoint, regular), and time limits for the two subtests for which time is critical. Also, the Test Booklet includes a worksheet allowing the examiner to transfer raw scores to standard scores easily; the back page of the UNIT Record Booklet contains the Interpretive Worksheet, which provides a number of tables to allow testing of various hypotheses using different levels of statistical significance (e.g., comparisons among global scale scores, comparisons of subtest scores with the mean of all subtests, comparisons of subtest scores with means obtained from specific scales, and comparison of pairs of subtests). With two exceptions—Cube Design and Mazes—subtests are scored dichotomously. Except for the first two items, each item from the Cube Design subtest is scored 1, 2, or 3, depending upon the correct placement of the block designs along three facets of the blocks. The Mazes subtest is also scored uniquely, based on the number of correct decision points transversed by the examinee. Each correct decision point is awarded one point credit, and correct decision points are shown on the separate Mazes Test Booklet.

Timing

Speed is deemphasized on the UNIT. Only two of the subtests—Cube Design and Mazes—provide bonus points for speed, and even then, bonus points for speed never exceed 2 points for any Cube Design item and 3 points for any Mazes item. All three memory subtests require that presentation of the stimulus materials be limited to 5 second(s).

Four Item Types

Demonstration items are presented by the examiner and are not scored. Sample items are completed by the examinee, with feedback from the examiner if needed, and are not scored. Checkpoint items are completed by the examinee and scored; feedback is provided if necessary. Regular items are completed by the examinee, and scored, with no feedback allowed.

Subtest-by-Subtest Rules of Administration

UNIT norms allow for administration of a two-, four-, or six-subtest battery. Completion of the six-subtest Extended Battery requires approximately 45 min. The two-subtest Abbreviated Battery takes about 15 min to administer; the four-subtest or Standard Battery requires about 30 min. The four-subtest Standard Battery is recommended for most purposes, including assessment leading to placement decisions.

All items from the UNIT must be administered completely nonverbally, using gestures, pantomime, and modeling, as described in the UNIT Manual. Only those examiners who have had proper training and experience should administer the test. Those individuals who have had formal graduate-level coursework in the administration and interpretation of individualized standardized cognitive tests may use the UNIT. These individuals can acquire the necessary administration skills by reading the Manual, viewing a training video, and practicing administration. There are detailed verbal directions and ample graphics in the Manual; in addition, there are supplemental training materials available, including the training video mentioned above, a Training Guide for individual and classroom use (Bracken & McCallum, 1999), and a training CD. In addition, each kit comes with an 8.5×11 in. $(21.6 \times 27.9$ cm) laminated sheet called "Administration at a Glance," which contains brief subtest directions and pictures of the gestures.

The eight gestures used during administration are very common and are easy for examinees to understand (e.g., nodding or "thumbs up" for yes or good effort, head shaking for no). The typical administration strategy for all subtests begins with the examiner ensuring that the examinee makes eye contact, presenting the stimulus materials, pointing to the materials, waving their hand over the stimulus materials, and shrugging (using the open-handed shrugging gesture). The gestures are shown in Figure 5.1.

Even though UNIT administration is nonverbal, it should not be stilted and artificial. Examiners can and should talk to examinees if there is a common language. It is helpful to talk to examinees to establish rapport, to obtain background information, and so on. However, the

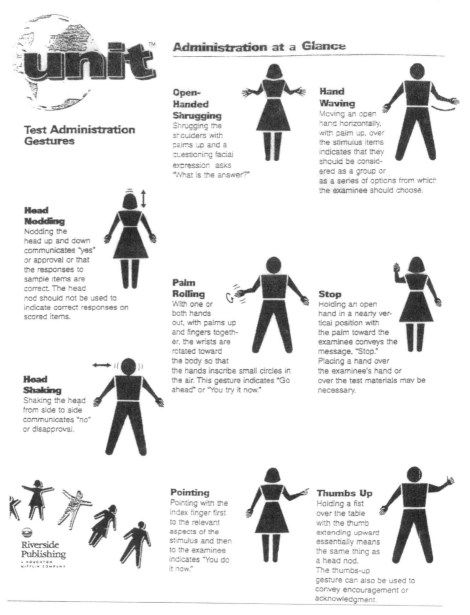

Administration at a Glance

Test Administration Gestures

Open-Handed Shrugging
Shrugging the shoulders with palms up and a questioning facial expression asks "What is the answer?"

Hand Waving
Moving an open hand horizontally, with palm up, over the stimulus items indicates that they should be considered as a group or as a series of options from which the examinee should choose.

Head Nodding
Nodding the head up and down communicates "yes" or approval or that the responses to sample items are correct. The head nod should not be used to indicate correct responses on scored items.

Palm Rolling
With one or both hands out, with palms up and fingers together, the wrists are rotated toward the body so that the hands inscribe small circles in the air. This gesture indicates "Go ahead" or "You try it now."

Stop
Holding an open hand in a nearly vertical position with the palm toward the examinee conveys the message, "Stop." Placing a hand over the examinee's hand or over the test materials may be necessary.

Head Shaking
Shaking the head from side to side communicates "no" or disapproval.

Riverside Publishing
A HOUGHTON MIFFLIN COMPANY

Pointing
Pointing with the index finger first to the relevant aspects of the stimulus and then to the examinee indicates "You do it now."

Thumbs Up
Holding a fist over the table with the thumb extending upward essentially means the same thing as a head nod. The thumbs-up gesture can also be used to convey encouragement or acknowledgment.

Figure 5.1 UNIT Administration at a Glance. (Copyright © 1998 by The Riverside Publishing Company. All rights reserved. Reproduced from the *Universal Nonverbal Intelligence Test, Administration at a Glance*, by Bruce A. Bracken and R. Steve McCallum with permission of the publisher.)

examiner must not talk to the examinee about UNIT test directions/responses.

Each UNIT subtest requires that the examiner present the stimulus material nonverbally. For the *Symbolic Memory* subtest stimulus plates are presented on an easel. The easel contains plates showing pictures of one or more of the following universal human figures, in a particular order: a green baby, a black baby, a green girl, a black girl, a green boy, a black boy, a green woman, a black woman, a green man, a black man. The examinee is presented the stimulus plate (for 5 s) and then is instructed, through modeling and gestures, to replicate the order shown on the stimulus plate. The examinee uses 1.5×1.5 in. (3.8×3.8 cm) response cards, each containing one of the universal human figures, to reproduce the array depicted on the stimulus plate. The task has no time limits and no bonus credit for rapid performance. Materials needed include Stimulus Book 1, 10 Symbolic Memory Response Cards, and a stopwatch. The subtest is discontinued after obtaining scores of 0 on both items for 1 and 2 or after five consecutive scores of 0 on Items 2–30.

The *Cube Design* subtest requires the examinee to use up to nine cubes to replicate one- or three-dimensional designs shown on a stimulus plate. A Response Mat provides a workspace for constructing the designs, and presents a diagonal line to allow the examinee to orient placement. Each cube contains six facets; two white sides, two green sides, and two sides, which contain diagonals (triangles), one green and one white. These cubes are arranged to replicate the one- and three-dimensional figures depicted on the stimulus plates. Items 1 and 2 are scored on one dimension (facet) only; items 3–15 are scored on each facet of the three-dimensional figures. Items are timed, but the time limits are liberal to emphasize the power, rather than the speeded nature of the task. Materials needed for the subtest include Stimulus Book 1, nine green and white Cube Design cubes, Cube Design Response Mat, and a stopwatch. Examiners should remember that for Items 1 and 2, the response cube is presented so that the correct face for completing the design is *not* up. For item 3, the response cube is presented with a solid white face up. For Items 4 and 5, one cube is presented with a solid face up and one with a two-color face up. For Items 6–15, the cubes are scrambled and presented so that at least one of each face is up. For each item, the examiner presents the correct number of cubes needed to complete the design. This number is presented in parentheses on the Test Booklet.

For the *Spatial Memory* subtest, the examiner presents a stimulus plate showing a random pattern of green dots and black dots on a 3×3 or 4×4 grid. After viewing the stimulus for 5 s, the examinee re-creates the pattern by placing green and black circular chips on a response grid. The examiner does not allow the examinee to touch the chips until the stimulus plate has been covered. Materials needed for this subtest include Stimulus Book 1, 16 Response Chips (8 green, 8 black), Response Grid (3×3 on one side and 4×4 on the other), and a stopwatch.

The *Analogic Reasoning* subtest requires the examinee to solve analogies presented in a matrix format. The examinee is directed to indicate which one of several options best completes a two-cell, four-cell, or nine-cell analogy.

Task solution requires the examinee to determine the relationships between objects. For example, in the four-cell matrix, the first cell might depict a fish, and the second water; the third cell might show a bird, and the fourth cell would be blank. The examinee would select from several options the picture that best completes the matrix. In this case, a picture of the sky would be a correct response. Materials needed for this subtest include Stimulus Book 1.

For the *Object Memory* subtest, the examiner presents pictures of common objects arranged on stimulus plates located on an administration easel. The easel is laid flat on the table, and the examinee is shown a plate containing pictures of one or more objects for 5 s, and the examinee is then shown a second plate containing pictures from the first plate *and* pictures of "distracter objects." The examinee identifies pictures on the second plate that were shown on the first plate; to create a semipermanent response, the examinee places black chips on the pictures selected. The examiner should not allow the examinee to touch the response chips until after the stimulus page has been turned. This memory task is not timed, other than the 5-s exposure. Materials needed for this subtest include Stimulus Book 2, eight Black Response Chips, and a stopwatch.

The *Mazes* subtest requires the examinee to complete a maze using a no. 2 lead pencil, minus the eraser. The examinee demonstrates successful completion initially, using a red-leaded pencil. Each maze shows a mouse in the center and one or more pieces of cheese on the outside of the maze. The cheese depicts one or more possible exits from the maze. The task is to determine the correct path from the center to the (correct) piece of cheese. The examinee is stopped after the first error, and the examinee is given one point credit for each correct decision up to the point of the first error. The Test Booklet shows successfully completed mazes and indicates correct decision points. Errors include entering a blind alley, crossing a wall, and retracing. Neither passing through a wall while rounding a corner nor briefly crossing a wall and returning to the alley is counted as an error. Examiners are instructed to give the examinee the benefit of the doubt in borderline cases. Items are timed, though the time limits are quite liberal, and 1–3 bonus points are possible for rapid performance on items 9–13. If the examinee stops before completing any maze, the examiner encourages completion by use of gestures. Materials needed for this subtest include the Mazes Response Booklet, a no. 2 graphite pencil without eraser, a red-leaded pencil, and a stopwatch. If an examinee aged 8–17 receives less than full credit on Sample 3, testing resumes with Demonstration 1.

INTERPRETATION

The UNIT allows three administration options: the Abbreviated Two-Subtest Battery, the Standard Four-Subtest Battery, and the Extended Six-Subtest Battery. All three batteries were designed to assess memory and reasoning as well as symbolic and nonsymbolic processing.

Interpretation begins with the examiner's consideration of which battery should be administered. Making a choice among the three batteries depends on several issues, including the purpose for conducting the assessment (e.g., screening, diagnostic testing, placement), the estimated attention span of the student, time available to conduct the assessment, and related concerns. Once the choice of batteries has been made, and the UNIT has been administered, actual test interpretation is conducted in multiple steps that consider data successively from the most global and reliable sources (e.g., FSIQ, Scale Scores) to increasingly more specific, yet less reliable, sources (e.g., subtests, items). The Abbreviated Battery is best suited for screening, the Standard Battery for placement decisions, and the Extended Battery for placement *and* diagnostic purposes.

It is possible to interpret results from an inter- and intrachild (ipsative) prospective. Both procedures have been employed by a variety of authors (Kaufman & Kaufman, 1983; McCallum, 1991; Sattler, 1988, 1992). The following discussion for interpreting the UNIT focuses on the guidelines outlined in the UNIT Manual (Bracken & McCallum, 1998). The strategies the UNIT authors suggest do include some attention to determining base rates of very common profiles in a manner similar to that recommended by McDermott and Glutting (1997), but their suggested procedures are not as inclusive. In their clinical experience, they have found the normative and ipsative strategies to be most helpful for examining an individual's strengths and weaknesses.

General Interpretation Guidelines

Traditional normative and ipsative interpretation should proceed from the most global and reliable scores to the most specific, least reliable scores. Test composites (e.g., FSIQs and scale scores) tend to be the most reliable scores because they include sources of variation from all of the subtests and scales that constitute the test. As such, these molar data sources are more reliable than the more molecular scores that result from individual subtests. Composite cognitive ability scores also are the best predictors of important real-world outcomes, particularly academic and vocational success (Sattler, 2001). Consequently, the most defensible interpretive strategy might be to address the overall composite score and stop the interpretive process. However, whenever there is considerable variability among examines' performance across individual subtests in a battery, the overall composite may not yield a good reflection of an examiner's true overall ability. When significant subtest and scale variation occurs, further interpretation of the test is warranted (Kaufman, 1979, 1999). Therefore, the UNIT interpretation scheme presented below follows the logical sequence of interpreting the instrument from the Full-Scale IQ, the Scales, and finally the subtests. Six specific steps include: (a) interpret the FSIQ; (b) determine the statistical significance of global score differences; (c) determine if the differences between global scores are abnormally large; (d) interpret the significant strengths and weakness of the profile; (e) interpret subtest abilities; and (f) generate hypotheses about fluctuation in the UNIT profile. The six steps of UNIT interpretation are described in more detail below.

Step 1: Interpret the Full-Scale IQ

First, describe the examinee's performance at the composite level (i.e., Full Scale) in both a quantitative (e.g., standard scores, confidence intervals, percentile ranks) and qualitative fashion (e.g., intelligence classifications). Quantitative descriptions are based on interpretation of obtained scores relative to population parameters (e.g., a population mean of 100 and standard deviations of 15). Scores on the UNIT conform to the traditional normal "bell" curve reasonably well, and UNIT standard scores can be compared with IQs and other standardized scores obtained on other tests based on the same metric (i.e., $M = 100$, $SD = 15$), such as the various Wechsler scales and the Woodcock–Johnson Psychoeducational Battery—Revised.

Variability in obtained scores comes from two sources (i.e., reliable variance and error variance); the error associated with the composite scores should be considered and communicated. Because error is assumed to be normally distributed, obtained scores should be considered within a band of confidence that frames the obtained score by one or more standard error(s) of measurement (SEM), as determined by the level of confidence desired (e.g., 68%, 95%, 99%). Confidence intervals built around obtained scores define the probability that a given range of scores would include the examinee's "true" score, that is, the hypothetical average that would be obtained upon repeated testing, minus the effects of error, such as practice, fatigue. In addition to the SEM, the UNIT also reports the band of error associated with the "estimated true score." This band of error takes into account regression to the mean, so the band becomes more elliptical as scores move toward the extremes. For the UNIT, the band of error (standard error of the estimate) can be found in Table B.10 in the Manual. Finally, qualitative descriptions are possible using the classifications provided in the UNIT Manual, also in Table B.10, and range from Very Superior to Very Delayed.

Step 2: Determining the Statistical Significance of Global Score Differences

Although the UNIT Full-Scale IQ is the first score to be interpreted, whenever there is significant variability in an examinee's subtest and/or scale scores, the FSIQ may not be a good representation of global ability. To determine the representativeness of the FSIQ as an estimate of overall intellectual ability, the examiner should consider first the comparability of the UNIT scale scores (i.e., Reasoning Quotient, Memory Quotient, Symbolic Quotient, or Nonsymbolic Quotient). If scale scores show considerable variability (i.e., significant difference among themselves), these differences should be interpreted if they are also abnormally large (see Step 3). If the difference between two scales is statistically significant, that is, so large that it would not likely occur by chance alone, such a difference should be considered important, at least initially. As suggested by

Kaufman and Lichtenberger (1999), we recommend that a probability level of 0.05 be used to determine significance. However, statistically significant differences are neither necessarily clinically meaningful nor rare. If differences exist, they should be checked to determine how rare they are in the population (see Step 3). See the UNIT Manual, table D.1, to determine values considered significant.

Step 3: Determine if the Differences between Global Scores are Abnormally Large

Relative frequency of differences addresses a separate issue from statistical significance. As mentioned above, statistical significance is described as the probability that the obtained score difference would be expected to occur in the population by chance alone. However, differences of that magnitude may occur in the normative population with considerable frequency due to real differences in the abilities of individuals within the population, rather than chance factors. Examiners should check the UNIT Manual, Table D.2, to find the relative frequency of score differences in the population. As a general rule, I recommend that differences exceeding 20 points be considered "abnormally large" because they typically occur only in the most extreme 15% of the population (Naglieri & Kaufman, 1983). If there are one or more abnormally large differences among the scale scores (e.g., Memory Quotient is significantly higher than the Reasoning Quotient, the Symbolic Quotient is significantly higher than the Nonsymbolic Quotient), the resulting UNIT FSIQ is a less-than-optimal index of the examinee's overall abilities. Consequently, scales should be interpreted as important indicators of (independent) abilities in their own right. However, if there is abnormal scatter among the three subtests within a particular global scale, that scale should not be interpreted as a unique and cohesive entity. Scatter is indicated by subtracting the lowest subtest score from the highest. If this range of scores is equal to or greater than 6 points, the scatter is abnormally large, that is, so large that only 15% of the standardization sample earned a value this large or larger.

The UNIT Manual provides some reasonable hypotheses describing characteristics of examinees who have particular strengths on the global scale scores. For example, those who have a stronger memory (than reasoning) should be able to reproduce visual stimuli better than they can problem-solve based on juxtapositions and relationships. Table 7.2 in the UNIT Manual shows many of these hypotheses.

Step 4. Interpret the Significant Strengths and Weaknesses of the Profile

If the scales exhibit statistically significant and abnormally large difference, interpretation proceeds along theoretical lines consistent with the UNIT model (e.g., Memory greater than Reasoning, or Symbolic greater than Nonsymbolic). Also, it may be important to consider non-UNIT based models; that possibility is investigated empirically in Step 5. For example, application of the Simultaneous-Successive model of processing, the

Cattell–Horn *gf–gc* model of intelligence, or Guilford's Structure of Intellect model may shed some important light on the child's unique abilities. Using other models to explain scores should follow the same general steps outlined above. Extra-test data should be considered to either support or refute the logic of using any particular model. Of particular importance, the examiner is obligated to discuss how this model might be applied to explain strengths and weaknesses and the relationship between those and real-world applications (e.g., educational strategies).

Step 5: Subtest Interpretation

Interpretation now focuses on individual subtests. Although significant scale deviation is considered an important index, examiners should be aware that nonsignificant variability among scales does not necessarily mean that a test profile contains no significant variability. *Subtest* scores may yield statistically significant but offsetting differences that result in similar scores across scales. That is, the MQ, RQ, SQ, and INSQ may be similar, but subtests may vary significantly. So, deciding on whether the FSIQ is a reasonable estimate of overall cognitive functioning should be not only based on scale scores but also considered at the subtest level. The examiner may refer to Table D.3 in the UNIT Manual to determine differences required for significance between each subtest and between a given subtest and the mean subtest score for the different scales, by battery.

The process of comparing individual subtest scores with the average subtest score should be completed for each scale (i.e., Memory, Reasoning, Symbolic, Nonsymbolic) and all subtests combined (i.e., all six subtests in a pooled fashion), as necessary. If scores between the global scales are not significantly or abnormally large, subtests should be compared with the overall mean in the pooled procedure, which considers the extent to which individual subtests deviate from the overall average subtest score. The process requires that the mean of all six UNIT subtests be computed, and each subtest score is individually compared with the mean of the six to identify "outliers," (i.e., scores that differ significantly from the overall subtest mean). In this case, the assumption is that variability within the UNIT cannot be characterized according to the model of abilities that underpin the test (i.e., memory, reasoning, symbolic and Nonsymbolic processing). The following guidelines are required to conduct the pooled interpretive process. First, the examiner should: (a) average all six subtest scaled scores; (b) create deviation scores by subtracting each respective subtest score from the mean subtest score; (c) identify subtests that deviate significantly from the average score (i.e., determine strengths and weaknesses); (d) determine whether individual subtests possess sufficient specificity to be interpreted as measuring some unique cognitive ability; (e) consider the abilities that underpin individual subtests to begin generating hypotheses or potential explanations for individual subtest strengths/weaknesses (e.g., conflicting subtest scores, inconsistent subtest patterns); (f) reconcile strong and weak abilities by examining comparable subtests (and abilities) assessed by other tests administered in the battery; and (g) consider additional extra-test variables, such as the referral problem, teacher/parent reports, class and assessment behavior observations, and students' work samples to support or refute hypotheses that are generated during the interpretation process.

These same guidelines can be followed for determining strengths and weaknesses within scales. For example, any subtest can be compared with its scale mean (i.e., spatial memory to the three memory subtests). The process of determining outliers and strengths/weaknesses within scales is the same.

Step 6: Generate Hypotheses about Fluctuation in the UNIT Profile

Scores consistent with the test model (i.e., that show little variability, or show significant and rare memory vs. reasoning or symbolic vs. nonsymbolic difference) lead to straightforward interpretation; but such patterns are not particularly common, and other models may be investigated (e.g., simultaneous vs. successive, Gf vs. Gc). When no model-based approach explains functioning, individual subtests scores must be examined. To facilitate generation of hypotheses about subtest strengths and weaknesses, see Table 7.3 in the UNIT Manual.

Importantly, sound test interpretation can be conducted only when tests possess reasonably good psychometric properties. Bracken (1987) and Bracken and McCallum (1998) recommend basic rules of thumb for acceptable psychometric criteria. For example, global scores used for making placement decisions should evidence reliability at a level of 0.90 or better; scores used for screening purposes should have reliability at a level of 0.80 or better. Also, item gradients should be sufficiently sensitive to capture small differences in actual ability. In addition, subtest specificity data must meet commonly accepted criteria before subtests can be considered as measures of unique abilities or skills. That is, even though subtests within an instrument contribute to the measurement of general cognitive ability, each subtest may be a reasonably good measure of some specific cognitive skills or ability. For example, the Cube Design subtest assesses reasoning, but it also assesses some unique ability not assessed by any other subtest. According to Kaufman (1979), if a subtest's unique variance, exceeds 25% of the subtest's total variance, and if its unique variance is greater than its error variance, the subtest can be interpreted as measuring some unique ability in addition to its contribution to subscales and full scale. See the specific information regarding subtest characteristics, including specificity, reliability, "g" loadings, and error in the UNIT Manual, Chapter 7. Finally, remember that intelligence tests scores should not be used in isolation. Critics such as McDermott, Fantuzzo, and Glutting. (1990) have failed to examine the clinical value of subtest analysis when it is employed as only one bit of data that is confirmed or refuted through other data sources. Thus, UNIT subtest analysis should be conducted to generate hypotheses about children's unique intellectual strengths and weaknesses and *never* used without additional extra-test information that will allow the examiner to evaluate further the hypotheses that are generated.

Steps 2–6 can be implemented by adhering to the procedures described in the Appendix. These procedures are most amenable to interpreting the Extended Battery, but the procedures for interpreting the Standard and Abbreviated Batteries should follow the same logic, as suggested below.

Interpreting the Standard and Abbreviated Batteries

The four-subtest Standard Battery lends itself to interpretation using the same strategies outlined for the Extended Battery, with minor modification. As with the Extended Battery, it is most appropriate to progress in interpretation from global scores to the most specific scores. Interpret all composite scores relative to normative data; then use a systematic strategy for the subtest interpretation. However, because the Standard Battery contains only four subtests, the extent of possible subtest interpretation is limited. The examiner can and should contrast the Memory Quotient with the Reasoning Quotient, and the Symbolic Quotient with the Nonsymbolic Quotient. Within-scale variability can be investigated in a paired-comparison fashion by contrasting one subtest with another.

The two-subtest Abbreviated Battery provides a good measure of "g" and has good psychometric properties. The two subtests included on the Abbreviated Battery are among the strongest subtests, that is, they have excellent psychometric qualities. The most reasonable interpretation for the Abbreviated Battery is to consider the FSIQ as a reasonably good estimate of overall intellectual functioning, then interpret the score in context, as with the Extended and Standard Batteries (i.e., obtain percentile ranks, confidence intervals, etc.)

The use of one memory subtest (i.e., Symbolic Memory) and one reasoning subtest (i.e., Cube Design) limits interpretation largely to the full-scale score. However, it is possible to compare Symbolic Memory with Cube Design to infer a memory/reasoning difference in abilities. If the difference is greater than 5 points, it can be considered large enough to be both "nonchance and rare." If such a difference exists, it may be useful to consider what that difference might mean. A reasonable hypothesis would be to assume that the Symbolic Memory subtest is influenced by memory more than any other ability and that Cube Design is influenced by reasoning more than any other ability; thus, the difference would be attributed to difference in memory and reasoning abilities. A second hypothesis might be related to symbolic (i.e., Symbolic Memory) versus Nonsymbolic (i.e., Cube Design) processing, or an interaction between the abilities assessed by the primary and secondary scales. Finally, intrasubtest variability should be considered (i.e., item response patterns). Consider that item variability may be related to attention problems, learning disabilities, or other conditions. A scoring and interpretive software program is available from the publisher.

STRENGTHS AND WEAKNESSES

The UNIT provides a relatively comprehensive and user-friendly assessment of intelligence. It is designed to be completely nonverbal, and it is the only multidimensional test that offers 100% nonverbal administration, using demonstration and sample items, gestures, and pantomime. The test offers a number of strengths. However, just like all other tests, it is not perfect. There are some salient weaknesses as well. Even though the test was published recently, there are already two independent reviews available (Fachting & Bradley-Johnson, in press; Fives & Flanagan, 2002). Fatching and Bradley-Johnson conclude their review by noting that the UNIT is a welcome addition to present methods of measuring intellectual functioning in a nonvocal manner. Fives and Flanagan conclude by noting that the UNIT "is theoretically driven ... psychometrically sound ... and appears to be highly useful." They also point out several specific advantages including the completely nonverbal administration, ability to measure multiple abilities, inclusion of Abbreviated, Standard, and Extended Battery forms, the comprehensiveness of the normative sample, the capability to distinguish between abstract tasks and those that require the use of internal verbal mediation, and an "exemplary" record form. In conclusion, they note that the UNIT "... appears to be highly useful instrument." Other specific strengths (and some limitations) are pointed out by both sets of reviewers in the body of their reviews. Strengths and weaknesses from their reviews and those identified by the UNIT authors are grouped into the following categories: test development, administration and scoring, standardization, reliability and validity, and interpretation.

Test Development

The UNIT was developed from a strong theoretical base, consistent with the models of Carroll (1993) and Jensen (1980), both of whom consider intelligence to be hierarchically structured and multifaceted. The UNIT authors consider intelligence as "the ability to problem-solve using memory and reasoning" (Bracken & McCallum, 1998; p. 12). The multifaceted and hierarchical model of the UNIT is supported by a wealth of research showing the hierarchical nature of intelligence *and* the importance of memory and reasoning as basic building blocks (see Bracken & McCallum, 1998; Jensen, 1980). Fives and Flanagan (2002) point out that the UNIT is unique in that its underlying theory is both correlational and experimental. Both correlational (e.g., factor analyses) and experimental (lab manipulation) methodologies were instrumental in producing the supportive literature for the UNIT.

Development of the UNIT was guided by 10 research and development goals. Some of the more salient goals include: ensure fairness by eliminating/reducing sources of bias, encourage efficient administration by including three formats; ensure 100% nonverbal administration; assess intelligence with psychometric rigor; and incorporate tasks that maximize examiner knowledge and experience. Similarly, the authors adopted a list of 10 item-selection criteria (see the UNIT Manual for elaboration). Those criteria require that: item presentation must be *entirely* nonverbal; item responses must be *entirely* nonverbal; task demands must be communicated *easily* through physical gestures, demonstration, sample, and checkpoint items; nonverbal stimuli (e.g., gestures) must be familiar to individuals from dominant world cultures; speeded responding must be deemphasized; items must be visually stimulating and interesting in order to elicit active participation; items must be sensitive to examinees regardless of gender, ethnic, or racial heritage; item presentation must be brief, simple and clear; and items must reflect the theoretical orientation of the subtest (recall of symbolic stimuli).

Some salient test development weaknesses include: (a) the age range extends from 5 years to 17 years 11 months only; (b) the art work for Matrix Analogies and Object Memory contain only black and white line drawings and may not be maximally engaging for young children.

Administration and Scoring

In their review, Fives and Flanagan (2002) note some of the administration/scoring innovations, including an excellent scoring procedure for the Mazes to increase variability, and inclusion of a helpful new item type, the "checkpoint" item, to ensure maintenance of the desired response set. Other strengths include: (a) three administration formats; (b) a clear, yet inclusive record booklet, complete with start and stop rules, correct responses, and other useful information; (c) a worksheet for subtest interpretation; (d) a video tape and CD showing administration of the test; a University Training Guide (Bracken & McCallum, 1999); a computer scoring/interpretation program released in 2001; use of a 8.5×11 in. $(21.6 \times 27.9$ cm) laminated "Administration at a Glance" sheet with abbreviated directions and pictures of the eight administration gestures; consistently applied scoring rules; use of the same exposure times for the stimulus plates on all three memory subtests; and pictures in the Manual showing the appropriate arrangement of test materials, examiner, and examinee for every subtest.

There are some limitations as well. Fives and Flanagan note that the administration directions are printed in the Manual and on the Administration at a Glance card, rather than on the easel, and consequently may not be as user-friendly for those familiar with easel-based directions. They also note that administration may begin at either end of the easel and go in either direction, which may be confusing to some examiners. That is, items are printed on both sides of each page (to reduce cost). However, to prevent confusion, the careful examiner will note that the easel cover lists in green font the subtests that can be administered in a particular direction; in addition, green tabs are used to orient the examiner.

Even though the examiner can talk to the examinee, the specific administration directions must be completely nonverbal, and may seem awkward initially. The use of the eight gestures may seem artificial initially. The use of nondichotomous scoring on the Mazes may seem somewhat difficult, particularly since the examiner must stop the child at the point of the first error, the first incorrect decision point in the maze.

Technical Properties

Internal/external reliability and validity data are reported in the UNIT Manual. For example, age-related growth curves and results from exploratory and confirmatory factor analyses are shown as evidence of internal validity. Correlations with other measures of intelligence and various measures of achievement provide evidence of external validity. Other item characteristics are reported as well (e.g., item gradients and floor/ceiling).

The internal consistency reliability indices are generally good; they are 0.91 and above for all of the full-scale IQs across all batteries. Composite (scale) scores range from 0.86 to 0.91 for the Standard Battery. As might be expected, subtest reliabilities are lower, ranging from 0.64 (Mazes) to 0.91 (Cube Design). Subtests on the Standard Battery range from 0.79 (Analogic Reasoning) to 0.91 (Cube Design). Also, the UNIT Manual reports consistently high reliabilities for the combined clinical populations taken from the various validity studies (e.g., 0.92 for the FSIQ). Split-half reliabilities are less impressive, ranging from 0.58 (Mazes) to 0.85 (Cube Design); again, the subtests in the Standard Battery yield more impressive values, though they range from only 0.68 (Spatial Memory) to 0.85 (Cube Design).

Raw scores on cognitive tests such as the UNIT should increase with age. Because W-score growth curves maintain the age-dependent relationship between cognitive sophistication and age, consistent W-score gains on all subtests as a function of age show construct validity, as is the case on the UNIT. Additional internal validity is shown via factor analyses. For example, the hierarchical structure of the UNIT, with "g" at the apex, is shown from an oblique rotation analysis, which yielded an eigenvalue of 2.33 for the first factor, and 0.64 for the second, indicating strong support for "g." Additional exploratory analyses also show support for the primary two-factor memory/reasoning structure in addition to a higher order "g" factor. Using a variety of goodness-of-fit statistics from confirmatory procedures, data support the overall structure, with support of "g," memory and reasoning, and the lower-order symbolic and nonsymbolic factors.

The floor and ceiling data are very positive, in general, with one exception The floor is somewhat problematic for very young (5-year-old) examinees who exhibit limited cognitive abilities, particularly for the Abbreviated Battery, which is not recommend for cognitively limited 5-year-old examinees. The problem is much less severe for the Standard and Extended Batteries.

Item gradients are good; care was taken to ensure that correct performance on each item changed the examinee's score by no more than 0.33. Extensive item gradient and floor/ceiling tables are presented in the Manual for the examiner's convenience. See Rapid Reference 4.3 for technical strengths and weaknesses. Additional strengths included: use of obtained correlation coefficients *and* those corrected for restriction and expansion in range, using Gulliken's formula; reliability coefficients are provided at two critical decision-making points for FSIQs (i.e., 70 and 130, are excellent at those points); practice effects are reported, and range from about 3 to 5 points over approximately 3 weeks for the Standard Battery; the UNIT Manual reports results of a number of concurrent validity studies with various measures of intelligence for different populations, with coefficients typically in the 0.70–0.80 range; the UNIT Manual reports correlations between UNIT scores and those from a variety of achievement tests; typically, coefficients range from 0.20 to 0.50 between global UNIT scores and various achievement scores; consistent with predictions from the UNIT theoretical model, coefficients between the Symbolic Quotient and various verbal and achievement measures are typically higher than the coefficients between the Nonsymbolic Quotient and verbal achievement measures. In fact, in the UNIT Manual, close to two thirds of the relationships show higher Symbolic Quotient – verbal/achievement coefficients. Specific variance values are sufficient for all subtests except Spatial Memory; thus, with the exception of this subtest, all can be interpreted on their own, that is, as measures of unique abilities. In spite of these significant strengths, some weakness should be highlighted: Some subtests yielded average subtest reliabilities below 0.80 (i.e., split-half reliabilities are 0.76 and 0.64 for Object Memory and Mazes, respectively; test–retest values for five of the six subtests are below 0.80); and because the floor is inadequate for cognitively limited 5-year-old examinees for the Abbreviated Battery, we recommend that examiners not use it for children suspected of having mental retardation.

Standardization

In general, standardization data are excellent. Data were collected from 108 sites in 38 states and included 2,100 children and adolescents. The data were collected based on a stratified random selection procedure and are representative of the 1995 census tract data (U.S. Bureau of the Census, 1995) and of the school-age population. Special-needs children were included to the extent that they were found in the school population. The following stratification variables were included: sex, race, Hispanic origin, geographic region, community setting, classroom placement, special education services, and parent education. Standardization data were collected by trained examiners, and data were checked against 33 criteria. Weaknesses include: standardization data were collected for school-age children only; and bilingual and ESL samples were under represented slightly (1.8% in sample, 3.1% in the population for the bilingual sample, 2% vs. 4% for the ESL sample).

Interpretation

The UNIT Manual provides extensive guidelines for normative and ipsative interpretation, along with an extensive number of tables showing step-by-step strategies for hypotheses generation. Conservative interpretation is suggested, taking error into account. UNIT authors acknowledge the controversy surrounding the practice of ipsative interpretation but recommend the procedure, noting that ipsative test data should be used carefully to generate hypotheses, which should be checked against extra-test data. Interpretive aids include tables showing abilities assumed to underlie subtest performance, test-age equivalents, floor/ceiling and item gradient data, subtest technical properties, base rates, and levels of statistical significance corresponding to various differences between subtest and scaled scores, test-age equivalents, prorated sums of scales scores when a subtest is substituted, and procedures for substituting a subtest when one is spoiled. In addition, the Record Booklet offers a number of user-friendly interpretative characteristics (e.g., interpretative worksheet lends itself to ipsative and normative analyses; descriptive categories are printed on the record form). A computer program is available to facilitate scoring and interpretation.

In spite of the interpretive strengths, some weaknesses are apparent. For example, there is little in the Manual describing base-rate interpretation procedures as presented by Glutting, McDermott, and Konold (1997), although Wilhoit and McCallum (2002) describe those procedures; the floors of the Symbolic Memory and Cube Design subtests are inadequate for cognitively delayed 5-year-old examines; the ceilings for the subtests Spatial Memory, Mazes, and Cube Design are slightly limited for very bright examinees at the oldest ages (e.g., 16- and 17-year-old examinees cannot earn a scaled score of more than 17 on Mazes and 18 on Cube Design and Spatial Memory); the interlocking design is conceptually spurious, that is, subtests are assigned to more than one conceptual category—thus, two major influences of subtest performance (i.e., memory/reasoning or symbolic/nonsymbolic processing) must be considered before more minor abilities are examined.

Fairness

The UNIT Manual includes a whole chapter devoted to describing test development efforts to ensure fairness and the results of fairness studies. Some of the major characteristics used to promote fairness include: elimination of language from test administration; assessment of multidimensional constructs; elimination of achievement influences; limited influence of speeded performance; use of variable response modes; use of ample teaching items; use of expert panels to select items; use of sophisticated item bias statistics to reduce content validity bias; comparison of psychometric properties across populations; use of sophisticated statistical techniques to reduce construct validity bias; comparison of mean scores across various populations; use of strategies to reduce predictive validity bias; and inclusion of children with handicapping conditions into the standardization sample. Importantly, means of minority group individuals are more similar to the means of the nonminority population on the UNIT than for other major intelligence tests (e.g., WISC-III).

In spite of the strong fairness data reported for the UNIT, there are limitations. Although the UNIT was developed and standardized to ensure cross-cultural fairness, it was not standardized for use in foreign countries. In addition, there are no specific methodological and statistical procedures in the UNIT Manual detailing how it can be adapted for use in foreign countries when full-scale restandarization is not possible (see McCallum, Bracken, & Wasserman, 2001 for some cross-cultural adaptation guidelines).

SUMMARY

This chapter has described the essential characteristics, strengths, and weaknesses of the UNIT. The test is multidimensional, and primarily assesses memory and reasoning using both a symbolic and nonsymbolic format. Examinees will find the UNIT easy to administer, score, and interpret. The Manual includes a wealth of data describing the technical properties of the test. In general, item and subtest properties are excellent, with few limitations. Riverside Publishing Company and the authors have developed a number of related materials, such as an administration video, a university training guide, a training CD, and a scoring and interpretative software package.

REFERENCES

Bracken, B. A. (1987). Limitations of preschool instruments and standards for minimal levels of technical adequacy. *Journal of Psychoeducational Assessment, 4*, 313–326.

Bracken, B. A., & McCallum, R. S. (1998). *Universal nonverbal intelligence test*. Itasca, IL: Riverside.

Bracken, B. A., & McCallum, R. S. (1999). *Universal nonverbal intelligence test: University training guide*. Itasca, IL: Riverside.

Bracken, B. A., McCallum, R. S., & Upson, L. (2003) Reducing minority-majority UNIT mean differences: Refining the Socio Economic Status matching procedure. Unpublished manuscript.

Brown, L., Sherbenou, R. J., & Johnsen, S. K. (1990). *Test of nonverbal intelligence* (2nd ed.). Austin, TX: PRO-ED.

Carroll, J. B. (1993). *Human cognitive abilities: A survey of factor-analytic studies*. New York: Cambridge University Press.

Cattell, R. B. (1963). Theory of fluid and crystallized intelligence. *Journal of Educational Psychology, 54*, 1–22.

Fachting, A., & Bradley-Johnson, S. (in press). A review of the Universal Nonverbal Intelligence Test (UNIT). *Psychology in the Schools*.

Fives, C., & Flanagan, R. (2002). *A review of the Universal Nonverbal Intelligence Test (UNIT): An advance for evaluating youngsters with diverse needs. School Psychology International, 23*, 425–448.

Glutting, J. J., McDermott, P. A., & Konold, T. R. (1997). Ontology, structure, and diagnostic benefits of a normative subtest taxonomy from the WISC-III standardization sample. In D. P. Flanagan, J. L. Genshaft, & P. L. Harrison (Eds.), *Contemporary intellectual assessment: Theories, tests, and issues* (pp. 349–372). New York: Guildford.

Horn, J. L. (1968). Organization of abilities and the development of intelligence. *Psychological Review, 75*, 242–259.

Jensen, A. R. (1980). *Bias in mental testing*. New York: The Free Press.

Kamphaus, R. W. (2001). *Clinical assessment of child and adolescent intelligence* (2nd ed.). Boston: Allyn and Bacon.

Kaufman, A. S. (1979). *Intelligent testing with the WISC-R*. New York: Wiley.

Kaufman, A. S., & Kaufman, N. L. (1983). *Kaufman assessment battery for children: Administration and scoring manual*. Circle Pines, MN: American Guidance Service.

Kaufman, A. S., & Kaufman, N. L. (1990). *Kaufman brief intelligence test manual*. Circle Pines, MN: American Guidance Service.

Kaufman, A. S., & Lichtenberger, P. O. (1999). *Essentials of WAIS-III assessment*. New York: Wiley.

McCallum, R. S. (1991). The assessment of preschool children with the Stanford–Binet Intelligence Scale: Fourth edition. In B. A. Bracken (Ed.), *The psychoeducational assessment of preschool children* (2nd ed., pp. 107–132). Boston: Allyn & Bacon.

McCallum, R. S. (1999). A "baker's dozen" criteria for evaluating fairness in nonverbal testing. *School Psychologist*, 40–60.

McCallum, R. S., Bracken, B. A., & Wasserman, J. (2001). *Essentials of nonverbal assessment*. New York: Wiley.

McDermott, P. A., Fantuzzo, J. W., & Glutting, J. J. (1990). Just say no to subtest analysis: A critique on Wechsler theory and practice. *Journal of psychoeducational assessment*, 8(3), 290–302

McDermott, P. A., & Glutting, J. J. (1997). Informing stylistic learning behavior, disposition, and achievement through ability subtests—Or, more illusions of meaning? *School Psychology Review*, 26, 163–175.

McGrew, K. S. & Flanagan, D. P. (1998). *The intelligence test desk reference (ITDR): Gf–Gc cross-battery assessment*. Boston: Allyn & Bacon.

Naglieri, J. A. (1985). Use of the WISC-R and K-ABC with learning disabled, borderline mentally retarded, and normal children. *School Psychology Review*, 22, 133–141.

Naglieri, J. A., & Kaufman, A. S. (1983). How many factors underlie the WAIS-R? *Journal of Psychoeducational Assessment*, 1, 113–119.

Raven, J. C. (1960). *Guide to using the standard progressive matrices*. London: H. K. Lewis.

Sattler, J. M. (1988). *Assessment of children* (3rd ed.). San Diego, CA: Author.

Sattler, J. M. (2001). *Assessment of children* (4th ed. rev.). San Diego, CA: Author.

U.S. Bureau of the Census. (1995). *Current population survey, March 1995*. Washington, DC: Author.

Wechsler, D. (1939). *Measurement of adult intelligence*. Baltimore, MD: Williams & Wilkins.

Wechsler, D. (1991). *Wechsler intelligence scale for children—third edition*. San Antonio, TX: The Psychological Corporation.

Wilhoit, B., & McCallum, R. S. (2002). Profile analysis of the Universal Nonverbal Intelligence Test (UNIT) standardization sample. *School Psychology Review*, 31(2), 263–281.

Woodcock, R. W. (1990). Theoretical foundations of the WJ-R measures of cognitive ability. *Journal of Psychoeducational Assessment*, 8, 231–258.

Woodcock, R. W., & Johnson, M. B. (1989/1990). *Woodcock–Johnson psycho-educational battery—revised*. Itasca, IL: Riverside.

APPENDIX: UNIT INTERPRETIVE WORKSHEET

Step 1: Interpret the Full-Scale IQ

Scale	IQ	Confidence interval (90/95 circle one)	Percentile rank	Descriptive category
Memory		90/95		
Reasoning		90/95		
Symbolic		90/95		
NonSymbolic		90/95		
Full Scale		90/95		

If there is at least one significant difference between the component parts of the Full-Scale IQ (i.e., among the following quotients: Memory [MQ], Reasoning [RQ], Symbolic [SQ], Nonsymbolic [NSQ]), the Full Scale should not be interpreted as the most meaningful representation of the individual's overall performance.

Step 2: Are There Any Significant Differences among the Quotients: Memory, Reasoning, Symbolic, Nonsymbolic (see Table 3.12)?

MQ vs. RQ difference	Significance: If yes, circle one	SQ vs. NSQ difference	Significance If yes, circle one
	0.05 0.01		0.05 0.01

If the answers are both no (there are no significant differences between either the MQ and RQ or the SQ and NSQ), first explain the meaning of the scales not being significantly different, then skip to Step 5. If either answer is yes (there is a significant difference between either the MQ and RQ or the SQ and the NSQ), then continue on to Step 3.

Step 3: Are the MQ vs. RQ or the SQ vs. NSQ Differences Abnormally Large?

MQ vs. RQ difference	Size needed for abnormality	Does size meet criteria?	
	20 points (extreme 15%)	Yes	No
	23 points (extreme 10%)	Yes	No
	27 points (extreme 5%)	Yes	No
	34 points (extreme 1%)	Yes	No
SQ vs. NSQ	20 points (extreme 15%)	Yes	No
	23 points (extreme 10%)	Yes	No
	27 points (extreme 5%)	Yes	No
	34 points (extreme 1%)	Yes	No

Step 3: Decision Box

If any abnormal differences exist, and if the scatter within any global scale is less than 6 points, interpret these abnormal differences in Step 4. If no abnormal differences exist, or if excessive scatter exists within one or more global scales, go to Step 5.

Step 4: Interpret the Global Memory vs. Reasoning and/or Symbolic vs. Nonsymbolic and Nonverbal Differences (If They Were Found to Be Interpretable)

Step 5: Interpret Significant Subtest Strengths and Weaknesses of Profile

A. Determine which mean you should use to calculate subtest strengths and weaknesses. MQ vs. RQ Discrepancy:

   0–20 points—Examine SQ vs. NSQ Discrepancy

   21 or more—Use mean of MQ subtests and RQ subtests separately

B. SQ vs. NSQ Discrepancy:

   0–20, and MQ vs. RQ < 20—Use mean of all subtest administered (Pooled Procedure)

   21 or more—Use mean of SQ subtests and NSQ separately.

Subtests	Scaled score	Rounded mean	Difference	Strength/weakness	%ile
Sym mem					
Cube Des					
Spa Mem					
Ana Rea					
Obj Mem					
Mazes					

6

Assessment with the Leiter International Performance Scale—Revised and the S-BIT

Gale Roid, Leah Nellis, and Mary McLellan

The *Leiter International Performance Scale—Revised* (Leiter-R; Roid & Miller, 1997) is a battery of individually administered subtests, administered nonverbally and designed to assess cognitive functions in children, adolescents and young adults, ages 2 years, 0 months to 20 years, 11 months. An abbreviated scale derived from the Leiter-R, known as the *Stoelting (Leiter) Brief Nonverbal Intelligence Test* (S-BIT) for ages 6–20 was recently published separately (Roid & Miller, 1999). These tests are widely used to operationalize nonverbal intelligence by assessing fluid reasoning and visualization as well as nonverbal memory and attention on the Leiter-R (McGrew & Flanagan, 1998). The foundational model for the tests is a hierarchical model of general nonverbal ability composed of the four dimensions of reasoning, visualization, memory, and attention. The battery was nationally standardized on a normative sample of 1,719 subjects; shows high reliability and has strong evidence of validity in correlating with other widely used intelligence measures and in clinical diagnosis.

Gale Roid, Department of Psychology, Peabody College of Vanderbilt University, Nashville, Tennessee 37325. At the time this chapter was written, Dr. Roid was Professor and Visiting Scholar in Residence at Simpson College and Graduate School, Redding, California.   Leah Nellis, Educational and Counseling Psychology, College of Education, University of Kentucky, Lexington, Kentucky 40506.   Mary McLellan, Department of Educational Psychology, Northern Arizona University, Flagstaff, Arizona 86011.

Handbook of Nonverbal Assessment, edited by R. Steve McCallum. Kluwer Academic/Plenum Publishers, 2003.

TEST MODEL AND PHILOSOPHY

The Leiter-R was revised to meet the growing need for nonverbal cognitive assessment in our increasingly multicultural society. The Leiter-R was designed to target the needs of children and adolescents with cognitive disabilities or exceptionalities who may not be accurately assessed by traditional verbally loaded tests. Some of the groups of children for whom the Leiter-R was specially developed include those with significant cognitive giftedness or cognitive delay or learning disability combined with communication disorders, English as a second language, hearing impairments, motor impairments, attention-deficit disorders, autism, elective mutism, or mutism due to traumatic experiences. Also, individuals with traumatic brain injury often need a comprehensive nonverbal battery to fully establish the effectiveness of their rehabilitation. For many years, the original edition of the Leiter International Performance Scale (Leiter, 1979), had served the needs of these children and their parents or guardians by providing an alternative to verbal assessments. The original Leiter was developed to provide a culture-fair, nonverbal measure of intelligence. The scale employed a series of wooden blocks that were manipulated by children to match sequences of figures and pictures depicted on a wooden "frame" containing "slots" to hold the reordered blocks. However, the original Leiter needed thorough revision, modernization, extended reliability and validity research, and national restandardization, all of which were provided in the Leiter-R.*

For the Leiter-R, nonverbal intellectual abilities were defined as those mental and cognitive skills and aptitudes involving a multitude of nonlanguage functions such as figural reasoning, spatial visualization, picture memory, or visual attention (van Zomeran & Brouwer, 1992). Nonverbal cognitive abilities were defined as those that do not require proficiency in perceiving, manipulating, or reasoning with words or numbers, printed materials, or with items requiring expressive or receptive language skills. Thus, with the Leiter-R, nonverbal abilities are tested with pictures, figural illustrations and coded symbols, and all administration instructions are given with gestures or pantomime by the examiner.

In addition, there were three primary rationales for the expansion of the Leiter-R to a full battery of assessment scales, as compared with the single, global score on the original Leiter: (a) the need for comprehensive, early identification of cognitive delays and learning difficulties; (b) the need for cognitive measures of change or "growth" sensitive to small increments of improvement; and (c) the need for assessment of adolescents and young

---

*Dr. Roid, is the senior coauthor of the Leiter-R. His motivation for working on the revision of the Leiter was to provide a helpful assessment tool for parents of children with special needs, given that he personally experienced the critical need for nonverbal assessment in his own family. Dr. Roid is currently the author of the Fifth Edition of the Stanford–Binet Intelligence Scale. The opinions expressed in this chapter are those of the authors and do not necessarily represent the opinions of the test publisher or the publisher of this volume.

adults transitioning from special education to the "world of work." First, most experts in special education agree that early intervention is key in preparing the child for school (e.g., Salvia & Ysseldyke, 1991). Researchers in special education have called for a stronger link between assessment and early intervention (e.g., Bagnato, Neisworth, & Munson, 1989; Meisels & Fenicel, 1996). In order to design effective interventions, a more thorough "profile" of nonverbal abilities was needed for the Leiter-R, including memory and attention because of their implications for the design of treatments.

Second, there is a critical need for a measure such as the Leiter-R to provide ability estimates sensitive to small increments of improvement in cognitive ability, rather than just a comparison with a norm-referenced standard. A number of investigators (Lohman, 1993; Miller & Robinson, 1996; Thompson et al., 1994) have called for growth measures to meet the mandate for measuring growth and recovery of cognitive functioning that go beyond traditional composite scores. Parents of children with disabilities, and the professionals that care for them, often express concern that the majority of measures of cognitive functioning that are currently available do not adequately document the quality and magnitude of gains achievable by children during the course of development. Although important gains in cognitive functioning are observed, most age-standardized test batteries are unable to document these gains for at least two reasons: (a) children with mild to moderate disabilities are functioning in the lowest standard-score category (two or three standard deviations below the mean) where measurement is imprecise; and/or (b) age-standardized, normative scores continue to categorize the child in the lowest score range at each successive year of age; hence, no "progress" is apparent from test scores. Notable exceptions are the ability scores of the Differential Ability Scales (DAS; Elliott, 1990), the W-scores of the Woodcock–Johnson Psychoeducational Battery—Revised (WJ-R; Woodcock & Johnson, 1989), the Scale Scores in the Pediatric Evaluation of Disability Inventory (PEDI; Haley, Coster, Ludlow, Haltiwanger, & Andrellos, 1992); and the Motor Organization scores in the Toddler and Infant Motor Evaluation (TIME; Miller & Roid, 1994) that are based on item-response theory scaling (Lord, 1980; Rasch, 1980) in addition to age-based standard scoring.

Third, the new Leiter-R was designed to provide a comprehensive profile of nonverbal abilities in the adolescent transitioning from special education to the work world. Transition services, as required by Individuals with Disabilities Education Act (1990) legislation, have been defined as "a coordinated set of activities for a student, designed within an outcome-oriented process, which promotes movement from school to post-school activities," including education, employment and independent living (Baroff, 1986). The team of professionals providing service to an adolescent with disabilities must include plans for transition services in the Individualized Education Program (IEP) by age 16, perhaps as early as age 14. Clearly, the cognitive abilities of adolescents are one part of an overall plan for such transition, and assessments should be sensitive to growth achieved by the individual during phases of the transition. Assessment of abilities in the Leiter-R, such as visualization, problem-solving, short and long-term memory, and attention-to-detail, are clearly relevant to future job performance or educational progress.

Theoretical Basis of the Test Batteries

A large body of research has developed during recent years linking the methods and concepts of cognitive science to the psychometric analysis of intelligence and aptitude (e.g., Carroll, 1993; Gustafsson, 1984; Horn, 1994; Hunt, 1976; Sternberg, 1977; Whitely, 1976). One of the main goals of development of the Leiter-R was to identify the cognitive components or processes that underlie the abilities that have been traditionally measured by intelligence tests. It is critical to understand the cognitive processes involved in test performance so that we can begin to ask how these abilities might be learned (Glaser, 1981).

Several lines of independent research have converged on a unifying model for the structure of cognitive abilities. Following several years of research on more than 450 data sets, including special-education and minority samples, Carroll (1993) has proposed a three-stratum theory of cognitive abilities that resembles the fluid-crystallized theory of Horn and Cattell (1966), Horn (1994) and the three-level hierarchical model of intelligence proposed by Gustafsson (1984). In the Gustafsson and Carroll models, the apex of the hierarchical model is a general intelligence or "g" factor. At the second level, a smaller number of broad factors have been identified (three or four by Gustafsson, seven by Carroll including the fluid and crystallized factors of Horn and Cattell that have also been verified independently by Woodcock, 1990). At the third level, a large number of "primary" factors are nested within the second-level factors.

Carroll (1993) provided strong verification of the hierarchical structure of intellectual abilities. Following several years of comprehensive study, involving more than 400 data sets, Carroll's (1993) hierarchical model provides detail and verification of the Gustafsson model by elaborating the three-stratum theory of cognitive abilities, with "g" at the apex. At the second level were eight ability domains similar to those identified by Horn (1994), Horn and Cattell (1966), Gustafsson (1984), Woodcock (1990) and McGrew and Flanagan (1998). These include fluid reasoning (Gf), crystallized ability (Gc), broad visualization (Gv), various memory and learning domains (Gsm), auditory ability (Ga), two factors of processing speed (Gs and decision speed), and long-term retrieval (Glr). At the third level are more specific abilities, such as inductive reasoning under Gf, or spatial visualization under Gv, memory span and associative memory under Gsm. Carroll's work was carefully studied during the design of the Leiter-R and, along with the Gustafsson model, guided the selection of domains such as fluid reasoning (nonverbal type), visualization, various aspects of memory, and the timed tasks of attention (related to immediate and delayed memory and to processing speed).

The final form of the Leiter-R model includes an increasingly complex set of subdomains, as the age of the child progresses, analogous to the differentiated model of the *Differential Ability Scales* (Elliott, 1990). Table 6.1 shows the major subdomains of the Leiter-R model. In the age range

Table 6.1   Factor Models of the Leiter-R by Age Group

Age group	Factors	Subtest with highest loading[a]
2–3	Reasoning	Repeated patterns
	Visualization	Classification
	Attention	Attention sustained
4–5	Reasoning	Repeated patterns
	Visualization	Figure ground
	Memory	Immediate recognition
	Attention	Attention sustained
6–10	Reasoning	Repeated patterns
	Visualization	Figure ground
	Memory: Recognition	Immediate recognition
	Memory: Associative	Associated pairs
	Memory: Span	Forward memory
	Attention	Visual coding
11–20	Reasoning	Sequential order
	Visualization	Paper folding
	Memory: Associative	Associated pairs
	Memory: Span	Forward memory
	Attention	Attention sustained

[a]Highest loading refers to the factor loading with the highest magnitude in the exploratory factor analysis tables reported in the Leiter-R manual (Roid & Miller, 1997). See the section on "Subtests" for an explanation of each subtest.

2–3 years, the major factors include Fluid Reasoning (Gf in the terminology of Carroll, 1993), Fundamental Visualization (Gv), and Attention. At ages 4–5, a separate factor of Recognition Memory appears, due to the introduction of the Immediate Recognition subtest at age 4. In the range of 6–10 years, the number of factors expands to six, as the number of available subtests increases. The factors are reasoning (Gf), visual/spatial (Gv), attention, and facets of short-term memory (Gsm) and retrieval (Glr), labeled Recognition Memory (Lezak, 1995), Associative Memory (Wilson, Bacon, Kaszniak, & Fox, 1982), and Memory Span (Lezak, 1995). In the range of 11–20 years, there are five factors due to the deletion of Recognition Memory (because it functions best in the younger age range), with names identical to those at ages 6–10.

Organization of the Leiter-R

The Leiter-R includes two groupings of subtests: (a) the Visualization and Reasoning (VR) Battery with 10 subtests of nonverbal intellectual ability related to visualization, reasoning, and spatial ability; and (b) the Attention and Memory (AM) Battery with 10 subtests of nonverbal attention and memory function. The testing time for each set of 10 subtests (with the AM Battery optional and not included in the IQ calculations) is 45–50 min. Examiners have the option of administering the VR and AM batteries separately or together, as determined by the clinical needs of the individual being assessed.

Also, four rating scales (Parent, Self, Teacher, and Examiner) provide multidimensional behavioral observations of the individual. There are four rating scales: Examiner Rating, Parent Rating, Teacher Rating, and Child's Self Rating. The domains that are included on the ratings are attention, activity level, organization/impulse control, sociability, sensory reactivity, emotions, anxiety, and mood. The ratings are on a Likert scale ranging from 0 to 3 points (parent-, teacher-, and self-rating) to 4 points (for examiner rating).

Test materials include three comprehensive stimulus easels, which include examiner directions, response picture cards, manipulatives, and printed materials. The Leiter-R employs a response mode highly similar to the original edition. To reduce the physical weight and provide improved hygienic testing materials, colorful "playing cards" and foam-rubber manipulatives have replaced the wooden blocks of the original Leiter. The child places the cards and manipulatives into the "slots" in the "frame," which is molded into the easel base of each stimulus booklet. Thus, the original nature of the Leiter has been maintained, while important changes, such as authentic national norms and modern illustrations, have been included in the Leiter-R. Two choices are available for the estimation of global intellectual ability or "g":

1. *Brief IQ (four subtests only)*. For tentative or reversible decisions (e.g., initial screening), a brief collection of four subtests in the VR Battery provides consistent measurement throughout the age range of 2–20. The subtests (see section below) are Sequential Order, Repeated Patterns, Figure Ground and Form Completion. This abbreviated IQ measure can be used as a rapid (about 25 min) estimate of global intellectual level, e.g., low, low–average, average, high–average, and high levels. This scale has been developed to meet the needs of examiners who are interested in a brief but reliable estimate of intellectual level when the Leiter-R is employed in a battery of other tests and assessments. Roid and Miller (1999) have recently published the Brief IQ subtests as a separate instrument called the S-BIT).

2. *Full-Scale IQ (six subtests only)*. High-reliability, full-scale estimates of global nonverbal intellectual level can be obtained (in about 40 min) for identification, classification, or placement decisions when such decisions are not easily reversed (e.g., placement in services for mental retardation). Two sets of six subtests are used: (a) one set for children aged 2–5 years (see list of subtests below, SO, RP, FG, FC, M, C) and (b) an overlapping set of six subtests for children and adolescents aged 6–20 (SO, RP, FG, FC, DA, PF).

When a comprehensive measure of nonverbal strengths and limitations is needed for treatment planning, additional subtests from both the VR and AM Batteries can be combined. Users should read the test manuals carefully (Roid & Miller, 1997, 1999) when deciding which combinations of VR and/or AM subtests to employ for specific purposes.

Subtests of the Leiter-R

The 20 subtests of the complete Leiter-R are listed below. The number preceding each subtest indicates its order of presentation in the Easel

Table 6.2 Primary Abilities Measured by the VR and AM Batteries

Visualization and reasoning (VR) battery: Brief IQ or S-BIT

1. *Figure Ground—FG (The Find It Game)*: Identification of embedded figures or designs within a complex stimulus.
2. *Form Completion—FC (The Put Together Game)*: Ability to recognize "whole objects" from a randomly displayed array of its fragmented parts.
3. *Sequential Order—SO (The Which Comes Next Game)*: Logical progressions of pictorial or figural objects and selection of related stimuli that progress in a corresponding order. This subtest includes several of the classic Leiter items.
4. *Repeated Patterns—RP (The Over and Over Game)*: Patterns of pictorial or figural objects that are repeated. Child supplies "missing" portion of pattern by moving response cards into alignment with easel.
5. *Design Analogies—DA (The Funny Squares Game)*: Classical "matrix analogies" items using geometric shapes, including 2×2, 4×2 and more complex matrices. Some of the more difficult items include mental rotation of figures; hence the relationship of this subtest to spatial ability.
6. *Matching—M (The Matching Game)*: Discrimination and matching of visual stimuli; selection of response cards or manipulative shapes that match easel stimuli.
7. *Picture Context—PC (The Belongs Together Game)*: Ability to recognize pictured objects that have been removed from a larger display (missing location indicated by markings), using visual contextual clues.
8. *Classification—C (The Goes Together Game)*: Categorization of objects or geometric designs.
9. *Paper Folding—PF (The Folding Game)*: Ability to mentally "fold" an object displayed in two-dimensions—unfolded—and to match it to a target (no actual paper is folded).
10. *Figure Rotation—FR (The Turn It Around Game)*: Mental rotation of a two- or three-dimensional object or geometric figure.

Attention and memory (AM) battery

11. *Associated Pairs—AP (The Partners Game)*: After pairs of pictured objects are displayed for 5 or 10 s and then removed, the ability to remember meaningful and non-meaningful associations is assessed. This is similar to a number of associative-learning tasks.
12. *Immediate Recognition—IR (The Something's Missing Game)*: After a stimulus array of pictured objects is shown for 5 s and then removed, the ability to discriminate between present and absent objects is assessed. This subtest reflects recognition rather than pure recall memory because the missing objects are shown on the response cards.
13. *Forward Memory—FM (The Remembering Game)*: Ability to remember a sequence of pictured objects to which the examiner points in a given sequence.
14. *Attention Sustained—AS (The Drawing Game)*: Measures consist of "boring" clerical tasks such as finding and crossing out all squares found in an array of geometric shapes printed on a page. Three parallel forms, of increasing difficulty, are included, a preschool "smiling face" form, a school-age animal-pictures form, and a more complex array of geometric shapes.
15. *Reverse Memory—RM (The Backwards Game)*: Ability to remember a sequence of pictured objects in the opposite order from that of the examiner. This subtest provides an important contrast to Forward Memory, just as forward and backward digits do.
16. *Visual Coding—VC (The Changing Game)*: A nonverbal version of the symbol to digit-coding task, using pictorial and geometric objects as well as numbers. Some of the more difficult items in this subtest have a reasoning, as well as a working-memory, component.
17. *Spatial Memory—SM (The Place Game)*: Increasingly complex displays of pictured objects, arrayed in a matrix format, are shown for 10 s and then removed. In response, cards are placed in the correct spatial location on a blank matrix grid.
18. *Delayed Pairs—DP (The Partners Game Again)*: After approximately a 20-min delay, the ability to recognize the objects associated in subtest AP is presented again.

Table 6.2   (*Continued*)

19. *Delayed Recognition—DR (The Something's Missing Game Again)*: After approximately a 20-min delay, the ability to recognize the objects present in the IR subtest is presented again. This and DP may tap incidental learning since the child is not previously asked to remember the pictures in either subtest.
20. *Attention Divided—AD (The Do Two Things At Once Game)*: This subtest measures the degree of persevering attention when divided attention is demanded. The materials include a cardboard sheath that holds a movable insert on which brightly colored objects (apples, bananas, fire-trucks, etc.) are pictured. When the insert is moved, the pictured objects appear in selected "windows" that expose a controlled number of targeted objects. The child's task is to point to the targeted objects in each trial. In addition, the child is taught a numerical card-sorting task. This subtest requires that the child divide their attention between pointing to objects in the sheath and sorting cards.

Books and on the Record Forms. A one- or two-letter abbreviation for the subtest name immediately follows the full subtest name. All subtests in the Leiter-R have been given "Game Names" to encourage examiners to interject a more fun atmosphere when testing young children. The primary ability being measured by each subtest is noted in the descriptions in Table 6.2.

It is important to note that *not all subtests need be administered at a given age*; rather, the clinician should administer only those subtests needed for selected composites at a specific age or those that will generate clinical hypotheses related to the specific case.

History of Test Development

When Russell Leiter developed the original scale in the 1930s, his goal was to create a scale that would be highly related to the Stanford–Binet but not include language requirements for either the examiner or the examinee (Leiter, 1966). The co-authors of the Leiter-R continued this nonlanguage tradition particularly targeting children with special needs and those from non-English backgrounds. During the 5-year development process, the Leiter-R was moved through the stages of planning/research, pilot studies, tryout testing, national standardization, and finalization for publication. Each of these stages will be described briefly in turn. However, the reader is referred to the comprehensive chapter in the test manual (Roid & Miller, 1997) for more details.

STAGES OF DEVELOPMENT

Planning/Research

The coauthors and publishing staff conducted an extensive review of the history of the original Leiter, including the literature cited in the comprehensive review by Levine (1982), and related neuropsychological literature (e.g., Lezak, 1995). Expert consultants were interviewed and asked to submit recommendations for the revision. A written survey of 100 frequent users of the original Leiter was collected, providing detailed comments on the strengths and weaknesses of the original scale. Tables of specifications showing the cognitive processes underlying performance on the various parts of the new scale were written and are provided in the test manual.

Pilot Studies

Small samples of subjects, including some clinical cases, elementary students in Colorado, and college freshmen in Oregon were employed to examine the first drafts of new items for the Leiter-R. In preparation for pilot studies of new subtests, new items were derived from a study of the item types in the original Leiter. Because of recent advances in research on intelligence, the Leiter-R employed the strategy of "taking apart" the items of the original Leiter and matching them to documented cognitive abilities (e.g., using Carroll, 1993). Then, sets of items were expanded to provide better coverage of each key dimension represented. For example, several items in the original Leiter tested a visual fluid-reasoning ability— seeing a sequential pattern in a series of figural objects. Such items were identified, several retained and reformatted, and expanded into a complete subtest called Sequential Order in the VR Battery. Some original Leiter items were clearly tapping a visual-matching ability, and these formed the core of the Matching subtest, also in the VR Battery. Another example is the original items that resemble the Coding test in the Wechsler scales, which were included and expanded into the Visual Coding subtest of the AM Battery. Since coding-type subtests are often included in factor scores labeled "distractibility," or "processing speed," they were seen as less central but supportive to the assessment of fluid reasoning and visualization, the most prominent factors in global intellectual ability (Carroll, 1993; Wechsler, 1991). Thus, subtests such as Visual Coding were placed in the diagnostic AM Battery rather than in the VR Battery where IQ is calculated.

Tryout Testing

During 1994–1995, a Tryout Edition of the Leiter-R, composed of 703 items in 23 subtests, was printed and administered to subjects by 59 trained and experienced examiners. Examiners from the Southern, Central and Western regions of the U.S. were given a 4-day training workshop in Aspen, Colorado, and administered the Tryout Edition to a total of 225 typical children and adolescents without disabilities and 325 with disabilities. With an unusually rigorous plan to conduct validity and reliability studies, results from the normative ("typical") cases were contrasted with cases of individuals with cognitive delays, communication disorders, delays in motor development, hearing impairments, traumatic brain injury or English as a second language. The sample included 46% Anglo, 22% African American, 25% Hispanic, 5% Native American, and

2% Asian American subjects from each socioeconomic level (measured by mother's number of years of education; 23% completed less than high school, 34% high school or the General Equivalency Degree (GED), which is given in the United States for those who obtain the equivalent of a high school diploma by examination as adults and 43% post-high school experience, which matched the 1993 Census quite well; U.S. Bureau of the Census, 1993). Extensive studies of item characteristics, item-response-theory scaling, factor analysis of scales and subtests, construct and criterion validity, internal-consistency, and test–retest reliabilities were all conducted. Additionally, extensive studies of potential item and test bias were examined. A few items or illustrations were deleted based on the item studies (e.g., Blair, 1996). The extensive Tryout studies are documented in Roid and Miller (1997) and included verification of the Reasoning, Visualization and Memory factors expected by the Gustafsson (1984) and Carroll (1993) models, in both exploratory and confirmatory factor studies. Extensive studies of item fit to the Rasch item-response model (Rasch, 1980; Lineacre & Wright, 1990) revealed an excellent model-data fit and revealed that the majority of the Tryout items fit the response model. Item calibrations were then employed in designing the sequence of items for the Standardization Edition. Initial versions of items for the Attention factor were found to be inadequate and were redesigned for the standardization phase. Also, four of the Tryout subtests were deleted due to a lower reliability or difficulties in administration or scoring.

STANDARDIZATION AND PSYCHOMETRIC PROPERTIES

The VR Battery was standardized on a nationally representative, stratified random sample of the United States, totaling 1,719 normative cases aged 2 years, 0 months to 20 years, 11 months (Madsen, Roid, & Miller, 1996). In addition, a nationally representative subsample of cases was given the AM Battery, totaling 763 cases. National representation of genders (49.9% female, 50.1% male) and geographic regions was maintained. The ethnic representation of the VR norming sample closely matched the targeted 1993 Census with Anglo/Caucasian (66.2%), African American (16.6%), Hispanic (12.6%), Asian American (3.2%) and Native American (1.3%) groups represented. Parental education levels of cases also closely matched the targeted Census (19.2% less than high school, 35.2% high school or GED, 45.7% post-HS). The separately published Brief IQ measure (four subtests), the S-BIT (Roid & Miller, 1999), was normed on a subsample of 983 cases, ages 6 years, 0 months to 20 years, 11 months, derived from the VR Battery national sample. Experienced examiners ($N = 114$) were trained in a 4-day workshop to administer the test and to collect data for the standardization. During 1995 and 1996, data collection on normative ($N = 1,719$) subjects, validity cases ($N = 701$) and test–retest reliability cases ($N = 163$) was closely monitored by coauthors and publishing staff and entered into computer files. Computer analyses were then conducted to produce the final item selections, normative calculations, and reliability and validity studies. In addition, all normative participants were rated for test-session behavior on the Examiner Rating Scale ($N = 1,719$), and subsamples of parents were administered the parallel behavioral checklist, the Parent Rating Scale ($N = 785$). A sample of 173 teachers completed parallel behavioral ratings on the Teacher Rating Scale, and 208 normative participants, ages 6–20, completed the Self Rating Scale.

Following extensive item-level and subtest-level empirical studies, the published edition of the Leiter-R was finalized. The VR Battery was shortened to allow for the most efficient testing time and effective rapport between examiner and examinee, while retaining a high reliability and validity. Criteria for item selection included a good fit to the item-response model, high point biserial correlations with total subtest scores, evidence of strong first factors in each subtest, and individual item validity in separating normative and clinical-validity cases (e.g., cases with mental retardation). Also, extensive studies of items and subtests in order to form Rasch-based "growth scales" were completed using software by Wright and Lineacre (1995). The "growth scales" are criterion-referenced scales provided as an alternative to normative standard scores, similar to the W-scores employed by Woodcock and colleagues (Mather & Woodcock, 2001). The growth scales are extremely useful in special education and treatment evaluation to study changes in cognitive performance over time. Roid and Woodcock (2000) recently demonstrated the consistency of the Leiter-R growth scales with the W-scale (Woodcock & Dahl, 1971) of the Woodcock–Johnson tests (Woodcock et al., 1977, 1989, 2001) and provided some additional validity evidence for the scales.

Comprehensive studies of reliability and validity were conducted on the Leiter-R and are detailed in the Leiter-R manual (Roid & Miller, 1997) and the S-BIT manual (Roid & Miller, 1999). The reliability and evidence for the content-, criterion- and construct validity, and fairness of the Leiter-R will be briefly described.

Reliability

Composite internal-consistency reliabilities of the Leiter-R were quite high, with Full-Scale IQ (six subtests) ranging from 0.91 to 0.93, and Brief IQ (four subtests) from 0.88 to 0.90, for age groups 2–5, 6–10, and 11–20. Thus, standard error of measurement values for IQ averaged 4.24–4.97. Test–retest reliabilities were quite high with Full-Scale IQ ranging from 0.90 to 0.96 and the Brief IQ ranging from 0.88 to 0.96. The Growth Scale equivalent of the IQ scores had very high test–retest reliabilities (0.93–0.96). Reliabilities of the composite scores for the VR Battery (Fundamental Visualization, Fluid Reasoning and Spatial Visualization) ranged from 0.88 to 0.92 across age groups. For the AM Battery, composite scores (Memory Screener, Recognition Memory, Associative Memory, Memory Span, Memory Process and Attention) ranged from 0.75 to 0.93, with a median of 0.87, across the age groups. For the summative scores of the Rating scales (Attention, Impulsivity, Activity Level, Sociability, etc.) internal-consistency reliabilities ranged from 0.73 to 0.99, with a median of 0.95 (most exceeded 0.90). Internal-consistency reliabilities (Cronbach,

1951) for 14 separate age groups are reported for the VR and AM Battery subtests. For the VR Battery subtests, average reliabilities across age groups ranged from 0.75 (Figure Ground) to 0.90 (Picture Context) with a median of 0.82. Thus, the standard error of measurement values for VR subtest scaled scores ($M = 10$, $SD = 3$) ranged from 0.95 to 1.50 with a median of 1.25. For the AM Battery, subtest reliabilities averaged from 0.67 (Attention Divided) to 0.87 (Attention Sustained) with a median of 0.84.

Content-Related Evidence of Validity

The content and factor relevance of each item and subtest in the Tryout and Standardization Editions were scrutinized by coauthors, consultants, and examiners ($N = 60$ and $N = 114$ for Tryout and Standardization, respectively) during the 5-year development project. Examiners completed extensive questionnaires rating each subtest for ease of administration, relevance to the intended cognitive factor, and acceptability to children and parents. Consultants representing various ethnic groups provided written reactions to illustrations and subtest task characteristics. McGrew and Flanagan (1998, pp. 446–453) analyzed the content and correlations for each Leiter-R subtest in their "Intelligence Test Desk Reference" using cross-battery comparisons and Horn, Cattell, and Carroll factor theories. McGrew and Flanagan concluded that several Leiter-R subtests measure Fluid Intelligence (Gf), either induction (e.g., Design Analogies, Repeated Patterns, Sequential Order, Classification) or general sequential reasoning (Picture Context, Visual Coding). Additionally, McGrew and Flanagan identified first-stratum factors within Visual-Processing ability (Gv): spatial relations in Figure Rotation, visualization in Form Completion, Paper Folding and Matching, flexibility of closure in Figure Ground, and visual memory in Immediate Recognition and Forward Memory. Thus, McGrew and Flanagan, as independent reviewers, gave expert judgment on the content validity and factorial alignment of the Leiter-R subtests. Empirical item analysis provided important evidence of content validity (as recommended by Kamphaus, 1993). The unifactorial nature of each subtest and composite domain (e.g., reasoning, visualization, memory) was inspected (along with SPSS factor analysis of items and statistical indexes of model-data fit for each item, using the Wright and Lineacre, 1995, computer routines). For example, model-data fit to the one-parameter logistic model was verified for the VR Battery across all 305 items by the overall chi-square of 179,066.3 (log likelihood method), which was much lower than the degrees of freedom (304,000), and mean-square fit values rarely exceeded 2.0.

Criterion-Related Evidence of Validity

Extensive studies of concurrent and criterion-group validity were detailed in the test manuals (Roid & Miller, 1997, 1999). The Leiter-R Full-Scale IQ correlated 0.86 with the WISC-III Full-Scale IQ in a sample of 122 children, ages 6–16, with Performance IQ (PIQ) correlated 0.85 and Verbal

IQ correlated 0.80. Mean scores on the two intelligence batteries were also quite consistent (Leiter-R 97.5, WISC-III 98.8) and well within the standard error of measurement of the scales, indicating the relative accuracy of the scaling and standardization of Leiter-R compared with WISC-III. The Brief IQ was correlated 0.85 with WISC-III Full-Scale IQ, 0.85 with PIQ and 0.78 with VIQ. In relation to the original Leiter, Leiter-R Full-Scale and Brief IQ, both correlated 0.85 with the Leiter IQ on a sample of 124 children and adolescents, ages 2–19. The Leiter-R Growth Scale (four subtests) correlated 0.93 with the original Leiter Mental Age score. Equating tables linking the Leiter-R to the original Leiter are provided in the test manuals. The consistency between the Leiter editions shows the historical trend predicted by Flynn (1987)—a higher ability in the world population with corresponding lowering of mean IQ by about 0.3 IQ points per year, resulting in a mean difference of 13.9 points in Full-Scale IQ between editions.

In terms of Leiter-R correlation with achievement measures, Full-Scale IQ and Brief IQ correlated between 0.62 and 0.83 with reading and math composites on the WIAT ($N = 17$), WJ-R ($N = 29$) and the WRAT-3 ($N = 33$), using samples of school-age children with recently archived scores in their cumulative files. Similarly, correlations between Leiter-R and group-administered achievement measures ranged from 0.24 to 0.70 on the same archived data.

Another aspect of criterion validity is evidence for the classification accuracy of the Leiter-R in identifying children with mental retardation, or children with intellectual giftedness at the other end of exceptionality. Optimal cutpoints on the IQ scale were examined in a comprehensive study of classification accuracy, sensitivity, and specificity (Roid & Miller, 1997). A double cross-validation design was employed to establish cutpoints in a smaller derivation sample (e.g., the AM Battery normative sample, $N = 724$) combined with 40 children previously identified with mental retardation, independently by school districts. Following derivation, results were cross-validated on the full standardization sample ($N = 1,719$ plus $N = 120$ children with retardation). The Leiter-R Full-Scale IQ was able to classify children with mental retardation (IQ less than or equal to 70) with an overall accuracy of 96%, classification of 84% of previously identified retarded (sensitivity), and 97% of typical normative cases (specificity). Errors of classification were small (1% true retarded classified as typical and 2.6% typicals classified as retarded). The classification accuracy of the Brief IQ was similarly accurate. Classification of gifted children showed a high overall accuracy (85%) but higher error rates (4–10%) and a lower ceiling (the optimal cutpoint was an IQ of 120). For the best results, the Leiter-R should be combined with multiple indicators in identifying giftedness. In addition, the Memory Process Composite (standard score of 90 or less) of the Leiter-R AM Battery, when combined with the Examiner Rating Scale (cutpoint 85), proved effective in identifying previously diagnosed attention-deficit hyperactivity disorder (ADHD; Barkley, 1990) cases (92% overall accuracy with 5–6% false positive errors).

Other studies in the literature that present criterion-related evidence of validity for the Leiter-R include Flemmer and Roid's (1997) study of Hispanic and speech-impaired adolescents, Quinn's (1999) study of children with traumatic brain injury, and Roid and Woodcock's (2000) demonstration of significant differences between normative and clinical groups on an experimental ratio IQ formed from the Leiter-R Growth scale. In addition, Olson (1998) showed evidence for the usefulness of the battery in identifying subtypes of learning disabilities, and Nordlund (1998) showed the validity of the Rating Scales for differentiating between normative and ADHD cases.

Construct-Related Evidence of Validity

Construct-related evidence of validity includes an extensive number of studies reported in detail in the test manuals (Roid & Miller, 1997, 1999) and recent publications (e.g., Roid & Woodcock, 2000). Studies included (a) documentation of age trends in raw scores and in the Rasch-based Growth Scale (Wright & Stone, 1979), (b) exploratory and confirmatory factor analyses of the Tryout and Standardization Editions, (c) analysis of common, specific and error variance of each subtest, and (d) cross-battery factor analysis.

Age trends in the mean raw scores of well-constructed cognitive instruments should show the classic "growth curve" when plotted on a graph by age group, as expected from cognitive-development theory. The Leiter-R and S-BIT normative tables show systematic increases in raw scores at the median score for all subtests, and the global scores (e.g., the Growth scale derived from the four subtests in the Brief IQ) clearly show the expected growth curve. Roid and Woodcock (2000) further showed that the age trends of the Leiter-R Growth scale consistently matched the progression of values for the W-scale from the Woodcock–Johnson Psychoeducational Battery (WJ-R, Woodcock et al., 1989) normative sample. Both the Growth scale and the W-scale are Rasch-based scores anchored with a value of 500 at age 10 years (5th grade), but the additional finding of matching values at younger (425 at age 2) and older (about 520 at age 20) ages provides evidence of construct validity for the Leiter-R.

An exploratory and confirmatory factor analysis of the subtests of the Leiter-R was conducted on both the Tryout Edition and the final subtests derived from the Standardization Edition. In addition, researchers external to the Leiter-R development project independently examined the factor structure of the Leiter-R (e.g., Bay, 1996; Bos, 1995; Bos, Gridley, & Roid, 1996). As shown in Table 6.1, the overall conclusion of these extensive analyses is that the Leiter-R VR and AM Batteries measure factors identifiable as Reasoning, Visualization, Attention, and various Memory factors (Recognition, Associative, and Span), with factor composition varying somewhat by the age level of the examinee. Differentiation of cognitive factors by age level has empirical support (Elliott, 1990; Garrett, 1946). Some variation in factor composition is due to subtests such as Immediate Recognition, which were designed to function within a range of ages (4–10 years), similar to the subtests of the Stanford–Binet Fourth Edition

(Thorndike, Hagen, & Sattler, 1986). Confirmatory factor analysis using LISREL (Jöreskog & Sörbom, 1993) and AMOS (Arbuckle, 1994) shows clear evidence for a five-factor structure (reasoning, visualization, attention, and two types of memory) in the age range of 6–20, with a four-factor structure at ages 4–5 (one less memory factor). Statistical findings for the five-factor structure included values of chi-square divided by degrees of freedom of 1.84 and 1.63, goodness-of-fit index of 0.90–0.92 and residual mean squares of 0.05–0.10, with samples of more than 200 subjects.

To verify the authenticity of interpreting profile patterns on the Leiter-R, factor-analytic studies of common, specific, and error variance of each subtest were completed, and details presented in Roid and Miller (1997). These analyses were computed from a series of principal-axis factor analyses of subtest scores with communalities estimated from the iterated, squared multiple correlations in SPSS factor analysis. Error values were obtained from the published, internal-consistency reliability estimates for each subtest. The overall percentages of variance, averaged across three age groups (ages 2–5, 6–10, and 11–20 with Ns of 310, 204, and 205) were 46% common, 34% specific, and 20% error variance. This pattern of variance percentages follows the classic C > S > E ideal (Sattler, 1992). And the pattern compares favorably with the overall averages for WPPSI-R (48%, 31%, and 21%) reported by Roid and Gyurke (1991) and for the WISC-III (42%, 37%, and 15%) reported by Roid, Prifitera, and Weiss (1993).

Cross-battery factor analyses is widely recognized as a key method in establishing the factorial validity of a cognitive battery (McGrew & Flanagan, 1998). Cross-battery analyses of the Leiter-R with the Woodcock–Johnson and with WISC-III have been conducted (Roid & Miller, 1997, 1999). Evidence for the construct validity of the Leiter-R for measuring the Fluid Reasoning (Gf) factor, described in the literature (Carroll, 1993; McGrew & Flanagan, 1998), was reported in a study of selected reasoning and visualization subtests of the Leiter-R, the WJ-R and the Stanford–Binet 4th Edition (SB-4 Matrices subtest). The Analysis-Synthesis subtest of the WJ-R was known to be an excellent marker for Fluid Reasoning, as was the Matrices subtest of SB-4 (Woodcock, 1990). The intercorrelations among the SB-4 Matrices, the four Brief-IQ subtests of the Leiter-R (FG, FC, SO, and RP), and the WJ-R subtests (Analysis-Synthesis, Spatial Relations, Picture Recognition, and Visual Closure) were subjected to a maximum-likelihood factor analysis (iterated multiple correlations in the diagonal) with Promax rotation. Results clearly showed two factors of reasoning and visualization, with the WJ-R Analysis-Synthesis and SB-4 Matrices subtests defining the first factor, where also the highest loadings were obtained for the Leiter-R subtests. The structure–matrix correlations showed that the visual subtests of Leiter-R (Figure Ground and Form Completion) correlated highly with the second visual factor dominated by the WJ-R Visual Closure subtest. Thus, the construct validity of the Fluid Reasoning element of Leiter-R Brief IQ (and the S-BIT) was demonstrated (see Roid & Miller, 1999, p. 109).

In the cross-battery analysis of the Leiter-R and the WISC-III, the Leiter-R VR subtests largely loaded with the WISC-III Performance scales, particularly Block Design and Picture Completion. A smaller third factor showed evidence that the Repeated Patterns subtest of Leiter-R functions separately from the Leiter-R visual subtests by loading on an apparent "visual sequential reasoning" factor along with Picture Arrangement of the WISC-III. McLellan, Nellis, and Roid (2000) recently conducted a confirmatory factor analysis with LISREL on data from 175 Navajo children (ages 6–12), who were administered both the Leiter-R VR Battery and the WISC-III. Results showed the best fit for a five-factor model representing the four factor dimensions of the WISC-III (verbal, perceptual, distractibility and speed), with the Leiter-R visualization subtests loading on the perceptual factor and the Leiter-R reasoning subtests (DA, RP, SO) loading on a fifth "fluid reasoning" factor.

Fairness of Assessment

Fairness across gender and ethnic groups for the Leiter-R subtests has been investigated extensively by Armenteros and Roid (1996), Blair (1996), Grant, Roid, and Fallow (1996), Mellott and McLellan (1995), McLellan and Walton (1996), Roid and Miller (1997, 1999), and Roid (1997). Roid and Miller (1999) presented a scatter plot showing the difficulty calibrations of the 62 items in the Repeated Patterns and Sequential Order subtests derived separately for male ($N = 500$) and female ($N = 483$) subsamples of the S-BIT normative sample. Difficulty calibrations were the locations parameters for the item characteristic curves calculated for the Rasch one-parameter logistic model (Wright & Lineacre, 1995). The scatter plot (Roid & Miller, 1999, p. 116) shows little departure from the ideal 45° regression line between the sets of calibrations, indicating a lack of differential item functioning (DIF; Holland & Wainer, 1993). In other words, no evidence for differential item bias was identified. These analyses and scatter plots were completed for all subtests of S-BIT across pairs of ethnic groups (Anglo vs. Hispanic; Anglo vs. African American) also, similarly demonstrating a lack of DIF. Similar analyses were completed for all Leiter-R subtests (excluding the speeded items of the Attention subtests), and scatter plots showed consistency and lack of evidence for item bias. Blair (1996) had previously examined DIF values for preliminary standardization versions of the picture-oriented subtests, Figure Ground (FG), Form Completion (FC), Picture Context (PC), and Classification (C); only one item from FC had a sufficiently large DIF to recommend deletion, and it was deleted from the final published Leiter-R.

In one of the most comprehensive studies of the fairness of Leiter-R scores, McLellan and Walton (1996) administered the WISC-III and Leiter-R to 175 children of Navajo background in northern Arizona. The Navajo children (ages 6–12) averaged 84.5 on the Verbal IQ, 106.0 on the Performance IQ, and 93.6 on the Full-Scale IQ of the WISC-III while averaging 98.0 on the Brief IQ and 97.3 on the Full-Scale IQ of the Leiter-R. While the WISC-III Full-Scale IQ is nearly one half a standard deviation below average, the Leiter-R Full IQ is within the approximate 3.0 standard error of measurement boundary around an average IQ of 100. Flemmer and Roid (1997) reanalyzed the Leiter-R standardization data showing that when children from Hispanic backgrounds are matched on parental education level with normative Anglo/Caucasian children, mean profile and IQ scores are quite complementary (e.g., for High School or GED parental level, Hispanic mean Brief IQ of 102 and Anglo mean 99.6). Roid (1997) showed further that predictions of math and reading achievement NCE scores from the California Achievement Test and Stanford Achievement Test from the Leiter-R Brief IQ (S-BIT IQ) were comparable in slope across Anglo and African American samples using the rigorous F-tests of Reynolds (1982).

ADMINISTRATION AND SCORING

This section will briefly address administration and scoring procedures of the Leiter-R. The Leiter-R and S-BIT manuals (Roid & Miller, 1997, 1999) and McCallum, Bracken, and Wasserman (2001) provide detailed information regarding subtest administration and scoring, and interested readers should consult these resources prior to using the Leiter-R. As previously mentioned, the Leiter-R contains 20 subtests representing a VR Battery with 10 subtests and an AM Battery also with 10 subtests. Also included are four rating scales, Examiner, Teacher, Parent, and Self, which provide information regarding behavioral observations. Examiners select which batteries and rating scales to administer based on the clinical needs of the examinee. In addition, since certain subtests were designed for specific age groups, subtest selection is based upon the child's age.

Within the VR and AM batteries, items vary in the type of response required from the examinee falling into one of three groupings: (a) items that require placement of response cards, (b) items that require arrangement of manipulative response shapes, and (c) items that require pointing to pictures on the easel. Items were designed to be administered in a non-verbal mode; thus, instructions are primarily communicated through pantomime consisting of a combination of hand and head movements, facial expressions, and demonstration. Specific examples of pantomime instructions are provided in the manual and on easel pages; however, examiners are also encouraged to be "creative and flexible" during the pantomiming of initial "teaching items" for each subtest. Verbalizations are to be avoided, but brief one- or two-word remarks may be required in rare circumstances on teaching items or to maintain rapport with an advanced examinee between subtests. However, no verbalizations were employed in the standardization of the tests. Teaching items are included on each subtest for all examinees, regardless of the starting point. Teaching items allow for repeated demonstration, if needed, in communicating what is expected of the examinee to promote fairness of assessment in the spirit of learning-potential test introductions (Feuerstein, Rand, & Hoffman, 1979). One subtest (Attention Divided) on the AM Battery is an experimental subtest that is not used in the calculation of any IQ index, and may require a brief verbal instruction in the teaching phase to communicate the nature of the dual task ("do this and that").

While most subtests are untimed, time bonuses are included on the more difficult items for three VR subtests (Design Analogies, Paper Folding, Figure Rotation). In addition, given the nature of the tasks, select AM Battery subtests have specific time requirements in exposure and delay recall conditions. For most subtests, responses are scored 0 (Failed) or 1 (Passed). Each response is scored, as opposed to sequences of responses in the original Leiter, and partial completion of a sequence is therefore credited. Exceptions to this scoring procedure are noted for subtests on the AM Battery, and users should consult the manual.

For subtests on the VR and AM Batteries, raw scores are converted to normalized scaled scores with a mean of 10 and a standard deviation of 3. A comprehensive computer scoring system (Roid & Madsen, 1998) for IBM computers is available and similar to other widely used scoring-assistant programs. Age norms are based on intervals reflective of the developmental changes that occur in young children over short periods of time. Age norms for children aged 2–3 years are available at 2-month intervals; for children aged 4–10 years, 3-month intervals; for individuals 11–15 years, 6-month intervals; and for individuals aged 16–20 years, 1-year intervals. In addition, there are eight Special Diagnostic scores that provide an in-depth analysis of a child's performance.

The VR Battery offers two IQ Scores, a Full-Scale IQ and a Brief IQ Screener, and three Composite Scores, Fluid Reasoning, Fundamental Visualization, and Spatial Visualization. The AM Battery offers six Composite Scores, Memory Screening, Associative Memory, Memory Span, Attention, Memory Process, and Recognition Memory. The Rating Scales all offer two Composite Scores, Cognitive/Social and Emotions/Regulation. All IQ and Composite Scores are standard scores with a mean of 100 and standard deviation of 15, and all profile and composite scores for VR and AM Batteries and the Rating Scales are calculated by the scoring software (Roid & Madsen, 1998). The Manual recommends that the examiner concentrate on the scores that contribute to one's understanding of the examinee and not simply calculate every contrast possible. Percentile ranks, confidence intervals, and age equivalents are also available to the examiner in the manual and in the software.

The Leiter-R also offers Growth Scale scores that provide an opportunity to collect criterion-referenced information regarding a child's performance. Growth scale scores are available for each subtest, composite, and IQ estimate on the Leiter-R, and tables can be found in the manuals and in the software. In addition, item growth values can be identified for each item passed or failed, which will explain the relative item difficulty of each item administered to the child. Item growth values can range from approximately 380 to 560 with a center of 500 at age 10 and with the degree of difficulty expressed by an item's location on the growth scale. Growth scores for subtests, composites, and IQs further provide a qualitative description of a child's nonverbal cognitive abilities as referenced to the skills measured by the Leiter-R.

INTERPRETATION

The following discussion regarding interpretation of the Leiter-R is based upon the recommendations presented in the manuals (Roid & Miller, 1997, 1999). In addition, McCallum, Bracken, and Wasserman (2001) provide interpretative guidelines and worksheets for comparing intraindividual differences. The test authors recommend a hierarchical method of interpretation that begins with a thorough review of developmental, clinical, and academic history, presenting concerns, and information collected via rating scales. Next, score examination begins with the most global estimates, that is, the Full-Scale Score, and proceeds to more specific estimates provided by the Growth Scale Scores, Composite and Subtest Scores.

The first stage of interpretation involves examining the global estimates of nonverbal intelligence as represented by the Full-Scale IQ and the Brief IQ Screener of the VR Battery. Such global estimates reflect the definition of intelligence as measured on the Leiter-R and is defined as "the general ability to perform complex nonverbal mental manipulations related to conceptualization, inductive reasoning, and visualization" (Roid & Miller, 1997, p. 103). Although attention is regarded as fundamental to cognitive performance, subtests of the AM Battery are not included in the Full-Scale or Brief IQ scores. Performance is interpreted using standard scores, confidence intervals, percentile ranks, and descriptive classification labels.

The examination of Growth Scores, especially for children who function at a low level of ability and/or are expected to be retested on the Leiter-R, is the next stage of interpretation. Designed using item-response theory (IRT; Rasch, 1980), Growth Scores provide an opportunity to measure small increments of growth along the continuum of ability (Embretson, 1996; Reckase, 1996) as measured by the Leiter-R.

Composite Score Interpretation

The next stage of interpretation involves examination of the Composite Scores of the VR and AM Battery. The VR Battery contains three composites: Fluid Reasoning, Fundamental Visualization, and Spatial Visualization; the AM Battery contains six composites: Memory Screener, Recognition Memory, Associative Memory, Memory Span, Attention, and Memory Process; each of the Rating Scales contains two composites: Cognitive/Social and Emotions/Regulation. Composite Scores are standard scores with a mean of 100 and standard deviation of 15. Confidence intervals, percentile ranks, and classification labels are provided in the manual and software to help in describing an examinee's performance.

Leiter-R subtests were designed to measure unitary constructs, are reliable, and are unbiased based on gender, race, ethnicity, and socioeconomic factors. Thus, interpretation of performance and abilities at the subtest level is supported and is the next stage of interpretation. The

Manual provides a comprehensive analysis of the abilities measured by each subtest as well as sets of subtests included in composites.

Interpretation of Score Differences

Tables in the test manuals and computer software (Roid & Madsen, 1998) are provided for the evaluation of statistically significant differences among scores and the frequency of occurrence of score differences in the normative sample. Approximately 12–14 points are required for significant differences among the Full-Scale IQ and the various composite scores of the VR Battery, and approximately 14–19 points among the composite scores of the AM Battery. When the Rasch-based Growth scores are employed in retesting during treatment, approximately 11–13 points are required for establishing a significant global change. Especially useful in plotting progress in special education is the "Growth Profile Booklet," which allows for the recording of mastery on all items and subtests, pretesting and retesting, in order to track small increments of improvement in children with special needs. As with other cognitive batteries employing subtest scaled scores ($M = 10$, $SD = 3$), approximately 3 to 4 points of difference are required to establish significance between subtest scores. Of course, examiners should be cautious in interpreting all profile differences and only report differences that are verified by other evidence in the child's cumulative record, from teacher or parent observations, other tests, or other information about the child.

Interpretation of Diagnostic Scores in AM Battery

In the spirit of "qualitative" (Matarazzo, 1990) or "cognitive process" assessment (Kaplan, Fein, Morris, & Delis, 1991), the memory and attention subtests of the AM Battery provide a rich source of neuropsychological (Lezak, 1995) and information-processing (Carroll, 1993; Larson, Merritt, & Williams, 1988; Larson & Saccuzzo, 1989) approaches to test interpretation. Guidelines and tables are provided in Roid and Miller (1997). For example, the Attention Sustained subtest is in the classic "cross out" or cancellation test format (Lezak, 1995; Rourke, 1985) in which the child finds and marks figures on a full page of illustrations that match the targeted figural object depicted at the top of the page. Examiners should watch the process of searching and marking done by the examinee. Neurological conditions such as visual neglect (Albert, 1973), where vision appears to be blocks to the right or left, up or down, can be identified when present. Tables of percentiles for the number of marks expected in each quadrant of the last (complex) page of Attention Sustained provide normative data for interpretation of visual neglect. In other examples, the pictorial objects that are paired together for the Associated Pairs memory subtest can be sorted into "familiar associations" versus "random associations" and scored separately, and forward touching of pictures on the Forward Memory subtest can be contrasted with touching them in backwards order on Reverse Memory.

Interpretation of the Rating Scales

The Rating Scales of the Leiter-R provide a rich source of information from examiner, teacher, parent, or the examinee themselves to assist in the interpretation of test results. The scales were developed using the temperament theory of Buss and Plomin (1984) and the "Big Five" factor model of normal personality (Goldberg, 1990; McCrae & Costa, 1989). Each of the four Rating Scales has two major composite scores, the Cognitive/Social and the Emotions/Regulation composites. Each has been normed and scaled with a mean of 100 and a standard deviation of 15, allowing clinicians to generate hypotheses about high (115+) and low (85−) scores. The Cognitive/Social composite includes attention, activity level, organization versus impulsivity, and social abilities. The child who scores at a high level is probably hard-working, attentive, focused, "high energy," and likeable, whereas the low scorer may be distractible, impulsive, disorganized, "low energy," and experience social difficulties. On the Emotions/Regulation composite, high scores imply confidence and calmness, and an ability to adapt and regulate one's emotional reactions, whereas low scores imply anxiety, worry, lower self-esteem and difficulties in regulating one's mood and emotional reactions.

STRENGTHS AND WEAKNESSES

Many strengths of the Leiter-R and S-BIT measures have emerged since their publication a few years ago. The tests provide the most comprehensive coverage of nonverbal cognitive abilities of any nationally standardized nonverbal battery. No other Battery provides both nonverbal IQ estimation and process diagnosis through investigation of attention and memory processes. Memory and attention difficulties often heighten or interfere with global intellectual functioning, such as in the child with giftedness who also has language or communication difficulties—the "twice exceptional" child (Kay, 2000). In addition, the strengths of the Leiter-R and S-BIT are as follows:

1. *Child- and Examiner-"Friendly"*: The quality of the manipulables, artwork and examiner directions of the Leiter-R were purposely designed to attract and engage the child in a "game like" interaction. Users have reported that the colorful artwork engages preschoolers and other children more than alternatives they have tried. Scoring is completely objective to relieve the examiner of the burden of subjective scoring. All examiner directions were refined through intense scrutiny with more than 60 Tryout examiners and 114 Standardization examiners. Also, nearly all Leiter-R items are untimed.
2. *Quick, Efficient IQ Assessment*: Although many potential users react when they hear that the Battery has a total of 20 subtests, most assessments require 4–8 subtests for any one age range.

The S-BIT and the Brief IQ (four subtests) or even the Full-Scale IQ (six subtests) of the Leiter-R can be completed more rapidly than comparable verbal intelligence batteries.

3. *Compare IQ to Memory and Attention*: The Leiter-R is the only battery that has both nonverbal IQ measures and nonverbal memory and attention measures. Full-Scale IQ with six subtests, plus Forward Memory and Attention Sustained subtests provides an excellent nonverbal assessment with just eight subtests.

4. *Thorough Cognitive Process Diagnosis Available*: As discussed in the introductory paragraph of this section, the Leiter-R AM Battery is highly unique in the field of assessment and provides a rich source of sophisticated qualitative assessment, such as contrasting immediate and delayed memory, analysis of errors versus number correct, and indicators of visual neglect.

5. *Valuable "Growth Scales"*: By employing a parallel system of scoring the Leiter-R and S-BIT with item-response theory scores called "Growth scales," the tests add a valuable dimension especially for clinical and special education settings where treatment interventions take time to show small increments of improvement in the child or client. Owing to the excellent characteristics of the scaling metric of the Growth Scales (Embretson, 1996), monitoring treatment outcomes becomes possible for the exceptional individual who would show no improvement in annual age-normative scores.

6. *Fairness of Assessment*: Perhaps the greatest strength of the Leiter–Rand S-BIT is the evidence for fairness of these assessments across ethnic groups. The nonverbal, pantomime administration of the tests inherently promotes fairness. Items have been shown free of differential item functioning, fairness of predicting achievement has been demonstrated, and the mean scores of ethnic groups matched for socioeconomic levels are quite comparable (Flemmer & Roid, 1997; McLellan & Walton, 1996).

With regard to potential weaknesses or critiques of the tests, the following points are offered:

1. *Difficulty in Learning the New Tests*: Some users have claimed that the new Leiter-R is complex to learn as it is different from the original Leiter. New editions of tests always pose a difficulty for the examiner that is used to the convenience of knowing the previous test. Upon further investigation, the objection of complexity is often centered on the misconception that all 20 subtests have to be used and mastered before one can use the tests. The four subtests that constitute the S-BIT are particularly easy to learn, and involve following the printed directions on the examiner easel pages, distributing the response cards to the child (6 years old and above), and scoring the test in the time-honored way of raw-score to scaled-score conversions. Also, examiners need to "take charge" of the materials and organize them before a formal testing by employing

a plastic box or case to hold the various manipulatives in the order of test administration. Certain of the memory subtests, such as Reverse Memory and Attention Divided, pose some challenges to the examiner but, once properly trained and mastered, are found to be easier than anticipated and extremely diagnostic clinically. These subtests are *not* included in the standard IQ scores and may not be used frequently by many examiners.

2. *"We Miss the Blocks"*: Some users lament that the wooden blocks of the original Leiter are gone, replaced by plastic pieces or "playing card" response cards. The original blocks, made of wood, were expensive to manufacture, varied in quality, posed a hygiene problem because of difficulty in sterilizing, and made the entire test kit heavy. Additionally, the original Leiter employed paper "strips" for item artwork, and these were easily damaged, misplaced, or difficult to maintain in order. More importantly, the strengths of the Leiter-R in providing comprehensive assessment of reasoning, visualization, attention and memory factors along with qualitative process diagnosis, and complete subtests profiles, could never have been accomplished with blocks since there are now more than 500 response pieces used in the new tests.

3. *Nonverbal Directions*: Some examiners have difficulty adapting to "not talking" when they first use nonverbal measures. They can be assured that verbal conversation can be done in the "rapport building" phase prior to testing, and can include saying something like "Let's play some games where I just motion and don't speak." Also, one reviewer claimed that the Leiter-R is not "100% nonverbal" because the test manual mentions in a footnote that brief words may have to be used for the supplementary subtest, Attention Divided (AM Battery), in extreme cases. All 10 of the VR subtests used for IQ assessment and all 10 of the attention and memory subtests can be administered with 100% nonverbal, and this was done in the standardization of Leiter-R. Therefore, the claim seems to be an overstatement.

4. *Is the Leiter-R Really Lighter?* Upon receiving the complete Leiter-R kit, many examiners feel that the kit is still quite heavy and reminds them of the previous wooden-block edition in weight. As with most test kits, the tests are packaged with all materials, a thick test manual with full norm tables, multiple copies of record forms and profiles, multiple copies of Rating Scales, and multiple copies of the Attention Sustained response booklets. Also, the easel books of the Leiter-R are constructed with a heavy-duty plastic. However, when the materials are sorted, and the test procedures learned, much of the kit material can be left behind when focusing on a specific client. When the purpose is to obtain an IQ assessment, the large AM Battery easel and response card box do not have to be carried. Profiles, the large manual, and other supportive materials can be left behind and are only needed after a testing session is completed.

5. *Cost of the Battery.* Although the cost of the complete VR and AM Battery kit is higher than other individual scales, its price is similar to that of the original Leiter and justified by the combination of features and age groups. Thus, the Leiter-R combines the age ranges of the WPPSI-R and WISC-III (Wechsler, 1989, 1991), with coverage of 4 years of the WAIS-III (Wechsler, 1997). Having extended age range and Memory subtests similar to other memory batteries, the Leiter-R thus combines about three other batteries into one kit. Finally, the costs of national standardization, extensive validity studies, and original, colored artwork cannot be underestimated.

SUMMARY

The Leiter-R is a comprehensive, nonverbal battery for ages 2–0 to 20–11, providing IQ, composite and profile scores based on a national standardization ($N = 1,719$). Each subtest has colorful artwork that engages children in a "game like" interaction using gestures and pantomime. The test is especially effective for preschoolers and low-functioning individuals. Teaching items are used to assure that each child thoroughly understands the tasks required in each subtest of the battery. The test is divided into a Visualization and Reasoning portion (where four or six subtests can be used to obtain an IQ) and an optional Attention and Memory portion with 10 subtests useful in cognitive process assessment. The Leiter-R Full-Scale IQ is correlated 0.86 with the WISC-III Full Scale IQ, and the IQ scores have reliabilities of 0.91–0.93.

Overall, the Leiter-R has brought the original Leiter back to the modern era and into a place of important usage particularly in special education and in the assessment of children with communication difficulties or English as a second language. The new edition is more comprehensive in providing a full profile of scores and was based on clinical-validity research in both the Tryout and Standardization phases of development—an extra step not always included in IQ test development projects. The extensive array of reliability, validity, and fairness analyses completed to establish the psychometric qualities of the tests are comparable in coverage and quality with those in the test manuals of other major intelligence batteries. The combination of the VR and AM Batteries allows for a richness of diagnosis and interpretation that is quite thorough, and will help examiners in making recommendations to teachers, parents, and professional colleagues.

REFERENCES

Albert, M. L. (1973). A simple test of visual neglect. *Neurology, 23,* 658–664.

Arbuckle, J. L. (1994). *AMOS version 3.6* [Computer program]. Chicago: Smallwaters Corporation.

Armenteros, E. C., & Roid, G. H. (1996). *Nonverbal abilities of Hispanic and speech-impaired preschoolers.* Paper presented at the meetings of the American Psychological Association, Toronto, August.

Bagnato, S. J., Neisworth, J. T., & Munson, S. M. (1989). *Linking developmental assessment and early intervention: Curriculum-based prescriptions.* Rockville, MD: Aspen.

Barkley, R. (1990). *Attention deficit hyperactivity disorder: A handbook for diagnosis and treatment.* New York: Guilford Press.

Baroff, G. S. (1986). *Mental retardation: Nature, cause and management* (2nd ed.). New York: Hemisphere.

Bay, S. M. (1996). *An exploratory factor analysis of the Leiter-R.* Unpublished doctoral dissertation, George Fox University, Newberg, OR.

Blair, R. J. (1996). *Item bias analysis of the Leiter-R for English as a second language populations.* Unpublished doctoral dissertation, George Fox University, Newberg, OR.

Bos, J. (1995). *Factor structure of the field edition of the Leiter International Performance Scale—Revised.* Unpublished doctoral dissertation, George Fox University, Newberg, OR.

Bos, J., Gridley, B. E., & Roid, G. H. (1996). *Factor structure of nonverbal cognitive abilities: Construct validity of Leiter-R.* Paper presented at the meetings of the American Psychological Association, Toronto, August.

Buss, A. H., & Plomin, R. (1984). *Temperament: Early developing personality traits.* Hillsdale, NJ: Erlbaum.

Carroll, J. B. (1993). *Human cognitive abilities: A survey of factor-analytic studies.* New York: Cambridge University Press.

Cronbach, L. J. (1951). Coefficient alpha and the internal structure of tests. *Psychometrika, 16,* 297–334.

Elliot, C. D. (1990). *Differential Ability Scales: Introductory and technical handbook.* San Antonio, TX: The Psychological Corporation.

Embretson, S. E. (1996). The new rules of measurement. *Psychological Assessment, 8,* 341–349.

Feuerstein, R., Rand, Y., & Hoffman, M. D. (1979). *The dynamic assessment of retarded performers: The Learning Potential Assessment Device.* Baltimore, MD: University Park Press.

Flemmer, D. & Roid, G. H. (1997). Nonverbal intellectual assessment of Hispanic and speech-impaired adolescents. *Psychological Reports, 80,* 1115–1122.

Flynn, J. R. (1987). Massive gains in 14 nations: What IQ tests really measure. *Psychological Bulletin, 101,* 171–191.

Gardner, H. (1983). *Frames of mind: The theory of multiple intelligences.* New York: Basic Books.

Garrett, H. E. (1946). A developmental theory of intelligence. *American Psychologist, 1,* 372–378.

Glaser, R. (1981). The future of testing: Research in cognitive psychology and psychometrics. *American Psychologist, 36*(2), 923–936.

Goldberg, L. R. (1990). An alternative description of personality: The big-five factor structure. *Journal of Personality and Social Psychology, 59,* 1216–1229.

Grant, G., Roid, G. H., & Fallow, G. (1996). *Fairness of intellectual assessment for children with speech impairments.* Paper presented at the meetings of the Western Psychological Association, San Jose, April.

Grossman, H. J. (1983). *Classification in mental retardation.* Washington, DC: American Association on Mental Deficiency.

Guilford, J. P. (1967). *The nature of human intelligence.* New York: McGraw-Hill.

Gustafsson, J. E. (1984). A unifying model for the structure of intellectual abilities. *Intelligence, 8,* 179–203.

Haley, S. M., Coster, W. J., Ludlow, L. H., Haltiwanger, J. T., & Andrellos, P. J. (1992). *Pediatric Evaluation of Disability Inventory (PEDI).* Boston, MA: New England Medical Center Hospital.

Holland, P. W., & Wainer, H. (Eds.). (1993). *Differential item functioning.* Hillsdale, NJ: Erlbaum.

Horn, J. L., & Cattell, R. B. (1966). Refinement and test of the theory of fluid and crystallized intelligence. *Journal of Educational Psychology, 57,* 253–270.

Hunt, E. (1976). Varieties of cognitive power. In L. B. Resnick (Ed.), *The nature of intelligence.* Hillsdale, NJ: Erlbaum.

Individuals with Disabilities Education Act. (1990) *20 U.S.C. 1400 et seq.: U.S. Statutes at Large, 104,* 1103–1151.

Jöreskog, K. G., & Sörbom, D. (1993). *LISREL 8 user's guide.* Chicago: Scientific Software.

Kamphaus, R. W. (1993). *Clinical assessment of children's intelligence.* Boston: Allyn & Bacon.

Kaplan, E., Fein, D., Morris, R., & Delis, D. C. (1991). *WAIS-R as a neuropsychological instrument* (WAIS-R NI manual). San Antonio, TX: The Psychological Corporation.

Kay, K. (Ed.). (2000). *Uniquely gifted: Identifying and meeting needs of the twice-exceptional student.* Gilsum, NH: Avocus.

Larson, G. E., Merritt, C. R., & Williams, S. E. (1988). Information processing and intelligence: Some implications of task complexity. *Intelligence, 12,* 131–147.

Larson, G. E., & Saccuzzo, D. P. (1989). Cognitive correlates of general intelligence: Toward a process theory of g. *Intelligence, 13,* 5–31.

Leiter, R. G. (1966). *Development of the Leiter International Performance Scale.* Unpublished audio recording. (Available from Dr. G. Roid, Box 183, Simpson College, Redding, CA 96003.)

Leiter, R. G. (1979). *Instruction manual for the Leiter International Performance Scale.* Wood Dale, IL: Stoelting.

Levine, M. N. (1982). *Leiter International Performance Scale: A handbook.* Los Angeles, CA: Western Psychological Services.

Lezak, M. D. (Ed.). (1995). *Neuropsychological assessment* (3rd ed.). New York: Oxford University Press.

Lineacre, J. M., & Wright, B. D. (1990). *The many-faceted Rasch model FACETS computer program manual.* Chicago: MESA Press.

Lineacre, J. M., & Wright, B. D. (1994). *FACETS: Many-facet Rasch analysis.* Chicago: University of Chicago MESA Press.

Lohman, D. F. (1993). Teaching and testing to develop fluid abilities. *Educational Researcher, 10,* 12–23.

Lord, F. M. (1980). *Applications of item response theory to practical testing problems.* Hillsdale, NJ: Erlbaum.

Madsen, D. H., Roid, G. H., & Miller, L. J. (1996). *Nonverbal intellectual assessment: Restandardization of a new measure, the Leiter International Performance Scale—Revised.* Paper presented at the meetings of the American Psychological Association, Toronto, August.

Matarazzo, J. D. (1990). Psychological assessment versus psychological testing. *American Psychologist, 45,* 999–1017.

Mather, N., & Woodcock, R. W. (2001). *Woodcock–Johnson III Tests of Cognitive Abilities: Examiner's manual.* Itasca, IL: Riverside.

McCrae, R. R., & Costa, P. T., Jr. (1989). *More reasons to adopt the five-factor model. American Psychologist, 44,* 451–452.

McGrew, K. S., & Flanagan, D. P. (1998). *The intelligence test desk reference (ITDR): Gf–Gc cross-battery assessment.* Boston: Allyn & Bacon.

McLellan, M. J., Nellis, L. M., & Roid, G. H. (2000). *Joint factor analysis of the WISC-III and the Leiter-R with Navajo children.* Unpublished paper, Northern Arizona University, Flagstaff, AZ.

McLellan, M. J., & Walton, M. J. (1996). *Concurrent validation of the Leiter-R with WISC-III with Navajo children.* Paper presented at the meetings of the American Psychological Association, Toronto, August.

Meisels, J., & Fenicel, E. (1996). *New visions for the developmental assessment of infants and young children.* Washington, DC: Zero to Three.

Mellott, M. J., & McLellan, M. J. (1996). *Using nonverbal cognitive scales with Navajo children.* Paper presented at the meetings of the Western Psychological Association, San Jose, April.

Miller, L. J., & Robinson, C. (1996). Strategies for meaningful assessment of infants and toddlers with significant physical and sensory disabilities. In S. J. Meisels & E. Fenichel (Eds.), *New visions for developmental assessment of infants & young children.* Washington, DC: Zero to Three.

Miller, L. J., & Roid, G. H. (1994). *Toddler and infant motor evaluation.* Tucson, AZ: Therapy Skill Builders.

Nordlund, C. B. (1998). *An examination of behavior ratings and rater differences of ADHD subjects on the Leiter-R Rating Scales*. Unpublished doctoral dissertation, George Fox University, Newberg, OR.

Olson, R. C. (1998). *Subtypes of learning disabilities on a nonverbal cognitive instrument*. Unpublished doctoral dissertation, George Fox University, Newberg, OR.

Quinn, D. C. (1999). *Nonverbal cognitive performance of children with traumatic brain injury using the Leiter-R Tryout Edition*. Unpublished doctoral dissertation, George Fox University, Newberg, OR.

Rasch, G. (1980). *Probabilistic models for some intelligence and attainment tests*. Chicago: University of Chicago Press.

Reckase, M. D. (1996). Test construction in the 1990s: Recent approaches every psychologist should know. *Psychological Assessment, 8*, 354–359.

Reynolds, C. R. (1982). Methods for detecting construct and predictive bias. In R. A. Berk (Ed.) *Handbook of methods for detecting test bias*. Baltimore, MD: Johns Hopkins.

Roid, G. H. (1997). *Validity and fairness of prediction in the Leiter-R*. Paper presented at the meetings of the American Psychological Association, Chicago, August.

Roid, G. H., & Gyurke, J. (1991). General-factor and specific variance in the WPPSI-R. *Journal of Psychoeducational Assessment, 9*, 275–289.

Roid, G. H., & Madsen, D. H. (1998). *Leiter-R computer scoring software system: User's guide*. Wood Dale, IL: Stoelting.

Roid, G. H., & Miller, L. J. (1997). *Leiter International Performance Scale—Revised (Leiter-R) manual*. Wood Dale, IL: Stoelting.

Roid, G. H., & Miller, L. J. (1999). *Leiter/Stoelting brief nonverbal intelligence scale manual (S-BIT)*. Wood Dale, IL: Stoelting.

Roid, G. H., Prifitera, A., & Weiss, L. G. (1993). Replication of the WISC-III factor structure in an independent sample. *Journal of Psychoeducational Assessment* (Special Issue on WISC-III), 6–21.

Roid, G. H., & Woodcock, R. W. (2000). Uses of Rasch scaling in the measurement of cognitive development and growth. *Journal of Outcome Measurement, 4*(2), 579–594.

Rourke, B. P. (1985). *Neuropsychology of learning disabilities*. New York: Guilford.

Salvia, J., & Ysseldyke, J. E. (1991). *Assessment* (5th ed.). Boston, MA: Houghton Mifflin.

Sattler, J. (1992). *Assessment of children: Revised and updated* (3rd ed.). San Diego, CA: Jerome M. Sattler.

Sternberg, R. J. (1977). *Intelligence, information processing and analogical reasoning*. Hillsdale, NJ: Erlbaum.

Thompson, N. M., Francis, D. J., Stuebing, K. K., Fletcher, J. M., Ewing-Cobbs, L., Miner, M. E. et al. (1994). Motor, visual–spatial and somatosensory skills and classic head injury in children and adolescents: A study of change. *Psychology, 8*, 333–342.

Thorndike, R. L., Hagen, E. P., & Sattler, J. M. (1986). *Technical manual for the Stanford–Binet intelligence scale* (4th ed.). Chicago: Riverside.

Ullman, R., Sleator, E., & Sprague, R. (1988). *Manual for the ADD-H comprehensive teacher's rating scale* (2nd ed.). Champaign, IL: MetriTech.

U.S. Bureau of the Census (1993). *Population profile of the United States 1993*. Washington, DC: U.S. Government Printing Office.

van Zomeren, A. H., & Brouwer, W. H. (1992). Assessment of attention. In J. R. Crawford, D. M. Parker, & W. W. McKinlay (Eds.), *A handbook of neuropsychological assessment*. Hove, UK: Erlbaum.

Wechsler, D. (1989). *Manual for the Wechsler preschool and primary scale of intelligence—Revised*. San Antonio, TX: The Psychological Corporation.

Wechsler, D. (1991). *Manual for the Wechsler intelligence scale for children* (3rd ed.). San Antonio, TX: The Psychological Corporation.

Wechsler, D. (1997). *Manual for the Wechsler adult intelligence scale—Third edition*. San Antonio, TX: The Psychological Corporation.

Whitely, S. E. (1976). Solving verbal analogies: Some cognitive components of intelligence test items. *Journal of Educational Psychology, 6*, 232–242.

Wilson, R. S., Bacon, L. D., Kaszniak, A. W., & Fox, J. H. (1982). The episodic–semantic memory distinction and paired associate learning. *Journal of Consulting and Clinical Psychology, 50,* 154–155.

Woodcock, R. W. (1990). Theoretical foundations of the WJ-R measures of cognitive ability. *Journal of Psychoeducational Assessment, 8,* 231–258.

Woodcock, R. W., & Dahl, M. N. (1971). A common scale for the measurement of person ability and test-item difficulty. *AGS Paper Number 10.* Circle Pines, MN: American Guidance Service.

Woodcock, R. W., & Johnson, M. B. (1977). *Woodcock–Johnson psycho-educational battery.* Itasca, IL: Riverside.

Woodcock, R. W., & Johnson, M. B. (1989). *Woodcock–Johnson psycho-educational battery—Revised.* Itasca, IL: Riverside.

Woodcock, R. W., McGrew, K. S., & Mather, N. (2001). *Woodcock–Johnson III.* Itasca, IL: Riverside.

Wright, B. D., & Lineacre, J. M. (1995). *BIGSTEPS: Rasch analysis for all two-facet models.* Chicago: MESA Press.

Wright, B. D., & Stone, M. H. (1979). *Best test design.* Chicago: MESA Press.

7

Comprehensive Test of Nonverbal Intelligence

Nils Pearson

The Comprehensive Test of Nonverbal Intelligence (CTONI; Hammill, Pearson, & Wiederholt, 1997) was designed to give examiners a means for nonverbally assessing reasoning skills of individuals from ages 6–0 to 89–11. Its six subtests (i.e., Pictorial Analogies, Geometric Analogies, Pictorial Categories, Geometric Categories, Pictorial Sequences, and Geometric Sequences) measure the ability to find relationships among pictures of familiar objects and unusual geometric designs. Test takers simply point to their answers; no manipulation of objects, reading, writing, or oral responses are required to take the test.

TEST MODEL AND PHILOSOPHY

This chapter describes the CTONI's (a) rationale, (b) administration and scoring, (c) interpretation, (d) psychometric properties, (e) strengths and weaknesses, and (f) reviewers comments. Readers who want a more complete description of the test should read the manual and the reviews. Readers who are interested in a detailed discussion about nonverbal assessment of intelligence and about issues surrounding it are referred to Volume 18, No.3, of the *Journal of Psychoeducational Assessment*, which provides a comprehensive view of nonverbal tests, the terms used to describe the tests, and how clinicians use them.

The first step in building the CTONI was to analyze the contents of a large collection of nonverbal intelligence tests. The tests that were

Nils Pearson, 403 W. 35th Street, Austin, Texas 78705.

Handbook of Nonverbal Assessment, edited by R. Steve McCallum. Kluwer Academic/Plenum Publishers, 2003.

analyzed are listed under the heading Nonverbal Cognition in Appendix B of *A Consumer's Guide to Tests in Print* (Hammill, Brown, & Bryant, 1992). Additional nonverbal tests can be found in books by Sattler (1988) and Salvia and Ysseldyke (1995).

In all, the contents of 36 different measures of nonverbal intelligence were analyzed. The tests were either unitary measures of a nonverbal ability (e.g., the *Test of Nonverbal Intelligence—Second Edition*, Brown, Sherbenou, & Johnsen, 1990) or specific subtests of a test battery (e.g., the Picture Arrangement subtest of the *Wechsler Intelligence Scale for Children— Third Edition*, Wechsler, 1991). All of the reviewed tests measured high-order thinking ability. No tests that measured low-order (i.e., nonreasoning) nonverbal abilities, such as those involved in perceptual matching, copying, eye–hand activities, parquetry, or puzzle completion, were included in the analysis. The status of each test relative to type of nonverbal test, ability measured, and context were reviewed.

Three principles emerging from these reviews were:

1. The test's instructions should be given orally or in pantomime, depending on which the examiner considers most appropriate.
2. The test should measure three kinds of intellectual abilities: analogical thinking, categorical formulation, and sequential reasoning.
3. The abilities should be measured in both pictured object and geometric design contexts.

Using these three principles, we decided to build a nonlanguage test with an oral instruction option that could measure all three intellectual abilities in both contexts. We built six subtests (i.e., Pictorial Analogies, Geometric Analogies, Pictorial Categories, Geometric Categories, Pictorial Sequences, and Geometric Sequences). The standard scores from the subtests are combined to form three composite quotients: Pictorial Nonverbal Intelligence Quotient, Geometric Nonverbal Intelligence Quotient, and an overall Nonverbal Intelligence Quotient.

Our decision to build a nonlanguage test with an oral instruction option that could measure all three intellectual abilities in both the pictorial and geometric contexts was consistent with the collective practice of professionals who have developed nonverbal tests of intelligence. This consistency is one type of evidence that the CTONI has content validity.

STANDARDIZATION AND PSYCHOMETRIC PROPERTIES

The psychometric properties of the CTONI are briefly described in this section and include a description of the norming sample, three techniques used to establish reliability, and evidence for validity.

Normative Sample

The CTONI was normed on a sample of 2,901 persons in 30 states and the District of Columbia. The entire sample was collected during the spring of 1995 ($N = 2,129$) and the fall of 1996 ($N = 772$). This resulted in a normative sample that is representative of the nation as a whole. The characteristics of the sample with regard to geographic region, gender, race, residence, ethnicity, family income, educational attainment of parents, and disabling condition are reported in the manual. The sample was stratified by age.

The percentages for these characteristics were compared with those reported in the Statistical Abstract of the United States (U.S. Bureau of the Census, 1997) for the school-age population (i.e., persons aged 6–0 through 18–11) and for those reported for persons aged 19 and older. The comparison of those percentages demonstrated that the sample was representative.

Test Reliability

The study of a test's reliability centers on estimating the amount of error variance associated with its scores. This error can be related to content sampling, time sampling, and scorer differences. The status of the CTONI subtests and composites relative to three sources of error variance content, time, and scorer is discussed below.

Content Sampling

Content sampling error (i.e., internal consistency reliability) of the CTONI was investigated by applying Cronbach's (1951) coefficient alpha method. Coefficient alphas for the subtests and composites were calculated at 19 age intervals using data from the entire normative sample. All but two of the coefficients for the subtests round to or exceed 0.80; coefficients for the composites are all greater than 0.90. One cannot always assume that because a test is reliable for a general population, it will be equally reliable for every subgroup within that population. The alphas for 10 selected subgroups within the school aged sample were examined. The subgroups studied were Caucasoids, African Americans, American Indians, speakers of English as a second language (ESL, mostly Hispanics), students with diagnosed learning disabilities, persons who are deaf or hard of hearing, Panamanians, males, females, and Asians. Again, all of the coefficients for the subtests round to or exceed 0.80; composite scores are all greater than 0.90.

Time Sampling

Time sampling or the stability of the CTONI was studied using the test–retest method with 33 of the students enrolled in the 3rd grade; 30 were in the 11th grade. In addition, pantomime instructions were used on the first testing; instructions were given orally on the second testing. With a single exception, the test–retest coefficients for the subtests were greater than 0.80; those for the composites rounded to or exceeded 0.90.

Scorer Differences

Scorer differences refers to the amount of test error due to examiner variability in scoring. Two staff persons in PRO-ED's research department independently scored a set of 50 randomly selected protocols ranging in age from 14 to 17. The results of the scoring were correlated, and the coefficients for the subtests rounded to or exceeded 0.95; those for composites rounded to or exceeded 0.98.

In summary, the magnitude of reliability coefficients relative to three sources of error variance indicates that the CTONI scores are highly reliable. The reliability studies also demonstrate that the CTONI scores are reliable for the subgroups studied, and it was demonstrated that, in the case of English-speaking, general class students, examiners may use either the pantomime or the oral instructions.

Validity of Test Results

Validity refers to the appropriateness or "truthfulness" of the interpretation of performance in a test, usually expressed in a test score (Reynolds, 1998). Unfortunately, it is far easier to define validity than it is to demonstrate conclusively that a particular interpretation of a test score is indeed valid. Most authors of current textbooks dealing with educational and psychological measurement—for example, Aiken (1994), Anastasi and Urbina (1997), Linn and Gronlund (1995), Salvia and Ysseldyke (1998), and Wallace, Larsen, and Elksnin (1992)—suggest that those who develop tests should provide evidence of at least three types of validity: content description, criterion prediction, and construct identification. The accumulated evidence regarding these three types of the validity of CTONI test score will be presented below.

Content-Description Validity

Content-description validity "procedures involve the systematic examination of the test content to determine whether it covers a representative sample of the behavior domain to be measured" (Anastasi & Urbina, 1997, pp. 114–115). Obviously, this kind of validity has to be built into the test at the time that subtests are conceptualized and items constructed. Those who build tests usually address content validity by showing that the abilities chosen to be measured are consistent with the current knowledge about a particular area. They will also demonstrate that the items hold up to particular statistical examinations. Two demonstrations of content validity are offered for the CTONI subtests and composites. First, the subtests and composites are shown to be readily identifiable with respect to popular theories of intellect. Second, the validity of the items is reinforced by the results of differential item functioning analyses used to show the absence of bias in a test's items.

Relationship of Subtests to Theories of Intellect

Evidence that the CTONI subtests do indeed measure cognitive abilities is fairly easy to demonstrate because the subtests are readily identifiable with respect to current theories of intelligence. Sattler (1988) briefly discussed models of intelligence that are most popular. Although the CTONI scores can be related to all these theories, they can be most clearly associated with the principles advocated by Horn and Cattell (1966), Das (1972), Jensen (1980), and Wechsler (1981, 1989, 1991). Each of the models is described briefly below.

Cattell and Horn's model postulated two types of intelligence—fluid and crystallized (Cattell, 1963; Horn, 1985; Horn & Cattell, 1966). Fluid intelligence emphasizes nonverbal mental operations that are relatively culture free. Crystallized intelligence emphasizes acquired skills taught directly or assimilated from the cultural milieu. Measures of arithmetic reasoning, inductive verbal reasoning, and syllogistic reasoning bridge both fluid and crystallized types. The CTONI subtests are easily identified with Cattell and Horn's fluid intelligence construct.

Das's model was based to some extent on those of Luria, Das and his colleagues (Das, 1972; Das, Kirby, & Jarman, 1975; Das & Molloy, 1975) and has categorized intelligence as involving simultaneous processing or successive processing. In the former, stimuli are arranged in a concurrent manner in order to make a decision. In the latter, stimuli are arranged sequentially to make a decision. The CTONI subtests are readily identifiable in terms of Das's concepts.

Jensen's (1980) model proposed a two-level theory of intelligence: associative (Level 1) and cognitive (Level 2). Abilities at the associative level and has the highest correspondence between the form of the stimulus input and the form of the response output, and abilities at the cognitive level involve transformation of the stimulus input. All of the CTONI subtests are readily assigned to Jensen's Cognitive Level.

Wechsler's (1958) model articulated no particular theory of intelligence other than to express a loose adherence to Spearman's concept of g, and the manner in which he grouped the subtests on his tests to form composites suggests an implicit theoretical orientation. On all of Wechsler's (1981, 1989, 1991) test batteries, each subtest is assigned to either a Verbal Scale or a Performance Scale. This is essentially a verbal and nonverbal dichotomy. The CTONI subtests are easily recognized as similar to Wechsler's Performance Scale subtests.

Differential Item Functioning Analysis

Camilli and Shepard (1994) recommended that test developers need to employ statistical techniques to detect item bias. For the purposes of detecting item bias, we specifically focused on the item performances of individuals in selected subgroups who took the test. We chose two methods to study item bias: (a) the Item Response Theory (IRT) approach and (b) the Delta Scores approach.

As a first test of item bias, the IRT approach was employed because it is the preferred procedure for detecting biased items in that it least confounds real mean differences in group performance with bias (Shepard, Camilli, & Williams, 1985, p. 77). This approach was used to compare item performance between five dichotomous groups: male versus female; African

American versus non-African American; American Indian versus non-American Indian; speakers of English as a second language (ESL) versus non-ESL; and learning disabled versus non-learning disabled. In all cases, the resulting comparisons identified less than 5% of the items with significant differences at the .001 level of confidence. Given the fact that no test will be completely unbiased in its items, we maintain that the relatively small number of CTONI items that were statistically significant suggests that any bias in the test is well within acceptable levels.

The second approach used to investigate the CTONI items for bias was developed by Jensen (1980) and is called the Delta Scores approach. Delta Scores (i.e., derived linear scales that relate to item difficulties) are linear transformations of the z scale (i.e., Delta = $4z + 13$). This procedure was applied to the five dichotomous groups that were described in the previous section and a deaf versus hearing dichotomous grouping. The resulting correlation coefficients for the six groups on the six subtests ranged from 0.97 to 0.99. Coefficients of this magnitude are considered as being very high (MacEachron, 1982) and provide further evidence that the CTONI items contain little or no bias in the groups investigated.

Criterion-Prediction Validity

Anastasi and Urbina (1997) refer to criterion-prediction validity instead of criterion-related validity. The definition for the new term is the same as that used previously for criterion-related validity, namely "criterion-prediction validation procedures indicate the effectiveness of a test in predicting an individual's performance in specific activities" (p. 118). They state that performance on a test is checked against a criterion that can be either a direct or an indirect measure of what the test is designed to predict. Thus, if the interpretation of the CTONI as a measure of nonverbal intelligence is accurate, CTONI scores should correlate highly with those of other intelligence tests known to be related to these abilities.

Three studies will be presented briefly. In the first study, the CTONI was correlated with three criterion tests that were already available on 43 elementary-level students diagnosed as having learning disabilities who were enrolled at the Winston School in Dallas, Texas. The school serves learning disabled students exclusively. The criterion tests were: the *Wechsler Intelligence Scale for Children—Third Edition* (WISC-III; Wechsler, 1991), the *Test of Nonverbal Intelligence—Second Edition* (TONI-2; Brown et al., 1990), and the *Peabody Picture Vocabulary Test—Revised* (PPVT-R; Dunn & Dunn, 1981). The second study correlated the CTONI with the WISC-III Performance Scale and subtest standard scores. Subjects were 32 deaf students ranging in age from 8 to 18 who were enrolled in regional day schools in Corpus Christi and McAllen, Texas. In the third study, the CTONI was correlated with the *Test of Nonverbal Intelligence—Third Edition* (TONI-3; Brown, Sherbenou, & Johnsen, 1997). The subjects of this investigation were 550 normal, nondisabled adults ranging in age from 20 to 89. The demographics of this sample were similar to those of the U.S. population in 1997 relative to race, ethnicity, social class, and gender.

Table 7.1   Correlations between CTONI and Selected Tests of Intelligence in Three Studies (Decimals Omitted)

Study and criterion measures	CTONI		
	PNIQ	GNIQ	NIQ
Learning Disability			
WISC-III			
Verbal scale	59	56	76
Performance scale	51	55	70
Full scale	64	64	81
TONI-2 quotient	43	84	82
PPVT-R quotient	66	41	74
Deaf			
WISC-III			
Performance scale	87	85	90
Normals			
TONI-3 form A	75	65	77
TONI-3 form B	73	65	75
Average correlation			
with nonverbal tests	69	73	80

Notes: PNIQ = Pictorial Nonverbal Intelligence Quotient; GNIQ = Geometric Nonverbal Intelligence Quotient; NIQ = Nonverbal Intelligence Quotient; WISC-III = Wechsler Intelligence Scale for Children—Third Edition (Wechsler, 1991); TONI-2 = Test of Nonverbal Intelligence—Second Edition (Brown et al., 1990); PPVT-R = Peabody Picture Vocabulary Test—Revised (Dunn & Dunn, 1981); TONI-3 = Test of Nonverbal Intelligence—Third Edition (Brown et al., 1997). All $ps < 0.05$.

The results of these correlational studies are presented in Table 7.1. The criterion tests used in these three studies measure a variety of intellectual abilities, including both verbal and nonverbal mental abilities. In addition, Table 7.1 includes the average correlation of the CTONI to the other nonverbal measures in these studies (i.e., WISC-III Performance Scale, TONI-2, and TONI-3). The coefficients in this table were corrected for attenuation to account for the lack of perfect reliability in the criterion measures and corrected for restricted range effects using formulas recommended by Guilford and Fruchter (1978). The correlation coefficients presented in the table are large. In particular, the average correlation between the CTONI and the other nonverbal intelligence scores ranges from 0.69 to 0.80. The magnitude of these correlations is high enough to provide convincing evidence that the CTONI is valid. In addition to the strong correlations among the tests, the three studies described are important because they establish the CTONI's criterion-related validity regarding two groups that are likely to be assessed frequently with the test (i.e., individuals who are deaf and those who are learning disabled) as well as with a normal representative sample.

Construct-Identification Validity

"The construct-identification validity of a test is the extent to which the test may be said to measure a theoretical construct or trait" (Anastasi &

Urbina, 1997, p. 126). As such, it relates to the degree to which the under-lying traits of the test can be identified and to the extent to which these traits reflect the theoretical model on which the test is based. Linn and Gronlund (1995) offered a three-step procedure for demonstrating this kind of validity. First, several constructs presumed to account for test per-formance are identified. Second, hypotheses are generated that are based on the identified constructs. Third, the hypotheses are verified by logical or empirical methods. For the purposes of this chapter, only three basic constructs thought to underlie the CTONI and three related testable ques-tions are presented:

1. Because intelligence is known to be strongly related to age in young children and less so in adolescents and adults, performance on the CTONI should be significantly correlated to age; the relationship will be greater for younger children than for older individuals.
2. Because the CTONI measures intelligence, its results should dif-ferentiate between groups of people known to be average and those known to be low average or below average in intellectual ability.
3. Because the CTONI subtests were built to conform with specific aspects of a model, a factor analysis of the subtests should confirm the relationship of the subtests to the constructs inherent in the model.

Age Differentiation

The means and standard deviations for the CTONI subtests at 19 age intervals are presented in Table 7.2. Coefficients showing the relationship of age to performance on the subtests are also shown in the table. The contents of the table demonstrate that the CTONI subtests are strongly related to age during the school years (i.e., the means become larger as the subjects grow older). This observation is verified by the correlations with age reported for this group, which, according to MacEachron's (1982) rule of thumb interpretations, range in size from moderate to high. These findings support our hypothesis about the relationship of the CTONI scores to age.

For adults, the pattern of raw scores is consistent with those asso-ciated with other tests of intellectual ability (e.g., the TONI-3 and the WAIS-R). The means for people between 19 and 59 are level; after age 60, however, the mean raw scores decline in size. This pattern has long been recognized (e.g., Wechsler, 1958) as a characteristic of adult performance on most tests that measure cognitive abilities. Scores rise steeply during younger ages, level off during adolescence and adulthood, and falloff past age 60. Not surprisingly, this same pattern was also noted on the *Wechsler Adult Intelligence Scale—Third Edition* (Wechsler, 1997), the *Test of Nonverbal Intelligence—Third Edition* (Brown et al., 1997), and the *Detroit Tests of Learning Aptitude—Adult* (Hammill & Bryant, 1991).

Table 7.2   Means (and Standard Deviations) for CTONI Subtests at 19 Age
Intervals and Correlations with Age

Age interval	CTONI subtest					
	PA	GA	PC	GC	PS	GS
6	3 (2)	2 (2)	7 (3)	8 (4)	6 (3)	4 (2)
7	4 (3)	4 (3)	9 (3)	10 (4)	9 (4)	6 (3)
8	6 (4)	5 (4)	10 (3)	11 (4)	10 (3)	7 (3)
9	7 (4)	7 (4)	10 (3)	13 (4)	11 (3)	8 (4)
10	9 (5)	9 (5)	11 (3)	13 (5)	12 (4)	9 (5)
11	11 (5)	10 (5)	11 (3)	14 (4)	13 (4)	10 (5)
12	12 (5)	11 (6)	12 (3)	15 (5)	13 (4)	11 (6)
13	14 (5)	14 (6)	13 (4)	16 (4)	15 (4)	13 (6)
14	14 (5)	14 (5)	14 (4)	16 (4)	15 (4)	13 (6)
15	15 (5)	14 (6)	14 (4)	16 (4)	15 (3)	13 (5)
16	15 (5)	16 (6)	14 (4)	17 (4)	16 (4)	14 (6)
17	15 (4)	16 (6)	15 (4)	17 (5)	16 (3)	14 (5)
18	16 (5)	17 (6)	15 (4)	17 (5)	16 (4)	15 (6)
Correlation with age	0.66	0.66	0.52	0.45	0.59	0.55
19–29	16 (5)	17 (6)	16 (4)	18 (5)	17 (3)	16 (6)
30–39	16 (5)	17 (6)	17 (5)	18 (5)	17 (4)	17 (6)
40–49	16 (5)	17 (6)	17 (5)	18 (5)	17 (3)	17 (6)
50–59	16 (5)	16 (6)	17 (5)	18 (5)	17 (4)	17 (5)
60–69	12 (6)	13 (7)	14 (5)	15 (6)	15 (5)	14 (6)
70–89	9 (6)	11 (7)	12 (4)	15 (5)	13 (4)	12 (6)

Notes: PA = Pictorial Analogies; GA = Geometric Analogies; PC = Pictorial Categories; GC = Geometric Categories; PS = Pictorial Sequences; GS = Geometric Sequences.

Group Differentiation

One way of establishing a test's validity is to study the performances of different groups of people on the test. Each group's results should make sense, given what is known about the relationship of the test's content to the group. Thus, in the case of the CTONI, a test of intelligence, one would expect that individuals with disabilities affecting mental ability, language, and academics would do less well than people who do not evidence such disabilities. One would certainly anticipate that persons who are diagnosed as having mental retardation would do very poorly on the test compared with other people.

In addition, even within the nondisabled population, we know that some groups include a disproportionate number of individuals who are seriously economically and educationally disadvantaged (e.g., African Americans, Hispanics, American Indians, Asians, and speakers of ESL). As a result of this impoverishment, the mean scores of these groups on tests of intelligence are almost always lower than average and often very much lower due to the verbal content of most intelligence tests.

Because deprived experiences do indeed adversely affect intellectual development in all groups of people, one would assume that groups with the most deprivation would have lower test scores than groups with lesser amounts of deprivation. However, in a test such as the CTONI, which was built to minimize the effects of cultural, linguistic, racial, and ethnic bias, any differences between minority and mainstream groups should be minimal, and all groups should have mean scores that are within the normal (i.e., average) range.

The mean standard scores for the school-age sample used to norm the CTONI as well as the mean standard scores for 11 subgroups are listed in Table 7.3. The numbers for the speakers of ESL, American Indians, and the learning disability groups were augmented by additional samples especially collected for validity purposes. Included are three mainstream subgroups (males, females, Caucasoids), five minority subgroups (African Americans, Hispanics, American Indians, Asians, speakers of ESL), and three disabled subgroups (learning disability, deaf, mental retardation). Although most individuals were members of more than one subgroup (e.g., many Hispanics and Asians were also in the ESL subgroup, and Caucasoids and African Americans were also in the male or female subgroups), the disabled individuals were assigned to discrete subgroups (e.g., a Hispanic male deaf subject was assigned only to the deaf subgroup). This was done in order to see the influence of cultural factors, rather than the effects of a disabling condition, on the scores of our subgroups. This analysis (and several reported later) was run using the school-age sample as subjects because some subgroups (i.e., the disability and speakers of ESL) were more readily identified in people of this age.

The mean scores in the table are very supportive of the construct validity of the CTONI. As expected, the mental retardation subgroup had scores that are characteristic of people with that condition (i.e., better

Table 7.3 Standard Score Means for Total School-Age Sample and 11 Subgroups

Group	Number of cases	CTONI subtest						CTONI composite		
		PA	GA	PC	GC	PS	GS	PNIQ	GNIQ	NIQ
School-age	2129	10	10	10	10	10	10	100	100	100
Males	967	10	10	10	10	10	10	101	101	101
Females	969	10	10	10	10	10	10	100	100	100
Caucasoids	1524	10	10	10	10	10	10	103	102	102
African Americans	313	10	9	10	9	9	9	97	97	97
Hispanic Americans	196	9	9	9	10	9	10	96	99	97
American Indians	107	9	10	9	9	9	9	96	94	95
Asians	67	10	10	10	10	10	10	101	104	103
ESL	158	9	9	9	9	9	9	92	93	92
LD	220	9	8	9	9	9	9	94	92	92
Deaf	74	8	9	8	9	9	9	89	92	90
MR	30	5	5	6	6	4	5	64	66	63

Notes: PA = Pictorial Analogies; GA = Geometric Analogies; PC = Pictorial Categories; GC = Geometric Categories; PS = Pictorial Sequences; GS = Geometric Sequences; PNIQ = Pictorial Nonverbal Intelligence Quotient; GNIQ = Geometric Nonverbal Intelligence Quotient; NIQ = Nonverbal Intelligence Quotient; LD = Learning Disability; MR = Mental Retardation; ESL = English as a Second Language.

than two standard deviations below average). The Caucasoids scored slightly above the other groups, but in all cases, the subtest standard scores rounded to 10, and their composite quotients were either 102 or 103. The minority subgroups did rather well on the CTONI. Their average scores for the subtests, with two exceptions, were within the standard error of measurement (SEM) for the test; their composite scores were all well within the normal range. These results both support the CTONI's validity and provide additional evidence that the test contains little bias.

Factor Analysis

Construct validity also relates to the degree to which the underlying traits of a test can be identified and the extent to which these traits reflect the theoretical model on which the test is based. One way of investigating this type of validity is to analyze the CTONI subtest performance of people in the normative sample using the principal-components method. Because all of the CTONI subtests measure some aspect of nonverbal mental ability, we would expect that all six subtests would load on a single factor and that such a factor would measure general nonverbal intellectual ability. In the CTONI, this factor would be best represented by the Nonverbal Intelligence Quotient (NIQ). Our factor analysis was computed, and the subtests did in fact all load on a single factor with subtests factor correlations ranging from 0.50 to 0.71.

ADMINISTRATION AND SCORING

The procedures for giving and scoring the CTONI subtests are described in this section. The first section discusses the appropriateness of the oral (i.e., verbal) or pantomime (i.e., nonverbal) directions when administering the test to specific groups. The second section details how to give instructions for the subtests and scoring.

Selecting Pantomime or Oral Administration

When administering the CTONI, the examiner can use either pantomime or oral directions. Individuals who are hearing impaired or speak a language other than English should always be tested using the pantomime directions. When the examinee is English proficient, instructions may be given orally. In cases where the examiner has any reason to think that the examinee might not understand the oral directions, the pantomime option should be used.

Some examiners may be tempted to translate the oral directions into sign language or another spoken language (e.g., Spanish). We strongly recommend that this not be done because the translations would vary from examiner to examiner and would necessarily vary in difficulty. As a result, the CTONI standardization would be violated.

Administration Instructions and Scoring

For the sake of brevity, only the oral directions for the six subtests will be presented in this section. The complete pantomime instructions are presented in the CTONI test manual along with illustrations of the appropriate facial expressions and gestures to be used during this form of test administration. An additional check to see that the examinee understands the directions takes place during the administration of the three example items that are presented at the beginning of each subtest. If the individual being tested cannot respond correctly to the example items, testing is discontinued. Scoring for each subtest is the same. Examinees all begin with the first item in each subtest, and testing continues until a ceiling is reached (i.e., 3 out of any 5 sequential responses are incorrect) or the last item is administered. Each item answered correctly up to the ceiling item is given 1 point.

Pictorial Analogies and Geometric Analogies

Figure 7.1 shows items contained in the analogies subtests. After the examiner opens the Picture Book, the examiner points to the first picture at the top of the page and says, "This is to (point to second picture) this (pause) as this (point to the third picture) is to which one of these (run your finger over the pictures at the bottom of the page)." "Point to your answer."

Pictorial Categories and Geometric Categories

Figure 7.1 shows items from the categories subtests. In these subtests, the examiner points to each of the two pictures at the top of the page and says, "These two are alike in some way." "Which one of these (run your finger over the alternatives at the bottom of the page) is most like these two and should go in the empty box (point back to the empty box between the top two pictures)?" "Point to your answer."

Pictorial Sequences and Geometric Sequences

Figure 7.1 shows items from the sequence subtests. The examiner points to each of the pictures at the top of the page and says, "Which one of these (run your finger over the boxes at the bottom of the page) goes in this box (point to the empty box at the top of the page)?" "Point to your answer."

INTERPRETATION

In this section, we provide a brief discussion about how to analyze the CTONI scores. This will include how to interpret the various scores derived from the CTONI, and what the CTONI measures.

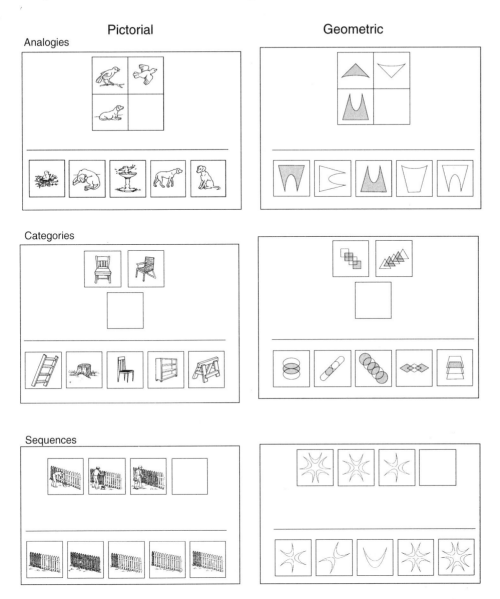

Figure 7.1 Examples of items from CTONI Subtests. (Reproduced by permission of PRO-ED, INC., Austin, TX.)

Test Scores

The CTONI yields three types of scores: percentiles, age equivalents, and standard scores for the subtests and composites. Each is described in this section.

Percentiles

Percentiles, or percentile ranks, represent values that indicate the percentage of the distribution that is equal to or below a particular score. Because this interpretation is easy to understand, percentiles are popular scores for practitioners to use when sharing test results with others.

Age Equivalents

Age equivalents associated with tests of mental ability (e.g., tests of intelligence or aptitude) are called mental ages. These scores are derived by calculating the average normative group's score at each 6-month interval. Through the process of interpolation, extrapolation, and smoothing, age equivalents are generated for each raw score point achieved on a subtest.

Standard Scores

Standard scores for subtests and composites provide the clearest indication of a person's performance on the CTONI. Guidelines for interpreting the standard scores that accompany the CTONI's subtests and composites follow.

The standard score of each CTONI subtest is constructed so that the mean is 10, and the standard deviation is 3. Therefore, a standard score on one subtest may be compared meaningfully with a standard score on any other subtest. The following guidelines for describing standard scores are suggested:

The "% Included" column refers to the percentage of the population that would be included within this category. Note that it corresponds to a normal or normalized distribution of the population. This column helps the examiner understand that most (nearly 50%) of the population is "average" and that scores considered "very superior" or "very poor" are sufficiently rare to warrant attention.

Standard scores provide the examiner with an intraindividual comparison of the measured abilities, and such scores are the best means of evaluating specific strengths and weaknesses across the six CTONI subtests. A discussion of the statistical significance of difference scores appears in the "Conducting a Discrepancy Analysis" section of the test manual.

The standard score of each CTONI composite is constructed to have a mean of 100 and a standard deviation of 15. Professionals who build tests generally call standard scores that are based on the 100:15 distribution "quotients," and we do the same. These quotients provide the most useful basis for interpreting test performance because they are highly reliable and because each is composed of representative subtests rather than only one. The quotients are formed by summing the standard scores of the subtests that comprise the composite and converting this figure to a quotient. The CTONI has three composites: Nonverbal Intelligence, Pictorial Nonverbal Intelligence, and Geometric Nonverbal Intelligence. Table 7.4 lists the descriptive ratings of the quotient scores.

Table 7.4   Interpreting CTONI Subtest and Composite Scores

Subtest score	Composite score	Description	Percentage included
17–20	131–165	Very superior	2.34
15–16	121–130	Superior	6.87
13–14	111–120	Above average	16.12
8–12	90–110	Average	49.51
6–7	80–89	Below average	16.12
4–5	70–79	Poor	6.87
1–3	35–69	Very poor	2.34

What Do the Subtests and Composites Measure?

The major value of the subtest scores is that they are necessary for calculating the quotients that correspond to the composites. Even though the reliabilities of the subtests are acceptably high, they are not as high as those of the composites. The content (as reflected in the items on a subtest) is not as broad or deep as the content associated with a composite, which is a conglomerate of the contents of several subtests. Also, performance on a subtest is more likely to be influenced by a momentary or transitory break in attention or outside distraction than is performance on a composite. Because of this, examiners must be cautious when considering the importance of low or high subtest scores or of discrepancies among subtest scores. Clinical skills should be reserved for interpreting the composite quotients. The subtests and the specific abilities they measure are as follows:

- *Pictorial analogies:* Measure the ability to recognize the relationship of two objects to each other and to find the same relationship between two different objects.
- *Geometric analogies:* Measure the ability to recognize the relationship of two geometric designs to each other and to find the same relationship between two different geometric designs.
- *Pictorial categories:* Measure the ability to select from a set of different pictures the one that is the most similar to two other related pictures.
- *Geometric categories:* Measure the ability to select from a set of different geometric designs the one that is most similar to two other related geometric designs.
- *Pictorial sequences:* Measure the ability to select from a set of pictures the one that completes a sequence of actions shown in three pictures.
- *Geometric sequences:* Measure the ability to select from a set of geometric designs the one that completes a sequence of action shown in three designs.

Because the quotients for the composites are the most clinically useful scores derived from the CTONI, guidelines for their interpretation are discussed in some detail. To reiterate, the composites are Nonverbal Intelligence, Pictorial Nonverbal Intelligence, and Geometric Nonverbal Intelligence.

The NIQ is the best index of what people mean when they say "nonverbal intelligence" (i.e., solving problems or reasoning that does not require words). This is because it represents a blend of three different cognitive abilities (analogical reasoning, categorical classifying, and sequential reasoning), all of which have been measured in two dissimilar contexts (pictorial objects and geometric designs). The multidimensional nature of this quotient makes it the most stable and clinically useful score produced by the CTONI. Individuals who do well on this composite exhibit an unusual ability involving spatial relationships and nonverbal symbolic reasoning. Although oral instructions may have been used in the directions for taking the subtests and although subvocalizing may have occurred, the fact remains that the contents of the subtests that constitute this composite can be mastered without verbal mediation.

High scores reflect the ability to see perceptual, logical, or abstract relationships; to reason without words; to solve mental puzzles that involve progressive elements; and to form meaningful associations between objects and designs. Low scores are made by people who have trouble managing nonverbal information, perceiving visual data, organizing spatially oriented material, or mastering the abstract properties of visually presented symbols.

One could argue that composite scores from tests of oral language might be equally useful, but often composites from such tests include no measures of verbal problem solving or reasoning and emphasize instead oral vocabulary, grammar, syntax, and articulation. Where comparisons are to be made between the CTONI and tests of verbal ability, the latter tests should also be measures that emphasize problem-solving and reasoning.

When comparing the NIQ to measures of verbal intelligence, several patterns are possible. These patterns and their diagnostic implications are as follows:

1. The nonverbal and verbal quotients are both 90 or above. The examinee is exhibiting normal (i.e., typical) intellectual behavior on the tests given. No cognitive problems are indicated. If the person is experiencing difficulties in school or other environments, subnormal intelligence is probably not the cause.
2. The nonverbal and verbal quotients are both below 90. General subaverage intellectual performance is indicated by such low scores. Major causes for subaverage scores are cultural deprivation or mental retardation. The duty of the examiner is to probe further using additional test data, interviews, and case histories to decide the likely cause of the problem. The lower the quotient, the greater the likelihood that the problem is mental retardation.
3. The nonverbal quotient is 90 or above, the verbal quotient is 89 or below, and the difference is significant (see CTONI manual for information on conducting discrepancy analyses). Numerous circumstances can produce this pattern of high nonverbal and low verbal. Examiners must rely on their clinical judgments and knowledge about the person tested to decide which of the following

circumstances is causing the problems. The examinee can be: (a) deaf or hard of hearing, (b) not sufficiently conversant in English, (c) from a home where verbal experiences are minimal, (d) dysphasic, (e) abnormally taciturn, or (f) disposed to block (i.e., to freeze up, forget, or panic) when confronted with verbal material

4. The nonverbal quotient is 89 or below, the verbal quotient is 90 or above, and the difference is significant. Numerous circumstances also can produce this pattern of low nonverbal and high verbal. It can be the result of: (a) a variety of visual (sight) impairments, such as strabismus, field defects, double vision, or reduced acuity, (b) visual perceptual problems (c) visual agnosia, or (d) emotional reactions to activities requiring the interpretation of visual material (e.g., freezing up, forgetfulness, panic).

5. Significant differences between nonverbal and verbal quotients are noted, but both quotients are above 90. A significant difference between verbal and nonverbal quotients where both quotients are in the average or better range (high nonverbal and high verbal) are considered to be of little clinical interest. Strengths and weaknesses within the average or better ranges are best thought of as being inconsequential preferences or variations rather than true deficits. Only significant differences in which one quotient is below average and the other is average or above or in which both quotients are in the below-average range should be considered worthy of diagnosis, discussion, or possible programming.

The Pictorial Nonverbal Intelligence Quotient is an index of problem-solving and reasoning for which representational pictures of familiar objects are used in the test formats. Because the pictured objects have names, examinees will likely verbalize to some extent while taking the subtests that contribute to this quotient. By verbalize, we mean that the examinees will talk about particular items while responding to them or silently think in words while pondering the items. In either case, persons being tested will probably enlist their verbal skills to reach an answer for the items. Because of this, verbal ability will influence the Pictorial Nonverbal Intelligence Quotient to some unknown degree. Although individuals could score high on this quotient without any verbal mediation at all, this is not likely in most cases.

The Geometric Nonverbal Intelligence Quotient is an index of problem-solving and reasoning for which unfamiliar designs are used as stimuli. Because examinees have no names for the designs, any tendency to verbalize about the items is inhibited considerably. The formats of subtests that contribute to this quotient were specially selected to avoid verbal contamination and therefore yield results that are the purest possible estimates of nonverbal intelligence. Although verbalization cannot be eliminated entirely from any test (i.e., no test format can completely keep an individual examinee from using words while thinking), the selected formats do reduce the probability that incidental verbalization (oral or silent) might influence a person's answers to any appreciable extent.

In the vast majority of circumstances, these two quotients will be approximately equal (i.e., the difference between them will be inconsequential). Where large differences do occur, we suspect that the Pictorial Nonverbal Intelligence Quotient will be the higher quotient because of the mitigating influence of language ability.

STRENGTHS AND WEAKNESSES

For a new test, the CTONI has been widely reviewed. Reviews of the CTONI have appeared in journals, books surveying current assessment practices, and *The Thirteenth Mental Measurements Yearbook* (Impara & Plake, 1998). Most of the reviewers' comments have been positive. The following is a selection of some of the other positive comments about the CTONI that have been published recently by reviewers:

- CTONI presents a welcome addition to measures of nonverbal intelligence, and the reviewer is excited about its appearance on the market (Van Lingen, 1998, p. 313).
- The CTONI represents a good positive attempt to measure nonverbal ability and does fill a void (Nicholson, 1998, p. 68).
- Overall, the manual provides a clear overview of the scores, their meaning and interrelationships, and appropriate cautions on the use of the results (Van Lingen, 1998, p. 313).
- The test seems particularly useful in testing bilingual students, and those with language deficits, auditory processing problems, motor impairments, or in children from socially disadvantaged households (Aylward, 1998, p. 312).
- The authors should be commended for conducting and presenting results from studies with minority groups (Drossman & Maller, 2000, p. 300).

Athanasiou (2000) provided the most exhaustive evaluation of the CTONI (see Table 7.5). She compared the technical adequacy, construct validity, and fairness of five current nonverbal tests. The comparisons were made using standards acquired from many sources: Bracken's (1987) six criteria for minimum levels of technical adequacy, Messick's (1995) six aspects of construct validity, and 10 indices of test fairness from Harris, Reynolds, and Koegel (1996), Reynolds and Kaiser (1990), and Jensen, (1980). The results from this evaluation, pertaining to the CTONI, are reported in Table 7.5. A cursory review of this figure shows that the CTONI met or exceeded all but one of the standards for technical adequacy, met all but one of the standards for test validity, and met all but two of the standards for fairness. Overall, the CTONI exceeded or met 82% of Athanasiou's standards, providing impressive evidence of the overall strength of the test.

Some reviewers have pointed out shortcomings of the CTONI, which are in fact not shortcomings, merely problems inherent in using a test format that requires people to interpret the meaning of visual stimuli. For

Table 7.5 Summary of Athanasiou's Evaluation of the CTONI

Standard and evaluation of adequacy

Evidence of technical adequacy
1. Median subtest reliability of .80 exceeded the standard
2. Total test reliability of .90, exceeded the standard
3. Test–retest stability of .90, exceeded the standard
4. Average subtest floor at or below 2 standard deviations below the mean and average subtest ceiling at or above 2 standard deviations above the mean; CTONI meets the standard for floors after age 8 and meets the standard for ceilings except for ages 30–49
5. Total test floor at or below 2 standard deviations below the mean, met the standard
6. Sufficient item difficulty gradients (i.e., no fewer than 3 raw score points per standard deviations of standard scores) met the standard

Evidence of test validity
1. Content aspect, met the standard
2. Substantive aspect, met the standard
3. Structural aspect, met the standard
4. Generalizability aspect, met the standard
5. External aspect, met the standard
6. Consequential aspect, did not meet the standard

Evidence of test fairness
1. Abilities assessed, met the standard
2. Emphasis on fluid abilities, met the standard
3. Use of nonverbal directions, met the standard
4. Response modes, did not meet the standard
5. Untimed administration, met the standard
6. Practice items, met the standard
7. Reliability, met the standard
8. Predictive validity, did not meet the standard
9. Construct validity, did not meet the standard
10. Item characteristics, met the standard

example, Drossman and Maller (2000), Nicholson (1998), and Van Lingen (1998) all cited that the test cannot be administered to individuals with visual difficulties. A larger number of reviewers have made suggestions for improving the test. These are most appreciated. First, Athanasiou (2000), Drossman and Maller (2000), and Nicholson (1998) have all noted that 6- and 7-year-old children cannot attain a standard score below 7 on the analogies subtests. Second, Athanasiou (2000), Drossman and Maller (2000), Salvia and Yssledyke (1998), and Van Lingen (1998) all noted that we did not study the CTONI's relationship to academic achievement. The thorough, thoughtful, and objective analysis of the CTONI by numerous reviewers has identified some problems.

For many examiners, the CTONI has become an essential complement to tests of verbal intelligence. The CTONI provides examiners with a measure of nonverbal reasoning that requires no spoken language or complex motor skills. Numerous studies have shown the test to be reliable, valid, and unbiased with regard to gender, race, and disability. Because of this, examiners can estimate the intelligence of at-risk or culturally different populations with little fear of contamination from social, ethnic, or disability bias.

The test is appropriate for a wide range of ages. In addition to the psychometric integrity of the CTONI, many examiners have praised the test format because they have found that most test takers seem to enjoy the challenge of solving picture puzzles with no time limit.

SUMMARY

The CTONI was designed to provide an estimate of the intelligence of individuals who are not proficient in English, or who are deaf, disadvantaged, language disordered, or motor impaired. Although no time limits are imposed on this test, most individuals complete all six subtests in 40–60 min. The test's formats and items were selected on the basis of statistical analyses; the results of these analyses also showed that the items contain little gender or ethnic bias and that the subtests are both reliable and valid.

REFERENCES

Aiken, L. R. (1994). *Psychological testing and assessment.* Boston: Allyn & Bacon.

Anastasi, A., & Urbina, S. (1997). *Psychological testing* (7th ed.). Upper Saddle River, NJ: Prentice Hall.

Athanasiou, M. S. (2000). Current nonverbal assessment instruments: a comparison of psychometric integrity and test fairness. *Journal of Psychoeducational Assessment, 18*, 211–229.

Aylward, G. P. (1998). Review of the comprehensive test of nonverbal intelligence. In J. C. Impara & B. S. Plake (Eds.), *The thirteenth mental measurement yearbook* (pp. 310–312). Lincoln: Buros Institute of Mental Measurements, University of Nebraska Press.

Bracken, B. A. (1987). Limitations of preschool instruments and standards for minimal levels of technical adequacy. *Journal of Psychoeducational Assessment, 4*, 313–326.

Brown, L., Sherbenou, R. J., & Johnsen, S. K. (1990). *Test of nonverbal Intelligence—Second edition.* Austin, TX: PRO-ED.

Brown, L., Sherbenou, R. J., & Johnsen, S. K. (1997). *Test of nonverbal intelligence—Third edition.* Austin, TX: PRO-ED.

Camilli, G., & Shepard, L. (1994). *Methods for identifying biased test items.* Thousand Oaks, CA: Sage.

Cattell, R. B. (1963). Theory of fluid and crystallized intelligence. *Journal of Educational Psychology, 54*, 1–22.

Cronbach, L. J. (1951). Coefficient alpha and the internal structure of tests. *Psychometrika, 16*, 297–334.

Das, J. P. (1972). Patterns of cognitive ability in nonretarded and retarded children. *American Journal of Mental Deficiency, 77*, 6–12.

Das, J. P., Kirby, J., & Jarman, R. F. (1975). Simultaneous and successive syntheses. *Psychological Bulletin, 82*, 87–103.

Das, J. P., & Molloy, G. N. (1975). Varieties of simultaneous and successive processing children. *Journal of Educational Psychology, 67*, 213–220.

Drossman, E. R., & Maller, S. J. (2000). Comprehensive test of nonverbal intelligence. *Journal of Psychoeducational Assessment, 18*, 293–301.

Dunn, L. M., & Dunn, L. M. (1981). *Peabody Picture Vocabulary Test—Revised.* Circle Pines, MN: American Guidance Service.

Guilford, J. P., & Fruchter, B. (1978). *Fundamental statistics in psychology and education.* New York: McGraw-Hill.

Hammill, D. D., Brown, L., & Bryant, B. (1992). *A consumer's guide to tests in print* (2nd ed.). Austin, TX: PRO-ED.

Hammill, D. D., & Bryant, B. (1991) *Detroit tests of learning aptitude—Adult.* Austin, TX: PRO-ED.

Hammill, D. D., Pearson, N. A., & Wiederholt, J. L. (1997). *Comprehensive test of nonverbal intelligence.* Austin, TX: PRO-ED.

Harris, A. M., Reynolds, M. A., & Koegel, H. M. (1996). Nonverbal assessment: Multicultural perspectives. In Suzuki, L. A., Meller, P. J., & Ponterotto, J. G. (Eds.), *Handbook of multicultural assessment: Clinical, psychological, and educational applications* (pp. 223–252). San Francisco: Jossey-Bass.

Horn, J. L. (1985). Remodeling old models of intelligence. In B. Wolman (Eds.), *Handbook of intelligence* (pp. 267–300). New York: Wiley.

Horn, J. L., & Cattell, R. B. (1966). Refinement and test of the theory of fluid and crystallized intelligence. *Journal of Educational Psychology, 57,* 253–270.

Impara, J. C., & Plake, B. S. (1998). *The thirteenth mental measurement yearbook.* Lincoln: Buros Institute of Mental Measurements, University of Nebraska Press.

Jensen, A. R. (1980). *Bias in mental testing.* New York: Free Press.

Kaufman, A., & Kaufman, N. (1983). *Kaufman assessment battery for children.* Circle Pines, MN: American Guidance Services.

Linn, R. L., & Gronlund, N. E. (1995). *Measurement and assessment in teaching* (7th ed.). Upper Saddle River, NJ: Prentice-Hall.

MacEachron, A. E. (1982). *Basic statistics in the human sciences.* Austin, TX: PRO-ED.

Messick, S. (1995). Validity of psychological assessment: Validation of inferences from a person's responses and performances as scientific inquiry into score meaning. *American Psychologist, 50,* 741–749.

Nicholson, C. L. (1998). Comprehensive test of nonverbal intelligence. *Diagnostique, 24*(1–4), 57–68.

Reynolds, C. R. (1998) Fundamentals of measurement and assessment in psychology. In C. R. Reynolds (Ed.), *Assessment,* Vol 4, pp. 33–56 of A. Bellak and M. Hersen (Eds.), *Comprehensive Clinical Psychology,* Oxford: Elsevier Science.

Reynolds, C. R., & Kaiser, S. M. (1990). Test bias in psychological assessment. In T. B. Gutkin & C. R. Reynolds (Eds.), *The handbook of school psychology* (pp. 486–525). New York: Wiley.

Salvia, J., & Ysseldyke, J. E. (1995). *Assessment* (6th edition). Boston: Houghton Mifflin.

Salvia, J., & Ysseldyke, J. E. (1998). *Assessment* (7th edition). Boston: Houghton Mifflin.

Sattler, J. (1988). *Assessment of children* (3rd ed.). San Diego, CA: Author.

Shepard, L., Camilli, G., & Williams, D. (1985). Validity of approximation techniques for detecting item bias. *Journal of Educational Measurement, 22,* 77–105.

U.S. Bureau of the Census. (1997). *Statistical abstract of the United States.* Washington, DC: Author.

Van Lingen, G. (1998). Review of the Comprehensive Test of Nonverbal Intelligence. In J. C. Impara & B. S. Plake (Eds.), *The thirteenth mental measurement yearbook* (pp. 312–314). Lincoln: Buros Institute of Mental Measurements, University of Nebraska Press.

Wallace, G., Larsen, S. C., & Elksnin, L. (1992). *Educational assessment of learning problems* (2nd ed.). Boston: Allyn & Bacon.

Wechsler, D. (1958). *The measurement and appraisal of adult intelligence* (4th ed.). Baltimore: Williams & Wilkins.

Wechsler, D. (1981). *Wechsler adult intelligence scale—Revised.* San Antonio, TX: Psychological Corporation.

Wechsler, D. (1989). *Wechsler preschool and primary scale of intelligence—Revised.* San Antonio, TX: Psychological Corporation.

Wechsler, D. (1991). *Wechsler intelligence scale for children—Third edition.* San Antonio, TX: Psychological Corporation.

8

The General Ability Measure for Adults*

Achilles N. Bardos

The assessment of individuals with diverse linguistic backgrounds has posed a challenge to psychologists for over 100 years. In the United States, the armed forces had a need for the evaluation of their recruits' cognitive ability as early as World War I. Nonverbal intelligence tests played a significant role in the psychological evaluations of that time, since many of the recruits were either non-English-speaking immigrants or individuals with little or no formal schooling. About a century later, psychologists are still facing similar issues when assessing the cognitive ability of individuals in the general population, who are either linguistically different from the English speaking population, and therefore are at a disadvantage when taking tests that have verbal directions, require verbal expressive skills, or exposure to formal schooling. The statistics presented in the various chapters of this book about the new and changing demographics of the United States clearly suggest that nonverbal intelligence tests are as important today as they were a century ago.

TEST MODEL AND PHILOSOPHY

The General Ability Measure for Adults (GAMA; Naglieri & Bardos, 1997) is an instrument that is accessible to persons with a wide variety of

*For a continuous update on research studies regarding the GAMA and to obtain a training CD, the reader is encouraged to contact the author at achilles.bardos@unco.edu.

Achilles N. Bardos, Division of Professional Psychology, University of Northern Colorado, Greeley, Colorado 80633.

Handbook of Nonverbal Assessment, edited by R. Steve McCallum. Kluwer Academic/Plenum Publishers, 2003.

backgrounds; it is a nonverbal test that is free of the confounding characteristics of expressive language skills and exposure to a formal English
speaking academic environment. Naglieri and Bardos (1997) stated that
the GAMA "evaluates an individual's overall general ability with items
that require the application of reasoning and logic to solve problems that
exclusively use abstract designs and shapes" (p. 1). In this respect, the
GAMA does not follow a particular theoretical model but rather attempts
to offer an alternative to the measure of general ability after recognizing
many inherent problems with tests of general ability that utilize lengthy
and wordy verbal directions (even for areas claimed or named nonverbal),
such as the Performance Scale of the Wechsler Adult Intelligence Test
(Wechsler, 1997).

The test comprises 66 items organized into four item types named
Matching, Analogies, Sequences, and Construction (See Figures 8.1–8.4).

The "Matching" subtest items require the subject to perceive the various shapes and color combinations, pay attention to details, and find the
two shapes that are identical.

The "Analogies" subtest requires the examinee to recognize the relationship between two abstract figures in the first pair and then identify
the option that completes the relationship in the second pair of designs.

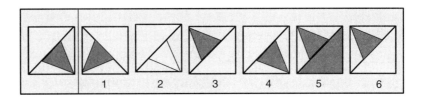

Figure 8.1 Matching Sample Item. (Copyright © 1977 NCS Pearson, Inc. All Rights
Reserved. Reproduced with permission from NCS Pearson. GAMA is a registered trademark
of NCS Pearson, Inc.)

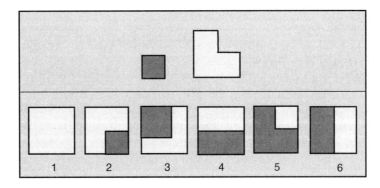

Figure 8.2 Construction Sample Item. (Copyright © 1977 NCS Pearson, Inc. All Rights
Reserved. Reproduced with permission from NCS Pearson. GAMA is a registered trademark
of NCS Pearson, Inc.)

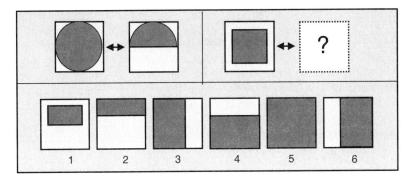

Figure 8.3 Analogies Sample Item. (Copyright © 1977 NCS Pearson, Inc. All Rights Reserved. Reproduced with permission from NCS Pearson. GAMA is a registered trademark of NCS Pearson, Inc.)

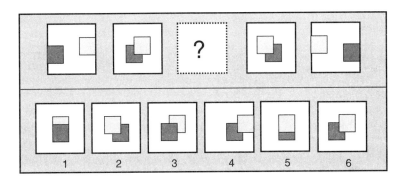

Figure 8.4 Sequences Sample Item. (Copyright © 1977 NCS Pearson, Inc. All Rights Reserved. Reproduced with permission from NCS Pearson. GAMA is a registered trademark of NCS Pearson, Inc.)

In the "Sequence" subtest, the subject is required to recognize the pattern, shape, and location of a design and complete the logical sequence of the presented pattern of designs.

Finally, in the "Construction" subtest, "items require the examinee to determine how several shapes can be combined to produce one of the designs" (Naglieri & Bardos, 1997, p. 5).

The four subtests and their scores do not represent different kinds of ability but rather represent four different ways to measure general ability by nonverbal means. All items use yellow, white, black, and blue print to enhance the presentation of the materials and reduce the effects of impaired color vision for some examinees.

History of Test Development

The primary goal for the development of the GAMA was to design a test that assesses general ability through a variety of nonverbal tasks that can be individually or group administered and with multiple formats using various item booklets (spiral bound, paper booklet, laminated booklet) and client response answer sheets (hand-scoring, scannable). Another goal was the development of a test that was normed on a large population so that age-specific and age-sensitive norms can be derived by including a sufficient number of individuals per age group. There were indeed a number of adult intelligence tests available at the time the GAMA was designed. However, a careful examination of their norming samples revealed serious and significant limitations in terms of both their sample size used to derive their norms at certain age groups and the methodology used to construct their norms. An additional goal was the reduction of the influence of motor requirements through the elimination of manipulatives as well as the reduction of the influence of speed at the item level.

Following pilot studies of approximately 200 test items in an initial item pool, the final test was selected on the basis of a series of psychometric studies. These studies included examining mean scores by age and gender, examining biased items, and computing the internal consistency coefficients for each item type as well as item difficulty and item discrimination values. Since this is a self-administered test that can be group administered as well, the amount of time necessary for test administration was examined. A 25-min time interval was selected.

STANDARDIZATION AND PSYCHOMETRIC PROPERTIES

According to the 1999 *Standards for Educational & Psychological Testing*, "validity refers to the degree to which evidence and theory support the interpretation of test scores entailed by proposed uses of tests" (p. 9). Tests are used to answer specific questions. The evidence presented in the technical manual and the information generated in the professional literature about a test allow users to judge the quality of inferences that can be made by a test's score(s) or, stated differently, how well the test answers those specific questions. In the next few paragraphs, evidence will be presented regarding the psychometric qualities of the GAMA in support of its claim as a measure of general cognitive ability.

A normative test requires a well-designed standardization sample. The GAMA standardization sample consisted of 2,360 people who ranged in age from 18 to 96 years and closely approximated the U.S. population according to the 1990 U.S. census (Bureau of the Census, November, 1992; Bureau of the Census, January, 1994) using gender, educational background, race or ethnic group, and geographic region as stratification variables. Standardization data were collected in 80 cities and 23 states across the United States. Eleven age groups were used to collect data allowing a sufficient number of individuals to represent each age group. The sample size ranged from 219 individuals for the 70–74 age group to 310 for the 25–34 years age group. This allowed for the calculation of sensitive age-specific norms.

The GAMA offers reliable scores. The median internal consistency across 11 age groups for the GAMA total score was 0.90, with values ranging from 0.79 for the older group (80 plus years) to 0.94 for the 35–44-year-olds. Reliability coefficients greater than 0.90 were observed in 7 out of the 11 age groups of the test. The average reliabilities for the four item types were 0.65, 0.66, 0.79, and 0.81 for the Construction, Matching, Sequences, and Analogies subtests, respectively. Stability coefficients were estimated with a test–retest study that included 86 adults tested across a 2–6-week test interval. With a mean test–retest interval of 25 days, the GAMA IQ Score produced a stability coefficient of 0.67. The four item types produced test–retest correlations that ranged from 0.38 (Construction) to 0.74 (Sequences). Gain scores of slightly less than one third standard deviation were consistent across the item types and GAMA IQ Score.

Multiple sources of evidence exist regarding the instrument's validity as a measure of overall cognitive ability. These include the examination of developmental trends across the 11 age groups, relationships with other intelligence tests measuring similar constructs, correlations with achievement tests, and performance of individuals of special populations (e.g., with learning disabilities, deaf, elderly nursing-home residents, individuals with traumatic brain injuries, individuals with mental retardation).

The trend of scores in the GAMA across the 11 age groups followed the expected pattern for adults, the pattern of diminishing ability over time in visual/spatial reasoning skills. Correlations of raw scores with age ranged from 0.43 to 0.56 for the subtests and 0.59 for the GAMA IQ total score.

The Appendix presents a summary of studies demonstrating the test's validity. Mean scores and correlations with individually administered comprehensive batteries such as the Wechsler Adult Intelligence Scales (Wechsler, 1981, 1997) and the Kaufman Adolescent & Adult Intelligence Scale (KAIT; Kaufman & Kaufman, 1990) were also examined. The GAMA IQ scores earned were consistently similar to scores in the WAIS-R, WAIS-III, and KAIT. In addition, high and significant correlations were obtained between the GAMA and the scale scores that measure similar constructs. This was the case for subjects selected from the regular population (Naglieri & Bardos, 1997), college age populations (Lassiter et al., 2000), individuals with learning disabilities (Naglieri & Bardos, 1997), individuals with mental retardation (Naglieri & Bardos, 1997), and individuals with traumatic brain injuries (Donders, 1999; Martin, Donders, & Thompson, 1999).

In studies using brief intelligence tests such as the Kaufman Brief Intelligence Test (K-BIT; Kaufman & Kaufman, 1990), the Shipley Institute of Living Scale (Zachary, 1991), and the Wonderlic Personnel Test (1992), the GAMA performed similarly to these instruments across a variety of samples as well (Festa, Sutton, Crawford, & Bardos, 1999). These studies illustrate that the GAMA offers cognitive ability scores similar to those of other instruments, thus leading to similar decisions.

The relationship between the GAMA and measures of academic achievement was also examined. Significant correlations were observed with the Nelson–Denny Reading Test (Crawford, Festa, Sutton, & Bardos, 1999) for a sample of college students and with the Mini-Battery of Achievement

(Bardos & Festa, 2000) for a sample derived from the general population. The magnitude of the coefficients observed is similar to that reported between other nonverbal reasoning as well as verbal tests and measures of achievement.

Ogard and Karr (1998) used the GAMA along with the MMPI-2 and 16PF in a personnel decision-making study "to develop baseline psychological information on the department's probation & parole staff ... that could be useful in the post job offer process of hiring new employees, in duty assignment decisions and in determining acceptability for arming." The inventories were administered to 62 staff members (31 males and 31 females), and the researchers concluded that "one of the two best predictors of supervisor ratings was the IQ score from the GAMA. ... The other best predictor was the L (Lie) scale of the MMPI-2."

In another study abroad, Petrogiannis, Bardos, Politikos (1999) reported that in a matched sample of Greek and U.S. subjects, the GAMA produced very similar scores, offering support that the GAMA might be able to be adopted by psychologists in other cultures with minimal effort.

In summary, the GAMA offers reliable scores, while numerous studies suggest that the GAMA provides scores very similar to individually or group administered, brief or comprehensive intelligence instruments offering support for the validity of the GAMA as a measure of general cognitive ability.

ADMINISTRATION AND SCORING

Administration and scoring of the GAMA are simple. Examiners who have completed a psychological assessment course and are eligible to administer intelligence and personality tests should have no difficulty with the administration and scoring of the GAMA. In addition, with proper supervision, examiner assistants can be trained to administer the test using the guidelines provided for the various settings and with the various test materials and answer sheets. In all cases, the examiner(s) must familiarize themselves with the test materials, which include: the technical manual, the item booklet (spiral bound) or the group item booklet and the two types of response forms, the scannable answer sheet, and the self-scoring answer sheet. The item booklets are printed in both English and Spanish. Directions for the administration of the test are printed in the last chapter of the manual to facilitate ease of use.

The test directions are read out loud by the examiner, who encourages the examinee to follow along in the test booklet and complete the four sample items. This affords the examiner the opportunity to teach the client the proper use of the response form.

Examinees with a second-grade reading ability should be able to read and understand the minimal printed instructions; however, for those who are unable to read in either English or Spanish, the examiner can pantomime the test directions. Upon completion of the samples, the examinee may begin the test with the exposure of the first item. The time allowed for the test administration is 25 min.

Scoring the GAMA is also very simple. If the Microtest Q (NCS Assessment, 1997) scoring software is used, scoring the GAMA involves entering the examinee's responses. This can be accomplished either manually or through a scanner. The use of a scanner is probably the more efficient method, especially in settings where numerous forms need to be processed. The software generates a report that includes all the scores and a narrative. If the self-scoring record form is used, all scoring steps needed are printed on the inside cover of the record form, thus obviating the need to refer to the technical manual. For example, in the self-scoring form, the examiner will find a section to score the test and obtain the appropriate subtest scale scores ($M = 10$, $SD = 3$) and the GAMA Total IQ score ($M = 100$, $SD = 15$) using the 11 norming tables, which are printed on the record form. Additional scores such as comparisons between subtest scores (an optional analysis), percentile scores, confidence intervals, and classification ranges of scores can be calculated on the form.

INTERPRETATION

Although the administration and scoring procedures of the GAMA are simple and can be accomplished by individuals with varying degrees of training in psychological testing and assessment, interpretation of the GAMA should always be made by individuals with formal training in psychological assessment. As always, it is best to consult the local licensing boards and/or regulatory agencies regarding test administration, test interpretation, and necessary supervisory arrangements.

The GAMA was designed to offer an estimate of a person's overall cognitive ability measured in nonverbal means. The GAMA total score represents this effort; it is the most reliable score across all age groups, so it is the score to use when interpreting the test. Consistent with other intelligence and achievement tests, the GAMA total IQ score is organized with a mean of 100 and a standard deviation of 15. Examiners are strongly encouraged to report confidence interval scores as well as classification ranges of a person's overall ability, thus enhancing the meaning of the GAMA total IQ score. Although intraindividual subtest scores can be calculated for the four item types to determine strengths and weakness, the four item types were not developed to represent separate cognitive abilities; rather, they are different means of assessing general cognitive ability in nonverbal means.

When a strength or a weakness is found in a client's profile, the score(s) should be interpreted considering both a normative and an intraindividual point of view. For example, a score of 9 might be a weakness in a person's profile, but the score is still ranked in the average range of ability when compared with individuals the same age. This weakness will be described as a relative weakness. A score of 6 identified as a weakness in an examinee's intraindividual profile analysis is best described as a cognitive weakness because it is ranked below one standard deviation when compared with individuals of the same chronological age.

The GAMA can also be used as a progress monitoring tool, especially for those examinees whose psychological evaluation and possible subsequent therapy are associated with a traumatic brain injury. A table was developed to assist the examiner in determining whether a change in scores from one administration to the other is a reliable change. The table offers the range of scores expected for such determination. Finally, in interpreting the GAMA test scores, especially when comparing the test score with other measures of cognitive ability (e.g., WAIS-III), the examiner should consider the unique features of the test. The GAMA requires no manipulatives and has very minimal directions requiring listening comprehension skills of the English language, and performance on the test is not affected by item-specific bonus points earned for speeded performance. A difference of 12 and 15 points in either direction is required to consider the scores between the GAMA and WAIS-III PIQ statistically significant at the 0.05 and 0.01 levels, respectively. Additional critical values with other cognitive and achievement tests are available from the author.

STRENGTHS AND WEAKNESSES

The GAMA with its administration format and excellent psychometric properties offers numerous advantages when an alternative instrument is needed to estimate a person's overall cognitive ability. Those in private practice who desire an estimate of their adult clients' cognitive ability can administer the test with minimal effort. Similarly, the individual and group booklets along with the scannable form can assist in testing small or large groups of individuals. This might be the case in correctional or personnel settings, in research studies or whenever an efficient measure of cognitive ability is desired. The evidence regarding the inferences that can be made by the GAMA score as a measure of general cognitive ability is overwhelmingly supportive.

Regarding its weaknesses, the GAMA does require minimal directions requiring second-grade-level reading ability and/or some receptive language skills, and it only offers item booklets printed in English and Spanish. Pantomime administration of the test addresses this limitation; however, a better alternative might be translations of these brief directions in various languages. This might make the GAMA more acceptable in cultures outside the United States or for those who live in the United States but do not speak English or Spanish. Additional cross-cultural investigations are needed to examine the instrument's ability to "cross borders" and be adapted by psychologists around the globe. The limited data in this area are supportive of such efforts. A computerized administration will also be a welcoming feature for the test.

SUMMARY

The GAMA is a nonverbal test designed to evaluate an individual's overall general cognitive ability; it does not require expressive language or exposure to formal English-speaking academic content to complete. It is short, consisting of 66 items; the items are organized in four item types: Matching, Analogies, Sequences, and Construction. Reliability and validity data are impressive. Administration and Scoring are easy, and scoring software is available.

REFERENCES

Bardos, A. N., & Festa, T. (2000, November). *The GAMA and its relationship to achievement*. Paper to be presented at at the 20th annual meeting of the National Academy of Neuropsychology, Orlando, FL.

Bardos, A. N., & Skinner, C. (1998, August). *Performance of traumatically brain-injured sample on the GAMA*. Paper presented at the annual meeting of the American Psychological Association, San Francisco, CA.

Crawford, N., Festa, T., Sutton, L., & Bardos, A. N. (1999, November). *The predictive validity of the General Ability Measure for Adults*. Paper presented at the annual meeting of the National Association of Neuropsychology, San Antonio, TX.

Donders, J. (1999). *Psychometric intelligence in patients with traumatic brain injury: Utility of a new screening measure*. Archives of Physical Medical Rehabilitation, 80, March, pp. 346–347.

Festa, T., Sutton, L., Crawford, N., & Bardos, A. N. (1999, November). *Measuring the cognitive ability of nursing home residents on the GAMA*. Paper presented at the annual meeting of the National Association of Neuropsychology, San Antonio, TX.

Kaufman, A. S., & Kaufman, N. L. (1990). *K-BIT (Kaufman Brief Intelligence Test) manual*. Circle Pines, MN: American Guidance Service.

Lassiter, K., Maher, C., Matthews, T., & Bell, N. (2000). *The general ability measure for adults: A measure of Gf?* Paper presented at the 108th annual convention of the American Psychological Association.

Martin, T., Donders, J., & Thompson, E. (1999). *Potentials and problems with new measures of psychometric intelligence after traumatic brain injury*. Paper presented at the annual meeting of the National Academy of Neuropsychology, San Antonio, TX.

Naglieri, J. A., & Bardos, A. N. (1997). *General Ability Measure for Adults (GAMA)*. Minneapolis, MN: National Computer Systems.

NCS Assessment (1997). *Microtest O Assessment System*. Minneapolis: National Computer Systems.

Ogard, C. M. & Karr, C. (1998). *Psychological testing and concurrent validity study of probation & parole staff for the department of juvenile and adult community justice*. Multnomah County, State of Oregon.

Petrogiannis, K., Bardos, A. N., & Politikos, N. (1999) *A cross cultural investigation of the General Ability Measure for Adults (GAMA) in Greece*. Paper presented at the International Conference of Test Adaptation, Washington, DC.

U.S. Department of Commerce. (1992, November). *1990 census of population, general population characteristics, United States (1 990 CP–1–1)*. Washington, DC: Author.

U.S. Department of Commerce. (1994, January). *1990 census of poulation, education in the United States (1 990 CP–3–4)*. Washington, DC: Author.

Wechsler, D. (1981). *WAIS-R (Wechsler Adult Intelligence Scale—Revised) manual*. San Antonio, TX: The Psychological Corporation.

Wechsler, D. (1997). *WAIS-III (Wechsler Adult Intelligence Scale—Third Edition) manual*. San Antonio, TX: The Psychological Corporation.

Wonderlic personnel test and scholastic level exam user's manual. (1992). Libertyville, IL: Wonderlic Personnel Test.

Zachary, R. A. (1991). *Shipley institute of living scale revised manual.* Los Angeles: Western Psychological Services.

APPENDIX: TABLES OF GAMA VALIDITY STUDIES

Correlations with Ability Tests

- Wechsler Adult Intelligence Scale® (WAIS-R®)
- Kaufman Adolescent & Adult Intelligence Test (KAIT)
- Kaufman Brief Intelligence Test (K-BIT)
- Wonderlic®
- Shipley

Table 8.1   Correlation Between GAMA™ and WAIS-R®, K-BIT

	Total sample			
	M	SD	N	R
GAMA IQ	104.5	13.8	194	
WAIS-R PIQ	106.7	15.9	194	0.74
WAIS-R VIQ	104.6	13.5	194	0.65
WAIS-R FSIQ	105.9	14.9	194	0.75
K-BIT matrices	106.7	10.9	189	0.72
K-BIT vocabulary	104.9	11.5	189	0.54
K-BIT IQ	106.4	11.1	189	0.70

Table 8.2   Descriptive Statistics for GAMA™ and KAIT

Test	M	SD	Correlations (corrected for restriction)
Fluid IQ	107.0	10.2	0.60
Crystallized	108.3	8.6	0.45
Composite	108.5	8.8	0.63
GAMA	106.2	10.0	

Table 8.3   Descriptive Statistics for GAMA™ and Wonderlic®, Shipley

	M	SD	r
Wonderlic	103.8	16.3	0.70
Shipley Vocabulary	97.2	14.1	0.56
Shipley Abstraction	109.1	12.8	0.73
Shipley Total	104.4	13.7	0.72
GAMA IQ	104.7	15.0	—

Note: Wonderlic scores converted to a mean of 100 and SD = 15.

Table 8.4 Descriptive Statistics for GAMA™,
K-BIT, and Nelson–Denny

	M	SD
GAMA™ IQ	108.4	11.0
K-BIT Vocabulary	105.5	6.7
K-BIT Matrices	105.3	10.6
K-BIT Composite	106.3	6.7
Nelson–Denny Vocabulary	104.7	11.6
Nelson–Denny Comprehension	103.7	11.1
Nelson–Denny Total	105.0	11.8

Gama/Nelson–Denny $r = 0.59$ $(p < 0.01)$. $N = 99$, mean age 19.5 $(SD = 2.6)$.

Table 8.5 GAMA™ and WAIS® Descriptive Statistics for
Adults with Learning Disabilities

		LD		Control	
	r	M	SD	M	SD
GAMA™ IQ		97.1	19.4	99.5	16.2
WAIS-R® VIQ	0.52*	96.7	11.6		
WAIS-R PIQ	0.66*	99.6	14.5		
WAIS-R FSIQ	0.65*	97.6	12.0		

$N = 34$ adults; 41.2% males; 58.8% females. * $p < 0.05$.

Table 8.6 GAMA™ Descriptive Statistics for
Adults Who Are Deaf (N 5 49)

	Deaf		Hearing	
	M	SD	M	SD
GAMA™ IQ	101.5	14.9	103.8	14.9

Table 8.7 GAMA™ and K-BIT Descriptive Statistics for
Nursing-Home Residents

	Nursing home		Control	
	M	SD	M	SD
GAMA™ IQ	93.6	9.4	100.9	13.4
K-BIT Vocabulary	98.7	10.0		
K-BIT Matrices	96.6	7.3		
K-BIT Composite	97.3	8.3		

$N = 43$; 86% female, 14% male.

Table 8.8 GAMA™ and K-BIT Descriptive Statistics for those with Traumatic Brain Injury

	TBI sample		Control group	
	M	SD	M	SD
GAMA™ IQ	83.6	13.4	101.4	15.3
K-BIT Vocabulary	87.1	12.3		
K-BIT Matrices	89.3	16.1		
K-BIT Composite	87.0	13.1		

$N = 50$ clients; mean age 38.8 years; 34% females; 66% males.

Table 8.9 GAMA™ and WAIS-R® Descriptive Statistics for Adults with Mental Retardation

	M	SD	r
GAMA™ IQ	66.2	6.7	
WAIS-R® VIQ	64.4	7.1	ns
WAIS-R PIQ	63.1	7.8	0.39*
WAIS-R FSIQ	62.1	5.7	0.36*

$N = 41$; mean age 37.8 years; 46.3% females; 53.7% males. * $p < 0.05$.

Table 8.10 GAMA™ Descriptive Statistics for Greece and the United States

	Greece		United States	
	M	SD	M	SD
Matching	11.0	2.7	10.9	2.7
Analogies	11.2	2.5	11.1	2.8
Sequences	11.8	5.4	11.1	2.8
Construction	10.4	3.1	10.8	3.0
GAMA IQ	105.8	12.1	106.3	13.4

$N = 88$; mean age 25.06 years; SD = 4.5.

9

Naglieri Nonverbal Ability Tests
NNAT and MAT-EF

Jack A. Naglieri

Jose is very smart, but you would not know that by observing him in class. His first-grade teacher says he just sits in class with a lost look on his face. During instruction times, he seems to want to participate, but he quickly loses interest and then starts to misbehave. The teacher has to tell him things repeatedly, and he seems not to understand. So it was quite a surprise to find out that Jose scored 128 (97th percentile) on a nonverbal test of ability! How could that be? The answer is that Jose has both a problem with intermittent hearing loss and limited English-language skills. This has resulted in poor communication skills and failure to follow what is going on in the classroom—when he does hear. This case illustrates the real advantage of a nonverbal test of general ability—to identify children's level of ability overcoming, in this case, the impediment of limited English-language skills and hearing problems that can pose a considerable obstacle to accurate assessment. In fact, nonverbal tests have been used to overcome limited English language since the early 1900s (Yoakum & Yerkes, 1920).

TEST MODEL AND PHILOSOPHY

This chapter will focus on two nonverbal tests—the 38-item Naglieri Nonverbal Ability Test (NNAT; Naglieri, 1997a) and the 72-item Naglieri

Jack A. Naglieri, Department of Psychology, George Mason University, Fairfax, Virginia 22030.

Handbook of Nonverbal Assessment, edited by R. Steve McCallum. Kluwer Academic/Plenum Publishers, 2003.

Nonverbal Ability Test-Individual Form (NNAT-I; Naglieri, 2003). The NNAT is an expansion and major revision of the 34-item Matrix Analogies Test Short Form (MAT-SF; Naglieri, 1985b), both of which were designed to provide a measure of general ability that comprises nonverbal items administered in group (NNAT; Naglieri, 1997a). The NNAT-I (Naglieri, 2003) is the individually administered version. In this chapter, the NNAT (group administered) and NNAT-I (individually administered) will be discussed. Despite the differences in administration format, each of these tests was built on the assumption that a nonverbal test of general ability will be appropriate for many different students because the completely nonverbal content puts every child on a level playing field.

Both the NNAT and NNAT-I comprise items that, to be solved, require that the patterns formed by shapes organized into colorful designs be understood to determine which answer completes the pattern. All items were printed using the colors white, yellow, and blue because these colors pose the least problems for children with color-impaired vision (Naglieri, 1985a). In both tests, items were written according to four different methods, which resulted in types labeled Pattern Completion, Reasoning by Analogy, Serial Reasoning, and Spatial Visualization. Each of these is described in the sections that follow.

Pattern Completion

Items of this type require that the child look at a design in a large rectangle and determine which answer completes the pattern (see Figure 9.1). The child must conceptually extend the pattern presented in the large rectangle to arrive as the answer. This requires paying careful attention to both the general orientation (e.g., the direction of the pattern) and the

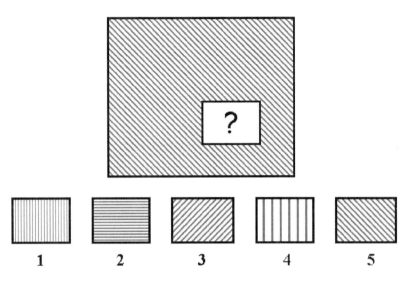

Figure 9.1 Pattern Completion Item Type.

specifics that may be involved (e.g., where a diagonal line would intersect the empty space or the spatial orientation of the lines within the empty space). These items typically appear more at the levels intended to be used for elementary school-age children because they are among the easiest of the several types of matrix items.

Reasoning by Analogy

The second type of item, called "Reasoning by Analogy," require that the child recognize a logical relationship between several geometric shapes. To determine which answer is correct the child must see how the objects change as one moves across the rows and down the columns of the design. These items also require the child to pay careful attention to the details of the design (e.g., notice the changes in the matrix designs) and work with more than one dimension (e.g., shape, orientation, and shading) simultaneously. Reasoning by analogy items becomes more difficult as the logic increases in complexity and number of dimensions involved. Figure 9.2 illustrates what this kind of item looks like. In this example, the student has to analyze the locations of the designs and determine that a rectangle with a shaded background is the answer because as one moves to the right, the shapes are turned 90° clockwise with a shaded background, and as one moves down, the shape changes from an oval to a triangle to a rectangle.

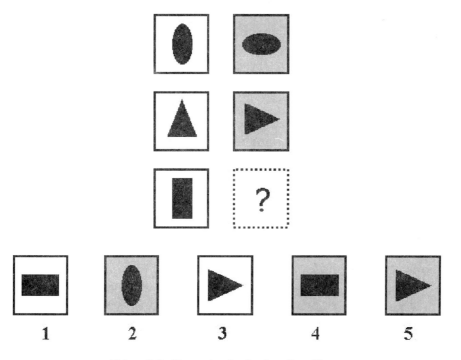

Figure 9.2   Reasoning by Analogy Item Type.

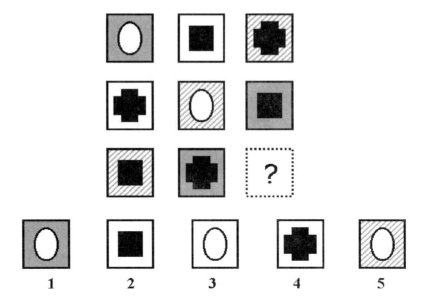

Figure 9.3 Serial Reasoning Item Type.

Serial Reasoning

Items are constructed using a series of shapes that change across the row horizontally and the columns vertically throughout the design. Figure 9.3 shows an example where there is the sequence circle–square–triangle that is presented in stages down the rows. As the design moves down the matrix, it also move one position to the right, creating a series of designs that change over the matrix. These items demand that the child recognize the sequence of shapes (in this example, circle–square–cross; shaded–white–stripped background) and that the sequence is staggered for each row. Serial Reasoning items become more difficult when there is more than one series included in the matrix. For example, more difficult items may use the circle–square–triangle sequence that moves from right to left with a sequence of coloring the shapes (e.g., white–blue–yellow) that moves in a left-to-right direction.

Spatial Visualization

The fourth type of item, called "Spatial Visualization," demands that the child recognize how two or more designs would look if combined, for example, in Figure 9.4, when the two triangles in the top row are combined within the square to yield two triangles, one above the other in the rightmost portion of the last box. Similarly, when the top two designs in the first row are combined, the bow-tie shape appears in the top of the leftmost box on the bottom row. This logic is extended throughout the matrix. The matrix provides the information that these shapes are combined in different ways along the vertical or horizontal dimensions.

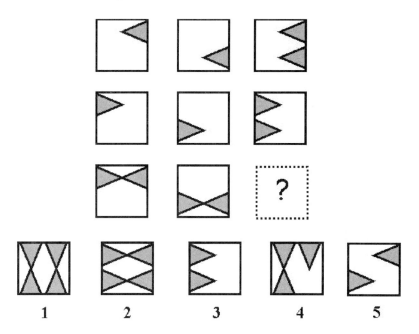

Figure 9.4 Spatial Visualization Item Type.

The child has to determine that the answer (four triangles in Option 2) is what is obtained. Spatial Visualization items are typically among the most difficult, especially when they involve shapes that intersect in ways that are difficult to recognize or involve rotation.

The four item types that appear in the NNAT and NNAT-I are intended to reflect different ways in which a figural progressive matrix can be constructed. They are *not* intended to represent different types of ability because these items are based on the concept of general ability, which, by definition, does not take a multidimensional view of intelligence. Users who wish to examine intelligence from a multidimensional perspective rather than the general intelligence model should consider alternatives such as the Cognitive Assessment System (Naglieri & Das, 1997), which posits four types of abilities, conceptualized as cognitive processes. Professionals who desire a single general intelligence score could use the NNAT or NNAT-I, keeping in mind that this approach yields one main score, and part scores should receive little emphasis. When these matrices tests are used, it is important to understand the perspective of ability they reflect.

What the NNAT and NNAT-I Measure

Practitioners often speak about nonverbal intelligence as a type of ability rather than as one way to measure general intelligence. This is logical if one's view of ability is framed by the work of David Wechsler, who developed his individual tests of intelligence from the Army alpha and beta tests described by Yoakum and Yerkes (1920) in the book *Army Mental Tests*. Wechsler (1939) followed the verbal nonverbal format and provided separate IQs for the verbal and nonverbal (Performance) intelligence scales. Implicit in this organizational structure are two types of intelligence, even though the concept of general ability developed during the early 1900s did not specify two specific "abilities." In fact, the general nature of the concept of intelligence is apparent in Wechsler's definition of ability as "the aggregate or global capacity of the individual to act purposefully, to think rationally, and to deal effectively with his environment." Note that there is no discussion of verbal and nonverbal intelligence in this definition. The verbal and performance scales are different methodologies used to assess the same general construct. Moreover, the vagueness of origin of the concept of general intelligence is clear in writings by Pintner (1925), who wrote, "we did not start with a clear definition of general intelligence ... [but] borrowed from every-day life a vague term implying all-round ability and knowledge, and ... we [are] still attempting to define it more sharply and endow it with a stricter scientific connotation" (p. 53). There is little reason to assume that those who originated tests of general ability conceptualized verbal and nonverbal types of intelligence. Rather, it is important to recognize that the verbal/nonverbal distinction was based on the Army Mental testing program, which contained verbal and nonverbal versions so that a wider variety of persons could be assessed effectively (Yoakum & Yerkes, 1920). The separation of tests by verbal/nonverbal content is an obvious and simple idea to address the problem of assessing persons from diverse linguistic and cultural populations. Thus, the distinction is a practical rather than a theoretical one (Bracken & McCallum, 1998).

My position is that general intelligence tests with verbal content and nonverbal content measure essentially the same construct as general ability tests that are all nonverbal or all verbal. That is, general intelligence can be assessed using tests with a variety of different types of items (verbal, quantitative, nonverbal, etc.). This view that general intelligence tests that differ in content (e.g., a nonverbal test and test with a variety of types of items) can actually both be considered measures of the same construct (general ability) can be examined empirically. For example, if it were true that a nonverbal test of general intelligence was less complete than a test of general intelligence composed of both verbal and nonverbal items, then the solely nonverbal instrument should have less validity. Naglieri (1999) addressed this type of question when he looked at the correlations between various tests of intelligence and achievement. He found that the median correlation between the *Wechsler Intelligence Scale for Children—Third Edition* (Wechsler, 1991) and the *Wechsler Individual Achievement Scale* (Wechsler, 1992) was 0.59 for the sample of 1,284 children who were administered both measures. This correlation can be compared with data reported in the manual of the NNAT (Naglieri, 1997b). In that manual, a median correlation of 0.61 between the NNAT and *Stanford Achievement Test* (9th ed.) (SAT-9) for 21,476 children in grades K-12. Similarly, Naglieri (1985a) reported the correlation between the MAT-EF and reading (0.55) and math (0.58) achievement standard scores for a sample of 2,050 children in grades 4–12. These data clearly show that nonverbal tests of general ability comprising one approach to item construction (NNAT and NNAT-I progressive matrices items) are as effective for predicting academic achievement as the individually administered verbal and performance WISC-III. The reason why these two tests correlate similarly with achievement is that, despite their different contents, they are both measures of general ability.

The findings summarized above augment the need to understand clearly the purpose of testing so that the appropriate instrument can be selected based upon the reason for testing, the characteristics of the child, and the administration format desired (group or individual). The NNAT-I is appropriate when a professional is conducting an individual assessment of a child and desires a measure of general ability. This approach will be appropriate for a wide variety of children, especially those with limited English-language skills. This includes those whose primary language is not English as well as children with communication impairments such as expressive or receptive language disabilities or the hearing impaired. When a fair assessment of a large number of children, for example identification of gifted children, especially gifted minority children is desired, a group nonverbal test such as the NNAT should be considered (see "Strengths and Weaknesses" section of this chapter). However, when a person is to be evaluated for determination of diagnosis, the potential for special programming, or for treatment planning, the NNAT would have to be replaced or augmented with others that are designed and validated for such purposes (e.g., Cognitive Assessment System; Naglieri & Das, 1997).

The strength of tests like the NNAT and NNAT-I is that the method of measuring general ability nonverbally excludes questions that involve verbal expression and/or reception, general information, math or reading skills, and with minimal motor requirements. The inclusion of verbal tests with strong achievement components poses a problem for assessment of diverse populations. In contrast, the structure of the NNAT and NNAT-I allows for a fair evaluation of ability for children from different cultural and linguistic groups (see "Strengths and Weaknesses" section later in this chapter) as well as those with motor or communication problems.

Practitioners might choose to give the nonverbal (Performance) portion of the widely used WISC-III (Wechsler, 1992) to meet the need for a nonverbal test. However, that individually administered test's Performance subtests have directions that are heavily laden with wordy verbal instructions, including basic language concepts (Bracken, 1986; Kaufman, 1990, 1994), which limits the Performance scale's utility as a nonverbal measure of general ability (Bracken & Naglieri, in press). Moreover, that solution is only possible for individual administration.

History of the Tests' Development

The NNAT-I (Naglieri, 2003) and NNAT (Naglieri, 1997a) were both built on the same set of types of items described earlier in this chapter.

These items were constructed with consideration of the nature of factors identified by Corman and Budoff (1974a, 1974b), Wiedl and Carlson (1976), Carlson and Jensen (1980), and other tests that use a progressive matrix approach. The 64-item MAT-EF (Naglieri, 1985a) was used as a base from which 34 items were chosen to form the Matrix Analogies Test Short Form (MAT-SF; Naglieri, 1985b). The NNAT is an enlarged version of the MAT-SF. The NNAT employs the same four abstract matrix item types (i.e., Pattern Completion, Reasoning by Analogy, Serial Reasoning, and Spatial Reasoning), used in the MAT-EF and MAT-SF but was designed to be a more effective (e.g., have higher ceilings and improved reliability across all ages) group administered test. To achieve this goal, the NNAT comprises seven levels, each of which contains items tailored to children's ability by grade.

NAGLIERI NONVERBAL ABILITY TEST (NNAT)

Structure

The NNAT is organized into seven levels, each containing 38 dichotomously scored items. Each level contains a carefully selected set of items that are most appropriate for children at the grade or grades for which that level is intended. Each level contains items that are shared with adjacent higher and/or lower levels as well as unique items. Shared items were used to develop a continuous scaled score across the entire standardization sample. The seven levels and corresponding grades for which they are appropriate are as follows: A/K; B/1; C/2; D/3 & 4; E/5 & 6; F/7–9; G/10–12.

Standardization

The NNAT was standardized on a nationally representative sample of 89,600 children in grades K through 12 (ages 5–18 years). The sample included 22,600 children tested in the fall of 1995 and 67,000 children testing in the spring of 1996. The final complete sample used to create the NNAT norms tables closely matches the U.S. population on the basis of geographic region, socioeconomic status, urbanicity, ethnicity, and school setting (private and parochial). The sample included children in special educational settings such as those with emotional disturbance, learning disabilities, hearing and visual impairment, and those who were mentally handicapped. Children with limited English proficiency were also included in the standardization sample. This standardization procedure also involved concurrent administration of the SAT-9. More details may be obtained from the NNAT Technical Manual (Naglieri, 1997b).

Administration

A regular classroom teacher typically administers the NNAT in a group format (if individual administration is required, the MAT-EF should be given by a school psychologist or similarly trained professional). Administration of the 38-item test is limited to 30 min, with about 10 min taken for completion of the demographic information on the answer document (levels D through G only). Children who are administered levels A, B, and C respond directly on the stimulus booklet.

Scoring

There are two ways in which the NNAT can be scored: by hand using scoring guides or using machine-scorable documents. In either case, each child's raw score is converted to a Nonverbal Ability Index (NAI) standard score, which is set at a mean of 100 and a standard deviation of 15. These standard scores are obtained through an intermediate Rasch value called a scaled score. Level D of the NNAT was used as the base level to which all other levels were equated. The appropriate equating constant was then added to the spring standardization Rasch item difficulties of each level to produce a continuous Rasch ability scale across all levels of the test. This method allows for greater flexibility, for example, so that a child of any age can be administered any NNAT level. For more information see Naglieri (1997b).

Scoring the NNAT involves three simple steps. First the raw score for a particular level is obtained. Next that raw score is converted to a scaled score, which is centered on Level D. The scaled scores are converted to standard scores with a mean of 100 and a standard deviation of 15 (called Nonverbal Ability Index) based on the age of a child. NAI scores can be converted to percentile ranks and stanine scores. All this scoring can be accomplished by hand or using machine scoring service from the publisher.

Reliability

The KR 20 internal reliability coefficients for the NNAT by Level and grade are reported in Table 9.1. These range from 0.83 to 0.93 and with an average internal reliability across all samples of 0.86. The NNAT total score, therefore, has acceptable reliability levels at all ages.

Interpretation

The NNAT yields an NAI score, which is set at a mean of 100, and a standard deviation of 15. This score can be interpreted as a traditional measure of general ability. The scale score system used to calculate the NAI scores links all levels of the test together, yielding a continuous scale that makes it possible to compare the scores children earn when taking different levels. Once a raw score is converted to a scaled score, the level that was given is no longer relevant because the NAI scores are based on age. This makes the NAI scores comparable across levels, which is especially helpful for out-of-level testing. In addition to NAI scores, percentile ranks, and stanine scores, cluster scores for the four types of items are

Table 9.1   NNAT Internal Reliability Coefficients (KR20) by
Level and Age ($N = 76,611$)

	Age group	N	Reliability
Level A	5	2,365	0.86
	6	3,243	0.86
Level B	6	2,929	0.85
	7	3,547	0.84
Level C	7	3,627	0.81
	8	4,066	0.83
Level D	8	3,745	0.83
	9	7,029	0.85
	10	4,579	0.87
Level E	10	2,676	0.87
	11	6,901	0.88
	12	4,730	0.86
Level F	12	2,565	0.86
	13	5,759	0.87
	14	5,978	0.88
	15	3,376	0.88
Level G	15	1,278	0.86
	16	3,395	0.87
	17	3,141	0.88
	18	1,682	0.88
All ages	5–18	76,611	0.86

Note: The all ages reliability is the mean of all age groups.

provided that describe the child's performance as "Below Average," "Average," or "Above Average." All these scores are summarized in a one-page report provided when the NNAT scoring service is utilized.

The NAI score obtained from the NNAT should be integrated with other relevant data and used appropriately like any other test score. That is, a child's performance on this test should be compared with academic performance, background experiences, and so forth, so that decisions are made with full consideration of all relevant information. When included as a portion of a larger picture of a child, the NNAT can play an important role as an estimate of ability obtained using nonverbal stimuli.

Strengths and Weaknesses

The strengths of the NNAT include practical issues such as a large standardization sample, brief administration time, and machine-scorable answer sheets, which allow for testing and scoring for large numbers of children in a short period of time. Other strengths related to practice but rooted in research include evidence of small differences between minority and white populations, evidence that the test is effective for identification of gifted minority children, and strong correlations with achievement. The research findings provide strong support for the practical utility of the NNAT and will be described in more detail.

Naglieri (1985b) and Naglieri and Ronning (2000a) provided a detailed study of mean score differences between matched samples of White ($N = 2,306$) and Black ($N = 2,306$); White ($N = 1,176$) and Hispanic ($N = 1,176$); and White ($N = 466$) and Asian ($N = 466$) children on the NNAT. The groups were carefully selected from a larger sample of children included in the NNAT standardization sample and matched on the demographic characteristics of the U.S. population, including geographic region, socioeconomic status, ethnicity, and type of school setting (public or private). Only small differences were found between the NNAT scores for the White and Black samples (Cohen's d ratio = 0.25 or about 4 standard score points). Minimal differences between the White and Hispanic (d ratio = 0.17 or about 3 standard score points), as well as White and Asian (d ratio = 0.02, less than one standard score point) groups were reported. Additionally, the correlations between NNAT and academic achievement were similar for the White and minority groups. The small mean score differences and the strong correlations strongly suggest that the NNAT has utility for fair assessment of White and minority children.

Naglieri and Ford (in press) reported further evidence that the NNAT is useful as a fair measure of general ability for minority children. They studied the percentages of White, Black, and Hispanic children who earned scores high enough to be used as one criterion for placement in classes for the gifted. Naglieri and Ford (in press) found that 5.6% of the White ($N = 14,141$), 5.1% of the Black ($N = 2,863$), and 4.4% of the Hispanic ($N = 1,991$) children earned an NNAT standard score of 125 (95th percentile rank) or higher. The authors found that the NNAT was effective at identifying diverse students for gifted education services and may help address the persistent problem of the underrepresentation of diverse students in gifted education.

Finally, two recent investigations of the NNAT have been completed. One included Native American children and the other children with limited English-language skills. In this study (Naglieri & Booth, 2002), 140 Hispanic children with limited English-language skills in grades Kindergarten through 12th grade were matched on sex, region, parental educational level, and NNAT level to 140 Hispanic children without limited English-language skills. The results of this study showed a minor difference between the two groups (d ratio = 0.13 or about 2 standard score points). Kaufman and Naglieri (2002) compared 793 Native American children with other race/ethnic groups. They found that the Native American children earned a mean score of 96.3, which differed by about 4 points (d ratio of 0.3) from the White (100.7) sample ($N = 41,995$). These data suggest that the NNAT scores of minority groups differ minimally from samples of White children.

The greatest weakness of the NNAT, as stated by Maller and Mowery (2000), is the need for more validity research on the instrument. Although research studies are beginning to appear (Naglieri & Ford, in press; Naglieri & Ronning, 2000a, 2000b), more are needed. Especially important will be concurrent validity studies that examine the relationship between the NNAT and other tests of general ability and examinations of the performance of special populations such as children with hearing impairments and limited English proficiency.

LEVEL 2: NAGLIERI NONVERBAL ABILITY
TEST–INDIVIDUAL FORM (NNAT-I)

Structure

The NNAT-I (Naglieri, 2003) is a general nonverbal measure of ability for children and adolescents between the ages of 5 and 17 years. The test has two 72-item Forms labeled A and B, each of which yields a total test standard score with a mean of 100 and standard deviation set at 15. The test is comprised of four different types of abstract designs labeled Pattern Completion, Reasoning by Analogy, Serial Reasoning, and Spatial Visualization. These progressive matrix item types are not intended to represent different kinds of ability, but rather four ways to measure general ability nonverbally.

Standardization

The NNAT-I was normed by a sample of 1,585 students aged 5 through 17 years. The sample was stratified to be representative of the U.S. population on the basis of age, gender, race/ethnicity, geographic region, and parental education level. The NNAT-I standardization sample included children in public and private schools. The resulting standardization sample closely matches the target population (for more details see Naglieri, 2003). Additionally, children who were receiving special educational services because of attention deficit disorder, emotional or behavioral disorders, learning disability, or speech, language, motor, and hearing impairment were also included in special validity studies.

Administration

Both Forms A and B of the NNAT-I are administered using brief verbal directions. Basal and ceiling rules and entry points based on the age of the child allow for efficient administration of the most appropriate items. Testing time is approximately 20 to 25 minutes.

Scoring

The NNAT-I is easily scored by converting the sum of the raw scores to a standard score (mean of 100, SD of 15) based upon the Form given. Confidence intervals are provided for NNAT-I standard scores at both 90 and 95% level of significance. All standard scores can be further described as percentile ranks and age equivalents.

Reliability

Internal consistency coefficients (Cronbach alpha) are reported for the normative sample of 1,585 students for each of the 12 age levels. Alpha

Table 9.2   NNAT-I Internal Reliability Coefficients
(Alpha) by Age (*N* = 1,585)

Age group	*N*	Reliability
5	140	.89
6	150	.90
7	150	.89
8	150	.89
9	150	.89
10	150	.90
11	140	.88
12	150	.92
13	105	.92
14	100	.94
15	100	.94
16–17	100	.95
5–17	1,585	.91

Note: The reliability for the 5–17-year group is an average of the separate ages.

coefficients for the NNAT-I presented in Table 9.2 range from a low of .88 to a high of .95. The average across the ages is .91.

Interpretation

Interpretation of the NNAT-I is focused on the total test standard score because it provides the best estimate of a child's general ability measured nonverbally. This score has the greatest reliability and validity and should be utilized, like any score, within the context of additional information about a child. For example, the score might be contrasted with achievement or other ability data to help the practitioner gain a more complete picture of a child.

The NNAT-I also provides a Parent Report Form. This is a two-page document on which the examiner can record information about the child's NNAT-I score. The form includes ability categories (e.g., Low Average, Average, etc.), standard scores, percentile scores plainly marked on a normal curve, and a written description of the purpose of the test and how it should be used as well as two sample items.

Strengths and Weaknesses

Like most nonverbal tests, the NNAT-I has the advantage that it can be administered to children who vary on the basis of linguistic and cultural backgrounds. The greatest strength of the NNAT-I, like the NNAT, is that researchers have found relatively small differences between the scores earned by different racial and ethnic groups. The NNAT-I manual Naglieri (2003) provides a summary of studies that have examined the differential performance of different racial/ethnic groups. In each of the studies the samples were matched on the basis of age, gender, parental education, and geographic region.

Naglieri (2003) compared the mean scores for 163 Hispanic children and 163 White children from the standardization sample and found that the mean scores for the Hispanic sample (97.0) was very similar to that obtained by the White sample (99.6). Naglieri (2003) also found that Hispanic children administered the NNAT-I directions in Spanish earned essentially the same mean score as those given the test in English (92.4 and 92.3, $n = 40$). In another study, Naglieri (2003) reported that children who did not speak English as their first language ($n = 77$) earned an NNAT-I score of 91.7, which was similar to the mean of 96.7 earned by a control group ($n = 77$). Finally, Naglieri (2003) reported similar findings for a study that examined mean scores differences between Black ($n = 205$) and White ($n = 205$) children. The Black and White groups earned mean scores of 92.7 and 101.1, respectively. In summary, the relatively small differences found across these studies suggest that an important strength of the NNAT-I is that it offers a viable means of assessing ability, non-verbally, for a variety of children and adolescents.

SUMMARY

The NNAT and NNAT-I are intended to provide a nonverbal test of general ability that provides a means of measuring ability that is fair to a wide variety of children and adolescents, especially those with limited educational skills, limited English-language proficiency, communication deficits (oral or expressive), or hearing impairment. In this chapter, I have summarized the two tests and provided a summary of the most relevant research that examines the reliability and validity of these tests. The NNAT and NNAT-I correlate with achievement at about the same level as the most widely used individually administered test of intelligence (WISC-III). Importantly, the NNAT and NNAT-I provide measures of ability that is minimally related to race and ethnic group (small mean score differences have been found), and the NNAT correlated with achievement similarly for all groups (evidence for fair assessment). Finally, evidence was summarized that suggests that the NNAT can be used for identification of gifted minority children. These findings provide considerable support for these brief nonverbal measures of general ability.

ACKNOWLEDGMENT. Research in support of this chapter was funded in part by a grant R215K010121 from the U.S. Department of Education.

REFERENCES

Bracken, B. A. (1986). Incidence of basic concepts in the directions of five commonly used American tests of intelligence. *School Psychology International*, 7, 1–10.
Bracken, B. A., & McCallum, R. S. (1998). *Universal nonverbal intelligence test*. Itasca, IL: Riverside.

Bracken, B. A., & Naglieri, J. A. (in press). Assessing diverse populations with nonverbal tests of general intelligence. To appear in C. R. Reynolds & R. W. Kamphaus (Eds.), *Handbook of psychological and educational assessment of children* (2nd Ed.). New York: Guilford.

Carlson, J. S., & Jensen, C. M. (1980). The factorial structure of the Raven Coloured Progressive Matrices Test: A reanalysis. *Educational and Psychological Measurement*, 40, 1111–1116.

Corman, I., & Budoff, M. (1974a). Factor structure of retarded and nonretarded children on the Raven's Progressive Matrices. *Educational and Psychological Measurement*, 34, 407–412.

Corman, I., & Budoff, M. (1974b). Factor structure of Spanish-speaking and non-Spanish speaking children on the Raven's Progressive Matrices. *Educational and Psychological Measurement*, 34, 977–981.

Kaufman, A. S. (1990). *Assessing adolescent and adult intelligence.* Boston: Allyn & Bacon.

Kaufman, A. S. (1994). *Intelligent testing with the WISC-III.* New York: Wiley.

Kaufman, J. C., & Naglieri, J. A. (in press). *Comparison of Native American children to other ethnicities on the naglieri nonverbal ability test.*

Maller, S. J., & Mowery, D. (2000). Naglieri Nonverbal Ability Test review. *Journal of psychoeducational assessment*, 18, 275–280.

Naglieri, J. A. (1985a). *Matrix analogies test—Expanded form.* San Antonio, TX: The Psychological Corporation.

Naglieri, J. A. (1985b). *Matrix analogies test—Short form.* San Antonio, TX: The Psychological Corporation.

Naglieri, J. A. (1997a). *Naglieri nonverbal ability test.* San Antonio, TX: The Psychological Corporation.

Naglieri, J. A. (1997b). *Naglieri nonverbal ability test technical manual.* San Antonio, TX: The Psychological Corporation.

Naglieri, J. A. (1999). *Essentials of CAS assessment.* New York: Wiley.

Naglieri, J. A., & Booth, A. (in press). *Comparison of Hispanic children with limited English proficiency and monolingual English speaking Hispanic children on the Naglieri nonverbal ability test.*

Naglieri, J. A., & Das, J. P. (1997). *Cognitive assessment system.* Itasca, IL: Riverside.

Naglieri, J. A., & Ford, D. (in press). Addressing under-representation of gifted minority children using the Naglieri Nonverbal Ability Test (NNAT). *Gifted child quarterly.*

Naglieri, J. A., & Ronning, M. E. (2000a). The relationships between general ability using the NNAT and SAT reading achievement. *Journal of Psychoeducational Assessment*, 18, 230–239.

Naglieri, J. A., & Ronning, M. E. (2000b). Comparison of White, African-American, Hispanic, and Asian Children on the Naglieri Nonverbal Ability Test. *Psychological Assessment*, 12, 328–334.

Pintner, R. (1925). *Intelligence testing.* New York: Holt.

Stanford Achievement Test (9th ed.). (1995). San Antonio, TX: Psychological Corporation.

Wechsler, D. (1939). *The measurement of adult intelligence.* Baltimore: Williams & Wilkins.

Wechsler, D. (1991). *Wechsler intelligence scale for children—Third edition manual.* San Antonio, TX: The Psychological Corporation.

Wechsler, D. (1992). *Wechsler individual achievement scale.* San Antonio, TX: The Psychological Corporation.

Wiedl, K. H., & Carlson, J. S. (1976). The factorial structure of the Raven Coloured Progressive Matrices Test. *Educational and Psychological Measurement*, 36, 406–413.

Yoakum, C. S., & Yerkes, R. M. (1920). *Army mental tests.* New York: Holt.

10

Test of Nonverbal Intelligence
A Language-Free Measure of Cognitive Ability

Linda Brown

The *Test of Nonverbal Intelligence* (TONI; Brown, Sherbenou, & Johnsen, 1982, 1990, 1997) was built 20 years ago in response to the increasing diversity and complexity of a society in which the evaluation of intellectual ability and aptitude was rapidly becoming a dominant motif. That trend has continued, and even burgeoned to the current day. Elementary and secondary schools, institutions of higher learning, business and industry, clinics, hospitals, and agencies in virtually every sector of our society routinely use measures of aptitude and ability not only in research but also in practical, everyday decision-making.

Not only does this broad use of intelligence measures call for a test that can be used by diverse professionals, but it also reminds us that intelligence tests are administered to a more diverse group of people than in the past. Less than a generation ago, large segments of the disability community could not be tested conventionally because sensory, language, and motor impairments made it impossible for them to interact with the content of the existing tests of intelligence and aptitude. In addition, the tasks constituting most intelligence tests administered in this country employ the common language and culture of the United States, under the dubious assumption that all "intelligent" people are able to identify, understand, and use the English language and American cultural icons. But in an increasingly diverse and complex society, many of the patients, clients, students, job applicants, and others who routinely take such tests may not be proficient in spoken or written English and may not be

Linda Brown, 1142 Limit Street, Leavenworth, Kansas 66048.

Handbook of Nonverbal Assessment, edited by R. Steve McCallum, Kluwer Academic/ Plenum Publishers, 2003.

familiar with many aspects of American culture. Individuals who do not use or understand standard English—such as those who are deaf or hard of hearing, who are fluent in a primary language other than English, who are electively mute, or who present a language or learning disability—and people who are not conversant with American pop culture, such as recent immigrants—will be penalized, regardless of their intellectual acumen, by intelligence tests on which the questions and answers are in English or which assume intimate knowledge of daily American life. Whether they are intelligent or not, they will score poorly on those tests of intelligence.

And so there was a need for a psychometrically sound test that could be administered reliably by professionals from many disciplines and would not equate lack of English-language proficiency or limited knowledge of American culture with low intelligence or poor aptitude for learning and achievement. The TONI was built to fill this niche. In this chapter, we will (a) examine the philosophy underlying TONI; (b) chronicle its development from the first edition in 1982 to the 1997 revision; (c) detail its psychometric characteristics, with particular attention to the reliability and validity of its results, the normative and standardization procedures governing its development, and empirical controls for bias; (d) describe TONI's administration and scoring; (e) offer suggestions and guidelines for the interpretation of the test results; and (f) summarize TONI's strengths and weaknesses.

TEST MODEL AND PHILOSOPHY

It should be noted from the outset that readers of this text do not need, and are not looking for, a history of intelligence testing, or for a recital of the prominent and influential theories of intelligence, nor even for definitions of intelligence. Those commentaries are available in greater detail and with more erudition than is possible in this limited space. Suffice it to say that the man who began the modern mental testing movement was driven more by pragmatism than by theoretical or philosophical inclinations. Alfred Binet began simply enough by observing his own little girls as they grew and learned, and later observed small groups of children (Binet, 1903, 1910). He and his colleagues (Binet & Henri, 1895a, 1895b, 1895c; Binet & Simon, 1905, 1909) then culled the behaviors that best differentiated children thought to be developing normally from those thought to be (in the term of the day) defective imbeciles.

Rather than philosophizing about what intelligence might be, or theorizing about its hypothetical constructs, the Binet team simply mined their catalogue of observed behaviors, validated their observations through scientific methods, and built an instrument with attention to simplicity, clarity, and consistency of administration. Their 30-item Metrical Scale (Binet, 1911; Binet & Simon, 1905, 1908, 1916), a diverse series of graduated tasks focusing on higher mental processes like memory, attention, and imagination, which were the best discriminators of learning potential, was "a triumph of pragmatism" (Tuddenham, 1962, p. 494).

Despite the absence of an elaborate theoretical base, the Binet–Simon scales were straightforward and functional. TONI follows in these practical and empirical shoes. TONI was not built to validate a theory of intelligence, but to achieve a particular purpose: to be a quick, reliable, and valid measure of global intelligence that required no reading, writing, speaking, or listening.

History of Test Development

Most measures of intelligence and aptitude depend heavily upon language: Some require test subjects to read the test items, others employ oral instructions or questions, many require oral responses, and a few require written responses. Even if such tests are psychometrically sound, they are inadequate for people who are not proficient in standard American English. They also tend to have heavy cultural loading, in part because of the pre-eminence of written or spoken English and in part because they presume intimate knowledge of the United States (i.e., noting the error on a map of the United States with Florida on the west coast, "Why are we tried by a jury of our peers?") or reflect learned knowledge (i.e., usage of upper- and lower-case letters, "What is the capital of France?"). However, many tests of intelligence that purport to control language also require significant manual dexterity, such as stringing beads, connecting dots, drawing a person, building with blocks, and manipulating objects.

> Language and motor skills are prominent components of most intelligence measures currently in use, yet such measures simply are not appropriate for many individuals. People who are unable to read or write, people who are deaf, people who have poor or impaired linguistic skills, people who are from different cultural or linguistic backgrounds, and people with limited motor ability require a testing format free of listening, speaking, reading, writing, and substantial motor responses. A large portion of the people who are evaluated by schools, clinics, and hospitals fall into at least one of these categories. They include non-English speakers, as well as individuals who are aphasic, learning disabled, deaf, or who have suffered severe neurological trauma and compromise through head injury, stroke, cerebral palsy, Alzheimer's disease, and similar conditions. (Brown et al., 1997, p. 28)

Very few tests filled this language-free niche 20 years ago when TONI was first built, and those that did possessed serious psychometric flaws. Most prominent among the existing measures were Raven's matrix tests (Raven, 1938, 1947, 1960, 1962, 1977), which were used widely despite old, nonrepresentative norms and modest estimates of reliability (particularly for children), flaws which were not corrected by a 1986 book reporting North American normative studies (Raven, 1986). *The Leiter International Performance Scales* (Leiter, 1948), designed for children with sensory, language, or motor deficits, were also in wide use when TONI was conceived. They were flawed by deficient normative and reliability data and reported a ratio IQ instead of a true standard score, deficits that were not substantially improved by Arthur's (1950) adaptation, nor even by the revision (Levine, 1982) contemporaneous with the publication of TONI. So, even those few tests that measured intelligence without the use of language were rendered largely useless in practice by the absence of representative normative populations, true normative scores, or acceptable evidence of reliability and validity.

Our goal, then, was to correct these problems and build a test that had acceptable norms, was reliable and valid, and estimated intellectual capacity without relying upon written or spoken language, without emphasizing American cultural familiarity, and without requiring complicated motor responses. We focused first on the test's format: the stimulus material and the administration and response modes. (a) The stimulus material could not use words, in either written or spoken form. The content had to be abstract in nature, something free of linguistic representation. We could have used pictures of a tube of Crest toothpaste or the golden arches of McDonald's, which would have avoided the use of words, but still would have introduced significant cultural bias into the test. And so the content also had to be novel, conferring no advantage or disadvantage on test subjects with more or less formal education or exposure to American culture. We settled on abstract/figural content. (b) Administration also had to be free of language. We elected to use pantomimed instructions. (c) Finally, the mode of response could not require speaking or writing. We settled on a multiple-choice format with a simple pointing response or any other meaningful gesture to indicate the test subject's choice from among the options offered.

With the format decided, content came next. Of all intelligent behaviors, we concluded that the one best measured in this manner is abstract reasoning and problem-solving. Not only does problem-solving lend itself well to the language-free, culture-reduced, motor-reduced format we stipulated, but there is also substantial empirical evidence that intellectual differences among individuals are most pronounced in higher complex mental processes like abstract reasoning and problem-solving, which were, therefore, likely to be powerful and stable predictors of overall, global intelligence.

We began building TONI with these qualifications in mind: (a) The test would measure a single intelligent behavior, problem-solving. (b) Administration would be pantomimed, requiring only a simple responsive gesture and no reading, writing, speaking, or listening. (c) The content would be abstract/figural in nature, thereby eliminating language and also reducing cultural loading. The evolution of TONI is abstracted here; full details are provided in the preface to TONI3 (Brown et al., 1997).

About the same time we were field-testing the prototype for TONI, Jensen (1980) published his book, *Bias in Mental Testing*, in which he recommended guidelines for language-free, culturally reduced measures. He advocated: (a) the use of performance tasks rather than paper-and-pencil tasks; (b) pantomimed instructions in lieu of oral or written instructions;

(c) inclusion of practice items; (d) abstract content, not pictures or reading passages; (e) content that required reasoning rather than recall of factual material; and (f) an untimed procedure. We had already incorporated these characteristics into TONI.

TONI (1982)

The first TONI (Brown et al., 1982) had two forms of 50 items each and consisted of an examiner's manual, a picture book with the stimulus drawings for the test items, and pads of Form A and Form B answer sheets to be completed by the examiner. Test items were selected empirically, assigned to Form A or Form B and arranged in easy-to-difficult order, parity between forms confirmed by coefficients of equivalence. TONI was normed on a sample of 1,929 individuals ages 5-0 years through 85-11 years who were demographically representative of the U.S. population (U.S. Bureau of the Census, 1980). Evidence for reliability and validity was provided in the manual.

TONI2 (1990)

TONI2 (Brown et al., 1990) was both a revision and an upward extension of the test. Ten more difficult items were added, but scoring and administration were unchanged, as were the kit components. The normative group was 50% larger, comprising 2,764 subjects, representative of the U.S. population (U.S. Bureau of the Census, 1985) across age, gender, race, ethnicity, geographic region, urban/suburban/rural domicile, parental education (for minor subjects), and educational attainment (for adult subjects). The equivalence of Forms A and B was verified by coefficients of equivalence. Coefficients Alpha, immediate and 7-day delayed alternate forms reliability, and extraction of content sampling error from time sampling error reflected good internal consistency and stability reliability. Acceptable coefficient Alphas, Kuder–Richardson Formula 21 coefficients, and immediate alternate forms coefficients were also reported for groups of subjects diagnosed with intellectual exceptionalities, learning disabilities, dyslexia, hearing loss, and closed head injuries, and for subjects who did not speak English or for whom English was a second language, including native Spanish speakers in Mexico and Chile, fully English-proficient bilingual speakers, limited-English proficient speakers, and non-English-proficient speakers. Validity data were extensive, incorporating our own research and independent, peer-reviewed research. Strong, positive relationships between TONI2 and 26 other tests of intelligence, aptitude, and achievement were demonstrated, along with item analytic data, factor analyses, multiple correlation/ regression, and convergent/divergent validity.

TONI3 (1997)

TONI3 is a strong measure of general intelligence that is not based upon one particular theory of intelligence. TONI3's abstract/figural problem-solving content and its language-free, culture-reduced format conform to various prominent theories of intelligence. These are summarized in Figure 10.1.

Gould (1981), in his classic book, *The Mismeasure of Man*, points out the logical fallacy committed by many people, lay and professional alike, when discussing intelligence tests, namely that intelligence is that which is measured by intelligence tests. If a test of intelligence requires a person to read or write English, or to speak or comprehend spoken English, to what extent is that test measuring intelligence, and to what extent is it measuring the learned skills of reading and writing, and not just reading and writing, but reading and writing, specifically, the English language?

- *Spearman's theory of intelligence*: The score generated by the TONI-3 is hypothesized to be a good representation of Spearman's *g*-factor.

- *The Thurstones' primary mental ability theory of intelligence*: The TONI-3 should measure their sixth primary mental ability, reasoning.

- *Guilford's SOI model*: The TONI-3 should tap, to some extent, all of Guilford's mental operations (i.e., cognition, memory, divergent and convergent thinking, and evaluation), although memory arguably contributes the least to TONI-3 performance. It also seems reasonable that all of Guilford's products, particularly classes, relations, systems, and transformations, are generated in solving TONI-3 problems. By choice, we limited the TONI-3 to one content, figural.

- *Piaget's theory*: It is difficult to classify the TONI-3 within the Piagetian model. The concepts of organization, adaptation, assimilation, and accommodation are strongly related theoretically to the TONI-3's problem-solving content. Clearly, too, any developmental component of intelligence would also be related to TONI-3 performance.

- *Cattell and Horn's two-factor theories*: The TONI-3 was built to measure fluid intelligence rather than crystallized intelligence.

- *Jensen's cognitive–associative model*: TONI-3 tasks, which require reasoning and do not demand rote memory or previous learning, would be measures of Jensen's cognitive level.

- *Das's simultaneous–sequential processing model*: The TONI-3 is difficult to classify within this model, because the thinking process cannot be observed; that is, there is no way to ascertain how a test subject arrives at an answer to a TONI-3 problem. Both sequential and simultaneous processes can yield correct solutions, although it is likely that as problem complexity increases, simultaneous solutions are more advantageous to the problem solver than sequential ones.

Figure 10.1   Relationship of TONI3 to Selected Theoretical Models of Intelligence (From *The Test of Nonverbal Intelligence* (3rd ed., p. 8) by L. Brown, R. J. Sherbenou, & S. K. Johnsen, 1997. Reproduced by permission of PRO-ED, Austin, TX.)

But can one conclude that a person who cannot read or write standard American English is not intelligent? Of course not. Likewise, there are disabilities that impair a person's language competence without impairing intellect. Language-based "tests are not only inappropriate for individuals who are deaf and hearing impaired, but also for people with aphasia, dyslexia, and other disorders related to spoken and written language, and for people who have excellent language skills but who are not proficient (in) ... English ... Cultural differences ... (also) may adversely affect test performance" (Brown et al., 1997, p. 14).

It is not surprising that language is represented so heavily in tests of intelligence because language is how we tend to store and retrieve information, but it can present an impediment in properly evaluating many people. Our goal in building TONI was to create a format that eliminated reading, writing, speaking, and listening from the measurement of intelligence; that reduced the impact of cultural familiarity upon test performance; and that minimized the motoric requirements of responding.

> We selected abstract/figural problem solving as the core of TONI3 for four reasons. First, problem solving appears to be a general and important component or construct of intelligent behavior rather than a splinter skill or subcomponent. Second, it is a pervasive activity that estimates the ... intellectual functioning of the problem solver. Third, the problem-solving process and the abstract/figural content both accommodate the language-free, motor-reduced testing format that we wanted to use in TONI3. Finally, abstract/figural content ensures that test items are novel and free of linguistic and cultural indicators.
>
> We then had format decisions to make. ... [M]any nonverbal tests rely on performance tasks, such as mazes, form boards, block designs, bead pattens, and paper folding or cutting. There is nothing inherently wrong with any of these formats, but we decided not to pursue them. One consideration that affected our decision was the bulkiness of the requisite components and paraphernalia. In addition, the cost of producing such equipment would increase the price of the test substantially. Further, although they suited our desire to eliminate language from the testing task, these formats impose heavy motor requirements and would have made the test inappropriate for subjects who presented a motor impairment of any kind. Finally, and more important, these formats are not particularly flexible. They limit the test developer to a narrow range of reasoning and problem-solving tasks. ...
>
> The matrix format overcame all of these obstacles. It is compact, cost efficient, and versatile. It can be administered to individuals who have no language skills and only the barest of motor abilities. By using figural matrices we could build great diversity into the test content without relying on language to do so and also could extend the range of difficulty from simple matching problems to extremely complex, multifaceted problems. (Brown et al., 1997, p. 24)

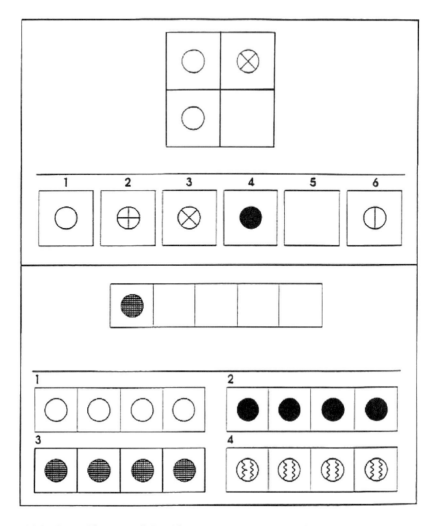

Figure 10.2 Four-Choice and Six-Choice Response Arrays. (From *The Test of Nonverbal Intelligence* (3rd ed., p. 38) by L. Brown, R. J. Sherbenou, & S. K. Johnsen, 1997. Reproduced by permission of PRO-ED, Austin, TX.)

Each test item poses a problem in a series of abstract figures in which one or more pieces of the figure are missing. The respondent is offered an array of four or six alternatives and asked, through pantomime, to select the one that solves the problem and completes the figure (see Figure 10.2). The particular reasoning strategies incorporated into TONI3 items are defined in Figure 10.3.

STANDARDIZATION AND PSYCHOMETRIC PROPERTIES

This section is concerned with the psychometric properties of TONI3, beginning with empirical item selection procedures and continuing with

- *Generalization and Classification*: These items require the identification of similarities. Given one example, the test subject must survey an array of other figures and symbols to find the one that is like it. These items may be as simple as matching a single characteristic or they may require a complex and sophisticated classification scheme.

- *Discrimination*: These items require the identification of differences, in particular the ability to review an array of stimuli and identify the figure or symbol that is different from the others presented.

- *Analogous Reasoning*: Analogies have an age-old format defined by the classic logical formula, "A is to B as C is to _____." The problem is to determine the relationship that exists between A and B and then to find something that bears a parallel, or analogous, relationship to C. In nonverbal tests the items usually depict figural or spatial analogies.

- *Seriation*: These items require the subject to perceive that the relationship among a series of stimuli is a sequential one and then to anticipate or complete the sequential relationship.

- *Induction*: Inductive reasoning involves the discovery of a governing principle that ties a set of figures together.

- *Deduction*: Deductive reasoning involves finding an example that illustrates a given governing principle or rule.

- *Detail Recognition*: The ability to focus on details is related to both speed and efficiency in solving problems. Salvia and Ysseldyke used the example of draw-a-person tests in which greater detail, such as facial features, hair, fingers, and toes, is equated with higher intelligence. Coding and symbol copying tasks also require detail recognition. But draw-a-person tests and symbol reproduction do not require problem solving. On measures of problem solving, detail recognition may be seen in the ability to identify parts that are mission or parts that are inferred but not actually represented. Increasing the number of details in a figure may also be used to increase the difficulty level of an item.

Figure 10.3 Reasoning Strategies Incorporated into TONI3 Items. (From *The Test of Nonverbal Intelligence* (3rd ed., p. 23) by L. Brown, R. J. Sherbenou, & S. K. Johnsen, 1997. Reproduced by permission of PRO-ED, Austin, TX.)

standardization and normative procedures. Support for the reliability and validity of the test's results is detailed, concluding with a discussion of test bias.

Item Selection

The original TONI was built from a pool of 307 items, winnowed by logical and empirical methods to 100 items and assigned to Form A or Form B.

The same methods were used to add 10 more difficult items in the 1990 TONI2 revision. By TONI3, we were concerned with three aspects of the existing test items: Was the original item order still appropriate more than a decade later, were the two forms still equivalent, and was there a way to make the test more efficient by reducing the number of items without compromising reliability and validity? To answer these questions, we returned to classic item analytic measures—item difficulty and item discrimination—and added differential item functioning analysis to detect items conferring advantage on the basis of extraneous variables such as gender or race.

A good test will discriminate subjects who possess more or less of the characteristic measured by the test, in this instance, intelligence. Discriminating power is observed in point-biserial correlations between individual item responses and total test scores. Item discrimination coefficients were calculated for every item in the TONI3 pool at every age interval. Items with coefficients below 0.35 were eliminated.

Item difficulty, the second criterion in classic item analysis, is simply the percentage of subjects who pass an item. The best discriminators are items passed by about 15–85% of people at a given age interval, with a mean 50/50 pass/fail rate. Item difficulty is also used to arrange test items in easy-to-difficult order and to assign items to different forms of a test to assure that the forms are of comparable difficulty.

Items that survived the classic item analytic techniques—those with item discrimination coefficients of 0.35 or greater and item difficulties of about 15–85%—were then subjected to differential item functioning analysis to study possible bias with regard to gender, race, ethnicity, disability, or principal language spoken. These measures included analyses of item curve characteristics, based upon hypothetical ability points, and correlation of delta values to estimate whole-test fairness.

The Standard Index of Bias is a nonparametric analysis of item curve characteristics which, according to Jensen (1980), is "one of the most direct and sensitive methods for detecting item bias" (p. 442). The theory is quite simple: If the characteristic being measured is intelligence, then a person who is more intelligent is more likely to pass any given item on TONI3 than a person who is less intelligent. Likewise, people of similar intelligence should have the same odds of passing any given item, and those odds should not be influenced by race, ethnicity, gender, socioeconomic status, or any personal qualities other than intelligence. The TONI3 normative group was dichotomized into five pairs, and differences between obtained and expected pass/fail frequencies within each subgroup were tested: (a) males and females, (b) African American subjects and subjects of all other races, (c) Hispanic subjects and subjects of all other ethnic groups, (d) gifted and talented subjects and all others, and (e) learning disabled subjects and all others. Very few of the hundreds of Standard Indices of Bias achieve significance at the 0.01 level, which means that the paired groups do not differ significantly from each other and "that the TONI3 items probably are not particularly biased with regard to gender, racial or ethnic group membership, or identified intellectual exceptionalities" (Brown et al., 1997, p. 94).

To look at whole-test bias, we analyzed Pearson product-moment correlations between Delta values (Δ) of seven dichotomous pairs in the normative sample: (a) males and females, (b) African American subjects and subjects of all other races, (c) Hispanic subjects and subjects of all other ethic groups, (d) gifted and talented subjects and all others, (e) learning disabled subjects and all others, (f) deaf subjects and all others, and (g) speakers of English as a second language and all others. The Pearson r values indicate "the degree of group resemblance in relative item difficulties when the rank order of the items is eliminated" (Jensen, 1980, p. 442). In other words, the higher the correlation, the lower the bias. For TONI3, all of the Δ-value correlations exceed 0.98, further evidence that bias has been largely controlled.

So, the 90 items of TONI3 were selected not only for their face validity as nonverbal problem-solving tasks, but also on the basis of empirical criteria: (a) strong point-biserial item-total correlations, (b) an acceptable pass/fail range, and (c) statistically insignificant indices of bias. Items were assigned to Form A and Form B and ordered from easy to difficult. Such rigorous attention to the selection and retention of items virtually ensured the reliability and validity of TONI3, the absence of bias in the test as a whole, and the equivalence of the two forms of the test even before norming was undertaken.

Standardization Procedures

TONI3 is both standardized and norm-referenced, meaning that it has specific administration procedures, objective scoring criteria, and an explicit frame of reference for interpreting its results, all of which reduce test error (Hammill, 1987). There would be a huge error variance, for instance, if each examiner gave the test differently (i.e., one examiner giving oral instructions and another pantomiming instructions), scored the test differently (i.e., one giving full credit for a human figure drawn with rudimentary stick limbs and another giving credit only for a drawing with shoulders, elbows, and knees), or interpreted the test scores differently (i.e., one calling a score of 10 normal and another calling 10 subnormal). Standardization ensures that, to the extent possible, each administration of the test is the same.

Normative Procedures

TONI3 has a large normative sample of 3,451 people ranging in age from 6-0 through 89-11 years and matched to the U.S. population (U.S. Bureau of the Census, 1990) on eight critical variables: region of the country, gender, race, ethnic group membership, urban/rural residence, disability status, family income and educational attainment of minor subjects' parents, and income and education of adult subjects (see Figure 10.4). The norm group is also stratified by age across geographic region, gender, race, and ethnicity, demonstrating not only that the normative sample is representative as a whole, but also that the stratified variables are dispersed throughout the sample's age range.

Demographic characteristics	School-age sample		Adult sample	
	Percentages of TONI-3 school-age sample	Percentages of U.S. school-age population	Percentages of TONI-3 adult sample	Percentages of U.S. adult population
Geographic region				
Northeast	20	18	20	20
Midwest	24	24	25	23
South	36	35	36	35
West	20	23	19	22
Gender				
Male	51	51	47	49
Female	49	49	53	51
Race				
White	79	79	82	84
Black	13	16	12	12
Other	8	5	6	4
Residence				
Urban	74	75	74	75
Rural	26	25	26	25
Ethnicity				
Native American	2	1	1	1
Hispanic	12	13	10	9
Asian	2	4	1	3
African American	13	15	12	11
Other	71	67	76	76
Disability status				
No disability	89	89	92	89
Learning disability	6	5	3	5
Speech–language disorder	1	3	2	3
Mental retardation	1	2	1	2
Other disability	3	1	2	1
Family income of parents of school-age subjects				
Under $15,000	17	14	NA	NA
$15,000–24,999	18	14	NA	NA
$25,000–34,999	18	14	NA	NA
$35,000–49,999	21	19	NA	NA
$50,000–74,999	17	20	NA	NA
$75,000 and over	9	19	NA	NA
Family income of adult subjects				
Under $15,000	NA	NA	19	21
$15,000–24,999	NA	NA	17	16
$25,000–34,999	NA	NA	17	14
$35,000–49,999	NA	NA	21	17
$50,000–74,999	NA	NA	17	17
$75,000 and over	NA	NA	9	15

Continued

Educational attainment of parents of school-age subjects				
Less than bachelor's degree	75	76	NA	NA
Bachelor's degree	19	16	NA	NA
Master's, professional, Doctoral degrees	6	8	NA	NA
Educational attainment of adult subjects				
Less than bachelor's degree	NA	NA	73	76
Bachelor's degree	NA	NA	20	16
Master's, professional, doctoral degrees	NA	NA	7	8

Age

6 ($N = 154$)	16 ($N = 170$)
7 ($N = 159$)	17 ($N = 180$)
8 ($N = 180$)	18 ($N = 132$)
9 ($N = 138$)	19–29 ($N = 277$)
10 ($N = 204$)	30–39 ($N = 252$)
11 ($N = 164$)	40–49 ($N = 330$)
12 ($N = 110$)	50–59 ($N = 202$)
13 ($N = 137$)	60–69 ($N = 127$)
14 ($N = 189$)	70–79 ($N = 91$)
15 ($N = 201$)	80–89 ($N = 54$)

Note: NA = Not applicable.

Figure 10.4 Demographic Characteristics of the TONI3 Normative Sample. (From *The Test of Nonverbal Intelligence* (3rd ed., pp. 73–76) by L. Brown, R. J. Sherbenou, & S. K. Johnsen, 1997. Reproduced by permission of PRO-ED, Austin, TX.)

Consumer's Guide Rating for Norms

In reading this or any other book, one should not rely upon authors' assurances that tests are well built: We behold our tests with a certain maternal affection and Lake Wobegon blindness. The psychometric properties of a test all can be evaluated objectively. Accepted psychometric standards for the normative characteristics, reliability, and validity of norm-referenced tests are detailed in *A Consumer's Guide to Tests in Print* (Hammill, Brown & Bryant, 1989, 1992), which operationalizes those objective standards to rate test scores as *Highly Recommended, Recommended,* or *Not Recommended* for use. An examiner must verify the psychometric adequacy of a norm-referenced test before using it, either by looking up the test's ratings in one of the two Consumer's Guide volumes, or by evaluating the test using the blank rating forms provided to rate tests that are not included.

Overall, TONI3 earns the highest Consumer's Guide rating, *Highly Recommended*, the only quick-score nonverbal measure of intelligence to meet the stringent psychometric criteria for this rating. The component ratings *Good* for norms, *Good* for reliability, and *Good* for validity are discussed throughout this chapter, beginning here with TONI3's normative characteristics.

The quality of a test's norms is critical: If the normative data are poor, the test's scores cannot be used with confidence. The Consumer's Guide evaluates four characteristics of a test's norms: the type of normative scores reported, the size and demographic characteristics of the normative sample, and the recency of the normative data. TONI3 earns a *Good* rating for its normative characteristics: It yields percentile ranks and deviation quotients, its norms are recent, and the normative sample, which matches the U.S. population on eight relevant demographic variables, has sufficient subjects at each age interval to calculate standard scores without interpolation and to ensure representativeness.

Reliability

Reliability is concerned with error variance in a test score. Error that is external to the test itself can be controlled in part by adhering to standardized administration and scoring guidelines, but even if a test were administered perfectly, there would still be error inherent in the test itself. Do the test's items perfectly reflect the construct being measured? Probably not. Is test performance perfectly stable over time? Again, that seems unlikely. Studies of a test's reliability estimate the variance that can be expected due to "content sampling error" (or the degree to which test items are not perfect measures of the construct in question) and to "time sampling error" (or the degree to which scores vary over time).

Content Sampling Error

Measures of content sampling error—sometimes referred to as a test's internal consistency—are concerned with the degree to which all test items measure the same thing. To a great extent, internal consistency was built into TONI3 by the manner in which items were selected in the first place, particularly the point-biserial item-to-total correlations, which helped to ensure both the validity and the internal consistency of TONI3. We also report coefficients alpha and immediate alternate forms correlations, both measures of content sampling error.

Coefficients alpha are intercorrelations of test items, a more sophisticated evolution of the venerable split-half technique. The coefficient alpha is, essentially, the average of all possible split-half correlations. Alphas are reported for Form A and Form B at each 1-year interval from 6 to 18 years and at each decade from 19 to 89 years. All of the 40 coefficients alpha for Form A and B exceed 0.89, and all but four are in the 0.90s, "supporting empirically the conclusion that TONI3 is a highly reliable, internally consistent test with minimal content sampling error, and that its results can be used with confidence to test individuals of all ages" (Brown et al., 1997, p. 80).

Because a test is reliable at all ages, it does not necessarily mean that the test is reliable with all of the various kinds of people to whom it may be administered. We therefore calculated coefficients alpha for seven subgroups within the normative sample: males, females, African

Americans, Hispanics, and subjects known to be deaf, learning disabled, or gifted/talented. These alphas are all in the 0.90s, indicating that the test is highly reliable when administered to diverse kinds of subjects.

Back-to-back administration of alternate forms provides another method to estimate internal consistency. If time elapses between administrations, time sampling error is also being measured, but the immediate alternate forms method eliminates this overlap. Form A and Form B were administered at the same time, alternating order of administration, and total scores for the entire norm group were correlated at 20 age intervals. The immediate alternate forms coefficients range from 0.74 to 0.95 ($\bar{x} = 0.84$ for all ages), further verification of the two forms' internal consistency.

Independent peer-reviewed research reports coefficients alpha, immediate alternate forms reliability, and Kuder–Richardson Formula #21 coefficients that corroborate the authors' own findings of TONI3's internal consistency reliability. These studies are cited fully in the test manual.

Time Sampling Error

Time sampling error usually is estimated through the delayed test–retest method, in which a period of time is permitted to elapse between two or more administrations of a test. Three studies of the 1-week test–retest reliability of Form A and Form B are reported. The coefficients range from 0.90 to 0.92 for Form A and from 0.89 to 0.94 for Form B; $\bar{x} = 0.91$ and 0.92, respectively), indicating that performance on TONI3 is relatively stable over time, with minimal time sampling error.

Error Due to Scorer Differences

TONI3 has explicit instructions for identifying correct answers, tabulating raw scores, and converting raw scores to standard scores, all of which reduce the probability of scorer error. Nevertheless, it is important to demonstrate the degree to which scorer differences affect test scores. We randomly selected from the normative group 25 test protocols for Form A and 25 for Form B to be rescored by two experienced scorers. The quotients reported by the two scorers were correlated, yielding coefficients of 0.99 for each of the two forms, evidence of nearly perfect interscorer reliability for TONI3. Virtually no error variance can be attributed to this factor.

Overall Test Reliability

Content sampling error, time sampling error, and scorer error were averaged using the z transformation method to estimate overall TONI3 reliability. The mean reliability for Form A with regard to content sampling error is 0.93, the mean with regard to time sampling error is 0.91, and the interscorer reliability is 0.99, yielding a mean overall reliability of 0.96. For Form B, the mean reliability with regard to content sampling error is 0.93, the mean with regard to time sampling error is 0.92, and the interscorer reliability is 0.99, also yielding a mean overall reliability of 0.96.

Reliability with Special Populations

Several studies establish the reliability of TONI3 with discrete populations, including those diagnosed with mental retardation, hearing loss, dyslexia, reading disability, and learning disabilities; those known to be gifted/talented; and English-fluent bilingual speakers, non-English speakers, or speakers of languages other than English with limited English-language proficiency.

Consumer's Guide Ratings for Reliability

Reliability is the degree to which a test is consistent in its measurements. It is typically studied through correlational procedures such as the split-half method, the Kuder–Richardson formulæ, coefficients alpha, interscorer correlations, the immediate and delayed test–retest and alternate forms methods. The Consumer's Guide criteria suggest minimum magnitudes of reliability coefficients, particularly when a test is used to make decisions about individuals, rather than simply to measure group performance, a use which demands less rigor and concludes "that 0.80 is the minimum acceptable level of reliability for highly standardized, norm referenced tests ... [but that] the more rigorous 0.90 is the preferred level" (Hammill et al., 1992, p. 11). It notes further that test authors should provide evidence of both internal consistency and stability reliability studied at individual age levels. TONI3's reliability rating is *Good*, with internal consistency and stability reliability coefficients generally above 0.90 at all ages studied.

Validity

Studies of validity are concerned with whether a test measures what it says it measures. By publication of TONI3, a true corpus of validity research had accumulated from the authors' own research and from independent sources. The discussion of these data is organized here into the traditional categories of content validity, criterion-related validity, and construct validity.

Content Validity

The content validity of TONI3 is established by logical and empirical methods. We began by perusing the literature of experimental psychology, which has been a rich area of theoretical research, and by examining earlier nonverbal tests of intelligence to create a large pool of potential test items conforming to the desired matrix format and abstract/figural problem-solving content. These logical methods were affirmed empirically by analysis of the difficulty and discriminating power of the items. The point-biserial discrimination coefficients reported in the manual are particularly powerful reflections of content validity, ensuring both that all test items are measuring the same construct and also that the items discriminate well between subjects who exhibit more or less skill at abstract/figural problem-solving. Empirical evidence of content validity is also found in the differential item functioning analyses, which show that the items are measuring the influence of intelligence upon test performance and not the influence of variables such as gender, race, ethnic group membership, or linguistic competence.

Criterion-Related Validity

If TONI3 is a valid nonverbal measure of mental ability, there should be robust correlations between TONI and other measures of intelligence and aptitude, especially nonverbal measures. We correlated TONI3 to the composite IQs of the *Wechsler Intelligence Scale for Children, Third Edition* (Wechsler, 1991); the composite IQs of the *Wechsler Adult Intelligence Scale—Revised* (Wechsler, 1981); and the Pictorial Nonverbal, Geometric Nonverbal, and Overall Nonverbal composite scores of the *Comprehensive Test of Nonverbal Intelligence* (Hammill, Pearson, & Wiederholt, 1996). The correlations are significant and large, particularly those associated with scores generated by subtests that resemble TONI3 in content and format (R_r: 0.51–0.76). In addition, all of the criterion-related validity work reported for TONI and TONI2 can be attributed to TONI3 because the "administration and response format is unchanged, and all TONI3 items were part of TONI and TONI2. ... Validity, after all, is not a one-time effort. It accrues over time and takes on particular importance as the body of research expands. The sheer volume of studies available is important because [different] researchers ... independently confirm each other's results" (Brown et al., 1997, p. 99). TONI and TONI2 were validated against scores from 19 criterion measures: the *Clinical Evaluation of Language Functions—Revised* (Semel, Wiig, & Secord, 1987), the *Comprehensive Test of Nonverbal Intelligence* (Hammill et al., 1996), the *Detroit Tests of Learning Ability—Adult* (Hammill & Bryant, 1991), the *Kaufman Assessment Battery for Children* (Kaufman & Kaufman, 1983), *The Leiter International Performance Scales* (Leiter, 1948), *The Otis–Lennon Mental Ability Test* (Otis & Lennon, 1970), *The Quick Test* (Ammons & Ammons, 1962), the *Scholastic Abilities Test for Adults* (Bryant, Patton, & Dunn, 1991), the *Screening Assessment for Gifted Elementary Students* (Johnsen & Corn, 1987), the *Slosson Intelligence Test for Children and Adults—Revised* (Slosson, 1985), the *Slosson Intelligence Test—Revised* (Slosson, 1991), the *Standard Progressive Matrices* (Raven, 1938), the *Test of Language Development—Intermediate, Second Edition* (Hammill & Newcomer, 1988a), the *Test of Language Development—Primary, Second Edition* (Hammill & Newcomer, 1988b), the *Vineland Adaptive Behavior Scales* (Sparrow, Balla, & Cicchetti, 1984), the *Wechsler Adult Intelligence Scale—Revised* (Wechsler, 1981), the *Wechsler Intelligence Scale for Children—Revised* (Wechsler, 1974), the *Wechsler Intelligence Scale for Children, Third Edition* (Wechsler, 1991), and the *Woodcock–Johnson Psycho-Educational Battery* (Woodcock, 1977). Readers are referred to the TONI3 manual for detailed descriptions of the subjects, research designs, and results.

Construct Validity

We formulated six hypotheses to study the construct validity of TONI3 and then designed analyses or cited independent research to reflect upon them. Full details are provided in the TONI3 manual. In summary, the hypotheses and findings related to content validity are:

1. *Hypothesis*: Because measured intelligence has a known developmental pattern, raw scores on TONI3 should be positively and significantly related to age, particularly in the first half of the test's age range. TONI3 correlates strongly and positively to age for school-aged subjects (TONI3-A = 0.63, B = 0.60) and raw scores show hypothesized developmental patterns, increasing sharply to about age 60 years, after which they decline slightly. This is true in an analysis of the entire normative sample and is confirmed by a separate ANOVA which, upon examination of the effects of age, gender, and socioeconomic status on test performance, finds a significant interaction effect only for age.

2. *Hypothesis*: Because intelligence and aptitude are strong predictors of academic success, TONI3 should correlate significantly and positively to measures of academic achievement, although those correlations should be more moderate than the correlations to measures of aptitude and overall intelligence. There are moderate, positive correlations (typically in the 0.40s and 0.50s) between TONI3 and the *Diagnostic Achievement Battery* (Newcomer & Curtis, 1984), the *Diagnostic Achievement Test for Adolescents* (Newcomer & Bryant, 1991), the *Diagnostic Achievement Test for Adolescents, Second Edition* (Newcomer & Bryant, 1993), the *Formal Reading Inventory* (Wiederholt, 1986), the *Iowa Tests of Basic Skills* (Lindquist & Heironymous, 1956; Heironymous & Hoover, 1985), the *Scholastic Abilities Test for Adults* (Bryant et al., 1991), the *SRA Achievement Series* (Naslund, Thorpe, & Lefevre, 1978), the *Stanford Achievement Tests* (Madden & Gardner, 1972), the *Test of Reading Comprehension—Revised* (Brown, Hammill, & Wiederholt, 1986), the *Test of Written Language—2* (Larsen & Hammill, 1988), the *Wide Range Achievement Test* (Jastak & Jastak, 1978), the *Wide Range Achievement Test, Revised* (Jastak & Wilkinson, 1984), and the *Woodcock–Johnson Psycho-Educational Battery* (Woodcock, 1977).

3. *Hypothesis*: Because it measures intelligent behavior, TONI3 should differentiate groups of subjects on the basis of known intellectual aptitude and ability. It is particularly important to show that TONI3 can differentiate subjects who vary in intelligence, because this is how the test is most likely to be used in practice. It is also important to demonstrate that TONI3 does not confer disadvantage or advantage on the basis of unrelated personal variables. Data show that TONI3 discriminates individuals with mental retardation, individuals classified as gifted, and individuals who have suffered closed head injuries from each other and from people of normal intelligence. There is also evidence that the test is free of bias with regard to gender, race, ethnicity, disability, and English-language competence. Normal test scores are reported for males and

females; for Hispanic and African American subjects; for subjects who have a primary language other than English; and for subjects who have hearing loss, dyslexia, learning disabilities, or attention deficits unrelated to intelligence.

4. *Hypothesis*: Because it measures similar constructs, TONI3 should predict performance on other measures of intelligence. In a multiple correlation and regression analysis, TONI2 scores were good predictors of the Full-Scale IQ of the *Wechsler Intelligence Scale for Children—Revised* (Wechsler, 1974), typically explaining a high percentage of the variance in the WISC-R scores.

5. *Hypothesis*: Because they measure global intelligence, TONI3 items should resolve into a single large factor. Promax rotation factor analysis produced three factors on each form of TONI3, accounting for 97% of test variance, with 60% of the variance loaded on a single factor, evidence of a strong *g* factor.

6. *Hypothesis*: Because they measure the same trait, TONI3 items should correlate strongly and positively to the total test score. Point-biserial item-to-total coefficients are all strong and positive.

Consumer's Guide Rating for Validity

TONI3's validity rating is *Good*, the Consumer's Guide criteria (Hammill et al., 1992), which work on the more-is-better principle: Validity is not established by a single piece of data, or even by a single type of data, but is inferred from a diverse body of accumulated evidence. A test score is rated *Acceptable* if there are "at least three different types of well-designed validity research yielding significant, hypothesized results" (p. 14); the *Good* rating is reserved for tests reporting five or more different types of empirical research. TONI3's validity is supported by multiple studies in eight of the research categories defined by the Consumer's Guide criteria.

Measures of Test Bias

Measures of bias were employed at the earliest stages of test development. TONI3 items were retained or rejected, in part, on the basis of their item curve characteristics, and whole-test fairness was subsequently confirmed by (Delta) Δ-value correlations during the norming of the test. Very few of the hundreds of Standard Indices of Bias, a nonparametric analysis of item curve characteristics, were significant, an indication of little or no bias with regard to gender, race, ethnicity, or language spoken; and all of the Δ-value correlations exceeded 0.98, confirming fairness of the total test score with regard to gender, race, ethnicity, hearing loss, and primary language spoken. In an independent study to determine the influence of personal variables on the test performance of elementary and secondary students, there were no significant interaction effects for gender or socioeconomic status, another indication of low bias.

In each TONI manual we cite all known independent reliability, the authors and validity research at the time of publication, including complete reference citations and descriptions of the research designs and results. Readers of this chapter are also referred to the following independent research published or discovered after TONI3: Barrett (2000); Coleman, Scribner, Johnsen, and Evans (1993); Frederick, Sarfaty, Johnston, and Powell (1994); Gonzalez (1995); Kamhi, Minor, and Mauer (1990); Kern, Cauller, and Dodd (in press); Lassiter and Bardos (1992); Lawrence (1993); Mackinson (1996); Mackinson, Leigh, Blennerhassett, and Anthony (1997); Schenck (2000); Valliant, Gauthier, Pottier, and Kosmyna (2000); Whorton and Morgan (1990); and Wu-Tien, Chung-chien, Jyh-fen, Hsin-tai, and Ching-chih (1995).

ADMINISTRATION AND SCORING

TONI3 is a highly standardized test, with well-defined protocols for administration and scoring. There are two equivalent forms of the test to accommodate situations in which multiple measures are needed, such as determining the effectiveness of a particular program or intervention or evaluating the progress of a student, patient, or client. In this section, we describe examiner and subject qualifications, the test's administration procedures, and the scoring procedures.

Examiner and Subject Qualifications

TONI3 can be administered by a wide range of qualified professionals, including psychologists, psychological associates, educational diagnosticians, teachers, rehabilitation specialists, and speech and language therapists, who have formal academic training and professional experience that make them competent to (a) review and evaluate the psychometric adequacy and utility of norm-referenced tests; (b) avoid tests that are not psychometrically sound or for which documentary information is incomplete or unacceptable; (c) choose a test that is appropriate for the intended purpose and for the person to be tested; (d) know the limitations and advantages of the chosen test and how those advantages and disadvantages might influence test performance; (e) administer, score, and interpret the chosen test; (f) understand the scale used to report and interpret test scores to make recommendations or decisions; (g) communicate the results to the person who took the test, to parents or guardians, to other professionals, and to the lay public, as appropriate; and (h) recognize unethical, illegal, or inappropriate uses of this information. In addition, examiners should be knowledgeable about the relevant local, state, and national laws regulating assessment and should adhere to accepted standards of professional conduct.

The examiner should be intimately acquainted with TONI3, including its proper uses, its psychometric characteristics, and its administration and scoring guidelines. It is critical to master the technique of the pantomime administration, which is unique to TONI3, before giving the test. We recommend that before examiners use the test formally, they practice until administration is fluid and smooth, which usually requires at least three practice sessions. The examinee must also meet some conditions to ensure proper test use. Obviously, subjects should be within the age range of the normative sample (6–0 to 89–11 years). Beyond that, training items help identify subjects for whom the test is not recommended: those who do not understand the pantomimed instructions, who cannot make a meaningful gesture to indicate response choices, or who choose not to respond.

Administering TONI

TONI3 is administered individually, usually in no more than 10–15 min. Some general procedures pertain in any testing situation: ensuring that the test site is private, comfortable, well-lighted, and free of distractions; assembling test materials in advance; and establishing rapport with the person being tested. Even before testing begins, the examiner should inform the person to be tested—or parents or guardians, as appropriate—about the purpose of testing, how the results may affect them, how the results will be recorded and stored, and who will have access to them. There should be a reasonable opportunity for questions. Assessment professionals—whether testers, scorers, or interpreters of test data—must at all times protect the due process and privacy rights of the examinee, in the test situation itself and in the subsequent dissemination of test results, including the release of summary information.

The examiner begins by pantomiming instructions for the training items, which are not scored but are used to determine whether the subject understands and is able to respond meaningfully. Because TONI3 requires only a minimal motor response, an examiner may test a subject who responds using a light beam, an eyelid switch, or other technological or mechanical means. In this special circumstance, examiners should ensure that the equipment is in working order before testing begins, and also that they understand the subject's choices as expressed in the preferred response mode. The training items can be employed constructively for this purpose, as can a prior meeting with the person to be tested.

TONI3 is not a timed test, and although dawdling should not be encouraged, test subjects should have all the time they need to make a response. TONI3 employs a ceiling but no basal, and so testing begins with item 1 for all subjects. Responses are noted on the Answer and Record Form. The correct response for each item is printed inside a circle, so examiners know immediately if a response is correct or incorrect. Items are arranged in easy-to-difficult order, and testing is discontinued when the subject reaches the ceiling by giving three incorrect responses within five consecutive items. Older and more able subjects may proceed through all 45 items without reaching a ceiling.

Scoring TONI

TONI is easily scored. The examiner is not called upon to make qualitative judgments about the correctness of a particular response: There is only one right answer to each item. A correct response is scored "1," and an incorrect response is scored "0."

The examiner must identify the ceiling item, which is the last of three errors in five consecutive items. The total score is the number of correct responses below the ceiling item, or the number of correct responses to all 45 test items if no ceiling is reached. Scoring is straightforward with minimal opportunity for error. Simple addition errors and improper use of the ceiling are the chief sources of scorer error, so examiners are encouraged to double-check their arithmetic and to review the test protocol to see that they did not inadvertently test past the ceiling.

INTERPRETATION

Test interpretation is a nuanced activity requiring sound data, a good knowledge base, and an open and enquiring mind. The examiner must accumulate multiple measures that are appropriate and credible, not only test scores but also observational and historical data and information from interested parties such as family members and other professionals involved in diagnosis or intervention.

TONI3 was not designed to measure academic progress, and it would be inappropriate to use its results as a criterion for promotion from one grade to the next, but one can argue that diagnosis is also a high-stakes decision and that the multiple measures issue is equally important in that context. How much information is enough when a diagnosis is being made or an intervention planned? When, if ever, can a single test score stand alone as the criterion on which a decision is made? What other data should be collected? Ethical standards are maddeningly bland. The Joint Committee on Testing Practices (1998) in its *Code of Fair Testing Practices in Education* encourages evaluators to look into "potentially useful" sources of information beyond standardized test scores. With similar vagueness, the National Council on Measurement in Education (NCME) (1995) says only that "multiple sources and types" of information should be used. A joint statement of the American Federation of Teachers, the NCME, and the National Education Association (1990) encourages the use of "accumulated" information. The American Psychological Association (APA) (1992) refers to undefined "multiple sources" in its standards, but it has commissioned a task force that is working now to refine those standards (APA President's Task Force on Psychology in Education, in press). Readers may also consult the standards of the American Educational Research Association (AERA) (AERA, 1992; AERA, APA, & NCME, 1985) and the recommendations of the National Research Council (1993).

In all instances where TONI3 is used to make decisions about individuals, multiple means multiple in all aspects: multiple types of data from multiple sources at multiple points in time. Test scores, grades in school, work products, job performance, self-report data, observation by the examiner and other interested parties, and other data should be accumulated over a reasonable period of time for the purpose in question; diagnosis, for instance, might be more urgent than ongoing program evaluation. But no diagnosis can be made, and no intervention planned, on the basis of one piece of data that is a snapshot at a given moment. Additional insight can be gained from Campbell, Voelkl, and Donahue (1997); Elmore, Abelmann, and Fuhrman (1996); Huebert and Hauser (1998); Kohn (2000); Madaus (1985); and Resnick and Resnick (1992). To stay abreast of this rapidly evolving issue, readers are referred to a recent and thoughtful article by Linn (2001) concerning assessment and accountability.

It is important at this point to distinguish between the examiner and the interpreter. The person who interprets assessment data is not always the examiner who administers TONI3. It is not unusual for several evaluators to be involved in the process—a psychologist might give TONI3, a psychology associate might administer other instruments, a therapist might undertake behavioral assessment, and a job counselor might contribute more data, all of which are amassed and interpreted by yet another person. In ongoing or cumulative assessment, test results from previous years might be reinterpreted or compared with current test results, with different examiners at each time. That makes it critical for each examiner to record all relevant information at the time the test is administered: the purposes for which the test was given, any accommodations made in administration, conditions that were not standard or were limiting to the test subject, and other information necessary for proper and accurate interpretation of the results by a person who was not present to observe them. It is also important to include complete information about how the test was scored; the adequacy and appropriateness of the norms; the kinds of normative scores reported, including the standard errors of measurement; known limitations of the test; proper interpretations and also likely misuses and misinterpretations of scores; and technical characteristics that affect the scores.

Understanding Test Scores

Standard Scores

TONI3 yields two standard scores, deviation quotients and percentile ranks. Deviation quotients are particularly versatile, with a distribution familiar to professionals and to the public at large, having a mean of 100 and a standard deviation of 15. As interval data, quotients are intrinsically more useful even than percentile ranks, which are also standard scores but which are ordinal data and therefore cannot be acted upon statistically. Quotients can be subjected to arithmetic operations and statistical procedures, which makes them particularly functional in research, profile analysis, and comparative interpretation. Percentile ranks, while not as versatile as quotients, are easily understood, quite simply, as the percentage of scores in the normative sample that are higher or lower than the score in question. Average or statistically normal test performance is represented by a percentile rank of 50.

The Meaning of Standard Scores

A table is provided in the test manual to assist examiners in interpreting quotients and percentile ranks in terms of Very Superior, Superior, Above Average, Average, Below Average, Poor, and Very Poor test performance. High scores and low scores both deviate significantly from the norm, and both deserve diagnostic consideration.

> Significantly low scores are percentile ranks below 16 or quotients below 85. Scores of this low magnitude may be indicative of mental retardation, developmental disabilities, or other cognitive disorders. If they are confirmed by additional diagnostic or clinical data, scores in this low range indicate a need for intervention, such as treatment, therapy, observation, or special programming.
>
> Significantly high scores are percentile ranks above 84 or quotients above 115. If confirmed, scores this high may be indicative of intellectual giftedness. Individuals with scores in this high range may benefit from accelerated content or enriched educational opportunities in school and may show a particular aptitude for professional pursuits. (Brown et al., 1997, pp. 62–63)

Age-Equivalent Scores

Age equivalents are worthless scores. They are not meaningful, they have inadequate statistical and psychometric properties, and they permit, one might even say they encourage, misinterpretation by professionals and laity alike. They are opposed by the professional organization primarily associated with psychological testing standards (American Psychological Association, 1992) and by all reputable psychometrists and educational statisticians (i.e., Aiken, 1994, 1996; Anastasi & Urbina, 1997; Sattler, 1992; and Wechsler, 1958; among many others). Nevertheless, they are inexplicably required by many states' education rules, which may even prevent the use of state dollars to purchase tests that do not report age equivalents, regardless of the tests' superior psychometric properties. We yielded to this commercial demand and added a table to TONI3 to generate age-equivalent scores for school-age test subjects, but we provide no place on the permanent record of the testing session to record age equivalents, and we provide no guidelines for interpreting them, as they are, for all intents and purposes, uninterpretable and without meaning.

Accounting for Test Error

Even the most well-built, psychometrically sound tests contain error. Therefore, one cannot say that the obtained test score is the one, true, and inerrant score. A test score is an estimate of test performance at a given time and place, and the quality of that estimate is affected by a number of variables.

Obviously, the subjects themselves bring variables that affect their performance. The test itself also contains error, which is discussed in terms of test reliability. Standard error of measurement (*SEM*) is a statistical means of accounting for within-test error and should always be reported when standard scores are reported so that any subsequent user of the data can calculate the upper and lower limits of the true-score range. The *SEM* values reported for 20 age intervals for TONI3 were computed using the coefficients alpha for the test's normative sample.

Foreign-Language, Alternate-Normed, and Cross-Validated Versions of TONI

TONI has been published in several foreign countries, sometimes with a complete renorming, and sometimes with equivalency or cross-validation research. TONI's unique language-free, culture-reduced content is appropriate for subjects without regard to their countries of residence or the languages they speak, but the test's U.S. norms may or may not be appropriate in these other settings. At this time, there are two complete foreign-normed versions of TONI2, one published in Spain (Brown, Sherbenou, & Johnsen, 1995) and one published in the Republic of China (Wu-Tien et al., 1995). Normative data are reported purporting to be representative of these countries, and there is preliminary work to establish the reliability and validity of the two tests in the respective countries.

Barrett (2000) cross-validated and established the equivalency of TONI3 in Jamaica. There have also been efforts at partial renorming and cross-validation in Chile (TONI and TONI2; Prado, 1988; Prado, Gatica, & Rojas, 1993), in Mexico (TONI; Garcia, 1988), and in India (TONI; Parmar, 1988). In addition to renorming and cross-validation in foreign countries, there have been some efforts to renorm or cross-validate the test with special populations including children who are deaf and hard of hearing (TONI; Mackinson et al., 1997), children who are deaf (TONI2; Mackinson, 1996), and children diagnosed with autism or pervasive developmental disabilities (TONI2; Kern, Cauller, & Dodd, in press).

STRENGTHS AND WEAKNESSES

It is difficult to discuss the strengths and weaknesses of a test like TONI3 out of context. A virtue in one situation might be a failing in another. If an examiner wants a quick measure, TONI3 is the best choice; if one wants an multifaceted measure, there are products on the market that better suit such purposes. There are general issues, though, that apply to any norm-referenced test: Is the test well-built? Does it possess excellent psychometric properties? Is there a sound theoretical base? Are there comprehensive and comprehensible administration and scoring guidelines? Is there a clear, convenient way to make a permanent record of the results? Are the components well constructed, durable, and attractive? Is the cost reasonable? All of these questions can be answered positively for TONI3.

Armed with reviews of TONI and TONI2, we removed 20 items from the test, streamlining its administration and simultaneously improving its psychometric properties. We gathered all-new normative data, almost doubling the size of the normative sample and improving its demography. We continued to report the burgeoning body of reliability and validity data and, for the first time, studied bias with regard to gender and cultural, ethnic, and linguistic characteristics. We also made cosmetic changes, with crisper, more sharply resolved drawings in the Picture Book and a new look to the Answer and Record Forms, expanding them from sheets to booklet format with more space to record information concerning the test situation, extended interpretations, and recommendations. We continued our efforts to write a clear, detailed, and fully descriptive test manual.

It appears that we were successful in creating a good measure. In fact, the TONI3 earns the highest possible overall Consumer's Guide rating, *Highly Recommended* for use (see Hammill et al., 1992). Reviews of TONI3 praise its psychometrics, its packaging, the comprehensive citation of research references, the documentation of TONI's historical evolution, our frank recognition of the test's limitations as well as its many strengths, and the overall clarity of writing and accessibility of the examiner's manual (Atlas, in press; DeMauro, in press; National Outcomes Work Group, 2000; Pierangelo & Giuliani, 2001; Salvia & Ysseldyke, 1998). The primary suggestion for improvement is more of the same: Additional reliability and validity research is always warranted, although TONI3 is supported by "validity and reliability estimates that already place it ahead of most 'tests' on the market" (DeMauro, in press). DeMauro suggests that the ceiling criterion might credit guesses; however, given the manner in which the test was standardized and normed, we believe this is a problem only if examiners misapply the criterion or apply it ex post facto. He also wonders if the pantomimed instructions might be "unnecessarily awkward" for people who are gifted or have no handicapping conditions. Examiners must decide from case to case if the format interferes with optimal performance.

Spragins (1998) reviewed TONI3 for the Gallaudet Research Institute. She identified three "disadvantages": (a) that the items all assess problemsolving; (b) that the test does not measure a broad array of intellectual skills (both of which she notes are "only a disadvantage if the test is improperly used"); and (c) that the authors tout the advantages of specialized norms for disability groups but do not provide them, encouraging their development independently. She goes on to say that the disadvantages are outweighed by six advantages: (a) the use of training items; (b) the use of the same item presentation throughout the test; (c) the extensive cautions against overgeneralization of the test results; (d) the use of abstract/figural content in lieu of reading passages; (e) the untimed format; (f) the availability of two equivalent forms; and (g) the citation of 20 years of research on TONI, TONI2, and TONI3.

SUMMARY

The *Test of Nonverbal Intelligence, Third Edition,* is a highly standard-ized, norm-referenced measure of abstract reasoning and problem-solving that requires no reading, writing, speaking, or listening. Not only is it completely language-free, but it is also culture-reduced and largely motor-free, requiring only a point, nod, or meaningful gesture as a response. It is appropriate for use with people ranging in age from 6–0 through 89–11 years of age, and its language-free format makes TONI3 particularly well suited for people who do not understand spoken or written English, either for cultural reasons or due to trauma, disease, or disability. It is also an ideal measure for people who are known, or believed, to have dis-orders of cognition or language or significant motor deficits arising from such conditions as aphasia, dyslexia, speech and language disabilities, hearing loss, learning disabilities, attention deficit, mental retardation/ developmental disabilities, autism, elective mutism, cerebral palsy, stroke, head injury, or neurological trauma. Indeed, TONI3 is suitable for use with almost all populations other than people who are blind or visually impaired.

TONI3 is administered individually in about 10–15 min. It yields two kinds of standard scores, deviation quotients, and percentile ranks. There are two equivalent forms of TONI3, Form A and Form B, each containing 45 items presenting a novel abstract/figural problem and arranged in easy-to-difficult order. Multiple response choices are offered to solve or complete each problem.

Finally, TONI3 is a psychometrically superior test, and based on my analysis, the only quick-score nonverbal measure of intelligence in publi-cation today that meets the stringent criteria for the highly recommended Consumer's Guide rating (Hammill et al., 1992). It is normed on a large, demographically representative and stratified sample of 3,451 people. The examiner's manual cites and describes an extensive body of more than 20 years of research establishing the reliability and validity of the test's results. Empirical evidence is also offered to demonstrate that the test is relatively free of bias with regard to gender, race, ethnicity, and other relevant variables.

REFERENCES

Aiken, L. R. (1994). *Psychological testing and assessment* (8th ed.). Boston: Allyn & Bacon.

Aiken, L. R. (1996). *Assessment of intellectual functioning* (2nd ed.). New York: Plenum.

American Educational Research Association. (1992). Ethical standards of the American Educational Research Association. *Educational Researcher, 21*(7), 23–26.

American Educational Research Association, American Psychological Association, & National Council on Measurement in Education. (1985). *Standards for educational and psychological testing.* Washington, DC: American Educational Research Association.

American Federation of Teachers, National Council on Measurement in Education, & National Education Association. (1990). *Standards for teacher competence in educational assessment of students.* Washington, DC: National Council on Measurement in Education.

American Psychological Association. (1992). *Ethical principles of psychologists and code of conduct* (rev. ed.). Washington, DC: Author.

American Psychological Association President's Task Force on Psychology in Education. (in press). *Learner-centered psychological principles: Guidelines for school redesign and reform.* Washington, DC: Author.

Ammons, R. B., & Ammons, C. H. (1962). The Quick Test: Provisional manual. *Psychological Reports, 11,* 11–161.

Anastasi, A., & Urbina, S. (1997). *Psychological testing* (7th ed.). Upper Saddle River, NJ: Prentice-Hall.

Arthur, G. (1950). *The Arthur adaptation of the Leiter international performance scales.* Chicago: Stoelting Company, Psychological & Educational Tests Division.

Atlas, J. A. (in press). Review of the Test of Nonverbal Intelligence, Third Edition. In J. Impara & B. Plake (Eds.), *14th Mental measurements yearbook* (Accession Number 14072077). Lincoln: Buros Institute of Mental Measurements, University of Nebraska Press.

Barrett, P. (2000). *Cross-Validation of the Test of Nonverbal Intelligence—Third Edition (TONI-3) for Jamaican students.* Unpublished doctoral dissertation, Auburn University, Auburn, AL.

Binet, A. (1903). *L'études expérimentale de l'intelligence.* Paris: Schleicher.

Binet, A. (1910). *Les idées modernes sur les enfants.* Paris: Flammarion.

Binet, A. (1911). Nouvelles recherches sur la mésure du niveau intéllectuel chez les enfants d'école. *L'Année Psychologique, 17,* 145–210.

Binet, A., & Henri, V. (1895a). La mémoire des mots. *L'Année Psychologique, 1,* 1–23.

Binet, A., & Henri, V. (1895b). La mémoire des phrases. *L'Année Psychologique, 1,* 24–59.

Binet, A., & Henri, V. (1895c). La psychologie individuelle. *L'Année Psychologique, 2,* 411–465.

Binet, A., & Simon, T. (1905). Méthodes nouvelles pour le diagnostic du niveau intéllectuel des anormaux. *L'Année Psychologique, 11,* 191–244.

Binet, A., & Simon, T. (1908). Le dévelopment de l'intelligence chez les enfants. *L'Année Psychologique, 14,* 1–94.

Binet, A., & Simon, T. (1909). L'intelligence des imbéciles. *L'Année psychologique, 15,* 1–147.

Binet, A., & Simon, T. (1916). *The development of intelligence in children.* (E. S. Kit, Trans.) Baltimore: Williams & Wilkins. (Original work published 1905)

Brown, L., Sherbenou, R. J., & Johnsen, S. K. (1982). *Test of nonverbal intelligence.* Austin, TX: PRO-ED.

Brown, L., Sherbenou, R. J., & Johnsen, S. K. (1990). *Test of nonverbal intelligence* (2nd ed.). Austin, TX: PRO-ED.

Brown, L., Sherbenou, R. J., & Johnsen, S. K. (1995). *Test de inteligencia no verbal: Apreciación de la habilidad cognitiva sin influencia del lenguaje.* Madrid: TEA Ediciones, S. A.

Brown, L., Sherbenou, R. J., & Johnsen, S. K. (1997). *Test of nonverbal intelligence* (3rd ed.). Austin, TX: PRO-ED.

Brown, V. L., Hammill, D. D., & Wiederholt, J. L. (1986). *Test of reading comprehension—Revised.* Austin, TX: PRO-ED.

Bryant, B. R., Patton, J., & Dunn, C. (1991). *Scholastic abilities test for adults.* Austin, TX: PRO-ED.

Campbell, J. R., Voelkl, K. E., & Donahue, P. L. (1997). *NAEP 1996 trends in academic progress.* Washington, DC: National Center for Education Statistics.

Coleman, M., Scribner, A. P., Johnsen, S., & Evans, M. (1993). A comparison between the Wechsler Intelligence Scale for Adults—Revised and the Test of Nonverbal Intelligence—2 with Mexican American secondary students. *Journal of Psychoeducational Assessment, 11*(3), 250–258.

DeMauro, G. E. (in press). Review of the Test of Nonverbal Intelligence, Third Edition. In J. Impara & B. Plake (Eds.), *14th Mental measurements yearbook* (Accession Number 14072077). Lincoln: Buros Institute of Mental Measurements, University of Nebraska Press.

Elmore, R. F., Abelmann, C. H., & Fuhrman, S. H. (1996). The new accountability in state education reform: From process to performance. In H. F. Ladd (Ed.), *Holding schools accountable: Performance-based reform in education* (pp. 65–98). Washington, DC: The Brookings Institution.

Frederick, R., Sarfaty, S., Johnston, J., & Powell, J. (1994). Validation of a detector of response bias on a forced-choice test of nonverbal ability. *Neuropsychology, 8*, 118–125.

Garcia, O. A. (1988). *Investigation del Test No Verbal de Inteligencia (TONI) en la Ciudad de Chihuahua.* Unpublished thesis, La Universidad Autonoma de Chihuahua, Chihuahua, Mexico.

Gonzalez, V. (1995). A model of cognitive, cultural, and linguistic variables affecting bilingual Hispanic children's development of concepts and language. *Hispanic Journal of Behavioral Sciences, 16*(4), 396–421.

Gould, S. J. (1981). *The mismeasure of man.* New York: Norton.

Hammill, D. D. (1987). An overview of assessment practices. In D. D. Hammill (Ed.), *Assessing the abilities and instructional needs of students* (pp. 5–37). Austin, TX: PRO-ED.

Hammill, D. D. (1998). *Detroit tests of learning aptitude* (4th ed.). Austin, TX: PRO-ED.

Hammill, D. D., Brown, L., & Bryant, B. R. (1989). *A consumer's guide to tests in print.* Austin, TX: PRO-ED.

Hammill, D. D., Brown, L., & Bryant, B. R. (1992). *A consumer's guide to tests in print* (2nd ed.). Austin, TX: PRO-ED.

Hammill, D. D., & Bryant, B. R. (1991). *Detroit tests of learning ability—adult.* Austin, TX: PRO-ED.

Hammill, D. D., & Newcomer, P. L. (1988a). *Test of language development—intermediate, second edition.* Austin, TX: PRO-ED.

Hammill, D. D., & Newcomer, P. L. (1988b). *Test of language development—primary, second edition.* Austin, TX: PRO-ED.

Hammill, D. D., Pearson, N. A., & Wiederholt, J. L. (1996). *Comprehensive test of nonverbal intelligence.* Austin, TX: PRO-ED.

Heironymous, A. N., & Hoover, H. (1985). *Iowa tests of basic skills.* Chicago: Riverside.

Huebert, J. P., & Hauser, R. M. (Eds.). (1998). *High-stakes testing for tracking, promotion, and graduation.* Washington, DC: National Academy Press.

Jastak, J. F., & Jastak, S. R. (1978). *Wide range achievement test.* Wilmington, DE: Jastak Assessment Systems.

Jastak, J. F., & Wilkinson, G. S. (1984). *Wide range achievement test, revised.* Wilmington, DE: Jastak Assessment Systems.

Jensen, A. (1980). *Bias in mental testing.* New York: Free Press.

Johnsen, S. K., & Corn, A. L. (1987). *Screening assessment for gifted elementary students.* Austin, TX: PRO-ED.

Joint Committee on Testing Practices. (1998). *Code of fair testing practices in education.* Washington, DC: Author.

Kamhi, A., Minor, J., & Mauer, D. (1990). Content analysis and intratest performance profiles on the Columbia and the TONI. *Journal of Speech and Hearing Research, 33*(2), 375–379.

Kaufman, A. S., & Kaufman, N. L. (1983). *K-ABC: Kaufman Assessment Battery for Children.* Circle Pines, MN: American Guidance Service.

Kern, J., Cauller, L. J., & Dodd, M. (in press). Application of the Test of Nonverbal Intelligence (TONI-2) in children diagnosed with autism/PDD. *Journal of Developmental and Learning Disabilities.*

Kohn, A. (2000). *The case against standardized testing: Raising the scores, ruining the schools.* Portsmouth, NH: Heinemann.

Larsen, S. C., & Hammill, D. D. (1988). *Test of written language—2.* Austin, TX: PRO-ED.

Lassiter, K. S., & Bardos, A. N. (1992). A comparison of learning-disabled children's performance on the Test of Nonverbal Intelligence, K-ABC, and WISC-R. *Journal of Psychoeducational Assessment, 10*, 133–140.

Lawrence, S. (1993). Is anything missing? An analysis of governmental training programs in California for disadvantaged youth (Doctoral dissertation, Golden State University). *Dissertation abstracts international, 54/05-A.* (University Microfilms No. 93-16614)

Leiter, R. G. (1948). *The leiter international performance scales.* Chicago: Stoelting Company, Psychological & Educational Tests Division.

Levine, M. N. (1982). *The leiter international performance scales handbook.* Los Angeles: Western Psychological Services.

Lindquist, E. F., & Hieronymous, A. N. (1956). *Iowa tests of basic skills.* Boston: Houghton Mifflin.

Linn, R. L. (2001). Assessment and accountability. In *ER online, 29*(2) [On-line]. Retrieved from http://www.aera.net/pubs/er/arts/29-02/linn01.htm

Mackinson, J. (1996). *Study of validity of the TONI-2 with deaf children.* Unpublished doctoral dissertation, Gallaudet University, Washington, DC.

Mackinson, J. A., Leigh, I. W., Blennerhassett, L., & Anthony, S. (1997). Validity of the TONI-1 with deaf and hard of hearing children. *American annals of the deaf, 142*(4), 294–299.

Madaus, G. F. (1985). Public policy and the testing profession: You've never had it so good? *Educational measurement: Issues and practice, 4*(4), 5–11.

Madden, R., & Gardner, E. F. (1972). *Stanford achievement tests.* New York: Harcourt Brace Jovanovich.

Naslund, R. A., Thorpe, L. P., & Lefevre, D. W. (1978). *SRA achievement series.* Chicago: Science Research Associates.

National Outcomes Work Group. (2000). *Evaluating the national outcomes: Children.* Tucson: National Outcomes Work Group, University of Arizona.

National Research Council. (1993). *Measuring what counts.* Washington, DC: National Academy of Sciences Press.

Newcomer, P. L., & Bryant, B. R. (1991). *Diagnostic achievement test for adolescents.* Austin, TX: PRO-ED.

Newcomer, P. L., & Bryant, B. R. (1993). *Diagnostic achievement test for adolescents, second edition.* Austin, TX: PRO-ED.

Newcomer, P. L., & Curtis, D. (1984). *Diagnostic achievement battery.* Austin, TX: PRO-ED.

Otis, A. S., & Lennon, R. T. (1970). *The Otis–Lennon mental ability test.* New York: Harcourt Brace Jovanovich.

Parmar, R. S. (1988). *Cross-cultural validity of the test of nonverbal intelligence.* Unpublished doctoral dissertation, North Texas State University, Denton.

Pierangelo, R., & Giuliani, G. A. (2001). *Special educator's complete guide to 109 diagnostic tests.* Upper Saddle River NJ: Prentice-Hall.

Prado, S. A. (1988). *Developing a slide projection group administration procedure for the TONI.* Unpublished manuscript, Universidad Austral del Chile, Valdivia, Chile.

Prado, S. A., Gatica, M. A., & Rojas, C. C. (1993). Instrumento de medición de actividad cognitiva libre del lenguaje: Test of Nonverbal Intelligence (TONI). *Revista Terapia Psicológica, 19,* 23–35.

Raven, J. C. (1938). *Standard Progressive Matrices: A perceptual test of intelligence.* London: Lewis.

Raven, J. C. (1947). *Coloured progressive matrices.* London: Lewis.

Raven, J. C. (1960). *Guide to standard progressive matrices.* London: Lewis.

Raven, J. C. (1962). *Advanced progressive matrices.* London: Lewis.

Raven, J. C. (1977). *The Raven progressive matrices.* San Antonio, TX: The Psychological Corporation.

Raven, J. C. (1986). *A compendium of North American normative and validity studies.* San Antonio, TX: The Psychological Corporation.

Resnick, L. B., & Resnick, D. P. (1992). Assessing the thinking curriculum: New tools for educational reform. In B. G. Gifford & M. C. O'Conner (Eds.), *Changing assessments: Alternative views of aptitude, achievement and instruction* (pp. 37–75). Boston: Kluwer Academic.

Salvia, J., & Ysseldyke, J. E. (1998). *Assessment* (7th ed.). Boston: Houghton Mifflin.

Sattler, J. M. (1982). *Assessment of children's intelligence and special abilities* (2nd ed.). Boston: Allyn & Bacon.

Sattler, J. M. (1992). *Assessment of children* (Rev. & updated 3rd ed.). San Diego, CA: Author.

Schenck, J. (2000). Before the memory fades: Measuring long term memory in older adults. *Proceedings of the 2000 adult education research conference.* Vancouver: University of British Columbia.

Semel, E., Wiig, E. H., & Secord, W. (1987). *Clinical evaluation of language functions—revised.* San Antonio, TX: The Psychological Corporation.

Slosson, R. L. (1985). *Slosson intelligence test for children and adults—revised.* East Aurora, NY: Slosson Educational.

Slosson, R. L. (revised by C. L. Nicholson & T. H. Hibpsham). (1991). *Slosson intelligence test—revised.* East Aurora, NY: Slosson Educational.

Sparrow, S. S., Balla, D. A., & Cicchetti, D. V. (1984). *Vineland adaptive behavior scales.* Circle Pines, MN: American Guidance Service.

Spragins, A. B. (1998). *Reviews of four types of assessment instruments used with deaf and hard of hearing students, 1998 update.* Washington, DC: Gallaudet Research Institute, Gallaudet University.

Tuddenham, R. D. (1962). The nature and measurement of intelligence. In L. J. Postman (Ed.), *Psychology in the making* (pp. 469–525). New York: Alfred A. Knopf Books.

U. S. Bureau of the Census. (1980). *Statistical abstract of the United States: 1980* (101st ed.). Washington, DC: U. S. Department of Commerce, Bureau of the Census.

U. S. Bureau of the Census. (1985). *Statistical abstract of the United States: 1985* (105th ed.). Washington, DC: U. S. Department of Commerce, Bureau of the Census.

U. S. Bureau of the Census. (1990). *Statistical abstract of the United States: 1990* (110th ed.). Washington, DC: U. S. Department of Commerce, Bureau of the Census.

Valliant, P. M., Gauthier, T., Pottier, D., & Kosmyna, R. (2000). Moral reasoning, interpersonal skills, and cognition of rapists, child molesters, and incest offenders. *Psychological Reports, 86,* 67–75.

Wechsler, D. (1958). *The measurement and appraisal of adult intelligence* (4th ed.). Baltimore: Williams & Wilkins.

Wechsler, D. (1974). *Wechsler intelligence scale for children—revised.* San Antonio, TX: The Psychological Corporation.

Wechsler, D. (1981). *Wechsler adult intelligence scale—revised.* San Antonio, TX: The Psychological Corporation.

Wechsler, D. (1991). *Wechsler intelligence scale for children, third edition.* San Antonio, TX: The Psychological Corporation.

Whorton, J. E., & Morgan, R. L. (1990). Comparison of the Test of Nonverbal Intelligence and Wechsler Intelligence Scale for Children—Revised in rural native American and white children. *Perceptual and Motor Skills, 70,* 12–14.

Wiederholt, J. L. (1986). *Formal reading inventory.* Austin, TX: PRO-ED.

Woodcock, R. W. (1977). *Woodcock–Johnson psycho-educational battery.* Allen, TX: DLM/ Teaching Resources.

Wu-Tien, W., Chung-chien, T., Jyh-fen, H. J. W., Hsin-tai, L., & Ching-chih, K. (1995). *The Chinese version of the Test of Nonverbal Intelligence (TONI-2) and its related studies.* Taipei: Taiwan Normal University.

11

Raven Progressive Matrices

John and Jean Raven

The *Raven Progressive Matrices* (RPM) tests measure "general cognitive ability" or, better, eductive, or "meaning making," ability (Raven, Raven, & Court, 1998a, 2000). The term "eductive" comes from the Latin root *educere*, which means, "to draw out." The basic version of the test, known as the *Standard Progressive Matrices* (or SPM), consists of five sets of items of the kind shown in Figures 11.1 and 11.2. Within each set, the items become progressively more difficult. At the beginning of each set, the items, although easy again, follow a different logic. The sets in turn become progressively more difficult. The five sets offer those taking the test five opportunities to become familiar with the method of thought required to solve the problems. In addition to the Standard series, there is the *Coloured Progressive Matrices* (CPM), which is designed to spread the scores of children and less able adults and the *Advanced Progressive Matrices* (APM), developed to spread the scores of the top 20% of the population.

TEST MODEL AND PHILOSOPHY

J. C. Raven developed the SPM because he was working with a geneticist, Lionel Penrose, on a study explaining the genetic and the environmental origins of mental deficiency (Penrose, 1938). This meant that adults as well as children had to be tested—and they had to be tested in homes, schools, and workplaces where there was often interfering noise and willing "helpers." Raven found full-length "intelligence" tests cumbersome to administer and the results impossible to interpret because scores

John and Jean Raven, 30 Great King Street, Edinburgh EH3 6QH, Scotland, United Kingdom.

Handbook of Nonverbal Assessment, edited by R. Steve McCallum. Kluwer Academic/ Plenum Publishers, 2003.

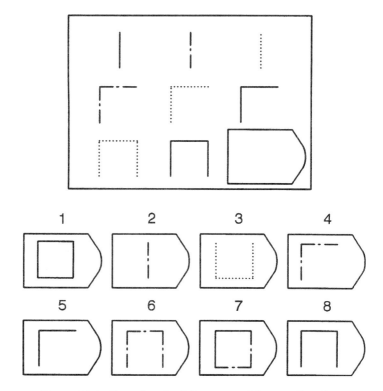

Figure 11.1 Easy Standard Progressive Matrices Test Item.

on many different abilities were composited into total scores, and the individual subscale scores were too unreliable to use. He therefore set about developing tests that would be easy to administer, theoretically based, and directly interpretable without the need to perform complex calculations to arrive at scores on latent, or underlying, "factors" or variables.

Raven was a student of Spearman's, and Spearman's formulations of intelligence influenced him. It is well known that Spearman (1927a, 1927b) was the first to notice that measures of what had previously been thought of as separate abilities tended to correlate relatively highly and to suggest that the resulting pattern of intercorrelations could be largely explained by positing a single underlying factor of general cognitive ability or *g*.

It is less well known that Spearman thought of *g* as being made up of two very different abilities which normally work closely together, one he termed eductive ability—meaning making ability—and the other reproductive ability—the ability to reproduce explicit information and learned skills. He did not claim that these were separate factors. Rather, he argued that they were analytically distinguishable components of *g*. Raven developed his RPM tests as measures of eductive ability and his Mill Hill Vocabulary (MHV) tests as measures of reproductive ability. (Raven, Raven, & Court, 1998d, 2000). These abilities are often, inappropriately, reffered to as "fluid" and "crystallized" intelligence.

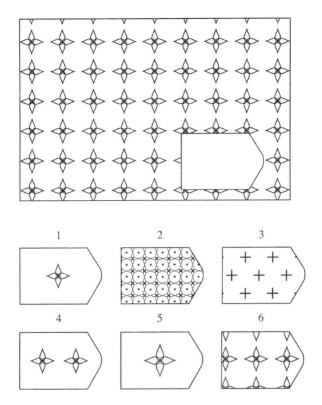

Figure 11.2   More Difficult Standard Progressive Matrices Type Test Item.

STANDARDIZATION AND PSYCHOMETRIC PROPERTIES

Standardization

Original normative data for Britain for the SPM were assembled by J. C. Raven and his colleagues immediately before and during World War II. The way in which the samples were combined is described in Raven (2000c). As also indicated in that article, sporadic (but, as it later turned out, inadequate) checks on the continuing appropriateness of these norms and their relevance to the United States were made by a number of researchers until the mid 1970s. Since then, many researchers, working largely with the present authors, have assembled a vast pool of international, ethnic, and time series norms that enable users to set the scores of groups and individuals they have tested in a variety of contexts. Many of these norms are included in the main Sections of the Manual (Raven, 2000b; Raven, Raven, & Court, 1998a, b, c, d; Raven et al., 2000), and others are summarized in its Section 7: Research and References (Court & Raven, 1995).

Internal Consistency

The appropriate model for assessing the internal consistency of the RPM and MHV is Item Response Theory. Given that the tests conform to what has come to be described as a three-parameter Rasch model, it does not make sense to intercorrelate the items to obtain the internal consistency of the tests. Because the items of the RPM both satisfy the requirements of IRT and are arranged in order of difficulty (at least within its five sets), one would anticipate high split-half reliabilities, and this is indeed the case: The majority of the coefficients reported in the literature exceed 0.90, having a modal value of 0.91 (Court & Raven, 1995; Raven et al., 2000).

Test–Retest Reliability

Reports of retest reliability are contained in over 120 articles, summarized in Court and Raven (1995). These studies differ widely in methodology, the populations studied (some being, for example, Native Americans or Africans and others psychiatric patients), and the intervals between the initial testing and retest. The retest intervals range from 1 week to 3 years. As would be expected, the test–retest correlations vary markedly with all these conditions. It would be misleading to report any single value. A textual summary of the main studies is presented by Raven et al. (2000) and concludes that well-conducted studies point to adequate retest reliabilities (i.e., 0.85 and upward) for intervals up to a year.

Validity

Establishing the validity of a test is somewhat difficult: How does one validate a test claiming to measure an ability—like eductive ability—when: (a) those concerned are only likely to display the ability when they are undertaking activities they care about; (b) the effective performance of such tasks as would lead them to display the ability also requires them to engage in a number of other activities which they may lack the ability or interest to perform; (c) the important contributions they are making to their school, group or organization are likely to be overlooked by their colleagues and their managers; (d) their behavior is constrained by organizational arrangements, the expectations which others have of them, and by what others do; and (e) the effects of their actions—and especially indices of their "profitability"—are heavily dependent on what others do?

In many real-world settings not only do many important contributions go unrecognized, but people are often not doing what others think they are doing and have recruited them to do. Thus, according to Hogan (1990, 1991), some 50% of American managers apply their minds to achieving personal goals—often personal advancement—which are to the detriment of their subordinates and their organizations. The problem is not that they lack intellectual ability, but the end to which they apply it. To find out what they are doing and how effectively they "think" about how to achieve it, one would have to interview them—and in a very nonjudgmental manner at that.

It follows that, as McClelland (1973) and Messick (1989, 1995) have been almost alone in emphasizing, the only way to validate tests is by undertaking a careful conceptual analysis of the nature of the qualities being assessed by the test, the psychological nature of the various criteria available for judging performance, the range of personal qualities required for "success" in terms of each of these criteria, and the factors that are likely to moderate the strength of observed relationships between test scores and criterion measures, and by making a conceptual analysis of a network of empirical relationships. In short, the way forward is to be found through complex, almost ethnographic, studies and not via the multivariate analyses that have such high prestige in psychology.

These problems are no less severe in school environments. Despite the fact that the word "education" comes from the same Latin root as "eductive" ability—and thus implies activities that "draw out the talents of" the students—most of what is passed off as education in schools and colleges involves "putting in" rather than drawing out. As Goodlad (1983) and Raven (1994) have observed, the activities that dominate schools do not merit description as "academic," "intellectual," or "educational."

In fact, to draw out the talents of the students, teachers would need concepts to think about multiple-talents—about diversity—and tools to help them design endless individualized developmental programs, monitor students' idiosyncratic development, take remedial action when necessary, and give the students credit for the particular talents they had developed. The concepts and tools required to do this are precisely those that psychologists have so conspicuously failed to develop to enable parents, teachers, managers, and other members of society to think about and assess aspects of competence outside the domain in which the RPM may be said to "work."

We have seen that people are only likely to display their eductive ability—their ability to make meaning out of confusion—while they are working at tasks they care about. A selection of activities that people may be strongly motivated to undertake is listed across the top of Figure 11.3 in our Model of Competence.[1] Down the side are listed a series of components of competence which, if the individual displays them, will help to ensure that the chosen activity is carried out effectively. These components of competence are cumulative and substitutable. The more of them an individual deploys to carry out any given activity, the more likely they are to carry out that activity effectively.

Three things follow directly from the theoretical model depicted in Figure 11.3:

1. Effective behavior is dependent on engaging in a range of other activities besides making meaning out of the situation in which one finds oneself.
2. It is only reasonable to seek to assess someone's meaning-making ability (and their ability to engage in the other activities that make for effective behavior) after one has identified the kinds of activity they are strongly motivated to undertake.

---

[1]The way in which this model has been built up from the work of David McClelland and his colleagues is described in Raven and Stephenson (2001).

Examples of components of effective behavior	Examples of Potentially Valued Styles of Behavior										
	Achievement					Affiliation				Power	
	Doing things which have not been done before.	Inventing things.	Doing things more efficiently than they have been done before.	Developing new formal scientific theories.	Providing support and facilitation for someone concerned with achievement.	Establishing warm, convivial relationships with others.	Ensuring that a group works together without conflict.	Establishing effective group discussion procedures.	Ensuring that group members share their knowledge so that good decisions can be taken.	Articulating group goals and releasing the energies of others in pursuit of them.	Setting up domino-like chains of influence to get people to do as one wishes without having to contact them directly.

Cognitive

Thinking (by opening one's mind to experience, dreaming, and using other subconscious process) about what is to be achieved and how it is to be achieved.

Anticipating obstacles to achievement and taking steps to avoid them.

Analyzing the effects of one's actions to discover what they have to tell one about the nature of the situation one is dealing with.

Making one's value conflicts explicit and trying to resolve them.

Consequence anticipated:
Personal: e.g. "I know there will be difficulties, but I know from my previous experience that I can find ways round them."
Personal normative beliefs: e.g. "I would have to be more devious and manipulative than I would like to be to do that."
Social normative beliefs: e.g. "My friends would approve if I did that": "It would not be appropriate for someone in my position to do that."

Affective

Turning one's emotions into the task:
Admitting and harnessing feelings of delight and frustration: using the unpleasantness of tasks one needs to complete as an incentive to get on with them rather than as an excuse to avoid them.

Anticipating the delights of success and the misery of failure.

Using one's feelings to initiate action, monitor its effects, and change one's behavior.

Conative

Putting in extra effort to reduce the likelihood of failure.

Persisting over a long period, alternatively striving and relaxing.

Habits and experience

Confidence, based on experience, that one can adventure into the unknown and overcome difficulties, (This involves knowledge that one will be able to do it plus a stockpile of relevant habits).

A range of appropriate routineised, but flexibly contingent behaviours, each triggered by cues which one may not be able to articulate and which may be imperceptible to others.

Experience of the satisfactions which have come from having accomplished similar tasks in the past.

Figure 11.3   A Model of Competence.

3.   To find out whether someone can be said to be behaving effectively, one first has to find out what it is that they are actually trying to do. (Making a statement that they do not undertake an activity one has set them—and especially developing this into a general statement about their incompetence—whilst not recording what they are good at is highly unethical—see Raven, 1991, 1997, 2000a.)

Raven, Raven, and Court (1998c) have used this model as a basis on which to build discussions of "problem-solving ability" and "intelligence" more generally. One of the most important conclusions to emerge is that "intelligence" is to be understood as *an emergent property of a group or culture*—a group or culture that taps and utilizes people with all the concerns listed across the top of Figure 11.3 and who bring to bear all the components of competence listed down the side to carry out those tasks effectively.

Reverting to the implications of what has been said for individual assessment, we may note that people have too often been branded as "unable to think" simply because they do not "think" in a math class or while undertaking tasks set by others in an assessment center (or during a Piagetian experiment). Such people may be able to think very effectively (i.e., make their own observations, learn without instruction, and make good judgments) on a football field, or on the job. As Spearman (1926) observed, the question that should be asked is, therefore, frequently not "How intelligent is this person?" but "While undertaking which kinds of activity does this person display his or her intelligence?" Only after that can one meaningfully ask: "Which of the competencies required for intelligent behavior do they display in the course of these activities?"

Some Correlates of RPM Scores

We have now made two apparently contradictory claims. On the one hand, we have argued that something that may be described as "general cognitive ability" or, better, "eductive" ability "exists" and that it can be measured directly by using the RPM instead of having to be calculated by applying mathematical formulae to weight the subscale scores obtained on tests constructed on the basis of other theoretical standpoints. On the other hand, we have argued that the effective assessment of eductive ability and exploration of its correlates would require us to adopt a much more sophisticated theoretical framework (see Figure 11.3), indeed a paradigm shift in psychometrics.

So, what do the RPM measure? What use are they? Because of their theoretical basis, the simplicity of their administration, and the directness of their interpretation, the RPM have been adopted as the tests of choice in a wide range of theoretical studies. But, perhaps more importantly, because of the care taken in their construction and their nonverbal nature, the RPM tests have been widely utilized in applied settings. Vast pools of data have been accumulated in some of these settings, and even more have been generated to provide the reference norms that are needed. In the end, reanalysis of some of these pools of data (accumulated for nontheoretical purposes) has yielded important insights into the nature of the qualities being assessed and the factors that influence them.

Correlations with "Intelligence" Tests

Detailed reviews of the intercorrelations between the RPM and MHV tests and full-length "intelligence" tests are found in Court and Raven (1995) and Raven et al. (1998c, 2000). The correlations vary with age group studied and the range of abilities represented within it. For English-speaking children and adolescents, reliable correlations between the SPM and the Binet and Wechsler scales range from 0.54 to 0.86. Correlations with verbal intelligence and vocabulary tests tend to be slightly lower, generally falling below 0.70. When compared with the British studies, the intertest correlations obtained in cross-cultural research with non-English-speaking children and adolescents tend to be lower although generally moderate, ranging from about 0.30 to 0.68. Intertest correlations for adult respondents are similar in magnitude and pattern to those for children.

Correlations with School Performance

Correlations between the RPM and performance on achievement tests and scholastic aptitude tests are generally lower than those with "intelligence" tests, and even more variable, ranging from negligible to very high. When the external criterion is school grades or teacher estimates, correlations generally fall between 0.20 and 0.60. The correlations tend to be higher with measures involving math and science skills than with language and overall academic achievement. The correlations with so-called achievement tests are not exactly a cause for jubilation because these tests tend to demand reproductive rather than eductive ability. Indeed, if users wish to predict school success among English-speaking children, they would do better to use language-loaded tests like the MHV test (Raven et al., 1998a), which is a companion test to the RPM and can also be administered even more quickly.

The use of the APM as one of several alternative criteria in selecting students for gifted education programs tends to admit a very different type of student from those who do well in traditional "academic" achievement tests, particularly in conditions where students are not familiar with English. However, if the talents of such students are to be nurtured and recognized, it will be necessary first to diversify the educational process.

Correlations with Occupational Performance

The correlations between the RPM and measures of occupational performance are, like those with school achievement, reviewed by Raven et al. (1998c, 2000). They vary with the preselection of the group studied, the range of ability represented, and, especially, with the extent to which performance on the criterion task depends upon eductive ability while making little demand for other components of competence. The pattern of results closely parallels that which emerges from such meta-analyses of studies relating to general cognitive ability as those prepared by Jensen (1998) and Schmidt and Hunter (1998). Briefly, the RPM predict proficiency within most types of work. Modal correlations are about 0.30 in each case. Strikingly, however, as such authors as Eysenck (1953) and Jensen (1998) have shown in multiple regression studies, all other tests known to psychologists improve these figures hardly at all. Thus, as Eysenck pointed out, a simple administration of the RPM gives almost as much information as a full assessment. This predictive capability is particularly impressive, given the complexity of many occupations, especially

managerial positions, which require the ability to make sense of complicated organizational, cultural, political, and legal environments.

Correlations with Ethnicity and Socioeconomic Status

As will shortly be shown, the RPM works—measures the same thing—
in a wide range of cultures. Some authors, such as Irvine (1969) and
Silvey (1972), have argued that the test ceases to work among some tribal
groups. However, doubt has been thrown on even this claim by item
analyses of data from some 4,000 Peruvian mountain children, which
yielded the lowest RPM norms we have seen (Raven, Raven, & Court,
1998b). The test scaled normally. It has now become clear that many of
the differences in mean score between cultural groups—such as that
between French- and Flemish-speaking Belgian adults and Brazilian and
European children—have not been eroded by the huge increase in the
scores achieved by successive generations in the groups concerned over
time. It follows from these observations that the suspicion that ethnic and
cultural differences stem from "bias" in test construction is ill founded.

Neurological and Neuropsychological Correlates

Despite claims in the popular psychological and scientific press to the
effect that the neurological base of g in the brain has been localized, a
careful review of the literature relating to neuropsychological applications
of the RPM by Court, Drebing, and Hughes (in Raven, 2000b) concludes
that "various brain functions are involved, i.e. visual-perceptual abilities,
logical reasoning, and concept formation, integration of processes, etc. As
a result localization is difficult as a number of regions of the
cortex appear to be involved." Despite this, comparisons between RPM
scores and those obtained on other tests do appear to be helpful in the
localization of brain injury.

In addition, RPM/MHV discrepancies have been widely advocated as a
means of distinguishing senile dementia from normal aging (Crawford,
Deary, Starr, & Whalley, in press; Deltour, 1993). However, the differential
change in RPM and MHV scores with age may be, in reality, a reflection of
increases in performance from date of birth. Consequently, the tendency
to infer premorbid eductive ability from MHV current scores into question.
Despite a review of the relevant literature in the MHV Section of the
Manual (Raven, Raven, & Court, 1998d), serious questions remain
unresolved at the time of writing.

Evidence of Fairness

Among young people in the 1979 British standardization (see Raven,
1981), the correlations between the item difficulties established separately
for eight socioeconomic groups ranged from 0.97 to 0.99, with the low of
0.97 being a statistical artifact. In the U.S. standardization (Raven, 2000b),
the correlations between the item difficulties established separately for

different ethnic groups (Black, Anglo, Hispanic, Asian, and Navajo) ranged from 0.97 to 1.00. Jensen (1980) reported similar results for the CPM. According to Owen (1992), the test has the same psychometric properties among all ethnic groups in South Africa—that is, it scales in much the same way, has a similar reliability, correlates in almost the same way with other tests, and factor analysis of these correlations yields a similar factorial structure. The correlations between the item difficulties established separately in the United States, United Kingdom, Germany, New Zealand, and Chinese standardizations range from 0.98 to 1.00. The test is therefore extremely robust and works in the same way (measures the same thing) in a wide range of cultural, socioeconomic, and ethnic groups despite the (sometimes huge) variation in mean scores between these groups.

ADMINISTRATION AND SCORING

The Progressive Matrices Tests

Six different tests make up the suite of RPM tests. Three of them are available in both educational and occupational versions.

The first form of the Progressive Matrices to be developed was the Standard series (SPM). This was designed to cover the whole range of ability from low-scoring respondents and young children, through high-scoring adults, to the lower scores of old age. To spread the scores—and thereby facilitate analysis—at, respectively, the lower and upper ranges of ability, the CPM and the APM were developed. (The APM is in fact made up of two separate booklets: Set I and Set II, the former being a practice set.) Together, at the time of their development, these three tests met most needs.

By the late 1980s, the well-established mentioned cross-cultural increase in scores (Flynn, 1984, 1987; Raven, 2000) had meant that there was a marked ceiling effect among young adults on the SPM, while the APM was yielding an excellent distribution across the entire adult population. In addition, some users felt that the existing CPM and SPM had become too well known for the scores to be trusted. Accordingly, work was carried out to develop versions of the tests that would (a) parallel the existing tests, on both an item-by-item and total score basis (so that all the existing normative and research data would be applicable) and (b) restore to the SPM the discriminative power at the upper levels of ability that it had when it was first developed.

The decision about what to do about the increase in scores was not straightforward. While the SPM lacked discrimination among able young adults, it also offered excellent discrimination among less able older adults and young children. In the end, it was decided to publish both exactly parallel versions of the SPM (SPM-P) and CPM (CPM-P) and a version of the SPM, which, while retaining most of the easy items, restored its discriminative power among more able young adults (SPM Plus).

Sometimes, it is important to know a person's speed of accurate intellectual work, as distinct from their capacity for orderly thinking. As the items of the SPM are arranged in five sets, each of which begins with simple problems but which grow progressively more difficult, a person's speed of intellectual work cannot be measured from the number of problems solved in a fixed time. Use of the SPM with an overall time limit results in an uneven and invalid distribution of scores because some people devote a great deal of time attempting the later problems of, say, Set D, while others skip over them and greatly enhance their scores by correctly solving the easier items of Set E. This problem can be overcome by timing each set separately. Until recently, this was the normal way of administering the test in Australia. However, the procedure is cumbersome, and, as explained more fully below, the desired information can be obtained more easily using the Advanced Progressive Matrices.

The CPM, from which Sets C, D, and E of the Standard series have been omitted, but into which an additional set of 12 problems (Set Ab) has been interpolated between Sets A and B, is designed to assess with greater precision the intellectual processes of young children, mentally retarded persons, and the elderly. The colored backgrounds on which the problems are printed attract attention, make the test spontaneously interesting, and obviate the need for too much verbal instruction.

As has been explained, the parallel versions of the CPM and SPM were developed to foil respondents who have memorized the correct answers. To help to ensure this, the position of the correct answer among the options on each item differs from that in the Classic versions of the tests. This is also the case for SPM Plus. It is therefore essential to ensure that the answer sheets and/or scoring keys selected correspond to the test used.

The APM offers a means of: (a) inquiring into the nature of high-level eductive ability; (b) spreading the scores of the more able, which has become particularly important in the light of the increase in scores over the years; and (c) assessing the speed of accurate intellectual work. Set I consists of only 12 problems. It is generally used to establish a field of thought for respondents and provide them with training in the method of working. However, it can also be used, under timed or untimed conditions, to obtain a rapid index of eductive ability or efficiency. Set I is normally followed immediately by Set II, although respondents can be allowed to take the first set away several days before testing in order to practice. Set II consists of 36 problems, arranged in ascending order of difficulty. As a result, it is not necessary for everyone to attempt every problem before stopping. By imposing a time limit, Set II can therefore be used to assess "intellectual efficiency." Although this is generally closely related to capacity for orderly thinking, this is not always the case, and the two must not be confused with each other.

Despite the fact that the APM now yields an excellent discrimination across the entire adult ability range, it cannot be recommended unreservedly for general use. This is partly because the cyclical format of the SPM offers five successive opportunities for those taking the test to acquire a sense of what is required and develop an appropriate method of working. The SPM is therefore to be preferred if it is considered that some respondents would benefit from practice. Other advantages of the SPM are:

- Lower-scoring respondents encounter fewer problems that are too difficult for them and, as a result, have a more positive experience.
- There are more research data for the SPM, including separate norms for different subpopulations.
- As an untimed test, it is less stressful for respondents.

Specific Administration Scoring Guidelines

The administration of all forms of the RPM is extremely easy, the main requirement being to ensure that those taking the test understand what they are to do. This is typically achieved by demonstrating the first five items as often as is necessary and allowing respondents to work at their own speed. Young children and those unable to cope with the answer sheets usually need to be tested individually. Eight- to 9-year-olds usually can be tested in small groups. Older children and adults can be tested in larger groups, but it remains desirable to have one administrative supervisor to about every 15 persons to be tested. When group testing is involved, respondents are normally asked to hand in their answer sheets when they have finished. These are then checked for such things as the answers having been displaced by one space from where they should have been, after which respondents normally leave the room individually.

Most respondents complete the SPM in less than 30 minutes. If it is necessary to set a time limit for Set II of the APM, this is normally set at 40 min. Note, however, that this seriously disadvantages those who work more slowly and carefully. Detailed instructions for administering the tests are available in the Manual.

Scoring the RPM is now by "easy-score" answer sheets. These are printed on two-part NCR paper and scored by separating the sheets to reveal (and count) the correctly marked answers.

INTERPRETATION

Percentile equivalents of the raw scores can be read off from a wide selection of reference data covering a range of age, nationality, ethnic group, and occupational groups. There is a special supplement—*Research Supplement No. 3* (year 2000 edition; Raven, 2000b)—devoted mainly to providing norms for a range of North American school districts. Users should select the norms they use carefully in relation to the uses to which the data are to be put. Indeed, depending on the objectives of the assessment, it may be desirable to adopt nonstandard procedures of administration.

Because of the criteria of eligibility for Special Education laid down in U.S. Federal statutes, detailed US norms are included in the Manual. However, their use is discouraged on the grounds that they incline users to attach importance to small differences in score—and too much importance to "intelligence" in general. Neither the discriminative power of the tests currently available, their reliability, nor the explanatory power of the constructs they are designed to assess justifies such usage. Worse, placing undue reliance on such scores undermines the quest for more comprehensive assessments and has the effect of absolving teachers, managers, and psychologists from responsibility for seeking ways of identifying and nurturing other talents.

The use of deviation IQs for reporting the results is discouraged for much the same reasons: In the first place, score distributions are typically bimodal or skewed rather than Gaussian. The result is that the same person, tested on the same test and compared with the same standardization group, can obtain wildly different "IQs" (having dramatically different legal consequences) depending purely on the assumptions made by the statistician who performed the calculations. Furthermore, as we have seen, the concept of "Intelligence" typically brings with it a range of associations that are devoid of scientific justification.

STRENGTHS AND WEAKNESSES

The RPM tests are perhaps the most researched of the measures of cognitive ability that have items presented in a nonverbal format. Their construct validity is, on the face of it, so well established that they are widely used as the criterion against which to validate other tests. Nevertheless, the tendency to describe them as "intelligence" tests has made for endless confusion. The tests are easy to administer, and there are a variety of tests and norms available for different purposes as well as tables to facilitate conversion of scores from one test to another. However, normative data for U.S. examinees are not as well developed as some critics would like (e.g., see Sattler, 2001).

The intergenerational increase in scores that has occurred on all measures of eductive ability has resulted in a ceiling effect among older adolescents and young adults on the Classic SPM. This has sometimes resulted in inappropriate conclusions being drawn in both research and individual assessment. Although the test's discriminative power at this level has been restored with the publication of the SPM Plus, the pool of normative data that are available for the new test is nothing like as extensive as that for the Classic SPM, and it is, in fact, important that the pool of normative data for all the tests be extended.

The chief limitations of the suite of Raven tests stem from psychologists' collective failure to operationalize the McClelland/Raven framework for thinking about competence and thus address Spearman's (1926) observation that "Every normal man, woman, and child is a genius at something ... it remains to discover at what." When the only tool one has is a hammer, all problems are treated as if they were nails. In the absence of an appropriate framework for thinking about and describing multiple talents, it is not only impossible to contextualize RPM scores appropriately, but it is also impossible to resist the pressures that result in measures of eductive and reproductive ability—and especially the latter—being used in ways that are altogether inappropriate.

SUMMARY

This chapter describes a suite of tests, primarily those collectively referred to as Raven's Progressive Matrices. They have been used extensively as operationalizations of intelligence for good or ill. The tests are generally considered to be good measures of eductive or fluid intelligence. The psychometric properties are good, and the tests are easily administered and scored. Raven's tests were developed over a period of years beginning in the 1930s, and a tremendous database has become available. Currently, the tests are used extensively over the world.

REFERENCES

Court, J. H., & Raven, J. (1995). *Manual for Raven's Progressive Matrices and Vocabulary Scales. Section 7: Research and references: Summaries of normative, reliability, and validity studies and references to all sections.* Oxford: Oxford University Press; San Antonio, TX: The Psychological Corporation.

Crawford, J. R., Deary, I. J., Starr, J., & Whalley, L. J. (in press). The NART as an index or prior intellectual functioning: A retrospective validity study covering a 66 year interval. *Psychological Medicine.*

Deltour, J. J. (1993). *Echelle de Vocabulaire Mill Hill de J. C. Raven: adaptation française et normes comparées du mill hill et du standard progressive matrices (PM38). Manuel et annexes.* Braine le Château, Belgium: Editions L'Application des Techniques Modernes SPRL.

Eysenck, H. J. (1953). *Uses and abuses of psychology.* Harmondsworth, UK: Penguin.

Flynn, J. R. (1984). The mean IQ of Americans: Massive gains 1932 to 1978. *Psychological Bulletin, 95,* 29–51.

Flynn, J. R. (1987). Massive IQ gains in 14 nations: What IQ tests really measure. *Psychological Bulletin, 101, 171–191.*

Goodlad, J. (1983). *A place called school.* New York: McGraw-Hill.

Hogan, R. (1990). Unmasking incompetent managers. *Insight, May 21,* 42–44.

Hogan, R. (1991). *An alternative model of managerial effectiveness.* Mimeo. Tulsa, OK: Institute of Behavioral Sciences.

Irvine, S. H. (1969). Factor analysis of African abilities and attainments: Continuities across cultures. *Psychological Bulletin, 71,* 20–32.

Jensen, A. R. (1980). *Bias in mental testing.* New York: Free Press.

Jensen, A. R. (1998). *The g factor: The science of mental ability.* Westport, CT: Praeger.

McClelland, D. C. (1973). Testing for competence rather than for "intelligence." *American Psychologist, 28,* 1–14.

Messick, S. (1989). Meaning and values in test validation: The science and ethics of assessment. *Educational Researcher, 18*(2), 5–11.

Messick, S. (1995). Validity of psychological assessment. *American Psychologist, 50*(9), 741–749.

Owen, K. (1992). The suitability of Raven's Standard Progressive Matrices for various groups in South Africa. *Personality and Individual Differences, 13,* 149–159.

Penrose, L. S. (1938). *A clinical and genetic study of 1280 cases of mental defectives (the 'Colchester Survey').* Medical Research Council. Republished by the Institute of Mental and Multiple Handicaps, 1975.

Raven, J. (1981). *Manual for Raven's Progressive Matrices and Vocabulary scales. research supplement no. 1: The 1979 British standardisation of the standard progressive matrices and mill hill vocabulary scales, together with comparative data from earlier studies in the UK, US, Canada, Germany and Ireland.* Oxford: Oxford University Press; San Antonio, TX: The Psychological Corporation.

Raven, J. (1991). *The tragic illusion: Educational testing.* New York: Trillium Press; Oxford, UK: Oxford Psychologists Press.

Raven, J. (1994). *Managing education for effective schooling: The most important problem is to come to terms with values.* Unionville, NY: Trillium Press; Oxford, UK: Oxford Psychologists Press.

Raven, J. (1997). Educational research, ethics and the BPS. Starter paper and peer reviews by P. Mortimore, J. Demetre, R. Stainthope, Y. Reynolds, & G. Lindsay. *Education Section Review, 21*(2), 3–26.

Raven, J. (2000a). Ethical dilemmas. *The Psychologist, 13,* 404–406.

Raven, J. (2000b). *Manual for Raven's Progressive Matrices and Vocabulary scales. Research supplement no. 3 (2nd ed.): A compendium of international and north American normative and validity studies together with a review of the use of the RPM in neuropsychological assessment by Court, Drebing, & Hughes.* Oxford, UK: Oxford Psychologists Press; San Antonio, TX: The Psychological Corporation.

Raven, J. (2000c). The Raven's Progressive Matrices: Change and stability over culture and time. *Cognitive Psychology, 41,* 1–48.

Raven, J., Raven, J. C., & Court, J. H. (1998a). *Manual for Raven's progressive matrices and vocabulary scales. Section 1: General overview.* Oxford, UK: Oxford Psychologists Press; San Antonio, TX: The Psychological Corporation.

Raven, J., Raven, J. C., & Court, J. H. (1998b). *Manual for Raven's progressive matrices and vocabulary scales. Section 2: The coloured progressive matrices.* Oxford, UK: Oxford Psychologists Press; San Antonio, TX: The Psychological Corporation.

Raven, J., Raven, J. C., & Court, J. H. (1998c). *Manual for Raven's progressive matrices and vocabulary scales. Section 4: The advanced progressive matrices.* Oxford, UK: Oxford Psychologists Press; San Antonio, TX: The Psychological Corporation.

Raven, J., Raven, J. C., & Court, J. H. (1998d). *Manual for Raven's progressive matrices and vocabulary scales. Section 5: The Mill Hill vocabulary scale.* Oxford, UK: Oxford Psychologists Press; San Antonio, TX: The Psychological Corporation.

Raven, J., Raven, J. C., & Court, J. H. (2000). *Manual for Raven's progressive matrices and vocabulary scales. Section 3: The standard progressive matrices.* Oxford, UK: Oxford Psychologists Press; San Antonio, TX: The Psychological Corporation.

Raven, J., & Stephenson, J. (Eds.). (2001). *Competence in the learning society.* New York: Lang.

Sattler, J. M. (2001) Assessment of children: Cognitive applications. (4th ed.). San Diego, CA: Jerome M. Sattler.

Schmidt, F. L., & Hunter, J. E. (1998). The validity and utility of selection methods in personnel psychology: Practical and theoretical implications of 85 years of research findings. *Psychological Bulletin, 124*(2), 262–274.

Silvey, J. (1972). Long-range predictions of educability and its determinants in East Africa (Chapter 42). In L. J. Cronbach & P. J. Drenth (Eds.), *Mental tests and cultural adaptation.* The Hague: Mouton.

Spearman, C. (1926). *Some issues in the theory of g (including the law of diminishing returns).* Address to the British Association Section J—Psychology, Southampton, England, 1925. London: Psychological Laboratory; University College: Collected Papers.

Spearman, C. (1927a). *The abilities of man.* London: Macmillan.

Spearman, C. (1927b). *The nature of "intelligence" and the principles of cognition* (2nd ed.). London: Macmillan.

III

Nonverbal Assessment of
Related Abilities

12

Nonverbal Assessment of Academic Achievement with Special Populations

Craig L. Frisby

Much of what transpires in the day-to-day activities of schools and classrooms involves the understanding and expression of ideas transmitted through the medium of spoken and written language. Academic instruction in nearly all content areas is often delivered orally or in a written format, and learners must communicate skills and competencies in the same manner. In order to be academically successful, students must demonstrate the ability to understand concepts through the medium of listening and reading, and must produce acceptable products using verbal and writing skills.

Most elementary, secondary, and postsecondary schools typically emphasize academic skill areas such as those listed in Table 12.1. These skill areas reflect typical expectations for nondisabled groups, since curriculum skills for disabled groups must necessarily have markedly different emphases and expectations (the degree of which is a function of the nature of the disability).

There are a wide variety of ways to assess academic achievement (e.g., see Frisby, 2001). The most common method of academic skill assessment in public education is through individual or group administered standardized achievement testing. Such testing involves a relatively structured situation in which the test-taker is administered a sample of tasks that require skills in decoding and understanding words, comprehending passages, spelling words correctly, writing coherent sentences

Craig L. Frisby, Department of Educational, School, and Counseling Psychology, University of Missouri, Columbia, Missouri 65211.

Handbook of Nonverbal Assessment, edited by R. Steve McCallum. Kluwer Academic/Plenum Publishers, 2003.

242   Craig L. Frisby

using acceptable handwriting skills, performing mathematical calculations, demonstrating application of mathematical concepts, and demonstrating a mastery of general information and critical thinking skills
within the content areas of science, social studies, and the humanities.

Given these realities, the concept of "nonverbal assessment of academic achievement" appears to be an oxymoron. Since most of what is
valued in schools involves reading, writing, and verbal expression, what
is the meaning of "nonverbal assessment," and how would nonverbal
assessment be of any value in educational contexts? Answers to these

Table 12.1   Skill Areas within the Academic Achievement Domain for
Non-Disabled Populations

Language/Communication

- Expressive (e.g., speaking in grammatically correct sentences; tailoring verbal expression
  of needs to the appropriate context)
- Receptive (e.g., understanding the meaning of words; successfully following multistep
  directions)

Reading

- Prereading skills (e.g., ability to visually discriminate similarities/differences in shapes
  and aurally discriminate between word sounds)
- Word Decoding (e.g., ability to apply phonetic and morphological rules in sounding out
  words)
- Reading Comprehension (e.g., understanding literal meaning, drawing implications, infer-
  ring cause/effect relationships within reading passages)
- Study/Research Skills (e.g., knowing how to use a dictionary; how to outline major points
  of a newspaper editorial)
- Functional Reading (e.g., recognizing the meaning of street and commercial signs)

Mathematics

- Knowledge of Math Concepts (e.g., understanding meaning of "more/less," understanding
  part–whole relationships)
- Math Calculation (e.g., ability to correctly add, subtract, multiply and divide numbers)
- Math Application (e.g., figuring out correct answer to math-word problems)
- Functional Math (e.g., making correct change at the grocery store; planning activities with
  a clock or a calendar)

Writing

- Handwriting Mechanics (e.g., learning to write in legible cursive)
- Spelling (e.g., using sentence context clues to correctly spell homonyms; knowing how to
  correctly spell words that have silent consonant/vowel sounds)
- Writing Composition (e.g., writing a letter that follows correct punctuation and capitaliza-
  tion rules)

Specialized Content Knowledge

- Recall/Recognition of Facts (e.g., knows the name and location of major rivers in the
  United States; knows the chemical composition of salt)
- Mastery of Complex Procedural Skills (e.g, designing a multimedia presentation on water
  pollution; putting together a car engine; testing a hypothesis in a science experiment that
  involves controlling variables)
- General Critical Thinking/Problem-Solving (e.g., applying criteria to distinguish fact from
  opinion; knowing how to recognize logical fallacies in reasoning; knowing how to break a
  problem into component parts; looking at an issue from multiple points of view)

difficult questions can be found within the context of adaptive education for disabled populations.

Large segments of school-age children experience a variety of disabling conditions that have adverse effects on their receptive/expressive language development, which in turn impacts development of the academic skills listed in Table 12.1.

ADAPTIVE EDUCATION FOR DISABLED POPULATIONS

Receptive and/or expressive language difficulties are often the result of four categories of etiologic conditions (King, 1999). *Congenital and/or developmental conditions* include cerebral palsy; severe sensory (vision or hearing) deficits; oral, verbal, or limb apraxias; and moderate to severe cognitive impairments. *Acquired disabilities* occur as a result of trauma from accidents, surgeries (i.e., laryngectomies), limb amputations, and spinal cord and/or brain damage. *Progressive neurological, neuromuscular diseases* such as amyotrophic lateral sclerosis, multiple sclerosis, muscular dystrophy, Parkinson's disease, Huntington's chorea or AIDS place serious limitations on the coordination and control of motor skills involved in writing or speech production, as do *temporary conditions* such as Guillain–Barré syndrome, Reye's syndrome, bodily burns, and laryngeal damage.

In the classroom context, children and youth with severe autism or cerebral palsy experience significant difficulties communicating verbally in ways that can be understood easily by others. Students with significant hearing impairments often cannot benefit from traditional methods of verbal instruction and therefore must receive instruction through largely nonverbal modes of communication. Disabled learners with serious physical impairments do not have the gross or fine motor skills to demonstrate achievement through writing, which necessitates alternative means of expression. Finally, individuals with significant mental impairments (e.g., mental retardation, traumatic brain injury) may have difficulty developing the cognitive skills necessary for becoming proficient in reading, performing calculations, and complex thinking—which would necessitate alternative ways of demonstrating that one has benefitted from an education. Adaptive educational services for learners with these various disabilities are required for those who receive the appropriate label under the Individuals With Disabilities Education Act—Part B (Pub. L. No. 105-17, 602, 111 Stat. 43 [1997]). Since academic instruction is altered due to the particulars of various disabling conditions, the assessment of academic achievement must necessarily differ as well.

THE MEANING OF NONVERBAL ASSESSMENT OF ACADEMIC ACHIEVEMENT FOR SPECIAL POPULATIONS

For the purposes of this chapter, "nonverbal assessment" of academic achievement is a heterogeneous concept that is broadened to include the following applications:

1. Due to examinees' cognitive, neurological, and/or emotional limitations, academic skills cannot be assessed through a structured interaction between an examiner and an examinee (i.e., in which the examiner gives verbal directions and the examinee performs a skill in compliance with these directions). In contrast, academic skills of examinees are assessed through examiner observations in naturally occurring settings.

2. Examinee's hearing impairments require test administration to be conducted in a nonverbal mode of communication that does not involve speaking, although the actual content of test items may require the perception and understanding of words.

3. Due to significant limitations in examinees' expressive language capabilities, extensive support is required to assist examinees in demonstrating academic competence in an alternative format.

The first of these applications is usually found within the context of adaptive behavior assessment. For a comprehensive treatment of the measurement of adaptive behavior of functional academic skills for students with moderate and severe disabilities, readers are encouraged to consult Browder (2001). The next two applications will be the focus in the next sections of this chapter.

The Development of Literacy and Deafness

More than 20 million persons in the United States have hearing impairments, and between 500,000 and 1 million persons are considered to be deaf, depending on the definition used (National Center for Health Statistics, 1994).

The central problem for profoundly deaf persons is the task of deciphering phonological codes in the absence of hearing. According to Leybaert, Content, and Alegria (1987), deaf children's word-decoding processes are developed through a combination of lip-reading, finger spelling, articulation patterns, and exposure to writing.

Individuals with mild hearing impairments can have an educational experience similar to hearing peers, with adequate support from speech therapy, hearing aids, and the use of note-takers and tutors (Brauer, Braden, Pollard, & Hardy-Braz, 1998). There are three basic methods of teaching communication skills to children with more severe deafness. The *oral method* emphasizes the acquisition of speech reading skills (i.e., interpreting the lip/mouth movements of others) and speech production skills, while discouraging the use of sign language. The *total communication method* emphasizes speech production skills but also emphasizes the development of manual communication, or "signing" skills. *American Sign Language (ASL)* is a standardized form of manual communication that employs hands, facial expressions, and body movements. ASL has its own morphological, syntactic, and semantic rules that differ from other forms of English signing. Embedded within sign language is letter-by-letter *finger spelling*, which becomes necessary whenever there is no conventional sign for a novel idea (Marschark, 1993). According to Brauer et al. (1998), the *bilingual–bicultural method* emphasizes written and signed forms of English only after mastery of ASL has been established first.

Deaf versus Hearing Populations

Some writers view the learning of reading and writing by deaf children as analogous to the learning of a second language (Charrow & Fletcher, 1974). Whereas a typical hearing 4-year-old child has a vocabulary of about 2,000–3,000 words, a prelingually deaf 4-year-old has a vocabulary of about 25 words. Deaf children's limited vocabularies, along with severe limitations in mastering syntax and grammar rules, limit acquisition of other academic skills. DiFrancesca (1972) found that reading scores increased only 0.2 grade levels per year of schooling in a large sample of 17,000 deaf children between the ages of 6 and 21. In contrast, the reading scores of hearing children gain 1 grade level for each year of schooling. As a result, the reading lags of deaf children relative to their hearing peers actually *increases* as they matriculate through school (Allen, 1986). The mean national reading level of deaf people has been estimated to be at the third- to fourth-grade level (Schmelter-Davis, 1984).

Compared with hearing students, the writing of deaf students lags behind their manual production skills and is characterized by shorter, less variable, and incomplete sentence structure (see review by Marschark, 1993). According to Kretschmer and Kretschmer (1978), the average deaf 18-year-old writes on a level comparable with that of a hearing 8-year-old. Marschark (1993) estimates that more than 30% of deaf students leave school functionally illiterate (e.g., displaying reading and writing levels below 4th grade) compared with fewer than 1% of their hearing peers. In summary, deaf children lag behind hearing peers of similar ages in a variety of academic areas related to the understanding of abstract relationships, conceptual categorization, mathematics, reading, and writing (see reviews by Marschark, 1993).

Comparisons between Deaf Subgroups

Deaf children's lag in academic achievement relative to hearing peers does not depend on differences in manual versus oral education (Marschark, 1993). However, children whose deafness occurred after the acquisition of language fundamentals make better educational progress than children whose deafness occurred before language fundamentals have been acquired. The marker age that generally divides pre- versus postlingual periods is approximately age 4 (Braden, 1994).

Deaf children of deaf parents display higher levels of academic performance than deaf children of hearing parents, although the specific reasons for this advantage remain unclear (see review by Marschark, 1993). What complicates this search is the finding that deaf parents have greater expectations for their deaf children than do hearing parents; they also seem likely to spend more time in educationally relevant interactions with their deaf children than do hearing parents, and their children develop in more "natural" social contexts than do the deaf children of hearing parents. In addition, deaf children of deaf parents appear to show more normal patterns of cognitive development than deaf children of hearing parents (Marschark, 1993). Calderon and Low (1998) found that young (3–6 years) deaf children whose father is present in the home had significantly better academic and language outcomes than those without a father present.

Based on extensive data collected by Gallaudet University's Center for Assessment and Demographic Studies during its 1990 standardization of the 8th Edition Stanford Achievement Test, deaf and hard-of-hearing (D/HOH) students who were integrated with hearing students, were Caucasian, had less-than-severe hearing loss, and had no cognitive handicap generally had the highest scores in reading comprehension and mathematics computation (Holt, 1994).

Achievement Testing without Norms for the D/HOH

In some instances, D/HOH students may be tested with achievement measures lacking the appropriate norms (i.e., standardized on hearing populations), simply because these tests do not require reading (unless designed to assess reading) or vocal responses. These tests are typically administered using the primary mode of communication used in the examinee's educational setting (e.g., see Yoshinaga-Itano & Downey, 1996). This practice should be avoided as much as possible if comparable tests normed on D/HOH students are available. If such measures are not available, diagnosticians should be aware of the following problems (Bradley-Johnson & Evans, 1991): (a) a number of stimulus words may not have signed equivalents in either the directions or the actual items. In such cases, the examiner would have to finger-spell the word or use several sign descriptors to accurately convey the concept, which may increase the difficulty level of the directions or items; (b) the signed response for a word, because of its form, may serve as a cue for the correct response, thereby decreasing the difficulty level of the item (e.g., see White & Tischler, 1999); (c) because of D/HOH students' greater difficulties with reading, tests that require students to read the items (instead of these being read by the examiner via sign) may be too difficult to comprehend, thus confounding results.

Selected Achievement Tests with Norms for the D/HOH

Tests with Older Norms

Some individually administered achievement tests have deaf norms that are over 15 years old (at the time of this writing) but continue to be currently used despite no updated norms (D. Gushleff, personal communication, June 4, 2001; T. Jones, personal communication, June 4, 2001).

These tests are considered "nonverbal" because they allow responses to be scored from the examinee's use of sign language. Examples of such tests are the *Carolina Picture Vocabulary Test* (a test of receptive vocabulary for hearing impaired students aged 2–8 to 18), the *Grammatical Analysis of Elicited Language* (a test of receptive and expressive grammar skills in either spoken or signed English for ages 3–12), and the *Rhode Island Test of Language Structure* (a test of syntax comprehension for hearing impaired students ages 5–17+). Bradley-Johnson and Evans (1991) describe these tests at length.

Test of Early Reading Ability

The *Test of Early Reading Ability: Special Edition for Students Who Are Deaf or Hard of Hearing (TERA-D/HH)* is an individually administered test of reading designed for young students (between the ages of 3–0 and 13–11 years) with moderate (41–62 DB) to profound (91 DB and above) sensory hearing loss (Reid, Hresko, Hammill, & Wiltshire, 1991). The TERA-D/HH was standardized on a sample of 1,146 children residing in 29 states and the District of Columbia. According to the examiner's manual, 72% of the standardization sample experienced onset of hearing loss at birth, 22% experienced hearing loss under 3 years of age, and 6% experienced hearing loss at 3 years of age or older.

According to the authors, the TERA-D/HH is available in two forms that measure three aspects of early reading skills: (a) construction of meaning, (b) knowledge of the alphabet and its functions, and (c) conventions of written language. *Construction of meaning* is assessed through items that require the student to "read signs, logos, and words frequently encountered in figural/situational contexts", as well as items that require the student to "select two words that are related to a stimulus word" (Reid et al., 1991, p. 5). Reading comprehension is assessed through cloze tasks (i.e., where the examinee supplies the missing word in a passage) and items that require the student to deduce the meaning of an unfamiliar word from its context. *Knowledge of the alphabet and its functions* is assessed through letter/number naming, alphabet recitation, and oral/signed reading items. *Conventions of written language* items measure the examinee's knowledge of punctuation in print, spatial concepts related to book handling and left–right orientation, and examinees' ability to recognize errors in printed material (i.e., proofreading skills).

Three kinds of normative scores are provided for the TERA-D/HH: percentiles, Normal Curve Equivalent scores, and quotients standardized to yield a mean of 100 and a standard deviation of 15. The authors purposely do not provide grade- or age-equivalent scores, due to their statistical limitations (e.g., see Salvia & Ysseldyke, 1998).

Stanford Achievement Test, 9th Edition

The SAT (abbreviated Stanford 9) is a group-administered measure of academic achievement in grades 1–9 (Traxler, 2000). It is one of the few group-administered achievement tests that includes norms for D/HOH students. In order to assign students to the appropriate level for testing, the Stanford 9 is partitioned into 8 difficulty levels corresponding to specific grade ranges for hearing students. Although the item content in the Stanford 9 is identical for both hearing and D/HOH students, the slower language development of D/HOH students necessitates that the test is administered differently to D/HOH students (Gallaudet Research Institute, 1996a).

For D/HOH, the Gallaudet Research Institute has developed eight brief screening tests, each containing a combination of sample items representative of three Stanford 9 subtests: Reading Comprehension, Mathematics: Problem-Solving, and Mathematics: Procedures (Gallaudet Research Institute, 1996b). The screening tests cover the full difficulty range of the eight Stanford 9 test levels. A school would administer and score the screening tests and, on the basis of the screening test scores, assign the appropriate Stanford 9 level to each of its students (Gallaudet Research Institute, 1996a). Due to the slower language development of D/HOH students, the Stanford 9 is usually not administered to D/HOH children under age 7.

Directions for test sections and individual test items (only for the lowest 2 levels) are communicated to D/HOH students via their usual mode of communication in the classroom. If the directions for the sample items are not clear, test users are permitted to use additional sample items (Gallaudet Research Institute, 1996c).

Similar to other group administered achievement tests for hearing students, the Stanford 9 yields raw, percentile, scaled, and grade equivalent scores. However, they are interpreted slightly differently for D/HOH students. For example, the "Primary 3" difficulty level is designed for hearing students between grades 3.5 and 4.5. If a 14-year-old D/HOH student achieves a grade-equivalent score of 6.2 on the Primary 3 Reading Comprehension test of the Stanford 9, it means that the student is performing comparable to how an average hearing student who is in the 6.3 grade would perform on the Primary 3 subtest (Gallaudet Research Institute, 1996a). Since the Stanford 9 was normed on D/HOH students, percentile rankings compare a D/HOH student with other D/HOH students of the *same age* who took that particular subtest area, regardless of the level of the subtest. Holt, Traxler, and Allen (1997) provide a comprehensive presentation of the more technical features of Stanford 9 score interpretation. Finally, Chaleff and Toranzo (2000) describe test-taking strategies that can assist deaf students in maximizing their performance on the Stanford Achievement Test (SAT).

Transition Competence Battery (TCB) for Deaf Adolescents and Young Adults

The TCB (Reiman & Bullis, 1993) was designed as a specialized assessment for transition competence of individuals who are deaf. The TCB was standardized on deaf students from both mainstreamed and residential settings. It comprises six subtests: Job-Seeking Skills for Employment, Work-Adjustment Skills for Employment, Job-Related Social/Interpersonal Skills, Money-Management Skills for Independent Living, Health and Home Skills for Independent Living, and Community-Awareness Skills for Independent Living. The average readability for the entire battery is at the 4th grade level, which is consistent with the estimated average reading level of the adult deaf population. The format permits individual or small group administration using a three-option multiple-choice format. Items are presented through a signed (Pidgin Signed English) or color videodisk presentation (Bullis, Reiman, Davis, & Thorkildsen, 1994) in combination with a simply worded and illustrated test booklet. The battery consists of 243 items, and the administration time is about 4 hours (h). A field testing of a shortened 46-item version of the TCB (i.e., "Mini-TCB") has shown internal consistency estimates that range between 0.61 and 0.78 across the six subtests. Correlations between the Mini-TCB and TCB subtests range between 0.40 and 0.85 (Bullis, Reiman, Davis, & Reid, 1997).

The Development of Literacy in Persons with Severe Speech and Physical Impairments (SSPI)

According to the American Speech–Language–Hearing Association, over 1 million individuals throughout the United States are severely speech impaired or nonspeaking as a result of neurological, physical, emotional, and/or cognitive factors (American Speech–Language–Hearing Association Position Statement on Non-Speech Communication, 1981). Many of these individuals suffer from cerebral palsy (CP), which is a general label given to a set of nonprogressive movement and posture disorders resulting from prenatal, perinatal, or postnatal brain trauma (Nagle & Campbell, 1998). The prevalence of CP is commonly reported to be 1.2–2.3 per 1,000 children at school age. According to Barnett (1982), CP can be distinguished by the quality of an affected person's movement (spastic, ataxic, or athetoid), the location of the affected areas (upper extremities, lower extremities, or one side of the entire body), or the degree of impairment (mild, moderate, or severe). About half of all people with CP have *spastic CP*, which is characterized by muscle tone that is too high or too tight. This form of CP is commonly associated with decreased intellectual functioning (Aroor, 1992). Individuals with spastic CP have stiff and jerky movements, difficulties moving from one position to another, or letting go of something in their hand. Persons with *ataxic CP* suffer from frequent shakiness and tremors, poor balance, muscle uncoordination, and unsteadiness in their gait. Persons with *athetoid CP* have difficulties from muscle tone that is sometimes too high and sometimes too low. Persons with athetoid CP have difficulty holding themselves in an upright, steady position for sitting or walking, and often show random, involuntary movements of their face, arms and upper body. CP can also be of a *mixed type* (Borowitz, 2000).

Although no supporting data are provided, Pierce and McWilliam (1993) argue that children with SSPI may have fewer opportunities to gain experience with play, reading and writing activities/materials that are crucial for adequate literacy development. In contrast, Koppenhaver, Evans, and Yoder (1991) used retrospective survey methods to show that literate adults with SSPI grew up in home and school environments with abundant reading/writing materials and regular exposure to print. Sandberg (1998) compared questionnaire responses from parents of 35 nonvocal children with CP, parents of a mentally retarded group matched for IQ and sex, and parents of a nondisabled group matched for mental age and sex. Although parents of the nonvocal children had fewer demands for active participation during story reading activities, she found few differences in the home literacy environment across these three groups. She concluded that individual differences in speech and language abilities, rather than home literacy variables, were better predictors of reading development.

Nonvocal children with CP demonstrate literacy levels that lag behind what would be expected from their intellectual levels (Berninger & Gans, 1986), even when early phonological awareness and intelligence are matched with nondisabled peers (Sandberg & Hjelmquist, 1996). For many persons with SSPI, emphasis on the explicit teaching of literacy skills does not occur until relatively late in their academic careers (e.g., Smith, Thurston, Light, Parnes, & O'Keefe, 1989).

Skill Assessment of Persons with SSPI

According to Barnett (1982), approaches to the psychoeducational assessment of individuals with SSPI fall within three categories: (a) adaptations of existing commercially available instruments, where every effort is made to administer the instrument under standardized conditions, except for situations that would require alteration of the test stimuli or response format; (b) the creation of new instruments that are specifically designed to accommodate persons with disabilities (such as designing tests that require only pointing responses); and (c) combining a variety of methods or instruments, in order to provide a comprehensive evaluation that would not be possible if any one method/instrument were used alone. Since persons with SSPI have serious speech production and motor deficiencies, assessment requires the use of special technologies to accommodate these deficiencies. These technological accommodations are described below.

Assistive Technology

Assistive technology (AT), can be broadly defined as tools, tool-related processes, helping devices, and equipment that is used to allow persons with special needs, disabilities, and challenges to participate in life activities along with others in their family, community, school, and worksite (King, 1999). As described by Public Law 100-407 (The Technology-Related Assistance Act of 1988), AT includes "any item, piece of equipment, or product system, whether acquired commercially off the shelf, modified, or customized, that is used to increase, maintain, or improve functional capabilities of individuals with disabilities" (Section 3.1).

King (1999) subdivides varied types of AT into 10 primary categories, two of which have direct application to nonverbal assessment of functional academic skills. *Augmentative and Alternative Communication (AAC)* refers to methods, strategies, and/or devices that are useful in supporting, augmenting, or replacing oral communication efforts of individuals whose speech capabilities are not adequate to meet their daily needs for exchanging meaning between themselves and others. Some AAC methods do not require sophisticated technology. These methods include, but are not limited to: manual sign language, finger spelling, or pointing to stimuli (e.g., pictures, symbols, words) on a board. Other highly technological AAC methods, such as voice output communication aids, translate letters and words on a computer screen into synthesized speech.

Adapted Computer Access methods involve creative adaptations for persons who have difficulty entering and/or reading out information from the computer (see Alliance for Technology Access, 2000, for a comprehensive treatment). Some disabled users have the use of their two hands, but regular typing becomes overly tiresome and/or painful. For these users, arm and wrist support devices (attached to a chair, table, or keyboard) can support the arms and wrists while the user is typing on a keyboard or using a mouse/trackball. For some disabled users, uncontrolled finger, hand, or arm tremors, spastic movements, or paralysis cause difficulties in interacting with a standard keyboard. In these cases, standard keyboard keys are experienced as either too far apart or too close together for effective input of information into the computer. *Access utilities* are software programs that modify various aspects of the standard computer keyboard. These modifications simplify operation of the keyboard by eliminating the need for a mouse, eliminating the need to press more than one key at a time, and providing visual or auditory cues in order to help users produce output. For example, "writing" a paragraph on the computer screen is a painfully slow process that produces excessive fatigue for some disabled persons. *Word-prediction programs* allow users to type on a keyboard the beginning letters of a word on the computer screen, and the program generates an on-screen list of all possible words that begin with the typed letters. The user simply selects the appropriate word needed, and the computer program inserts the word into the on-screen text, thereby increasing typing speed and reducing keystrokes. *Abbreviation-expansion programs* allow the user to assign a series of letters, words, or sentences to one or more keystrokes. When the assigned keys (i.e., the abbreviations) are entered, the program will automatically insert the expanded text on the computer screen. *Macros* allow users to record a long series of commands and assign them to a function key or combination of keys. Once a macro is recorded, the user can "execute" a complex series of procedures exactly as recorded by simply typing the assigned key(s).

Some users have no capabilities for using their hands to interact with a computer keyboard. For these individuals, mouth and head sticks allow users to strike keys on a keyboard without the use of hands. Computers can be adapted with interface devices and software that connects a switch to the computer, which then enables the computer to interpret the operation of the switch. Switches can be designed to accommodate a wide range of activation stimuli from users. Switches can be mounted on, and activated from, any part of the human body. Switches can be activated by a light touch, a pulling motion, by squeezing, or even by the blink of an eye. In addition, switches can be activated by sound or by the interruption of a beam of light. Enabled by the use of a switch, *automatic scanning programs* allow cursors on the computer screen to slowly scan through charts of letters, numbers, and/or symbols on the computer screen. The user simply activates the switch when the cursor appears over a particular symbol, and the symbol is transferred to another part of the screen. Some users may not be able to use a hand-operated switch and must rely instead on head movements. For these users, headgear can be worn, which shines a beam of light on a keyboard shown on the computer screen. With the use of *dwelling software*, the beam of light "dwells" on a key for a specified amount of time, and the computer types the letter on the screen. For users whose speech capabilities are fairly good, *voice-recognition systems* allow users to simply speak their thoughts, and the computer translates this speech into "typed" words on the computer screen.

Blissymbolics is the name given to a symbolic/pictorial system of communication called "semantography." This system was originally developed by Charles K. Bliss (1897–1985) for the purpose of international communication (Bliss, 1978). The Bliss symbols are currently composed of over 2,000 graphic symbols (simple shapes and/or lines) that can be combined in a variety of ways to create even newer symbols. These symbols can be sequenced to express thoughts in the form of words and sentences. This communication system was first applied to the communication of children with physical disabilities by an interdisciplinary team at the Ontario Crippled Children's Centre (now the Bloorview MacMillan Centre) in 1971 (http://home.istar.ca/~bci/intro.htm). For those who have a communication impairment, Blissymbols can be used on simple communiction boards mounted on wheelchairs, or on electronic devices with synthetic speech and within computer software.

Select Case Studies of Assessment of Persons with SSPI

Due to the wide range of functional levels and multiple problems experienced by persons with SSPI, nonverbal assessment is highly individualized. At the lowest end of the functional spectrum, quadriplegic persons with cerebral palsy cannot speak, write, manipulate keyboards, or sign beyond the most primitive gestures (Sappington, Reedy, Welch, & Hamilton, 1989). A typical dilemma in the assessment of persons with SSPI is that an accurate diagnosis of cognitive and academic skills is often hindered by unreliable communication skills, and the lack of data about cognitive/academic functioning frustrates the design of communication interventions (Goossens, 1989). As a result, assessment of persons with SSPI typically begins with a determination of whether or not the examinee is capable of the most rudimentary forms of receptive communication.

Assessment at this level often involves *binary questioning*, where the therapist/examiner asks an extended series of questions that require only a "yes/no" response. The examinee uses one gesture for "yes" and another gesture for "no." Sappington et al. (1989) have shown empirically that this method accurately reflects communicative intent of persons with SSPI.

Some studies suggest that rudimentary IQ scores can be obtained from nonverbal quadriplegic persons with cerebral palsy through the use of the Peabody Picture Vocabulary test (e.g., Sappington et al., 1989), which is a pictorial receptive vocabulary test that can be administered by binary questioning.

In many cases, initial functional skills are so low that assessment and training are enmeshed. For example, Goossens (1989) describes the case of Jessica, a 6-year-old nonspeaking, nonambulatory, quadriplegic Korean girl. Prior to intervention, Jessica had been living in America for only 3 months. She was initially diagnosed as also mentally retarded. Jessica had limited use of her upper extremities, poor head control, unreliable eye-gaze responses, and a spoken vocabulary of less than 10 English words, all of which was confounded by a language barrier. Her cognitive skills were estimated to be at approximately 16–20 months; hence, the first task was to teach Jessica to communicate using picture symbols (see Mayer-Johnson, 1984, 1985) accessed through eye gazes. This was accomplished by extensive interviewing of Jessica's adoptive parents to ascertain her communication needs within the context of the home. Picture symbols were chosen that would effectively mediate communication during key home routines. Each picture symbol contained a simple word (i.e., "eat") and a simple drawing of the word (i.e., picture of a person eating). During these routines, Jessica was exposed to picture symbols from two sources. Some picture symbols were mounted on a "sandwich-board" vest worn by any adult working with Jessica (see Goossens & Crain, 1986). Each vest consisted of six displays, with each display containing multiple picture symbols attached by velcro to the vest and categorized by activity. When there was a switch to a different activity, each display could be accessed and "flipped" much like pages in a book. Other picture symbols were mounted on a transparent acrylite frame attached to Jessica's wheelchair and positioned directly in front of her face (which was gently held in one position by head braces attached to the wheelchair). The frame had the middle cut out so that Jessica could see the adult (wearing the vest). For example, during the activity of washing dishes, picture symbols representing the concepts "sponge," "wet," "rinse," and "clean" were clearly visible. The adult demonstrated the activity and simultaneously pointed to the corresponding picture symbol in teaching receptive vocabulary. Eventually, Jessica was trained to activate a homemade wheelchair-mounted switch by simply turning her head to her left. This switch was capable of advancing picture slides on a projector while an audiotaped story was being read. The tape would play a bell sound to indicate when the next slide should be shown. The switch could also be programmed to activate and stop a rotating pointer mounted on a picture wheel. This apparatus would allow Jessica to communicate her needs by forming elementary "picture sentences."

As a result of these preliminary training interventions, a more accurate assessment of functional academic skills was facilitated. To assess word comprehension, Peabody Picture Vocabulary items (four cards for each item) were mounted on four corners of the acrylite frame within Jessica's eye gaze. The pictures were positioned far enough apart to discriminate which picture is the focus of Jessica's eye gaze. When a target word was spoken by the examiner, Jessica would gaze at the picture that represented her response to the item. Although Jessica was in the United States for only 7 months at the time of testing, she was able to achieve a score comparable with the average performance of a 2-year, 5-month-old child.

The Columbia Mental Maturity Scale—Third Edition (Burgemeister, Blum, & Lorge, 1972) was used to assess Jessica's cognitive level, also using eye gaze as the response mode. The test required reasoning skills to determine which of three to five stimuli on a card did not belong. By shifting the card slowly back and forth, along with the reminder to "keep looking at the one that does not belong," Jessica's visual target could be easily interpreted (Goossens, 1989). Goossens (1989) reports an average level of measured intelligence using this method, which eventually resulted in a mainstreamed placement in a regular kindegarten class and an abandonment of the mentally retarded label.

Smith, Thurston, Light, Parnes, and O'Keefe (1989) describe a method for assessing written communication in a higher functioning sample of six congenitally, physically disabled individuals between the ages of 13 and 22 years. These subjects did possess functional receptive language skills necessary for daily living; they had been trained in the use of Blissymbols for face-to-face communication; they had been using a microcomputer and keyboard as a written communication system in the home for a period of at least 5 months; they were familiar with traditional keyboard letters for written communication, and evidenced spelling abilities of at least the third-grade level; and they were competent in the use of basic computer word-processing programs, which included basic skills in deleting errors, saving, and printing text.

The researchers collected all written output (printed from micro-computers) completed in the each of the subjects' homes over a 4-week period. They analyzed these data in two categories. First, questionnaires were given to the subjects themselves and to their facilitators. These questionnaires were designed to assess four areas: (a) the quantity of output, (b) the amount and nature of assistance required to produce writing samples, (c) the amount of time spent writing each sample from idea generation to editing, and (d) the intended function of the sample. Second, the form of the writing samples was analyzed using both commercial diagnostic tests (e.g., Test of Written Language; Hammill & Larsen, 1978) and more informal diagnostic methods of writing analysis (e.g., Weiner, 1980).

Data were collected in four areas: (a) total words per sample; (b) frequency and accuracy of use of grammatical morphemes; (c) total number of sentences per sample; and (d) complexity of sentence type (i.e., simple, compound, or complex).

The researchers found that, on average, more than 80% of all writing was completed independently by the subjects. Each of the subjects required a considerable amount of time to plan, generate, and revise their written output, as typified by a mean writing rate of 1.5 words per minute. Although subjects were able to make the transition from Blissymbols to traditional orthography, all subjects had difficulties with their use of morphological endings and formulating sentences beyond the simple sentence level. Although the transition from Blissymbols to traditional orthography allowed these subjects to develop a basic level of proficiency in grammar and syntax, the authors hypothesize that they did not develop a precise understanding of more complex sentence formulation or morpheme use (Smith et al., 1989).

SUMMARY

Current accountability systems in national and state education agencies place a high value on the inclusion of all students in evaluation efforts (Browder, 2001). The Gallaudet Research Institute has taken the lead in developing state-of-the-art norms for deaf students taking individual and group standardized achievement tests. For those educators who will be administering tests to deaf students, the Registry of Interpreters for the Deaf has developed a Code of Ethics (Burns, 1998), which insures that translators convey accurately the meaning of the test items, do not unethically help or advise test-takers, and accurately record responses when necessary. As demonstrated in this chapter, planning alternate assessments for students with SSPI is a complex affair. Many of these students do not pursue a regular high-school diploma, do not have a common curriculum, and have only a life-skills IEP for a "curriculum" (Browder, 2001). Especially problematic is that the measurement of life skills and functional equivalents of academic skills do not lend themselves well to standardized testing. However, it is incumbent on professionals who work with this population to understand that adherence to strict standardization can be relaxed in lieu of what is effective in eliciting maximum performance. With time, rapid technological advancements will move us closer to this goal.

ADDITIONAL RESOURCES

Organizations

Blissymbolics Communication International (BCI) is a nonprofit charitable organization that has the worldwide exclusive license for the use and publication of Blissymbols for persons with communication, language, and learning difficulties. BCI supports Blissymbol use through the training of professionals, assistance to Blissymbol users, consultation, publications, technology and software development, and projects related to Blissymbol applications. "BlissInternet" has been developed to allow Bliss users to communicate with anyone with Internet access and BlissInternet software. All Bliss materials within North America can be obtained from Betacom/Bridges 2999, King St. W., Inglewood, Ontario, L0N 1K0, Canada. Phone: 1-800-353-1107; Internet: http://home.istar.ca/~bci/ intro.htm

The Gallaudet Research Institute (GRI), a subsidiary of Gallaudet University, is internationally recognized for its leadership in deafness-related research. GRI researchers gather and analyze data concerning the demographic and academic characteristics of deaf and hard-of-hearing populations, primarily to provide information needed by educators in the field. One of the research initiatives of GRI is assessment. GRI is the source for information, materials, and research related the academic achievement and literacy of deaf students who took the SAT (6th, 7th, 8th, and 9th editions). GRI also provides recommendations for the best academic/readiness tests to use with deaf students. The GRI mailing address is: Gallaudet Research Institute, Gallaudet University, 800 Florida Avenue, NE Washington, DC 20002, USA. Phone: 1-202-651-5575 (V/TTY), Internet: http://gri.gallaudet.edu/

Periodicals

Closing the Gap is a resource magazine devoted to computer hardware and software technology in special education and rehabilitation, and is published bimonthly in February, April, June, August, October, and December. The annual Resource Directory issue represents a year-round search for computer-technology-related products for children and adults with special needs. Address all correspondence to Closing The Gap, PO Box 68, Henderson, MN, 56044, or contact them at http://www.closingthegap.com

BOOKS

Alliance for Technology Access (2000). *Computer and web resources for people with disabilities: A guide to exploring today's assistive technology* (3rd ed.). Alameda, CA: Hunter House.
Lazzaro, J. J. (1996). *Adapting PCs for disabilities.* New York: Addison-Wesley.

REFERENCES

Allen, T. E. (1986). Patterns of academic achievement among hearing impaired students: 1974–1983. In A. N. Shildroth & M. A. Karchmer (Eds.), *Deaf children in America* (pp. 161–206). San Diego, CA: College-Hill Press.
Alliance for Technology Access (2000). *Computer and web resources for people with disabilities: A guide to exploring today's assistive technology* (3rd ed.). Alameda, CA: Hunter House.

American Speech–Language–Hearing Association Position Statement on Non-Speech Communication (1981). *Asha, 23,* 577–581.

Aroor, S. R. (1992). Assessment of cerebral palsy. *Indian Journal of Pediatrics, 59,* 159–164.

Barnett, A. J. (1982). Designing an assessment of the child with cerebral palsy. *Psychology in the Schools, 19,* 160–165.

Berninger, V., & Gans, B. M. (1986). Language profiles in nonspeaking individuals of normal intelligence with severe cerebral palsy. *Augmentative and Alternative Communication, 2,* 45–50.

Bliss, C. K. (1978). *Semantography (Blissymbolics): A simple system of 100 logical pictorial symbols, which can be operated and read like 1 + 2 = 3 in all languages.* Sydney: Semantography (Blissymbolics) Publications.

Borowitz, K. C. (2000). Different types of cerebral palsy. Retrieved from http://hsc. virginia.edu/cmc/tutorials/cp/type/type.html

Braden, J. P. (1994). *Deafness, deprivation, and IQ.* New York: Plenum.

Bradley-Johnson, S., & Evans, L. D. (1991). *Psychoeducational assessment of hearing-impaired students: Infancy through high school.* Austin, TX: PRO-ED.

Brauer, B. A., Braden, J. P., Pollard, R. Q., & Hardy-Braz, S. T. (1998). Deaf and hard of hearing people. In J. S. Sandoval, C. L. Frisby, K. F. Geisinger, J. D. Scheuneman, & J. R. Grenier (Eds.), *Test interpretation and diversity: Achieving equity in assessment* (pp. 297–316). Washington, DC: American Psychological Association.

Browder, D. M. (2001). *Curriculum and assessment for students with moderate and severe disabilities.* New York: Guilford Press.

Bullis, M., Reiman, J., Davis, C., & Reid, C. (1997). National field testing of the "Mini" version of the Transition Competence Battery for Adolescents and Young Adults Who are Deaf. *Journal of Special Education, 31*(3), 347–361.

Bullis, M., Reiman, J., Davis, C., & Thorkildsen, R. (1994). Examination of administration and response formats in the videodisc assessment of deaf adolescents' transition skills. *Exceptional Children, 61,* 158–173.

Burgemeister, B. B., Blum, L. H., & Lorge, I. (1972). *Columbia mental maturity scale* (3rd ed.). New York: Harcourt Brace Jovanovich.

Burns, E. (1998). *Test accommodations for students with disabilities.* Springfield, IL: Charles C. Thomas.

Calderon, R., & Low, S. (1998). Early social-emotional, language, and academic development in children with hearing loss: Families with and without fathers. *American Annals of the Deaf, 143*(3), 225–234.

Chaleff, C., & Toranzo, N. (2000). Helping our students meet the standards through test preparation classes. *American Annals of the Deaf, 145*(1), 33–40.

Charrow, V., & Fletcher, J. D. (1974). English as a second language of deaf children. *Developmental Psychology, 10,* 463–470.

DiFrancesca, S. (1972). *Academic achievement test results of a national testing program for hearing-impaired students—United States, Spring 1971.* Office for Demographic Studies, Gallaudet College.

Frisby, C. (2001). Academic achievement. In L. A. Suzuki, J. G. Ponterotto, & P. J. Meller (Eds.), *Handbook of multicultural assessment* (2nd ed., pp. 541–568). San Francisco: Jossey-Bass.

Gallaudet Research Institute (1996a). *Achievement testing of deaf and hard-of-hearing students: The 9th edition Stanford Achievement Test.* Washington, DC: Gallaudet Research Institute.

Gallaudet Research Institute (1996b). *Stanford Achievement Test, 9th edition. Screening procedures for deaf and hard-of-hearing students.* Washington, DC: Gallaudet Research Institute.

Gallaudet Research Institute (1996c). *Stanford Achievement Test, 9th edition. Administration procedures for deaf and hard-of-hearing students.* Washington, DC: Gallaudet University.

Goossens, C. (1989). Aided communication intervention before assessment: A case study of a child with cerebral palsy. *Augmentative and Alternative Communication, 5*(1), 14–26.

Goossens, C., & Crain, S. (1986). *Augmentative communication intervention resource.* Chicago, IL: Don Johnston Developmental Equipment.

Hammill, D. D., & Larsen, S. C. (1978). *Test of Written Language (TOWL)*. Austin, TX: PRO-ED.

Holt, J. (1994). Classroom attributes and achievement test scores for deaf and hard of hearing students. *American Annals of the Deaf, 139*(4), 430–437.

Holt, J. A., Traxler, C. B., & Allen, T. E. (1997). *Interpreting the scores: A user's guide to the 9th edition Stanford Achievement Test for educators of deaf and hard-of-hearing students*. Washington, DC: Gallaudet Research Institute.

King, T. W. (1999). *Assistive technology: Essential human factors*. Boston, MA: Allyn & Bacon.

Koppenhaver, D. A., Evans, D. A., & Yoder, D. E. (1991). Childhood reading and writing experiences of literate adults with severe speech and motor impairments. *Augmentative and Alternative Communication, 7*(1), 20–33.

Kretschmer, R. R., & Kretschmer, L. W. (1978). *Language development and intervention in the hearing impaired*. Baltimore: University Park Press.

Kucherawy, D. A., & Kucherawy, J. M. (1978). Pen and share it. *Education and Training of the Mentally Retarded, 13*(3), 342–44.

Leybaert, J., Content, A., & Alegria, J. (1987). *The development of written word processing: The case of deaf children*. Workshop presentation, ISPL Congress, University of Kassel.

Marschark, M. (1993). *Psychological development of dear children*. New York: Oxford University Press.

Mayer-Johnson, R. (1984). *The picture communication symbols*. Solana Beach, CA: Mayer-Johnson.

Mayer-Johnson, R. (1985). *The picture communication symbols—Book II*. Solana Beach, CA: Mayer-Johnson.

Nagle, R. J., & Campbell, L. H. (1998). Cerebral palsy. In L. Phelps (Ed.), *Health-related disorders in children and adolescents* (pp. 145–153). Washington, DC: APA Books.

National Center for Health Statistics (1994). *Data from the national health interview survey*. Washington, DC: U.S. Department of Health and Human Services.

Pierce, P. L., & McWilliam, P. J. (1993). Emerging literacy and children with severe speech and physical impairments (SSPI): Issues and possible intervention strategies. *Topics in Language Disorders, 13*(2), 47–57.

Reid, D. K., Hresko, W. P., Hammill, D. D., & Wiltshire, S. (1991). *Test of Early Reading Ability—Deaf of Hard of Hearing (TERA-D/HH): Examiner's manual*. Austin, TX: PRO-ED.

Reiman, J., & Bullis, M. (1993). *Transition competence battery for deaf adolescents and young adults*. Santa Monica, CA: James Stanfield.

Salvia, J., & Ysseldyke, J. E. (1998). *Assessment* (7th ed.). Boston: Houghton Mifflin.

Sandberg, A. D. (1998). Reading and spelling among nonvocal children with cerebral palsy: Influence of home and school literacy environment. *Reading and writing: An interdisciplinary journal, 10*, 23–50.

Sandberg, A. D., & Hjelmquist, E. (1996). Phonologic awareness an literacy abilities in nonspeaking preschool children with cerebral palsy. *Augmentative and Alternative Communication, 12*(3), pp. 138–153.

Sappington, J., Reedy, S., Welch, R., & Hamilton, J. (1989). Validity of messages from quadriplegic persons with cerebral palsy. *American Journal of Mental Retardation, 94*(1), 49–52.

Schmelter-Davis, L. (1984). *Vocational evaluation of handicapped college students: Hearing, motor, and visually impaired* (ISBN 0-916855-01-5). Lincroft, NJ: Brookdale Community College (ERIC Document Reproduction Service No. ED 264 390).

Smith, A. K., Thurston, S., Light, J., Parnes, P., & O'Keefe, B. (1989). The form and use of written communication produced by physically disabled individuals using microcomputers. *Augmentative and Alternative Communication, 5*(2), 115–124.

Traxler, C. B. (2000). The Stanford Achievement Test, 9th Edition: National norming and performance standards for deaf and hard-of-hearing students. *Journal of Deaf Studies und Deaf Education, 5*(4), 337–348.

Weiner, E. (1980). Diagnostic evaluation of writing skills. *Journal of Learning Disabilities, 13*, 48–53.

White, A., & Tischler, S. (1999). Receptive sign vocabulary tests: Tests of single word vocabulary or iconicity? *American Annals of the Deaf, 144*(4), 334–338.

Yoshinaga-Itano, C., & Downey, D. M. (1996). The psychoeducational characteristics of school-aged students in Colorado with educationally significant hearing losses. *Volta Review, 98*(1), 65–96.

13

Functional Behavioral Assessment of Nonverbal Behavior

Christopher H. Skinner and Ruth A. Ervin

Interest in functional behavioral assessment (FBA) procedures may be traced to several factors. First, a long-established and evolving research base has demonstrated that FBA procedures can play an important role in preventing and remedying problem behaviors, particularly in people with disabilities (Ervin, Ehrhardt, & Poling, 2001). Second, psychologists and educators have often sought to enhance service delivery by linking assessment procedures to interventions, thereby unifying these primary service activities (Batsche & Knoff, 1995; Gresham & Lambros, 1998). Third, recent statutory changes in how students with disabilities are served have enhanced interest in functional behavioral assessment across psychoeducational professionals (Nelson, Roberts, Rutherford, Mathur, & Aaroe, 1999; Telzrow, 1999; Yell & Shriner, 1997).

Researchers and practitioners have demonstrated how FBA procedures can be used to identify the function of various behaviors, thus leading to interventions that have successfully reduced inappropriate behaviors. Because functional behavioral assessment procedures do not require clients or students to provide verbal or written reports of their behavior or conditions surrounding those behaviors, FBA procedures are particularly well suited for determining the function of behaviors of

Christopher H. Skinner, Department of Educational Psychology and Counseling, University of Tennessee, Knoxville, Tennessee 37996.   Ruth A. Ervin, Department of Psychology, Western Michigan University, Kalamazoo, Michigan 49008.

Handbook of Nonverbal Assessment, edited by R. Steve McCallum. Kluwer Academic/Plenum Publishers, 2003.

students with communication skills deficits (e.g., students with severe and profound disabilities who are nonverbal, students with autism who have poor receptive and expressive language skills). Although some FBA procedures do require assessor–student verbal or written communication, throughout this chapter we will describe and provide examples of how FBA procedures can be used to identify the function of various behaviors in nonverbal students.

FOUNDATIONS OF FBA

Psychoeducational professionals employ FBA procedures and traditional psychometric assessment procedures for similar reasons (e.g., to identify or confirm problems and collect data that enhances their ability to develop more effective procedures to prevent and remedy problems). Furthermore, FBA and traditional assessment models depend on similar assessment techniques such as checklists and rating scales and direct observation (Shapiro & Kratochwill, 2000).

Although FBA and traditional models of assessment have similar broad goals and employ similar data-gathering techniques, FBA is based on a different set of assumptions. Many traditional psychoeducational theories view problem behaviors as symptoms of deeper, underlying, within-student problems. For example, disruptive behaviors may be caused by intraindividual traits, conditions, or disorders (e.g., attachment disorders, attention-deficit/hyperactivity disorder). Generally, these causal variables are thought to be stable and somewhat resistant to change (Hartmann, Roper, & Bradford, 1979; Nelson & Hayes, 1979). In many instances, it is not possible to directly observe these within-subject causal variables, conditions, or traits. Thus, traditional assessment procedures often rely on student communications to collect data related to these within-student variables. For example, a teenager may keep a diary, a young child may be asked to respond verbally to vague stimuli (e.g., ink blots, pictures, sentence fragments), or a clinical interview is often used as part of the assessment or diagnostic process. Because students' verbal (e.g., clinical interview) or written (e.g., sentence completion) responses are often used to assess these internal (within-subject) causal variables, determining if a student has these underlying problems can prove challenging when student–assessor communication is hindered. However, as the current text indicates, researchers have made, and continue to make, important advances in this area.

Under a behavioral model, specific problems are not viewed as mere symptoms of underlying, within-student traits or disorders. Rather, the behaviors themselves are of interest, and altering these behaviors is considered a valid psychoeducational goal (Nelson & Hayes, 1979). Furthermore, under an operant behavioral model, behaviors are assumed to be caused by or maintained by an interaction between current environmental conditions and an organism's past learning history (McComas, Hoch, & Mace, 2000; Sprague, Sugai, & Walker, 1998). Therefore, the focus of a *functional* behavioral model of assessment is to identify the current environmental conditions that are maintaining or reinforcing behaviors of interest (i.e., target behaviors).

Identifying environmental conditions that maintain specific behaviors may allow one to make inferences with respect to a student's past learning history. These inferences may be useful in that they may allow the researcher to determine what events in the subject's past may contribute to current problems, which in turn may allow researchers to develop prevention programs. Although preventing problems is an important goal, in many cases it is often difficult to determine when and why a specific behavior first presented itself. For example, it may not be possible to determine why a person first began to engage in echolalic speech (repeating words and phrases) or hand flapping (e.g., repetitive waving of hands in front of one's eyes). Regardless of etiology, it is often possible to determine what current environmental conditions are *maintaining* these behaviors (Townsend, 2000). When attempting to remedy problems, FBA procedures tend to focus on current environmental conditions that are maintaining current aberrant behaviors (Hartmann et al., 1979).

Although there are many behavioral theories (Malone, 1990; Staddon, 1993), FBA procedures are most closely associated with B. F. Skinner's operant psychology (Ervin, Ehrhardt et al., 2001). Operant psychology is concerned with how behaviors operate on the environment. Environmental conditions that maintain behaviors are positive reinforcement and negative reinforcement. Positive reinforcement occurs when, under specific antecedent stimulus conditions, consequent stimuli (e.g., reinforcing stimuli) are delivered contingent upon behavior, *and* this process increases the probability of that behavior reoccurring when those antecedent conditions reoccur. Negative reinforcement occurs when stimuli are removed contingent upon behavior, *and* this process increases the probability of that behavior reoccurring when those antecedent stimulus conditions reoccur. FBA procedures are designed to specify reinforcement contingencies that are currently maintaining target behaviors. Specification includes delineating antecedent conditions, target behaviors, and consequent events that are contingent upon target behaviors.

Specifying maintaining contingencies may allow psychoeducational professionals to develop more effective treatments (Bergan & Kratochwill, 1990; Sprague et al., 1998). For example, suppose that FBA data suggest that a student's hand-flapping behavior is being maintained or reinforced by teacher attention. Treatment may then be constructed whereby teachers remove attention contingent upon hand flapping, but maintain or deliver attention contingent upon more desirable behavior (e.g., differential reinforcement of other behaviors, DRO; differential reinforcement of incompatible behaviors, DRI). Now, suppose that hand flapping is being maintained by the removal of teacher attention (i.e., negative reinforcement). In this situation, the DRO and DRI interventions are likely to strengthen, rather than reduce, the hand-flapping behavior (Townsend, 2000).

NONVERBAL BEHAVIORAL ASSESSMENT PROCEDURES

FBA procedures differ from traditional assessment procedures and general behavioral assessment procedures because the focus is on identifying and specifying the contingencies that are reinforcing target behaviors within the natural environment (Carr, 1993). Interviewing target students and other self-report techniques (e.g., checklist and rating scales) may allow one to gather data designed to specify these contingencies. These self-report measures can provide rich and detailed information. However, in the current chapter, we exclude these assessment procedures for several reasons. First, when communication is problematic (e.g., the subject does not speak), collecting this type of data can be extremely difficult. One of the primary advantages of FBA procedures is that they do not rely on subject reports. Thus, FBA is particularly useful for assessing nonverbal behavior and the contingencies that may be maintaining these behaviors.

If students have strong verbal skills, they may be able to identify quickly and accurately why they are engaging in a target behavior (Sprague et al., 1998). For example, suppose that Johnny's disruptive outburst is being reinforced with teacher attention. Asking Johnny why he is engaging in these behaviors could yield a response "because when I do the teacher notices me." However, in many instances, students may not be *conscious* of the contingencies that are reinforcing and consequently maintaining their behavior. Thus, in our previous example, the student may not be intentionally manipulating teacher attention with their disruptive behavior. Additionally, demand characteristics of assessment situations may bias student responses with respect to function. Thus, in many instances, it may be extremely difficult for students to identify, specify, and report the functions (i.e., reinforcement contingencies) of their own behavior.

In other situations, students simply do not have the verbal and/or cognitive skills to provide FBA data via self-report. Given FBA's roots in operant conditioning research and the study of lower-level organisms' behavior (e.g., laboratory pigeons), it is not surprising that FBA procedures have been developed and successfully applied across human behavior where students or clients have limited verbal skills or severe communication disorders. FBA procedures have been used to identify the function of specific behaviors in students with severe disabilities and communication deficits, including students with severe mental retardation, students with autism, and students with severe mental illness (e.g., Durand & Crimmins, 1987; McComas et al., 2000; Townsend, 2000). Although FBA procedures can be used across behaviors and students, one strength of these procedures for assessing behavior when verbal communication is hindered (e.g., students with speech or hearing deficits, students with autism, students who do not speak) is that many FBA procedures do not require verbal communication between the assessor and the student being assessed.

For these reasons, FBA procedures have been developed that rely less on self-reports for identifying the function of student behaviors. Rather, procedures used to identify extra-subject variables (e.g., positive and negative reinforcement contingencies) that may be maintaining target behaviors in the natural environment typically include informant reports (e.g., interviews, rating scales), direct observation in natural environments (e.g., antecedent–behavior–consequent (A–B–C) recording, scatter-plot recording), and observation in modified or analog environments (e.g., experimental functional analysis). Next, these types of functional assessment techniques will be described and analyzed.

Informant Reports: Interviews and Rating Scales

FBA Interviews

Perhaps the most common and most researched procedures for collecting functional assessment data via informant interviews are based on the structured interview format developed by Bergan (1977) and expanded on by others (e.g., Bergan & Kratochwill, 1990; Sheridan, Kratochwill, & Bergan, 1996). There are three structured interviews that are essential to Bergan's behavioral consultation model of service delivery.

Initially, the series of interviews focuses on the target behaviors and related goals. These goals include defining target behaviors, estimating target behavior levels, and developing data collection systems designed to measure target behaviors. However, in this first interview, the focus is also on soliciting information from informants that may indicate contingencies of reinforcement that are maintaining target behaviors within natural environments. Thus, structured interviews are design to collect data that (a) indicate when and where target behaviors are more likely to occur, (b) specify sequential events that precede and follow target behaviors, and (c) identify procedures that have been attempted to remedy problems.

Also, behavioral interview data can allow one to identify other variables that may impact treatment selection and implementation. These variables include (a) teacher or parent skills, (b) acceptability or perceptions regarding specific interventions, (c) resources (time, other responsibilities) available to apply to the problem, (d) goals with respect to immediacy, levels, and stability of desired behavior, (e) priorities when multiple behaviors are problematic, and (f) maintenance issues and generalization procedures.

Strengths and Limitations of FBA Interviews

Initial referrals often fail to provide information that specifies target behaviors. The flexible verbal exchange that occurs during structured interviews with referring agents (e.g., teachers or parents) may be the most efficient procedure for obtaining clear, operational definitions of target behaviors, especially when these behaviors are atypical or unusual. Through verbal exchange, these interviews also can be used to develop data collection procedures that can be used to (a) confirm problems, (b) evaluate and precisely measure characteristics of target behaviors (e.g., rate, variability, duration, intensity), (c) establish treatment objectives and goals, and (d) provide baseline data that allow one to evaluate the effects of interventions (Bergan, 1977).

Interviews also allow psychoeducational professionals to determine when and where the behavior is most likely to occur. Data on variability across settings, activities, and time allow one to schedule direct observation sessions. Additionally, this type of data may assist in identifying the function of target behaviors. For example, suppose a target behavior is most likely to occur only during a specific activity (e.g., communication training). These data suggest that the conditions during communication training differ from other conditions and somehow reinforce this target behavior. For example, the target behavior may be reinforced in this setting because it allows the student to escape or avoid this activity or some specific stimuli associated with this activity (e.g., the instructor who conducts communications training). Perhaps the communication instructor is more likely to attend to or reinforce target behaviors during these instructional activities.

Interview data can be used to collect reports on sequential events that immediately precede target behaviors and those that immediately follow target behaviors. Because reinforcement is stronger when it immediately follows target behaviors, establishing this sequence of events may help identify consequent events (i.e., positive and negative reinforcing events) that are maintaining target behaviors (Neef, Mace, & Shade, 1993; Neef, Shade, & Miller, 1994). Obtaining sequential data is critical because many reinforcing events are conditioned. Therefore, an event that serves as a reinforcer for some behaviors, under some conditions, for some children, may serve as a neutral stimulus or punishing event across other conditions, behaviors, or children (Kazdin, 2001). The flexibility of verbal exchanges provided via interviews allows one to specify atypical idiosyncratic contingent relationships.

However, not all events that immediately follow behaviors are functionally related to those behaviors. One of the primary advantages of interview data is that they allow psychoeducational professionals to collect data on events that do not immediately follow target behavior but may be reinforcing target behaviors. For example, during a specific activity a child may engage in destructive behavior (e.g., throwing educational materials on the floor), which is followed by a teacher or parent reprimand. However, this reprimand may not be functionally related to the target behavior. Instead, by eventually giving up and ceasing all attempts to engage the child in the educational activity, the teacher may reinforce the behavior. Thus, the reinforcing event that is maintaining the behavior (e.g., withdrawal of the educational demand, thus the function of the behavior is escape avoidance) may be more temporally distant from the target behavior than another event (e.g., social attention in the form of the reprimand) that frequently tends to occur immediately after the target behavior but is not functionally related to the target behavior.

Temporally distant antecedent events also can impact functional relationships. For example, Ray and Watson (in press) found that inappropriate classroom behaviors served different functions dependent upon whether the student woke on time or late. When the student woke late, aggressive behaviors were maintained by escape, and when the student woke on time, aggressive behaviors were maintained by access to tangible reinforcers. Interviews provide a means to collect data on delayed reinforcers and antecedent events or establishing operations that are functionally related to target behaviors.

Interview data also can help determine if the behavior is being reinforced intermittently. Researchers have shown that behaviors on thin and intermittent schedules of reinforcement may be more resistant to extinction (Kazdin, 2001). Interviews with individuals who have a long history of interacting with the target student may be able to provide reports of these intermittent reinforcers by providing information on events that typically follow target behaviors and events that *occasionally* follow target behaviors.

Interview data also may allow one to determine what interventions have been previously implemented and the impact of these interventions. The significance of determining what has been tried in the past is clear. For example, an educator may report that they have tried to consequent a target behavior with time out and that this procedure increased the child's target behavior. Such a report may suggest that the target behavior is being reinforced by escape avoidance, as opposed to attention.

Reports of previous interventions and their success should be interpreted with caution. Some interventions require high levels of integrity for them to be effective. However, research on treatment integrity suggests that many interventions are not carried out accurately or consistently (Noell, Witt, Gilbertson, Ranier, & Freeland, 1997; Sterling-Turner, Watson, Wildmon, Watkins, & Little, 2001; Watson & Robinson, 1996). Additionally, some interventions may have a gradual effect that is difficult to detect without precise measurement. Therefore, sometimes when informants report that an intervention failed, the intervention may have actually been working, but the effect was gradual and subtle. Consequently, when an informant reports that an intervention was not effective, this lack of effectiveness may have little implication for determining the function of the behavior unless the treatment was implemented with integrity, and evaluation of intervention effectiveness was precise. Again, the flexibility inherent in the interview process may allow one to discern whether previous interventions were implemented with integrity and evaluated appropriately.

FBA Rating Scales

Checklists and rating scales have long played a role in diagnosing students. These instruments include general or broad-band assessment instruments (e.g., Devereux Behavior Rating Scale; Naglieri, LeBuffe, & Pfeiffer, 1993) and narrow-band instruments designed to measure specific behaviors (e.g., Social Skills Rating System; Gresham & Elliott, 1990) or disorders (e.g., ADHD Rating Scale—IV; DuPaul, Power, Anastopoulos, & Reid, 1998). Psychometric properties associated with these instruments and the ability to compare response patterns with a normative sample have allowed practitioners to use these instruments for screening, diagnostic, and treatment evaluation purposes. However, few data have been collected to show how they lead to more effective interventions (Merrell, 2000).

Recently, researchers have begun to develop informant report measures designed to indicate the function of target behaviors. The Motivational Assessment Scale (MAS; Durand & Crimmins, 1988b) is a teacher report instrument that can be used after target behaviors have been identified. Teachers respond to a series of questions across a 7-item Likert scale (never to always) designed to indicate conditions when target behaviors are more likely to occur. Scores are summed across four possible functions of the target behavior, including sensory stimulation, negative reinforcement or escape avoidance, positive reinforcement—social attention, and positive reinforcement—access to tangibles. For example, a score of always on the item that asks if the target behavior occurs following a request to perform a difficult task suggests that the behavior may be serving an escape-avoidance function. However, a response of always to an item that asks if the behavior occurs whenever the teacher ceases attending to the child would suggest that the behavior is being reinforced with attention.

The Problem Behavior Questionnaire (PBQ—Lewis, Scott, & Sugai, 1994) is similar in that the target behavior is already defined, and responses are based on how often this behavior occurs under specific conditions. However, this measure focuses on five conditions. Four conditions are concerned with the consequence of the behavior including escaping peers, obtaining peer attention, escaping adults, and obtaining adult attention. The last category focuses solely on antecedent or settings events that may consistently precede target behaviors (e.g., is the behavior more likely to occur following disruptions of schedules?). Again, scores are summed, and results are designed to indicate the function of specific behaviors.

Strengths and Limitations of FBA Rating Scales

Once a target behavior is specified or defined, perhaps the most obvious advantage of checklists and rating scales is that they provide a time- and resource-efficient procedure for identifying the function of that behavior. Although these instruments may provide a general indication of behavioral function (e.g., escape avoidance), typically these instruments do not indicate specific antecedent and consequent events, conditions, or stimuli that are functionally related to that behavior within the specific environment of concern (e.g., escaping feedback from a teacher versus avoiding doing a task). Therefore, other data-collection procedures (e.g., interview) may be needed to identify these variables more precisely.

In one of the earliest investigations of the validity of checklist and rating scales, Durand and Crimmins (1988a) collected MAS, direct observation data, and experimental functional analysis data to attempt to determine the function of self-injurious behavior in eight participants. Results showed that the three assessment procedures tended to correlate. These results suggest that the MAS is a valid procedure for determining the function of a student's self-injurious behavior.

Crawford, Brockel, Schauss, and Miltenberger (1992) conducted a study where eight staff members (four residential and four vocational trainers) completed the MAS for four subjects who engaged in high rates of stereotypic behavior. MAS results showed agreement (i.e., results indicated the same function) among all four vocational staff. However, MAS results from the residential staff were inconsistent as identification of function varied across staff completing the instrument. Furthermore, direct observation data (A–B–C) did not always suggest the same function as MAS data. Similarly, Townsend (2000) found that MAS results identified different functions of echolalic behaviors than experimental functional analysis results.

Research and development of FBA checklists and rating scales has just begun. While some studies have found evidence supporting the reliability and validity of these measures, results from other studies suggest psychometric weaknesses with these instruments (Akande, 1994; Crawford et al., 1992; Sigafoos, Kerr, & Roberts, 1994; Thompson & Emerson, 1995; Townsend, 2000). Clearly, more research is needed to establish the validity and reliability of these instruments (Sturmey, 1994). The limitations of informant report rating scales are well known. Merrell (2000) summarizes these limitations including response bias (i.e., halo effects, leniency/severity effects, and central tendency). However, these effects have been primarily investigated with respect to measures of target behaviors or within-student constructs (e.g., diagnostic measures). Researchers should conduct similar studies of FBA checklists and rating scales to determine if these limitations impact informant reports designed to indicate the function of the behavior, as opposed to the presence, level, or severity of behaviors, symptoms, or disorders.

Merrell (2000) discusses error variance that can be attributed to source (who provides the ratings), settings (ratings vary across settings where the child is observed), and temporal variance (ratings change over time). When constructs of interest are assumed to be relatively stable, variance across source, settings, and time is assumed to be an index of error. However, variance across source, settings, and time is not always viewed as error under behavioral models. In fact, variability across conditions is often necessary for determining the function of a behavior. Thus, many procedures used to evaluate traditional measures may have to be adjusted. Regardless, as Shriver, Anderson, and Proctor (2001) indicate, FBA procedures are used to assess a construct (i.e., a functional relationship), and if these procedures are to have applied value, they must accurately indicate those variables that are maintaining target behaviors within natural settings. Because FBA checklist and rating scales are relatively more structured than other FBA procedures (e.g., interviews), these instruments may prove invaluable in developing procedures for evaluating the quality (e.g., reliability and validity) of FBA data.

Direct Observation in Natural Environments

One of the advantages of an operant model of psychology is that both target behaviors and variables that are functionally related to target behaviors can often be directly observed. Thus, behavioral psychology has long employed direct observation procedures as an integral part of assessment. There are many procedures that can be used to record direct observation data (see Skinner, Freeland, and Shapiro, in press, for a comprehensive review). Below, we will discuss and provide examples of narrative and empirical procedures for recording FBA data.

Narrative Recordings

Narrative recordings merely require an observer to write a description of student behaviors and events surrounding those behaviors. Narrative recordings can provide a flexible and rich description of a child's behavior. These recordings that describe target behaviors can be used to help specify or operationally define target behaviors. Furthermore, narrative descriptions of target behaviors can provide general information about the behavior (e.g., rate, intensity, and topography) that may be necessary for developing empirical data-collection systems that allow one to measure target behavior levels and evaluate the effects of intervention procedures more precisely.

One example of a narrative recording is a communications log that may be used by parents and teachers to communicate with each other (Skinner, Freeland, & Shapiro, in press). Thus, a parent may send daily narrative reports that describe a student's behavior and events surrounding that behavior to a teacher. For example, a narrative report from a parent may indicate that a student wet his bed last night, had difficulty falling asleep, or was noncompliant during preschool morning routines. These data may provide information on setting events that may influence the student's behavior in school (Ray & Watson, in press).

When serious behaviors occur, educators are often required to write an incident report or a narrative description of the behavior that includes events that preceded the behavior, and how they reacted to or dealt with the behavior. This form of narrative recording is similar to narrative A–B–C recording. During A–B–C recording, an observer may use the occurrence of a previously defined target behavior or class of target behaviors (often based on interview data or previous observations) as a stimulus or cue to write a description of the target behavior (e.g., Ralph began to slap his face repeatedly), general conditions that preceded the target behavior (e.g., Mrs. Smith was conducting picture communication training with Ralph, while Mrs. Jones was providing food preparation training to the other four students), specific events that immediately preceded the target behavior (e.g., Mrs. Smith took a picture card away from Johnny that he was chewing on), and events that immediately followed the target behavior (e.g., Mrs. Smith ceased picture communication training and held Johnny's hands next to his side).

Strengths and Limitations of Narrative Recordings

Narrative recordings of events surrounding target behaviors may allow one to identify antecedent and consequent events that are functionally related to target behaviors. Thus, in our above example, narrative recording data suggest that the self-injurious behavior may be positively reinforced by the teacher holding Johnny's hands to his side or negatively reinforced by the cessation of sight–word training. Additionally, these data suggest that taking the flash card away from Johnny is an antecedent event that often precedes self-injurious behavior.

Narrative recording takes time and therefore often results in discontinuous observations. Thus, while observers are busy writing descriptions, they may miss the opportunity to observe and record important events that may be functionally related to target behaviors (Skinner, Dittmer, & Howell, 2000). Additionally, data are likely to be influenced by the observer's writing skills, vocabulary, and training. For example, a trained observer may be more skilled in observing and recording subtle events that may be functionally related to target behaviors (e.g., the student sitting next to Jane looked at her and smiled after she began hand flapping). Thus, it may be difficult to confirm narrative data.

It is often impossible to translate narrative recordings to empirical data. Therefore, it may be difficult to use narrative data to measure behaviors with enough precision so that these data can be used to evaluate gradual changes or trends in target behaviors. This limits the utility of narrative recordings for evaluating intervention effects. Additionally, without empirical data, it may be difficult to determine if target behaviors are more likely to occur under some conditions than others (Skinner, Dittmer, et al., 2000). These conditional probability data are often useful, if not critical, for determining the function of a behavior.

Empirical Recording Procedures

Empirical recording procedures typically require an observer to record the presence of a previously defined behavior or event with a tally. Thus, the first step in constructing empirical recording procedures is to operationally define the behaviors or events to be recorded. Next, a data-recording system must be established. For low-rate, discrete behaviors, frequency counts are often used, which can be translated into rate data (e.g., two disruptive outbursts in 30 min). However, for high-rate or continuous behaviors, interval recording systems are often used to estimate durations of behavior. With whole-interval recording, a behavior or event must occur for an entire interval for it to be recorded as present. With partial interval recoding, the behavior or event must be present only for an instant during the interval for it to be recorded as present. With momentary time sampling, the behavior or event must be observed at the moment an interval begins for it to be recorded as present (Powell, Martindale, Kulp, Martindale, & Bauman, 1977).

Strengths and Limitations of Direct Observation in Empirical Recording Procedures

Empirical recording procedures yield more precise data that allow for more immediate evaluation of treatment effects and conditional probabilities. Additionally, empirical recordings allow target behaviors to be verified with a level of precision that may be necessary when important decisions are being made. Finally, with empirical recording systems, observers typically record the presence of a behavior or event by tallying (i.e., writing a slash in a specified place) as opposed to providing written descriptions of behavior. These characteristics of empirical recording allow observers to collect more precise data on multiple behaviors and events in a more continuous manner than narrative recording (Skinner, Rhymer, & McDaniel, 2000). Collecting data on multiple behaviors and events (e.g., teacher directions, teacher feedback) in a continuous manner allows observers to obtain a record of the temporal sequence of these events that may assist with identify antecedent and consequent conditions that surround target behaviors.

Researchers have developed various direct observation systems (e.g., *State-Event Classroom Observation System*; Saudargus, 1992). However, their utility for establishing functional relationships has not been empirically validated across cases. Furthermore, because settings, target behaviors, and consequent conditions may vary across cases, researchers often develop their own direct observation system. In order to do this, interview data and narrative recordings may be used to establish observation targets (e.g., target behaviors and antecedent and consequent events) and characteristics of these targets (rates, levels, intensity, continuity) that should be considered when developing interval recording systems (Skinner, Rhymer et al., 2000).

Empirical recording observations in natural environments may be ideal when target behaviors are being reinforced immediately. However, these systems may be less useful for collecting data on delayed reinforcement. For example, a child may misbehave and immediately receive a teacher reprimand contingent upon the misbehavior. However, the reprimand may have no functional relationship to the behavior. Instead, the child may be misbehaving in order to receive delayed peer attention at recess (Skinner, Rhymer et al., 2000).

Data collected in natural settings is often considered more valid than data collected in analog settings because one does not have to assume that behaviors would be constant across artificial and natural conditions. However, the process of observing behaviors can cause reactivity, which may impact the validity of assessment data. For example, when an independent observer enters the classroom to record behaviors, the classroom environment has been altered, and the presence of this observer may impact target student behavior, teacher behavior, and peer behavior.

Researchers have identified a variety of variables that impact subject or target student reactivity including (a) what the child is told about the observers presence, (b) perceived power of the observer, and (c) obtrusiveness of the observer and their behaviors. There are several procedures that can be used to reduce reactivity. Independent observers should not orient themselves directly and continuously toward target students, respond to any activities that occur during observation periods, or communicate with students (Skinner, Dittmer et al., 2000). They should enter the room as unobtrusively as possible (e.g., before class begins) and station themselves where they are less likely to command student attention (e.g., the back of the room). Finally, reactivity tends to fade over time. Thus, initial assessments may produce behaviors and events less typical (i.e., more reactivity) than subsequent assessments.

In order to reduce reactivity, teachers should not inform target students or peers why the observer is in the room. However, it is difficult to reduce teacher reactivity, as they typically know why you are present, which student is the focus of your observations, and what behaviors and events may be of particular interest. While direct observation data in natural environments may yield precise and verifiable data, caution is required when interpreting these data because it is not possible to determine the precise impact of reactivity. For example, a teacher who typically reprimands a student who fails to follow directions may be more likely to redirect the student or ignore the student when an independent observer is present. This reactivity may mislead observers in their attempts to identify the function of a particular behavior under typical (e.g., nonreactive) environmental conditions.

EXPERIMENTAL FUNCTIONAL ANALYSES IN ANALOG OR NATURAL CONTEXTS

As described above, data gathered through interviews, rating scales, and/or observations are analyzed and interpreted to formulate hypotheses regarding functional relations between environmental variables and target behaviors. In some cases, when data are clear and consistent, it may be sufficient to develop hypotheses and intervention strategies directly from these data sources. In other cases, particularly when data gathered from various descriptive sources (interviews, observations, rating scales) are ambiguous and difficult to interpret, it may be necessary to actually *test* hypotheses through an "experimental functional analysis." According to Cone (1997), the process of verifying causal hypotheses can be accomplished through formal systematic manipulations (e.g., withdrawal designs, alternating treatments designs) or through less formal means (e.g., structuring observations to compare naturally occurring situations associated with low and high rates of the target behavior).

A recent review of the research literature on school-based applications of functional assessment (Ervin, Radford et al., 2001) suggests that this verification phase is almost always (i.e., 90% of cases) included in research studies, making it a critical feature of functional behavioral assessment.

Analog Experimental Functional Analyses

One purpose of an experimental functional analysis is to use experimental methods to infer a causal relationship (always an approximation) between the environmental events (context) and a specified response (target behavior) to further our understanding of these relationships. In 1977, Carr reviewed the research on self-injurious behavior and hypothesized that there was a functional relationship between self-injury and its consequences in certain settings. This hypothesis sparked subsequent studies wherein experimental methods were used to evaluate this premise (e.g., Carr & Newsom, 1985; Iwata, Dorsey, Slifer, Bauman, & Richman, 1982/1994). For example, Iwata et al. (1982/1994) conducted systematic manipulations of environmental variables to examine four proposed functions of self-injurious behavior (i.e., escape from demands, gaining adult attention, access to tangible items, and access to sensory stimulation) across nine individuals with developmental disabilities. In order to establish tight experimental control (i.e., precisely control independent variables or reinforcement procedures and precisely measure the dependent variable, student behavior levels), manipulations were conducted in modified or analog environments. Conditions were randomly scheduled in a multielement design, and session length was also held constant and kept brief (i.e., 15 min) for each of the conditions. Results indicated that self-injurious behavior was functionally related to different environmental consequences across different individuals. Data indicated clearly distinguishable outcomes for seven of the nine participants and inconclusive outcomes for two participants.

Other studies have continued this line of analog experimental functional analysis research, extending applications across behaviors, populations, and settings (e.g., Carr, Newsom, & Binkoff, 1980; Derby et al., 1994; Northup et al., 1991). A variety of procedures for conducting analog experimental functional analyses are available in the literature. For example, procedures developed by Iwata and colleagues (1982/1994) have been modified to include the use of protective equipment (i.e., helmets, padding) and consultation from medical professionals when conducting experimental manipulations of variables that covary with self-endangering behavior. Other researchers have included the manipulation of antecedent events (events that precede the occurrence of problem behaviors) such as instructional demands (e.g., Durand & Crimmins, 1987) and task preference (e.g., Cooper et al., 1992) in addition to the traditional emphasis on the manipulation of consequences. Across studies, analog experimental manipulations can vary on several dimensions, including: (a) what variables should be manipulated (antecedents, consequences), (b) how they should be manipulated (e.g., schedules of reinforcement, length of sessions, sequence of sessions, number of sessions), and (c) how to record and interpret data. These factors need to be considered when preparing to collect experimental functional assessment data.

Experimental Functional Analyses in Natural Contexts

When the primary purpose of a functional assessment is to develop an intervention strategy, it may not be necessary to confirm the hypothesized behavior function through an analog functional analysis, unless descriptive data regarding function (interviews, ratings scales, observations) are ambiguous. If sufficient evidence (interviews, observations) indicates a clear functional relationship between problem behavior and environmental events, it may be appropriate to consider the selection of an assessment-based, functionally relevant intervention strategy (Dunlap & Kern, 1996).

Functionally relevant interventions will directly address the behavioral function (e.g., escape from task) in a number of ways. First, an intervention strategy may consider accommodations to reduce motivation for the problem behavior by addressing the antecedent context/situations (e.g., changing task demands). Second, the intervention strategy might focus on teaching an acceptable alternative behavior that serves the same purpose as the problem behavior (e.g., using a picture card to request a break when behavior is maintained by escape from task). Third, the intervention strategy might focus on weakening the functional relation between the problem behaviors and maintaining consequences (e.g., disconnecting the link between aggression and escape from task demands). Alternatively, the intervention might focus on strengthening the connection between an appropriate behavior that is incompatible with the problem behavior and access to the identified reinforcer.

Working from a functional assessment model, a number of specific, functionally relevant interventions might be useful. When selecting specific interventions, careful consideration should be given to how the intervention addresses functional relations, as well as to practical constraints (time, resources), and individual teacher and/or student preferences. An experimental analysis of the effects of hypothesized intervention strategies can be conducted to determine which intervention strategy should be selected. This can be accomplished through comparisons across various interventions (alternating treatments design) or through comparisons between a hypothesized intervention strategy and baseline conditions (no intervention).

Several studies have employed this intervention hypothesis testing approach to functional assessment. For example, Dunlap, Foster-Johnson, Clarke, Kern, and Childs (1995) examined the effects of systematically manipulating functionally relevant curricular variables that were identified by teachers of three elementary students with various disabilities (i.e., autism, mental retardation, emotional and behavior disorder). Results supported hypotheses that the modified classroom activities would lead to reductions in problem behaviors and increases in on-task behavior. In another study, Lalli, Browder, Mace, and Brown (1993) successfully evaluated the effects of functionally relevant intervention strategies during ongoing classroom activities across three children with severe to profound mental retardation. In this study, Lalli et al. also trained teachers to conduct experimental analysis to confirm hypothesized functions of behavior (teacher attention) in the classroom.

Strengths and Weaknesses of Analog and Natural Experimental Functional Analyses

Experimental functional analyses data can be used to empirically confirm behavior function and/or the utility of functionally relevant intervention strategies. When experimental analyses indicate clear and consistent functional relations between environmental variables (e.g., task demands, attention, hypothesized intervention strategies) and target behaviors (e.g., off-task, aggression, compliance), these analyses contribute to our understanding of behavior environment relations and our ability to influence these relations to promote desired change. Whether these analyses are conducted in analog or natural settings may be of issue depending on the purpose of the assessment.

Analog functional analyses allow for more control of extraneous variables than might be possible in more natural contexts. Thus, it may be helpful to conduct manipulations in modified environments, particularly when preliminary information (e.g., unstructured interviews, rating scales, direct observation data) is ambiguous or unclear. Further, because analog analyses allow for careful control of the context (environmental conditions) under study, it is sometimes possible to conduct these analyses over relatively brief time periods. The potential utility of brief, analog analyses is illustrated in the findings of assessments conducted across 79 outpatients with mild to severe mental retardation who exhibited various behaviors (self-injury, aggression, destruction, and stereotypy). Across these cases, manipulations of environmental contingencies demonstrated behavioral control during 84% of cases, supporting generalizability and utility of brief experimental functional analyses for high-frequency behaviors exhibited by individuals with developmental disabilities (Derby et al., 1992).

This tight experimental control and brevity of assessment may, however, come at the cost of what Cone (1997) refers to as "representational validity," the extent to which a measure faithfully portrays the target of assessment. According to findings of a study conducted by Derby et al. (1994), brief functional analyses are useful in generating hypotheses about distinct functions of high rate behaviors, but extended functional analyses are preferable to brief functional analyses when screening for multiple functions of behavior and in determining functional response classes. Another criticism is that functions identified by analog probe sessions may not agree with functions identified by functional analysis interviews or naturalistic direct observations (e.g., Conroy, Fox, Crain, Jenkins, & Belcher, 1996). These potential limitations are the subject of continued debate and research in functional assessment.

Practical applications of functional experimental analyses should be conducted with consideration of potential limitations of this methodology. Although these experimental analyses can contribute to the "believability" of functional assessments, they may be especially difficult to conduct in practical settings for several reasons. First, many practitioners (educators, clinicians) are not trained in such techniques. Second, such techniques require time and resources (space, extra personnel) that may not be readily available in applied settings (e.g., residential treatment centers, outpatient clinics, schools). Third, such techniques, which are often used several times each day, may deprive students of access to appropriate learning, employment, and/or social environments. Finally, research has yet to directly compare the cost–benefit ratios of experimental functional analysis procedures with those of other methods of assessment and intervention selection.

CASE EXAMPLE

Mark is a 7-year-old boy who was diagnosed with autism by local psychiatric and school personnel using criteria outlined in the *Diagnostic Statistical Manual of Mental Disorders*, 4th ed. (American Psychiatric Association, 1994). Although Mark could follow simple one-step verbal requests and gesture or manually sign in order to communicate basic needs (e.g., need to use the bathroom), his verbal communication skills were extremely limited. Mark attended a self-contained K-3 classroom in a public-school setting and lived at home with his mother, father, and 12-year-old sister.

Mark's stereotypic behaviors included head weaving, body rocking, and hand waving. Mark's parents and teacher were concerned that his stereotypy interfered with learning, so he was referred to the school psychologist for consultation. In order to assess the factors that contributed to the maintenance of Mark's stereotypy, the school psychologist conducted teacher and parent interviews, direct observations, and an experimental functional analysis.

According to teacher and parent interviews, Mark's stereotypic behaviors occurred across most settings and situations. Mark's parents indicated that he was less likely to engage in stereotypy when he was involved in an activity. He was more likely to engage in stereotypy when he was at the store or while waiting for assistance with an activity or task. Mark's teacher reported that Mark seemed to be more likely to engage in stereotypic behaviors when he was presented with school work.

In order to directly assess the possible functions of Mark's stereotypy, an experimental functional analysis was designed, which included four conditions: (a) free play, (b) attention, (c) no attention, and (d) demand (see Iwata et al., 1982/1994). During the free-play condition, Mark was provided with various preferred activities that were identified by his teacher and parents, and he was praised every 15 s with an absence of stereotypy. In the attention condition, Mark and his teacher sat at a table, and his teacher worked on some paperwork while Mark was provided with the same preferred activities he was given during the free-play condition. If Mark engaged in stereotypy during this condition, his teacher provided 5 seconds (s) of social attention, including asking him not to engage in stereotypy. The teacher responded to each occurrence of stereotypy in the same manner in order to assess the effects of positive reinforcement (in the form of social attention) on stereotypic responding. During the no-attention condition, the teacher was present in the room, but Mark was seated at a table alone without any activities. To assess the degree to which stereotypy occurred in the absence of environmental stimulation, no social attention was provided during this condition. Finally, in the demand condition, Mark's teacher provided a verbal task demand every 15 s. If Mark responded correctly to the task demand, the teacher praised his correct responding. If he did not respond within 5 s, his teacher provided a physical prompt. If Mark engaged in stereotypy during this condition, the teacher ceased providing task demands for a period of 30 s. This condition was designed to assess the degree to which Mark's stereotypic responding was sensitive to escape from task demands.

Each condition was presented for 10 min each day for a period of 5 days. The school psychologist conducted observations of the occurrence of Mark's stereotypy during these conditions through the use of a 5-s partial-interval recording procedure.

Results of the experimental functional analysis are presented in Figure 13.1. These results indicate that, consistent with the parent and teacher report, Mark's stereotypy occurred across all of the conditions, but differential effects were noted. More specifically, elevated levels of stereotypy were noted during the demand and no-attention conditions, and very low rates were noted during the free-play and attention conditions. When each of the topographies of stereotypy (i.e., head weaving, body rocking, and hand waving) was examined separately, the same patterns emerged. These data suggested that Mark's stereotypical behaviors functioned primarily to avoid/escape task demand conditions and also occurred at high rates during low levels of environmental stimulation. Given the differentially low rates of stereotypy during the attention and free-play conditions, social attention did not appear to be a maintaining factor for Mark's stereotypy.

The school psychologist met with Mark's parents and teacher to discuss the assessment results and implications for intervention. All parties agreed that the data gathered through teacher interviews and observations clearly and consistently indicated that Mark's stereotypic behaviors (i.e., head weaving, body rocking, and hand waving) occurred at higher rates during demand situations and were more likely to occur during low levels of environmental stimulation. Because the data were fairly clear and consistent, it was decided that the next step would be to develop an intervention based on the assessment results.

First, the team (i.e., parents, teacher, school psychologist) considered intervention components that might reduce Mark's motivation for engaging in stereotypy to escape or avoid task demands (e.g., enriching the

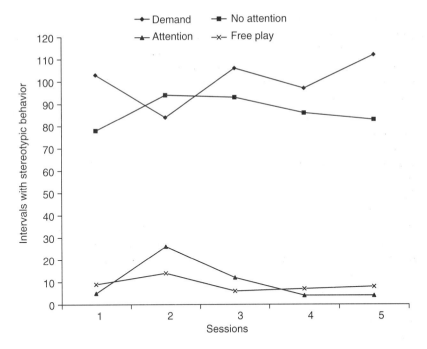

Figure 13.1   Experimental FBA Data for Mark's Stereotypic Behavior Across Conditions.

environment during task demands by playing music during certain less preferred activities, incorporating more hands-on activities, and interspersing preferred and less preferred tasks). Second, the team discussed the possibility of teaching Mark a more acceptable way of requesting escape from task demands (e.g., signing for a break, using a picture card to request assistance or a break from task demands). Third, strategies for weakening the functional relation between stereotypy and escape from task demands were explored, and strategies for strengthening the connection between task engagement and escape from tasks (i.e., scheduled breaks contingent on periods of task engagement) were considered.

Additionally, the team considered procedures designed to reduce stereotypic behavior during conditions of low levels of environmental stimulation. Specifically, they considered adding to Mark's communication program procedures that would allow Mark to make requests for specific stimuli (e.g., a preferred toy) or for the opportunity to engage in preferred behaviors (e.g., listen to music) during times when stimulation was low (e.g., free time).

Mark's case demonstrates how FBA data can be used to form hypotheses with respect to the function of target behaviors within natural environments. Equally as important is how FBA data can be used to rule out interventions. In Mark's case, the data suggested that attention was not reinforcing Mark's stereotypic behavior. Thus, interventions designed to reduce attention contingent upon stereotypic behavior and to provide attention contingent upon no stereotypic behavior (e.g., DRO) were ruled out, as FBA data suggested that these would not have been effective and may have actually exacerbated the problem (i.e., increased Mark's stereo-typic behavior). In this manner, FBA data may help prevent professionals (e.g., teachers) and others (e.g., parents) from developing and implement-ing interventions that are unlikely to be successful. Such failures can cause professionals and parents to become frustrated and have a debili-tating effect on a future problem-solving behavior. For example, Mark's teacher, parents, and/or school psychologists may be less likely to engage in future systematic problem-solving and/or less likely to carry out future interventions with integrity if they had employed a DRO intervention that exacerbated Mark's stereotypic behavior.

FBA data provide information about idiosyncratic reinforcement. In addition to providing directions for interventions designed to address pre-senting problems, this information can be used to make other psycho-educational decisions. In Mark's case, FBA data suggested that parent and teacher attention is a neutral stimulus or a low-quality reinforcer. This is important because, relative to other reinforcers, attention is inexpensive, easy to deliver immediately, and less susceptible to satiation effects. Because psychoeducational programming and instruction may be more effective and efficient when attention is reinforcing, in Mark's case the FBA data may encourage the team to consider implementing procedures designed to enhance the reinforcing value of parent and teacher attention (e.g., pairing teacher and parent attention with high-quality reinforcers). If the team is successful, specific psychoeducational programming may become more effective and efficient. Additionally, both teachers and par-ents may be able to reinforce incidental (unplanned) appropriate behaviors more successfully within natural occurring environments (e.g., praise inci-dental prosocial or appropriate communication behaviors).

SUMMARY

Although covert behaviors such as thoughts and feelings (self-efficacy, optimism) are considered important to behaviorists (see Skinner, 1974), FBA is based on an operant model of psychology where overt behaviors are maintained by their effects on the environment. Because covert behaviors cannot impact the environment (some researchers inves-tigating extrasensory perception such as telekinesis may disagree), behav-ioral assessment procedures have traditionally measured observable behaviors and how they operate in their environments (e.g., observable reinforcement delivered contingent upon target behaviors). Thus, behav-ioral assessment and FBA have traditionally been less dependent upon self-reporting to assess variables of interest. This has led to numerous demonstrations of the effectiveness of FBA indicating the function of behav-iors in individuals who are nonverbal or who have other communication-skill deficits.

In the current chapter, we indicate how FBA procedures can be used to identify natural environmental contingencies that are maintaining the

behavior of individuals who lack the verbal skills to communicate information about the function of their behavior (e.g., nonverbal students).
These data can then be used to develop interventions based on this
within-subject data. Although FBA procedures are based on sound theory,
the development and evaluation of such procedures is in its infancy, and
future research is needed to improve the quality of these procedures so
that psychoeducational professionals can efficiently determine the function of target behaviors. Additionally, combining FBA and treatment effectiveness research may allow researchers to develop function-by-treatment
models of linking assessment to intervention, which may allow psychoeducational professionals to develop more effective prevention and remediation procedures *across subjects*, based on the assessed function of
target behaviors.

REFERENCES

Akande, A. (1994). The motivation assessment profiles of low-functioning children. *Early Child Development and Care, 101*, 101–107.

American Psychiatric Association. (1994). *Diagnostic statistical manual of mental disorders* (4th ed.). Washington, DC: Author.

Batsche, G. M., & Knoff, H. M. (1995). Linking assessment to intervention. In A. Thomas & J. Grimes (Eds.), *Best practices in school psychology—III* (pp. 569–586). Washington, DC: National Association of School Psychologists.

Bergan, J. R. (1977). *Behavioral consultation*. Columbus, OH: Merrill.

Bergan, J. R., & Kratochwill, T. R. (1990). *Behavioral consultation in applied settings*. New York: Plenum.

Carr, E. G. (1977). The motivation of self-injurious behavior: A review of some hypotheses. *Psychological Bulletin, 84*, 800–816.

Carr, E. G. (1993). Behavior analysis is not ultimately about behavior. *The Behavior Analyst, 16*, 47–49.

Carr, E. G., & Newsom, C. (1985). Demand-related tantrums. *Behavior Modification, 9*, 403–426.

Carr, E. G., Newsom, C. D., & Binkoff, J. A. (1980). Escape as a factor in the aggressive behavior of two retarded children. *Journal of Applied Behavior Analysis, 13*, 101–117.

Cone, J. D. (1997). Invited essay: Issues in functional analysis in behavioral assessment. *Behaviour Research and Therapy, 35*, 259–275.

Conroy, M., Fox, J., & Crain, L., Jenkins, A., & Belcher, K. (1996). Evaluating the social and ecological validity of analog assessment procedures for challenging behaviors in young children. *Education and Treatment of Children, 19*, 233–256.

Cooper, L. J., Wacker, D. P., Thursby, D., Plagmann, L. A., Harding, J., Millard, T., & Derby, M. (1992). Analysis of the effects of task preferences, task demands, and adult attention on child behavior in outpatient and classroom settings. *Journal of Applied Behavior Analysis, 25*, 823–840.

Crawford, J., Brockel, B., Schauss, S., & Miltenberger, R. G. (1992). A comparison of methods for the functional assessment of stereotypic behavior. *Journal of the Association for Persons with Severe Handicaps, 17*, 77–86.

Derby, K. M., Wacker, D. P., Peck, S., Sasso, G., DeRaad, A., Berg, W., Asmus, J., & Ulrich, S. (1994). Functional analysis of separate topographies of aberrant behavior. *Journal of Applied Behavior Analysis, 27*, 267–278.

Derby, M., Wacker, D., Sasso, G., Steege, M., Northup, J., Cigrand, K., & Asmus, J. (1992). Brief functional assessment techniques to evaluate aberrant behavior in an out-patient setting: A summary of 79 cases. *Journal of Applied Behavior Analysis, 25*, 713–721.

Dunlap, G., Foster-Johnson, L., Clarke, S., Kern, L., & Childs, K. E. (1995). Modifying activities to produce functional outcomes: Effects on the problem behaviors of students with disabilities. *Journal of the Association for Persons with Severe Handicaps, 20*, 248–258.

Dunlap, G., & Kern, L. (1996). Modifying instructional activities to promote desirable behavior: A conceptual and practical framework. *School Psychology Quarterly, 11*, 297–312.

DuPaul, G. J., Power, T. J., Anastopoulos, A. D., & Reid, R. (1998). *ADHD Rating Scale—IV: Checklists, norms, and clinical interpretation.* New York: Guilford Press.

Durand, V. M., & Crimmins, D. B. (1987). Assessment and treatment of psychotic speech in an autistic child. *Journal of Autism and Developmental Disorders, 17*, 17–28.

Durand, V. M., & Crimmins, D. B. (1988a). Identifying variables maintaining self-injurious behavior. *Journal of Autism and Developmental Disorders 18*, 99–117.

Durand, V. M., & Crimmins, D. B. (1988b). Motivational Assessment Scale. In M. Hersen & A. Bellack (Eds.), *Dictionary of behavioral assessment techniques* (pp. 309–310). Elmsford, NY: Pergamon.

Ervin, R. A., Ehrhardt, K. E., & Poling, A. (2001). Functional assessment: Old wine in new bottles. *School Psychology Review, 30*, 173–179.

Ervin, R. A., Radford, P. M., Bertsch, K., Piper, A. L., Ehrhardt, K. E., & Poling, A. (2001). A descriptive analysis and critique of the empirical literature on school-based functional assessment. *School Psychology Review, 30*, 193–210.

Gresham, F. M., & Elliott, S. N. (1990). *Social skills rating system.* Circle Pines, MN: American Guidance.

Gresham, F. M., & Lambros, K. M. (1998). Behavioral and functional assessment. In T. S. Watson & F. M. Gresham (Eds.), *Handbook of child behavior therapy* (pp. 3–22). New York: Plenum Press.

Hartmann, D. P., Roper, B. L., & Bradford, C. C. (1979). Some relationships between behavioral and traditional assessment. *Journal of Behavioral Assessment, 1*, 3–21.

Iwata, B., Dorsey, M., Slifer, K., Bauman, K., & Richman, G. (1982/1994). Toward a functional analysis of self-injury. *Journal of Applied Behavior Analysis, 27*, 197–209. (Reprinted from *Analysis and Intervention in Developmental Disabilities, 2*, 3–20, 1982.)

Kazdin, A. E. (2001). *Behavior modification in applied settings* (6th ed.). Belmont, CA: Wadsworth.

Lalli, J. S., Browder, D. M., Mace, F. C., & Brown, K. (1993). Teacher use of descriptive analysis data to implement interventions to decrease students' maladaptive behavior. *Journal of Applied Behavior Analysis, 10*, 141–150.

Lewis, T. J., Scott, T. M., & Sugai, G. (1994). The problem behavior questionnaire: A teacher based instrument to develop functional hypotheses of problem behavior in general education settings. *Diagnostique, 19(2–3)*, 103–115.

Malone, J. C. (1990). *Theories of learning: A historical approach.* Belmont, CA: Wadsworth.

McComas, J. J., Hoch, H., & Mace, F. C. (2000). Functional analysis. In E. S. Shapiro & T. R. Kratochwill (Eds.), *Conducting school-based assessment of child and adolescent behavior* (pp. 78–101). New York: Guilford Press.

Merrell, K. W. (2000). Informant reports: Theory and research in using child behavior rating scales in school settings. In E. S. Shapiro & T. R. Kratochwill (Eds.), *Behavioral assessment in schools: Theory research and practice* (2nd ed., pp. 233–256). New York: Guilford Press.

Naglieri, J. A., LeBuffe, P. A., & Pfeiffer, S. I. (1993). *Devereux Behavior Rating Scales—School Form.* San Antonio, TX: Psychological Corporation.

Neef, N. A., Mace, F. C., & Shade, D. (1993). Impulsivity in students with serious emotional disturbance: The interactive effects of reinforcer rate, delay, and quality. *Journal of Applied Behavior Analysis, 23*, 37–52.

Neef, N. A., Shade, D., & Miller, M. S. (1994). Assessing the influential dimensions of reinforcers on choice in students with serious emotional disturbance. *Journal of Applied Behavior Analysis, 24*, 389–408.

Nelson, R. O., & Hayes, S. C. (1979). Some current dimensions of behavioral assessment. *Behavioral Assessment, 1*, 1–16.

Nelson, J. R., Roberts, M. L., & Rutherford, R. B., Mathur, S. R., & Aaroe, L. A. (1999). A statewide survey of special education administrators and school psychologists regarding functional behavioral assessment. *Education and Treatment of Children, 22*, 267–279.

Noell, G. H., Witt, J. C., Gilbertson, D. N., Ranier, D. D., & Freeland, J. T. (1997). Increasing teacher intervention implementation in general education settings through consultation and performance feedback. *School Psychology Quarterly, 12,* 77–88.

Northup, J., Wacker, D., Sasso, G., Steege, M., Cigrand, K., Cook, J., & DeRaad, A. (1991). A brief functional analysis of aggressive and alternative behavior in an outclinic setting. *Journal of Applied Behavior Analysis, 24,* 509–522.

Powell, J., Martindale, B., Kulp, S., Martindale, A., & Bauman, R. (1977). Taking a closer look: Time sampling and measurement error. *Journal of Applied Behavior Analysis, 10,* 325–332.

Ray, K. P., & Watson, T. S. (in press). Analysis of temporally distant events on school behavior. *School Psychology Quarterly.*

Saudargus, R. A. (1992). *State-Event Classroom Observation System (SECOS).* Knoxville: University of Tennessee, Department of Psychology.

Shapiro, E. S., & Kratochwill, T. R. (2000). Introduction: Conducting a multidimensional behavioral assessment. In E. S. Shapiro & T. R. Kratochwill (Eds.), *Conducting school-based assessments of child and adolescent behavior* (pp. 1–20). New York: Guilford Press.

Sheridan, S. M., Kratochwill, T. R., & Bergan, J. R. (1996). *Conjoint behavioral consultation: A procedural manual.* New York: Plenum Press.

Shriver, M. D., Anderson, C. M., & Proctor, B. (2001). Evaluating the validity of functional behavioral assessment. *School Psychology Review, 30,* 180–192.

Sigafoos, J., Kerr, M., & Roberts, D. (1994). Inter-rater reliability analysis of the MAS: Failure to replicate with aggressive behavior. *Research in Developmental Disabilities, 15,* 333–342.

Skinner, B. F. (1974). *About behaviorism.* New York: Knopf.

Skinner, C. H., Dittmer, K. I., & Howell, L. A. (2000). Direct observation in school settings: Theoretical issues. In E. S. Shapiro & T. R. Kratochwill (Eds.), *Behavioral assessment in schools: Theory research and practice* (2nd ed., pp. 19–45). New York: Guilford Press.

Skinner, C. H., Freeland, J., & Shapiro, E. S. (in press). Applying behavioral assessment procedures to the problem solving process. In C. R. Reynolds & R. Kamphaus (Eds.), *Handbook of educational and psychological assessment of children: Personality, behavior, and context* (2nd ed.). New York: Guilford.

Skinner, C. H., Rhymer, K. N., & McDaniel, E. C. (2000). Naturalistic direct observation in educational settings. In E. S. Shapiro & T. R. Kratochwill (Eds.), *Conducting school-based assessments of child and adolescent behavior* (pp. 21–54). New York: Guilford Press.

Sprague, J., Sugai, B., & Walker, H. (1998). Antisocial behavior in schools. In T. S. Watson & F. M. Gresham (Eds.), *Handbook of child behavior therapy* (pp. 451–474). New York: Plenum Press.

Staddon, J. E. R. (1993). *Behaviorism: Mind, mechanism and society.* London: Duckworth.

Sterling-Turner, H. E., Watson, T. S., Wildmon, M., Watkins, C., & Little, E. (2001). Investigating the relationship between training type and treatment integrity. *School Psychology Quarterly, 16,* 56–67.

Sturmey, P. (1994). Assessing the functions of aberrant behaviors: A review of psychometric instruments. *Journal of Autism and Developmental Disorders, 24,* 293–304.

Telzrow, C. F. (1999). IDEA amendments of 1997: Promise or pitfall for special education reform? *Journal of School Psychology, 37,* 7–28.

Thompson, S., & Emerson, E. (1995). Inter-informant agreement on the motivation assessment scale: Another failure to replicate. *Mental Handicap Research, 8,* 203–208.

Townsend, B. J. K. (2000). *A functional analysis of the echolalic behavior of three children with autism in a residential school setting.* Unpublished doctoral dissertation, Mississippi State University, Starkville.

Watson, T. S., & Robinson, S. L. (1996). Direct behavioral consultation: An alternative approach to didactic consultation. *School Psychology Quarterly, 11,* 267–278.

Yell, M. L., & Shriner, J. G. (1997). The IDEA amendments of 1997: Implications for special and general education teachers, administrators, and teacher trainers. *Focus on Exceptional Children, 30,* 1–19.

14

Nonverbal Assessment of Personality and Psychopathology

John D. Wasserman

The appraisal of personality and psychopathology through nonverbal methodologies is distinguished by its widespread practice among psychologists, in spite of a dearth of empirically supported tests and procedures. As part of the assessment process, the vast majority of professionals use projective drawings (e.g., Camara, Nathan, & Puente, 2000) and implicitly observe nonverbal behaviors during interviews and test sessions (e.g., facial expressions, motor behaviors, and problem-solving approaches). At the same time, these approaches are often interpreted informally and unsystematically and relegated to a secondary status behind norm-referenced self-report and other-report procedures in arriving at diagnostic and treatment-related inferences. In this chapter, some historical perspectives are recounted and a framework offered for thinking about nonverbal tests within the domain of personality and psychopathology assessment. Several approaches to nonverbal assessment of personality are reviewed, including some traditional and enduring techniques as well as some newer pioneering efforts. Finally, areas of promising research are described that may suggest a new era in the use of nonverbal personality assessment procedures to augment language-based measures.

In psychological assessment, the appraisal of personality and psychopathology typically has the objectives of describing an individual's

John D. Wasserman, Center for Cognitive Development, Department of Psychology, George Mason University, Fairfax, Virginia 22030.

Handbook of Nonverbal Assessment, edited by R. Steve McCallum, Kluwer Academic/Plenum Publishers, 2003.

current state and symptomatology, underlying characterological and interpersonal styles, the content and focus of associated problems in living, and available intrapsychic coping resources and environmental supports. While the proximal goal of assessment is to answer specific referral questions and facilitate diagnosis, the ultimate goal is to produce a deeper understanding of the client's internal experience to facilitate effective intervention. Once problems are thoroughly understood, it becomes easier to formulate and implement an appropriate therapeutic intervention.

In general, the use of nonverbal tools in the appraisal of personality and psychopathology is indicated for any individual who cannot or does not respond accurately to linguistically loaded measures, or when the inclusion of language in the task negatively impinges upon test score validity or reliability. Nonverbal personality assessment may be indicated with (a) individuals with neurologically based acquired language disorders (e.g., aphasia, language-based learning disabilities), (b) individuals with varied cultural, linguistic, or national backgrounds (e.g., non-English speakers), (c) individuals who are illiterate or poorly educated, (d) individuals who are deaf or hard of hearing, (e) individuals with forms of emotional disturbance that are manifested through an inability or unwillingness to produce an adequate and unconstrained sample of verbal behavior (such as may be found in cases of severe depression, some psychoses, or selective mutism), or (f) individuals who are prone to misrepresent themselves on verbal self-report measures.

As defined here, a test is operationally nonverbal if it involves a relatively brief verbal instructional set (and therefore makes limited demands on the examinee's receptive language) and requires little or no verbal response (thereby involving minimal expressive language) on the part of the examinee. These criteria exclude popular measures such as the Rorschach Inkblot Test (Rorschach, 1921) and Thematic Apperception Test (TAT; Morgan & Murray, 1935), both of which involve the presentation of nonlinguistic pictorial stimuli and the elicitation of many verbal responses. It is noted, however, that this operational definition is not uniform, as Paunonen and Ashton (in press) consider the Rorschach and TAT to be nonverbal on the basis of the pictorial nature of the test stimuli.

Also excluded from the category of nonverbal assessment are tests that require reading of printed semantic material, such as the Beck Depression Inventory—II (BDI-II; Beck, Steer, & Brown, 1996) and the Minnesota Multiphasic Personality Inventory—2 (MMPI-2; Butcher, Dahlstrom, Graham, Tellegen, & Kaemmer, 1989). Reading is an inherently verbal and linguistically demanding process with strong word-knowledge requirements, even if little or no spoken language is involved in test administration. Reading skills are frequently impaired in individuals with language-related disorders. Additionally, most printed self-report tests are designed for use with adolescents at least 13 years of age because test content is at or above a sixth-grade reading level, leaving preschool and young school-aged children untestable through written self-report methods. Even sixth-grade reading levels may be too high for many adolescents referred for psychological evaluations, since they may have language-based learning problems or disabilities that impinge upon their reading skills. Nonverbal assessment techniques using no printed verbal instructions or semantic test stimuli provide a useful alternative to the limitations of language-based self-report instruments.

HISTORICAL ANTECEDENTS

The belief that personality and psychopathology may be most clearly understood through language probably traces its origins to Josef Breuer and Sigmund Freud's written accounts in the 1890s of the psychoanalytic "talking cure." The foundations of psychoanalysis placed a heavy emphasis on language expression and content, as per the admonition of psychoanalysts to their clients to "Say whatever comes into your mind."

The earliest psychometric attempts to measure personality were predominantly verbal self-report measures (e.g., Bernreuter, 1931; Woodworth, 1917) and rating scales (Scott, 1919), the latter increasing in popularity when easy-to-use graphic rating scales became accepted (Freyd, 1923). Isolated early efforts to use nonverbal methodologies to measure honesty and trustworthiness included Hartshorne and May's (1928) nine groups of tests, several of them nonverbal, which intentionally provided examinees with opportunities to cheat as a test of honesty. A few unsuccessful nonverbal adaptations of verbal tests were also available in the 1920s.

However, the nonverbal assessment of personality can be most easily traced to Florence L. Goodenough's (1926) publication of the Draw-a-Man test as a measure of intelligence, laying the groundwork for numerous derivative human figure drawing systems. In the editor's introduction to Goodenough's test, Lewis M. Terman explicitly noted its nonverbal qualities, having become sensitized to the issues of language-loaded assessments by criticisms of his Stanford–Binet intelligence scale. Goodenough speculated about the use of drawings in the assessment of personality, but it would remain for pioneers like John N. Buck (1948) and Karen Machover (1949) to more fully explore the nonintellective value of drawing tests.

With the advent of the projective testing movement, nonverbal assessment techniques showed substantial growth. Projective techniques purport to reveal the private world of the individual in a manner about which the examinee is typically unaware. Frank (1948), who coined the term *projective methods*, suggested that "The essential feature of a projective technique is that it evokes from the subject what is in various ways expressive of his private world and personality process" (p. 47). Nonverbal personality assessment techniques spawned in this era included drawing tests, fingerpainting techniques, expressive movement, and other visual–motor activities, as well as specialized methods such as the Szondi Test, Mosaic Test, and World Test (Bell, 1948).

Challenges to psychoanalytic theory (e.g., Eysenck, 1990; Holt, 1992), doubts about the theoretical assumptions behind the projective methods

(Exner, 1993; Wagner, 1999), and poor psychometric properties for many projective tests (e.g., Dumont & Smith, 1996; Smith & Dumont, 1995) have thrown into question the utility of projective measures. It is beyond the scope or intent of this chapter to defend the concept of projective testing, but it may not be necessary to accept the assumption of unconscious projection in order to find value in many so-called projective tests. For example, Exner (1993) has reconceptualized the Rorschach as a problem-solving task in which examinee perceptions of the inkblots and the nature of articulated responses reveal both state- and trait-based aspects of psychological operations; the role of projection has been relegated to a relatively minor role. A similar evolution in thinking has occurred with the projective drawings, which have been shown to have value in the discrimination of clinical groups even after the psychoanalytically oriented sign approach is abandoned in favor of a holistic or polythetic approach to interpretation (e.g., Tharinger & Stark, 1990). Accordingly, it is possible to use the projectives without accepting their implicit theoretical assumptions, so long as contemporary psychometric standards are met. We now turn our attention from theoretical limitations to specific nonverbal tests.

APPROACHES TO NONVERBAL ASSESSMENT OF PERSONALITY AND PSYCHOPATHOLOGY

In this section, a number of predominantly nonverbal measures of personality and psychopathology are described, including their theoretical approaches, administration and scoring, interpretation, technical adequacy, and strengths and weaknesses. The nonverbal assessments of personality and psychopathology described below are classified in three broad classes of tests adapted from those offered by Frank (1948) and Lindzey (1961), who emphasized the kind of response the technique elicits from the examinee:

- *Drawing techniques.* Drawings, depictions, or reproductions of persons, objects, and figures (e.g., Bender–Gestalt Test, Draw a Person, House–Tree–Person, Kinetic Family Drawing)
- *Object placement and play techniques.* Arrangement of materials and manipulatives in meaningful and interpretable ways (e.g., Erica Method, Family System Test, Mosaic Test, SandPlay, World Technique)
- *Self-rating and self-report techniques.* Rating a pictorial stimulus as it personally relates to oneself (e.g., Five-Factor Nonverbal Personality Questionnaire, Nonverbal Personality Questionnaire, Visual Analog Mood Scales).

To these could be added expressive/aesthetic techniques (e.g., finger-painting, expressive movement) and preference/choice techniques (e.g., Szondi Test). While tests belonging to these classes have been developed, none are used with any frequency or approach current standards of psychometric adequacy (Bell, 1948; Camara et al., 2000).

Although it remains to be proven, nonverbal methods may be sufficiently indirect so as to avoid a major limitation of verbal personality assessment methods—that they tend to be highly susceptible to deliberate efforts by examinees to misrepresent or manage their self-presentation by selectively endorsing items in a given direction. As Hutt (1985) observed, "Many of our personality tests are based on verbal responses to test stimuli. This can sometimes prove to be a serious limitation in cases in which verbal defense of façade can conceal, rather than reveal, pathology" (p. 113). Alternatively as Frank (1939) commented with respect to projective tests, "The most important things about an individual are what he cannot or will not say" (p. 395).

DRAWING TECHNIQUES

Drawing is a commonplace and familiar activity during development, and drawing tests offer a nonthreatening start to many psychological evaluations. The study of children's drawings dates back to the 1880s, but the first popular Draw-a-Man test was offered by Goodenough (1926). Norm-referenced and standardized updates of this drawing procedure as a measure of cognitive–intellectual ability are available in the Goodenough–Harris Drawing Test (Harris, 1963), Koppitz's (1968) Developmental Items, and the Draw a Person: A Quantitative Scoring System (Naglieri, 1988). Our focus is on personality assessment, however, and Goodenough's work spawned three main projective drawing techniques: Draw a Person, House–Tree–Person, and Kinetic Family Drawing.

Surveys of test usage show that several drawing measures still rank among the most popular with psychologists conducting assessments of personality and psychopathology: House–Tree–Person (ranked 4th), Bender–Gestalt Test (ranked 5th), Human Figures Drawings (ranked 9th), and Kinetic Family Drawings (ranked 15th) (Camara et al., 2000). Vass (1999) reports that 6,530 studies on drawing tests have been published since 1950, with about 100–170 studies published per year.

In spite of their long-standing popularity, the scientific status of drawing techniques remains in question. Reviews of evidence supporting the validity of human figure drawings for personality assessment have generally been mixed or negative (Cummings, 1986; Kahill, 1984; Klein, 1986; Knoff, 1993; Motta, Little, & Tobin, 1993a; Smith & Dumont, 1995; Thomas & Jolley, 1998). Leading criticisms include problems with the theoretical underpinnings of the projective hypothesis, interpretation that is susceptible to interpreter biases, inadequate test score reliability, inadequate normative bases, inadequate evidence of incremental validity, poor prediction of future behavior and long-term outcome, and inconsistent identification of and discrimination between contrasting clinical groups. Several researchers have gone so far as to assert that the use of projective drawing techniques for personality assessment is professionally unethical (Martin, 1983; Motta, Little, & Tobin, 1993b; Smith & Dumont, 1995), especially for practitioners without specific competence and training in the use of drawing techniques.

At the same time, some newer scoring and interpretive methodologies hold promise, particularly those that supplant the cookbook, psychoanalytically informed sign approach. The value of holistic, integrative approaches in reliability and validity studies has been frequently supported (Handler & Habenicht, 1994; Swenson, 1968; Tharinger & Stark, 1990), whereas others have provided preliminary support for actuarial polythetic approaches (involving total scores across multiple criteria, as opposed to the single projective criterion, or sign approach) that are derived through the capacity of individual items to effectively discriminate emotionally disturbed from normal comparison children (McNeish & Naglieri, 1993; Naglieri & Pfeiffer, 1992). Rating schemes that consider drawings as a whole and use composite item sets are frequently able to make clinical discriminations at statistically significant levels (Swenson, 1968). Computerized scoring algorithms also offer a new approach that may improve test score reliability (Vass, 2001).

The continued publication of findings that provide equivocal support, at best, for drawing tests suggests that a major reconceptualization of their utility is in order. The evidence is fairly clear that interpretation of individual signs cannot be supported empirically, but interpretation of sets of signs may be of value. It is also possible that drawing techniques are useful only in certain types of clinical decisions, or with specific populations, or with specific age groups. The quest to identify a very heterogeneous group such as emotionally disturbed children with a single measure is likely misguided. Moreover, the assumption of projection may be irrelevant to the mental processes that contribute to drawings (e.g., Wagner, 1999). Having noted the limitations, we now describe specific drawing tests.

Draw a Person Technique

The early leading proponent of the projective human figure drawing test was Karen Machover (1949), whose *Personality Projection in the Drawing of the Human Figure* sold over 25,000 copies in the next 50 years (Fagan & Wilson, 1997). Machover's work utilized a systematic approach to analysis of projective signs, emphasizing the value of the figure drawing test in revealing the impulses, anxieties, conflicts, and compensations of the individual doing the drawing. She describes the formulation of the test as owing much to projective methods and psychoanalytic theory, and in support of the projective aspects of this test she wrote, "In the production of a drawing, there emerges out of the individual's total experiential background a unique pattern of movement and idea. Its significance for personality stems from the fact that there are involved processes of selection out of the infinite pool of experience and imagery potentially available in combination with a dynamic organization of movement and percept" (Machover, 1949, p. 9).

Machover's administration procedure involves the presentation of a 21.6×27.9 cm sheet of unlined paper and a pencil with eraser and instructions to simply "Draw a person." When one drawing is completed, the examinee is given another sheet and instructed to draw the other sex with "Now draw a man" or "Now draw a woman." The examiner separately notes questions and spontaneous comments by the examinee, approximate time, and sequence of the parts drawn. Resistant or reluctant examinees are encouraged with examiner reassurance: "This has nothing to do with your ability to draw. I am interested in how you *try* to make a person" (p. 29).

According to Machover (1949), interpretation of human figures is linear and literal: "The process of drawing the human figure is for the subject, whether he realizes it or not, a problem not only in graphic skill, but one of projecting himself in all of the body meanings and attitudes that have come to be represented in his body image. Consequently, the drawing analyst should feel free to extract from the graphic product what the subject has put into it. He should feel free to interpret directly aspects which, with striking literalness, often reflect real life problems and behavior of the individual who is drawing." (p. 35). For example, any degree or type of shading is considered an expression of anxiety. Depression may be evident in the omission of arms, emphasis on the head, emphasis on (or omission of) the mouth, low placement on the page, and a small figure. Machover's (1949) approach has been preserved in some interpretive cookbooks (Urban, 1963) but has received little support in systematic reviews of the more research literature (Roback, 1968). The poor reliability of individual signs may act to constrain validity (Swenson, 1968). Following Knoff (1993), it is suggested that an isolated sign-based approach to human figure drawings be used primarily for hypothesis generation, at most.

Moving beyond the work of Machover, Elizabeth M. Koppitz (1968, 1984) offered a norm-referenced, psychodynamically oriented, developmental, and psychopathologically aligned scoring system for the human figure drawings of elementary- and middle-school children. Normed on 1,856 children from ages 5 through 12 years of age, Koppitz's Human Figure Drawing (HFD) method includes 30 dichotomously scored indicators of emotional disturbance, each of which was required to differentiate between children with and without emotional problems, be relatively infrequent (less than 16%) in normal children, and not significantly related to developmental maturation. The 30 emotional indicators are divided into quality signs, special features, and omissions. Interscorer reliability tends to be adequate (Koppitz, 1968; Fuller, Preuss, & Hawkins, 1970).

Using a 21.6×27.9 cm blank sheet of paper and No. 2 pencil with eraser, Koppitz's (1968) examiner instructions are: "On this piece of paper, I would like you to draw a whole person. It can be any kind of a person you want to draw, just make sure that it is a whole person and not a stick figure or a cartoon figure" (p. 6). Koppitz's (1968) instructions leave selection of the gender of the drawing to the examinee if further explanation is needed: "You may draw a man or woman or a boy or a girl, whichever you want to draw" (p. 7). There is no time limit.

Koppitz (1968) offered dynamically informed interpretive principles for HFDs: "(1) How a child draws a figure, regardless of whom he draws, reflects his own self-concept. ... (2) The person whom the child draws is the person who is of greatest concern and importance to the child at the time he is making the drawing. ... What a child is saying in his HFD may be twofold; it may be an expression of his attitudes and conflicts, or it may be a wishdream, or both" (pp. 75–77). An overall interpretation should include: observation of the child's behavior while completing the drawing; an overall impression of the drawing; determination of the maturity of the drawing; determination of the consistency, extent, and number of emotional indicators; analysis of drawing content; and signs of neuropathology (Koppitz, 1984). The emotional indicators may be conceptually grouped and interpreted in clusters tapping impulsivity, insecurity and feelings of inadequacy, anxiety, and shyness and timidity. Koppitz (1968) deplored the cookbook approach to interpretation, agreeing with the "consensus among the experts on HFDs that no one-to-one relationship exists between any single sign on HFDs and a definite personality trait or behavior on the part of the boy or girl making the drawing" (p. 55).

Contemporary demands for an objective, standardized, and psychometrically sound Draw a Person with clinical discriminability has led to the development of the Draw a Person: Screening Procedure for Emotional Disturbance (DAP:SPED; Naglieri, McNeish, & Bardos, 1991), essentially an incremental improvement on the model provided by Koppitz. Naglieri et al. (1991) set as their objectives the development of a system that could be consistently and accurately scored, norm-referenced with a nationally representative sample, empirically capable of differentiating normal and disturbed populations, and used in conjunction with a scoring system intended to tap cognitive ability.

Instructions include some variations on other human-figure drawings, including instructions to draw three drawings each on the record form and allowance of 5 min per drawing. For individual administration, the initial instructions are: "I'd like you to draw some pictures for me. First I'd like you to draw a picture of a man. Make the very best picture you can. Take your time and work very carefully, and I'll tell you when to stop. Remember, be sure to draw the whole man" (p. 21). These instructions are reiterated for a second drawing of a woman and a third drawing of "yourself." Instructions for group administration are also included.

The scoring system is based on two types of items, those dealing with figure dimensions and those dealing with drawing content. The same set of 55 scoring criteria is used for each of the three drawings. Each criterion is dichotomously scored. Ten scoring templates are included to measure figure size or location on the page. The total raw score across the drawings of the man, woman, and self may be converted to age- and gender-specific T scores ($M = 50$ and $SD = 10$). The interscorer reliability is adequate ($r = 0.844$), and the median coefficient alpha is 0.73. Test norms consist of a nationally representative standardization sample of 2,260 children and adolescents between the ages of 5 and 17 years.

Interpretation is made for the score across all three drawings, with the higher the T score, the greater the likelihood that emotional disturbance exists. The authors recommend that the DAP:SPED be used as a screening measure to identify individuals who would likely benefit from further evaluation. Recommended cutoff scores are $T < 55$ (further evaluation is not indicated), $55 \le T \le 64$ (further evaluation is indicated), and $T \ge 65$ (further evaluation is strongly indicated).

With a few exceptions, most investigations have supported the use of the DAP:SPED in differentiating emotionally disturbed children and adolescents from normal samples, albeit with modestly sized differences between normative and clinical groups. Four validity studies reported in the test manual (two of these studies have been separately published as McNeish & Naglieri, 1993; Naglieri & Pfeiffer, 1992) show that across samples and settings of older children and adolescents with heterogeneous emotional disturbances, the DAP:SPED produces mean T scores from 54.8 to 57.0 compared with the performance of normative samples that is close to $T = 50$. In independent investigations, Matto (2001) showed that the DAP:SPED was a significant predictor in explaining behavioral disturbance and hostility in latency aged children (ages 6–12 years) receiving outpatient and residential mental-health treatment, and Matavich (1999) reports that the DAP:SPED shows significant differences between incarcerated juvenile delinquents and a normal comparison sample. Poorer discriminability has been reported in two investigations. Briccetti (1994) reported that the DAP:SPED was not a valid discriminator between emotionally disturbed and undisturbed deaf samples. Wrightson and Saklofske (2000) could distinguish between Canadian regular education, alternate education, and the behavior class students but had a comparatively lower discriminability than behavior rating scales.

As the best normed and developed of the human figure drawing tests, the DAP:SPED realizes the objectives recommended by Roback (1968), who called for the development of standardized and validated human figure drawing scales and concluded that "the ultimate fate of the DAP test will be one of a rough screening device for determining 'gross level of adjustment'" (p. 17). At the same time, its capacity to discriminate between normal and abnormal groups tends to be limited, based upon relatively small discrepancies between normal and clinical groups.

House–Tree–Person Technique

While developing an intelligence test, John N. Buck (1948) originated the House–Tree–Person (H–T–P) projective drawing technique. Intended to involve common things that were familiar to even young children as well as to stimulate open verbalization, the H–T–P was found to tap both intellective and nonintellective factors, leading Buck to devise a quantitative scoring system for intellectual assessment and qualitative approach for personality assessment.

The H–T–P is most suitable for use with individuals over 8 years of age (Buck & Warren, 1992). Administration involves at least two steps, the first a nonverbal and unstructured series of drawings, followed by a semi-structured verbal inquiry. An optional third and fourth step require redrawing a house, tree, and person (using colored crayons) and another postdrawing verbal inquiry. An optional drawing of a person of the opposite gender to that of the first person drawn may also be requested.

At the outset, the examiner says, "I want you to draw a picture of a house. You may draw any kind of house you wish, and do the best you can. You may erase as much as you like. You may take as much time as you need. Just do your best" (p. 4). While the examinee draws, the examiner should record contemplation time (time elapsed between the end of instructions and the commencement of drawing), the order of details drawn, the length of any pauses and associated details, any spontaneous verbalizations or displays of emotion, and the total time to completion of each drawing. Once each drawing is completed, the examiner uses some standard suggested questions to gain an understanding of the examinee by eliciting as much information as possible about each drawing's content and context.

Scoring involves completion of an interpretive concepts checklist for each drawing, providing common clinical hypotheses. The interpretive concepts checklist includes lists of normative features, as well as general observations, proportion, perspective, detailing, nonessential details, and irrelevant use of details. Characteristics of the use of color are also checked if the crayon administration option is included. Buck and Warren (1992) caution that the signs included in the checklist are not exhaustive and should only be interpreted in combination with patient history, presenting problem, and responses to other assessment tools.

In general, the H–T–P is intended to tap an individual's "personality, maturity, integration and efficiency" (p. 151). The H–T–P has been used as a way of detecting behavior problems, an evaluation aid for students who are entering school, and in the screening of employee applicants (Buck, 1948). The house is considered to be a reflection of home life and the interpersonal dynamics of the family (Buck & Warren, 1992). The tree is considered to be a graphic expression of the examinee's felt experience and a view of his or her personality resources for deriving satisfaction from the environment (Buck, 1948). The drawing of the person is considered more than the other drawings to elicit conscious and direct feelings of body image and self-concept (Buck, 1948). The colored crayon drawings are thought to evoke a deeper level of experience than pencil drawings. The test manual also includes specific H–T–P features associated with physically and sexually abused children. Developmental differences in interpretation of drawing features are also provided for the life span, from young children through older adults (Buck & Warren, 1992).

Buck's (1948) system was originally derived from study of the drawings of 150 adult clinical patients in specified diagnostic categories, as compared with drawings from 500 normal adults. Its leading advocate in the United States has been Emanuel F. Hammer (1958, 1986), a student of Buck's, whose interpretive approaches have primarily taken the analytically informed sign-based approach with the limitations previously discussed. The HTP represents a technique with a rich clinical history awaiting the development of a holistic or polythetic scoring system with representative norms, reliability, and validity. Until such a system is available, its use is most defensible for hypothesis generation or as a nonthreatening prelude to formal assessment.

Kinetic Family Drawings

Family drawing tests date back to Hulse (1951) but were observed to often produce static depictions of isolated family members. In order to facilitate the generation of family drawings that depicted family dynamics and interactions, Burns and Kaufman (1970, 1972) introduced the Kinetic Family Drawing (KFD) technique. This has spawned parallel tasks in school environments (Prout & Phillips, 1974) and even a Kinetic–House–Tree–Person task (Burns, 1987). In this section, the KFD technique is described across multiple administration and interpretive systems (Burns & Kaufman, 1970, 1972; Klepsch & Logie, 1982; Knoff & Prout, 1985; Reynolds, 1978).

The KFD is usually considered appropriate for school-aged children but not particularly useful with adults. The examinee is given a 21.6×27.9 cm blank sheet of paper, usually in a landscape (horizontal) orientation, and No. 2 pencil with eraser. Instructions emphasize the portrayal of family members performing an action: "Draw a picture of everyone in your family, including you, doing something. Try to draw whole people, not cartoons or stick people. Remember, make everyone doing something—some kind of action" (Knoff & Prout, 1985, p. 4). There is no time limit, and the performance phase is completed when the examinee indicates that they are finished.

A verbal inquiry phase may follow the drawing phase, aimed at clarifying the examinee's drawing and investigating associated thought processes as well as building rapport. Over 50 inquiry questions have been suggested for the inquiry in the different KFD systems. The value of these questions has yet to be established, and they certainly limit the "nonverbal" utility of the KFD.

The KFD is generally scored according to a number of individual indicators, and several interpretive systems are available. Burns and Kaufman (1970, 1972) interpreted *actions, styles*, and *symbols* in the drawings. Reynolds (1978) reported 37 signs that may indicate family dysfunction, such as the lack of physical proximity between figures. For Knoff and Prout (1985), diagnostic inferences may be drawn from areas of and between figures; figure characteristics; position, distance, and barriers; style; and symbols.

As with other drawing systems, the individual or cumulative sign approach with the KFD has generally yielded poor differentiation of children with and without emotional disturbance (Cummings, 1986; Knoff & Prout, 1985; Tharinger & Stark, 1990). Accordingly, the KFD may be best described as a clinically rich test useful in hypothesis generation but without an existing scoring system that meets contemporary standards of psychometric adequacy.

Bender Visual–Motor Gestalt Test

The Bender–Gestalt Test (BGT; Bender, 1938) is a simple paper-and-pencil design copy test that has become one of the best known tests in psychological assessment. It consists of nine gestalt figures that were

originally selected by Lauretta Bender from those used by Max
Wertheimer (1923) in his studies of gestalt visual perception. Bender
began using the figures with some modifications in 1929 with schizophrenic adults at the Springfield State Hospital of Maryland, later extending their use to neurotic patients and children in the Psychiatric Division
of Bellevue Hospital. Although the BGT is primarily used as a screener for
neurological dysfunction (e.g., Lacks, 1999), multiple systems have been
developed for its use in the appraisal of personality and psychopathology
(Hutt, 1985; Koppitz, 1963, 1975; Lerner, 1972; Pascal & Suttell, 1951;
Reichenberg & Raphael, 1992).

In conjunction with her developmental scoring system, Koppitz (1963,
1975) described 12 BGT emotional indicators that differentiate children
with and without socioemotional problems. The emotional indicators tend
to be associated with externalizing problems (chiefly impulsivity) or internalizing problems (chiefly anxiety). Koppitz (1975) recommends that three
or more emotional indicators is suggestive of the need for further evaluation and that more emotional indicators does not necessarily connote
more severe disturbance. She cautions that any single emotional indicator does not indicate any serious emotional problem, and that the
emotional indicators cannot be combined into a single scale because they
lack internal consistency.

The fate of Koppitz's BGT emotional indicators is much the same as
her HFD emotional indicators. Problems with the reliability of the emotional indicators have been reported (Goff & Parker, 1969), and inadequate
evidence of concurrent validity has been reported among women diagnosed
with mental retardation (Dixon, 1998) and emotionally disturbed adolescents (Oliver & Kronenberger, 1971). Buckley (1978) reviewed research on
the use of the BGT and failed to find support for its use in the diagnosis of
emotional disturbance. At the same time, Rossini and Kaspar (1987)
reported findings that with developmental level controlled, children with
adjustment disorders and behavior disorders produced Bender–Gestalt
reproductions with significantly more emotional indicators than a normal
control sample. These mixed findings are likely indicative of the general
limitations of a pathognomic sign-based approach.

Hutt (1985) has also offered preliminary evidence supporting the use
of the BGT as a measure of psychopathology. He derived 17 indicators
(labeled as "factors") as constituting a psychopathology scale. Hutt (1985)
also utilized the personality dimension termed perceptual adience–
abience to represent a primary defensive personality operation marked by
an openness or closedness to one's internal and external worlds. Adient
individuals are thought more likely to be open to new varieties of learning
experience and better able to profit from them than abient individuals,
who tend to block out new experiences and profit less from exposure to
new experiences. Investigations of the psychopathology and the perceptual adience–abience scales in the last decade have yielded mixed findings, with Wasserman (1995) failing to find support for their use in a
sample of individuals diagnosed with posttraumatic stress disorder,
whereas Lee and Oh (1998) reported support for their use in elucidating

differences between traumatic brain-injured and neurotic samples. Sangster, Rogers, and Searight (1993) reported convergence between Hutt's indices and measures of aggressiveness.

Other Drawing Tests

In addition to the tests described above, there are numerous additional drawing techniques available. Most lack formal scoring systems and psychometric rigor, although they appear to potentially tap constructs beyond those found in traditional drawing techniques. These techniques include the Bicycle Drawing (e.g., Sharma, 1972), Bridge Drawing (Hays & Lyons, 1981), Circus Phenomenon (Hanes, 1997), Map of My World (MMW; Gurycka, 1996), Most Unpleasant Concept Test (Harrower, 1950), and Rey's "Une dame qui se promène et il pleut" ("A lady walking in the rain"; Taylor, 1959).

Several drawing test batteries are also published or in development. The *Children's Self-Report and Projective Inventory* (CSRPI; Ziffer & Shapiro, 1992) is an idiographic, individually administered inventory intended to assess social–emotional functioning in children between the ages of 5 and 12. It is not normed. It consists of eight components, some nonverbal and some verbal, including four drawing tasks (color how you feel, color how others make you feel, draw a child in the rain, and a kinetic family drawing) and two self-report measures with optional pointing response formats (choosing cards with printed words, e.g., "Very much like me"). The coloring tasks involve the association of different colors with different emotions (e.g., green with worry). The drawings include an adaptation of Rey's drawing of a person walking in the rain, intended to tap functioning under environmental stress. The entire battery requires about 90 min to administer; the nonverbal elements can be administered in about 60 min. The *Diagnostic Drawing Series* (DDS; Cohen, Hammer, & Singer, 1988) consists of three drawings administered with paper and pastels. The examinee is directed to make any picture, then a picture of the tree, and then a picture of how they feel using lines, shapes, and colors. A modification of the DDS for children (DDS-C) is also available (Gulbro-Leavitt & Schimmel, 1991). The *Levick Emotional and Cognitive Art Therapy Assessment* (LECATA; Levick, 2000) includes six drawing tasks and covers the ages of 3–11 years. The five tasks are a drawing of anything and a story about the drawing, a self portrait, a scribble using one color and a picture created from the scribble, a drawing of a place the examinee "would like to be" (for ages 3–5; draw an "important place" for children 6 years and up), and a drawing of a family. A normative sample for the LECATA is currently being collected (Levick, personal communication, October 10, 2001).

Of the assessment methodologies described in this chapter, none has proliferated like the drawing techniques. Drawings are easy and inexpensive to administer, a ready bridge from assessment to intervention, and an efficient form of nonverbal expression. Their long-standing popularity for three-quarters of a century suggests that they may offer information of value to clinicians. The failure to produce more clear-cut evidence to support their use suggests that new approaches, more circumscribed indications for use, and additional research and development are needed.

OBJECT PLACEMENT AND PLAY TECHNIQUES

Just as paper-and-pencil drawing tasks may be used for the nonverbal appraisal of personality and psychopathology, so may object placement tasks. These types of tasks involve a meaningful arrangement or placement of a set of symbolic manipulables within structured or unstructured spatial parameters. In the Family System Test (FAST; Gehring, 1998), the examinee is instructed to place schematic male and female figures at varying heights and proximity on an 81-square checkerboard. Results may be interpreted as providing a representation of family relations, cohesiveness, and hierarchy. In the World Technique (e.g., Lowenfeld, 1979) and its many derivative tests, examinees are typically given numerous small objects (such as people, animals, fantasy items, and items with which to build landscape or scenery) and told to do what they like with them, often constructing sandtray panoramas that are thought to symbolically represent a "miniature world" that is associated with the child's interpersonal and intrapsychic systems and ways of perceiving and thinking about experiences. These types of procedures usually require little verbalization by examinees, although additional inquiry options are available. These object placement techniques will now be described in detail.

Family System Test (FAST)

The FAST (Gehring, 1998) is a standardized figure placement technique for individuals and families with members 6 years or older. It was formulated based on structural family systems theory, and its scores yield spatial representations of family cohesion and hierarchy. Its scores are intended to describe family-oriented psychosocial issues and to facilitate the planning, execution, and evaluation of therapeutic interventions. Structural family therapy conceptualizes psychopathology as being seated in the family (and not the identified patient), with the objective of the therapist being to restructure family subsystems and transform dysfunctional transactional patterns between members (Minuchin, 1974).

Administration

The FAST requires about 10 min to administer to individuals. Its materials include a 45×45 cm board, divided into 81 squares. Schematic male and female figures are used, as are cylindrical blocks of three different heights that may be placed under the schematic figures to depict elevation in a hierarchy.

Verbal explanations are long in duration, although little expressive language is required of the examinee. At the outset, the examiner says, "I would now like to explain a procedure we use for representing family relations. With this board and these figures and blocks you can show how close the members of your family are to one another and how much power or influence each member has in the family. Members of the same family usually evaluate their relations differently" (Gehring & Page, 2000, p. 437).

The examiner explains the concepts of emotional closeness and distance (i.e., cohesion) by placing figures side by side on adjacent squares (minimum distance), at diagonally adjacent squares (second closest distance), and at diagonally opposed corners of the board (maximum distance). The examiner also explains power or influence within the family (i.e., hierarchy) by using the blocks of different sizes to elevate the figures already positioned on the board, conveying that the greater the difference in height between two figures, the more hierarchical is their relationship. Two figures at the same height have balanced or equal power within the family.

Once these concepts are understood, the FAST is administered under three conditions. First, examinees are asked to represent their current family relations (typical representation), followed by a semistructured verbal interview. Second, examinees are asked to portray their desired family structures (ideal representation), again followed by an interview. Finally, examinees are asked to depict their family in an important conflict (conflict representation), again followed by an interview.

Scoring and Interpretation

The three-dimensional configurations yielded on the FAST may be scored to determine the range of emotional connectedness and the degree of influence perceived to exist within and across generations for each of the three family circumstances. Cohesion and hierarchy scores can also be combined to classify family structure in each situation and can be compared across situations to determine family flexibility. Cohesion is represented by the distance between figures on the board, and hierarchy is represented by the elevation of figures with blocks. As a criterion reference, healthy families are thought to have a balanced relationship structure (cohesive and with a balanced hierarchy), clear generational borders, and a flexible organization. Pathological family organization is suggested by a number of configurations, such as when the elevation of a child figure surpasses that of a parent figure (a hierarchy reversal).

Normative FAST representations of typical family relations among nonclinical respondents are based upon a sample of nearly 600 children, adolescents, and parents from the San Francisco Bay Area, about two thirds from intact families and one third from single parent or blended families. Racial and ethnic composition appears to be nationally representative, with the exception of African Americans who are underrepresented (6% of the total sample). The nonclinical sample is predominantly middle class.

Strength and Limitations

Gehring's (1998) objective in the development of the FAST was to create a flexible instrument that meets high clinical standards and that has an association for family-based intervention, and toward these ends, the instrument holds considerable promise.

The FAST shows early evidence of psychometric adequacy. FAST validity studies include convergent validity with common measures of family functioning (Family Cohesion and Adaptability Scale, or FACES III; and the Family Environment Scale or FES). Comparisons between the results of these instruments are suggestive that FAST indices of cohesion are relatively convergent with those offered by the FACES III and the FES, although indices of hierarchy are weakly related (Gehring & Page, 2000). Discriminant validity is supported by differences between FAST representations of nonclinical respondents and members of families attending a child psychiatric outpatient clinic (Gehring & Page, 2000). Based on individual representations of typical, ideal, and conflict situations by fathers, mothers, and children in the two groups, members of clinically identified families were more likely than nonclinical respondents to report their family structures as unbalanced. In eight of nine comparisons, clinical and nonclinical samples differed at statistically significant levels in their family perceptions of current family relations across situations. FAST reliability has been investigated through test–retest stability over a 1-week period with children and adolescents. Results range from $r = 0.63$ to 0.87 at the family level for cohesion and hierarchy (Gehring & Page, 2000).

Some weaknesses of the FAST include its lengthy and somewhat stilted verbal instructions, as well as the lengthy verbal follow-up interviews to the three test conditions (typical, ideal, and conflict representation). Unless these interviews can be demonstrated to improve test validity incrementally, they may be unnecessary to the test (just as the lengthy inquiries following drawing tests have questionable value). The FAST offers the major assets of an efficient nonverbal depiction of family dynamics, and the excess verbiage serves only to distract from these assets and make the test less universal.

Development of the FAST began in the early 1980s in Zurich and later California, making it a relatively new international and cross-cultural endeavor. Although it clearly needs further psychometric development, the FAST is closely aligned with a well-articulated theory and family-based intervention approach. As an instrument that can both identify the nature of family pathology and direct the focus of therapeutic interventions, it offers a connection between assessment and intervention that is rare among psychological tests.

World Techniques

Assessment procedures in which examinees are directed to arrange an array of toys and objects as they wish are sometimes referred to as *world tests*, after prototypal tests initially developed by Erikson (Homberger, 1938) and Lowenfeld (1939). Examinees usually construct panoramic constructions that are considered to reflect their perceptions of their world.

Like projective tests, the world techniques trace their origins to psychoanalytic theory and practice. Some of the earliest attempts to develop diagnostic play assessments that could be used seamlessly with play therapy were created in England by child psychoanalyst Margaret Lowenfeld, whose nonverbal techniques (the Mosaic Test, the World Technique, and Sandplay) were predicated on the belief that young, pre-school children are not able to express their thoughts and feelings in con-structive language although thoughts and feelings are indeed present. Preverbal (or nonverbal) thinking was considered to represent a form of pictorially based thinking preceding spoken language. In spontaneous play with pictures and toys, Lowenfeld reasoned, children symbolically express their ideas and feelings about the world. Through close observa-tion of the play of emotionally disturbed children, it is possible to under-stand and gain access to the intrapsychic representations of early experiences that contribute to emotional disturbance.

Variations on the world technique include Erikson's Dramatic Productions Test (Homberger, 1938), the Erica Method (Sjolund, 1981, 1993; Sjolund & Schaefer, 1994), and Buhler's (1951a, 1951b; Buhler & Kelly, 1941) World Test. Diagnostic play assessments are reported to be more popular in Europe than in the United States (Gitlin-Weiner, Sandgrund, & Schaefer, 2000), presumably because of their association with psychoanalytic theory and their comparative lack of psychometric rigor. A scant amount of research on these measures has appeared in main-stream American psychology journals in the last 30 years. Nevertheless, object placement represents an assessment paradigm that has come to have a prominent role in the nonverbal process of play therapy.

Administration

Materials for Lowenfeld's (1939, 1979) world technique include a $75 \times 50 \times 7$ cm metal sand tray, containing sand so that the examinee can model contours and place objects as desired. Water also needs to be available. Tools to manipulate the sand, such as shovels, funnels, and molds, are nearby. Materials that can be shaped easily are also provided. The child has a wide array of miniature objects from various classes to use in developing the world, including people and animals, fantasy figures, scenery and landscape, items of transportation, and equipment. Other adaptations of this technique use a wooden tray instead of a sand tray. Buhler and Kelly (1941) include 150 small objects in their World Test. The Erica Method uses two metal trays (one with dry sand and one with wet sand) and 360 miniature toys including people of different ages and sizes, genders, and occupations; farm animals and wild animals; vehicles; and various objects such as fire, explosions, guns, buildings, furniture, trees, fences, and traffic signs (Sjolund, 1981). A small piece of play-dough is also provided if the child wishes to create an object not available.

In Lowenfeld's world technique, the materials are introduced with a naturalistic and simple sequence of ideas that are explained in the buildup to the task: that children think differently than adults, that many ideas and experiences that do not translate into words (Lowenfeld termed this "picture thinking" with children), that many things are easier to understand in pictures and actions than in words, that this is a natural way of thinking, and that the examiner-therapist wants to make a bridge between the worlds of children and the world of adults. The world materials are introduced, and the child is invited to make "whatever comes into your head." There are otherwise few limits put upon the child, and Lowenfeld emphasizes the need for the construction of many successive worlds or worlds created over several therapeutic sessions.

The Erica Method is administered on three or four occasions in order to establish consistency and allow patterns to develop. Instructions are deliberately unstructured: "Here you see a lot of toys. You may use whatever you want and build with them in the sandbox. Here is a sandbox with dry sand and here is one with wet. Which one do you want to build in?" (Sjolund, 1981, p. 323). The examiner does not provide any more comments or encouragements.

Scoring and Interpretation

The process of scoring the World Techniques typically begins with a graphical or photographic representation of the worlds produced by the examinee. Scoring in some adaptations includes the number and choices of toys and pieces, the various forms of interaction included in the world, items used and rejected, and salient behaviors and verbalizations during and after construction. Interpretation is based upon both qualitative and objective indices. Lowenfeld (1979) described the interpretive process as beginning with attempts to understand what the objects used signify to the child: "Having drawn the 'World' we then substitute in it the qualities and concepts the child has given. When these are reassembled together the result is a picture of affect, concept, memory and experience inextricably woven together into the presentation of a total state" (p. 7). She described categories of worlds, including realistic or representational worlds, worlds in which real objects are put together in an unreal fashion, demonstrations of fantasies, and mixed types of worlds. Michael and Buhler (1945) described six objective types of abnormal worlds that may be observed in both children and adults:

- *Aggressive*: worlds in which killing, accidents, and violence occur
- *Unpopulated*: worlds in which people are omitted
- *Empty*: worlds in which few objects appear
- *Closed*: worlds in which many boundaries, fences, and enclosures are prominent
- *Chaotic or disorganized*: worlds in which the elements are poorly planned or incoherently organized
- *Rigid*: worlds in which elements are overly organized and overly symmetrical.

These types of worlds tend to be associated with emotional disturbance. Buhler and Kelly (1941) suggested that construction of two or more symptom worlds is indicative of psychopathology, with the most clinically significant world being closed and unpopulated.

The Erica Method yields information concerning the child's developmental and functional level (recognition, sorting, groupings, and relationships between toys), as well as his or her perception of the world (i.e., through realistic, fantasy, aggressive, chaotic, or bizarre themes). For example, the nature of relationships between the toys may be classified as conventional, meaningful, chaotic, and/or bizarre. Content analysis involves the identification of themes in one or more of the child's worlds, such as high levels of aggression (Sjolund, 1981).

Strengths and Weaknesses

Although Lowenfeld (1979) considered her technique to be objective, recordable, and interpretable, with standardized materials and procedures, it was not originally normed-referenced, and few studies of its psychometric qualities have been conducted. Buhler (1951a) offered norms (now considered outdated), and the Erica Method includes performance norms by age (Sjolund, 1981, 1993; Sjolund & Schaefer, 1994). Aoki (1981) has reported adequate test–retest reliability of a world test in adjusted and emotionally disturbed primary and middle-school students in the only study of this type. In general, the world technique represents a promising approach in need of further psychometric development before it can meet existing psychometric standards. As described by Sjolund and Schaefer (1994), the Erica Method currently "combines the hardiness of a formal, reality-based observation with the softness and fragility of empathic contact with the child" (p. 231).

SELF-RATING AND SELF-REPORT TECHNIQUES

Nonverbal assessment paradigms that do not have clear counterparts in verbal personality assessment have thus far been described, but one may ask if there are nonverbal counterparts to the so-called objective broad-band and narrow-band verbal self-report measures, like the MMPI-2 (ranked second in usage among clinical practitioners, according to Camara et al., 2000) and the Beck Depression Inventory—II (ranked tenth in clinical usage). In this section, two relatively new nonverbal self-report paradigms are described that parallel verbal measures and that offer broad-band and narrow-band assessments of personality and psychopathology.

Nonverbal Personality Questionnaire

Just as verbal self-report personality inventories require examinees to respond "true" or "false" to a lengthy series of sentence-based items according to whether the items apply to them, it is possible to respond to a series of pictorial depictions of behavior and rate their personal applicability. Pictures take more space than sentences, so fewer items may be administered so as to avoid overwhelming the examinee with an overly lengthy inventory. At the same time, psychometric properties may be maintained with fewer items when an expanded rating of response options (e.g., Likert rating scales) is offered.

The 136-item Nonverbal Personality Questionnaire (NPQ; Paunonen & Jackson, 1998; Paunonen, Jackson, & Keinonen, 1990) and the 60-item Five-Factor Nonverbal Personality Questionnaire (FF-NPQ; Paunonen, Ashton, & Jackson, 2001) represent the first instruments in a new generation of pictorial self-report inventories. These measures are distinguished by the absence of verbal content, while tapping into familiar personality constructs including Murray's (1938) need-based traits and the "big five" factor structure of personality (e.g., Goldberg, 1993).

The NPQ was developed from the identification of a series of behavioral acts thought to represent exemplars of common personality traits. The behavioral acts were intended to portray the needs (traits) described in Murray's (1938) system, with many of these needs having been previously measured through verbal self-report in Jackson's (1984) Personality Research Form (PRF). Following the system of personality scale development suggested by Jackson (1971), a pool of pictorial items was first generated according to the 17 traits depicted in Murray's (1938) system of needs. For each item, a line drawing was made of a central character performing a behavior in a specific situation corresponding to the designated trait. The requirement that the examinee respond with self-ratings suggested that NPQ item contents be limited to exemplars of trait expression, with the rating describing the likelihood that the examinee would engage in the *type* of behavior pictured (rather than the specific behavior itself). Items were also created for an Infrequency validity scale, consisting of items that are likely to be endorsed by someone who completes the questionnaire randomly. NPQ items were then winnowed down through elimination of items that failed to meet minimum psychometric standards and retaining items with the best composite psychometric qualities. The NPQ has been subjected to a number of cross-cultural studies described below. Replication of a five-factor factorial structure across cultures led to the development of the abbreviated FF-NPQ scale, with most items selected from the lengthier NPQ and a few new items created.

Administration

For both the NPQ and the FF-NPQ, examinees are presented with a picture booklet and asked to "look at each illustration and rate the likelihood that you would engage in the type of behavior shown." Representative items are shown in Figure 14.1. Examinee responses are given on a 7-point numerical rating scale, with 1 representing "extremely unlikely that I would perform this type of behavior" and 7 labeled "extremely likely that I would perform this type of behavior." The NPQ requires approximately 25–30 min to complete, and the FF-NPQ requires approximately 10 min to complete. Although the instruction page gives verbal directions, the questionnaire items are inherently nonverbal and can be administered to individuals with different cultural and linguistic backgrounds.

Figure 14.1 In the NPQ, examinees are asked to "Look at Each Illustration and Rate the Likelihood That You Would Engage in the Type of Behavior Shown." Ratings are give on a 7-point scale. Item 12 Depicts Nurturance, and Item 127 depicts Thrill-Seeking Behavior. (NPQ Sample Items Copyright © 1998 by Sigma Assessment Systems. Used with permission.)

Scoring and Interpretation

Scoring is currently accomplished by hand. In the NPQ, eight items are used to score each of the Murray need-based scales, as well as the Infrequency scale that is used to detect random or dissimulated response patterns. The FF-NPQ consists of 60 items, with 12 items assigned to each of the five factors. FF-NPQ scales correspond to the "big five" personality factors: Neuroticism (N), Extraversion (E), Openness to Experience (O), Agreeableness (A), and Conscientiousness (C). Pending nationally representative normative studies, the NPQ and FF-NPQ should be considered research-based instruments. Based upon the psychometric characteristics and validity evidence described below, however, it is clear that these instruments hold considerable promise for expanding the breadth of cross-cultural and nonverbal personality assessment.

Strengths and Weaknesses

The NPQ and FF-NPQ were developed according to rigorous contemporary standards, and they appear to yield much the same information as verbal self-report measures without the attendant limitations. As the NPQ pictorial paradigm undergoes evaluation by independent researchers in the coming years, it may lead to further expansion of nonverbal techniques in the assessment of personality disorders and psychopathology.

Both the NPQ and the FF-NPQ demonstrate adequate reliability. In spite of the relative brevity of NPQ scales, internal consistency tends to be adequate, with mean coefficient alpha across scales of 0.75 in a Canadian sample, 0.78 for an English sample, 0.67 across four European cultures, 0.61 for a Hong Kong sample, and 0.59 for an Israeli sample (Paunonen et al., 1996, 2000). These reliability findings tend to compare favorably with various translations of the PRF verbal scales. The FF-NPQ scales have been reported to have a mean internal consistency of 0.80 (Paunonen et al., 2001).

Convergent validity also appears to be good. Convergence of the NPQ with PRF verbal self-report indices translated across multiple languages tends to cluster at or above $r = 0.50$, although there is variability across cultures (Paunonen et al., 1996; Paunonen, Zeidner, Engvik, Oosterveld, & Maliphant, 2000). The FF-NPQ scales have been reported to have a mean correlation with the corresponding scales on the NEO-FFI of $r = 0.52$, with self-ratings and peer ratings of $r = 0.41$, and with 14 external behavior criteria a multiple $R = 0.25$ (Paunonen et al., 2001).

The factor structure of the NPQ has been found to be generally invariant across cultures as well as across verbal and nonverbal methods (Paunonen, Jackson, Trzebinski, & Forsterling, 1992). Exploratory principal-components analyses generally yield five orthogonal factors across cultures, corresponding to the big five factors of personality. When intercorrelation matrices are compared across cultures, coefficients of congruence are consistently high (>0.80), suggesting a robust and generalizable factor structure (Paunonen et al., 1996). Metafactor-analytic methodologies are suggestive that the NPQ has robust structure across 10 or more cultures and language groups, including Canada, England, Finland, Israel, Germany, the Netherlands, Norway, Poland, Russia, and Hong Kong (Paunonen et al., 1996, 2000).

The test's psychometric properties have been reported to be best in North American samples (Paunonen et al., 2000), presumably because some of the behaviors represented may be culture specific. For example, items portray people dreaming about graduation from the university, attending a party with dancing and drinking, playing pool, and even flying a hang-glider! The degree to which these activities are predominantly Western has not been evaluated, but an international bias and review panel might recommend that some of these items be considered for deletion because they may not exemplify familiar activities to members of non-Western cultures.

As normal-range research instruments, the NPQ and FF-NPQ are in need of a nationally representative normative sample before they can be used for applied purposes. Items with strong cultural associations should be considered for deletion in favor of more universal types of items, and the item stimuli should be redrawn with more realistic figures depicted instead of stick figures. Murray's (1938) need-based traits and the big five model of personality both have limited value in the appraisal of known or suspected psychopathology, so it may eventually prove useful to develop a self-report depression inventory or multiaxial inventory utilizing this nonverbal paradigm. The NPQ's major advantages over comparable verbal measures include better cross-cultural transferability without the need for item translations, as well as potential utility with illiterate populations or individuals with language-based learning disabilities (Paunonen et al., 1996).

Visual Analog Scales

Another approach to nonverbal administration of self-report measures is to utilize graphic rating scales anchored by self-explanatory pictures. This methodology was first described by Aitken (1969) and typically requires examinees to mark on a unipolar or bipolar graphic rating scale how they feel at a given time. The location of the mark on a standard 100-mm line relative to the polar extremes yields an interpretable score. For example, examinees may be asked to indicate how they currently feel by placing a line on "X" at the appropriate segment of a scale with a happy face at one end and a sad face at the other.

Deceptive in their simplicity, visual analog scales may be used with a wide range of populations. They are readily understood by neurologically impaired individuals (Stern, Rosenbaum, White, & Morey, 1991) and generally yield convergent findings with more language-loaded measures. The reliability of visual analog scales tapping psychiatric experiences of anxiety or depression has been shown to be robust across raters and across categorical or continuous scales (Remington, Tyrer, Newson-Smith, & Cicchetti, 1979). Visual analog scales offer a simple nonverbal alternative to narrow-band self-rating measures.

A search of the *Mental Measurements Yearbook* database shows that there are few commercially available normed visual analog scales, with most containing considerable verbal test stimuli in addition to the analog scales. For example, the Derogatis Stress Profile (Derogatis, 1987) includes but a single item 100-mm visual analog measure, tapping the examinee's subjective evaluation of their current level of stress (Subjective Stress Score). The Dissociative Experiences Scale (Bernstein & Putnam, 1986) features a 100-mm response line for each item verbally describing a dissociative experience, requiring the respondent to mark an "X" on the spot representing the percentage of occurrence between 0 and 100. Both measures are embedded in longer verbally loaded tests.

The only norm-referenced visual analog scales are the Visual Analog Mood Scales (VAMS; Stern, 1997). The VAMS includes unipolar, vertically presented scales tapping eight mood states (afraid, sad, energetic, happy, confused, angry, tired, and tense), each anchored by a neutral face at the top end and a specific mood face at the bottom end.

Administration

The VAMS may be administered to individuals or groups for whom conventional language-loaded measures are inappropriate, especially those with language or other cognitive deficits. It is suitable for self- or examiner administration, with examinees instructed to make one mark across the line to show how they feel, following a brief verbal explanation and demonstration. The examiner's vocal intonation and facial expression should match the valence of the mood being assessed. Administrative accommodations are provided in the manual for examinees who are unable to write. The VAMS typically requires no more than 5 min to administer.

Scoring and Interpretation

The VAMS is scored using a ruler that measures the distance (from 0 to 100 mm) from the neutral end of the line to the middle of the examinee's mark. For example, an examinee who makes a mark at the 34-mm mark receives a raw score of 34 on that scale. Raw scores for each scale may be converted to age- and gender-appropriate linear-transformed T scores ($M = 50$, $SD = 10$), and the T scores may be graphically represented in the response booklet. The VAMS is normed for ages 18–94 years. The VAMS was normed in its self-administered form on 579 adults between the ages of 18 and 94 years. The normative sample was representative of age, gender, and race, according to 1990 census results. Reference norms for 290 psychiatric inpatients and outpatients, including groups with major depression, mild depression, and anxiety disorders, are also available.

Six VAMS scales measure predominantly negative mood stages (fear, confusion, sadness, anger, and fatigue), and two scales measure positive mood states (vigor and happiness). Stern (1997) recommends that scores on the negative mood scales be interpreted as follows: $59T$ or lower is within normal limits, 60–$69T$ is borderline, and $70T$ or greater is abnormal. For the positive mood scales, scores above $40T$ are within normal limits, scores of 31–$40T$ are borderline, and scores at or below $30T$ are abnormal.

A cutoff raw score of 50 on the Sad scale has been reported to maximize the aggregate sensitivity, positive predictive power, and negative predictive power in the differentiation of major and mild depressive disorders from demographically matched normal standardization participants. Approximately 86% of respondents who score 50 or greater on the Sad scale would likely be diagnosed with a depressive disorder.

The VAMS may also be used to track changes in mood over time. A change of more than $30T$ may be interpreted as reflecting both a reliable and a clinically significant change in level of mood. The VAMS has been shown to be as sensitive to the therapeutic changes from electroconvulsive therapy (ECT) as verbal self-report rating scales (Arruda, Stern, & Legendre, 1996).

Strengths and Limitations

At this early stage, the VAMS shows promising psychometric evidence of validity (Stern, 1997). Several investigations have provided convergent and discriminant validity for the VAMS, through the use of multitrait–multimethod studies (Nyenhuis, Stern, Yamamoto, Luchetta, & Arruda, 1997; Stern, 1997; Stern, Arruda, Hooper, Wolfner, & Morey, 1997). In two geometrically separate samples administered both the VAMS and the Profile of Mood States (POMS; McNair, Lorr, & Droppleman, 1981), convergent validity was supported by statistically significant correlations between corresponding scales of the two methods relative to correlations between noncorresponding scales. Convergent validity with an adapted version of the POMS was again demonstrated with stroke patients. Correlations with the Beck Depression Inventory (BDI; Beck & Steer, 1987) in two samples yielded the highest correlations with the VAMS Sad scale (ranging from $r = 0.53$ to 0.54). The VAMS has also been found to be highly correlated with the clinician's Clinical Global Improvement rating and patient self-report using a modified Center for Epidemiological Studies Depression Scale (Arruda et al., 1996). Correlations with the State-Trait Anxiety Inventory (STAI; State form; Spielberger, Gorsuch, & Lushene, 1970) predictably yielded a high correlation with the VAMS Tense scale ($r = 0.66$).

As reported above, the VAMS shows a good capacity to discriminate between groups with mood disorders and normal comparison samples (Stern, 1997). The VAMS also has been shown to be sensitive to the treatment effects of ECT (Arruda et al., 1996). The reliability of the VAMS has been examined through two test–retest reliability studies conducted with 15-min test–retest intervals, the brief interval intended to minimize state-based fluctuations in mood state (Stern, 1997). In a sample of 75 college students, reliability coefficients ranged from 0.49 (Sad) to 0.78 (Anxious, later renamed Tense). In a sample of 27 acute stroke patients, reliability coefficients ranged from 0.43 (Confused) to 0.84 (Afraid). These score reliabilities are somewhat more variable than expected.

The VAMS includes printed verbal descriptors at the poles (e.g., the word "Neutral" at one end and "Afraid" at the other), in addition to the schematic pictorial representations. The use of printed words reduces the nonverbal nature of the VAMS, insofar as word knowledge and reading ability requirements are increased. In an investigation reported by Stern et al. (1997), a group of 96 college students were administered a "no words" version of the VAMS followed in 15 min by the version with printed words. Correlations were statistically significant between each scale without words and the same scale with words, ranging from $r = 0.42$ (Tired) to $r = 0.90$ (Happy), with the exception of a low correlation for one scale that was later changed ($r = 0.26$ for the Anxious scale, later renamed Tense).

The authors concluded that the VAMS has adequate content validity and can be completed accurately by patients with impaired language comprehension (Stern et al., 1997).

Finally, the VAMS is probably more vulnerable to intentional misrepresentation of an examinee's mood than any of the nonverbal instruments described in this chapter because of its obvious and transparent content. Accordingly, the VAMS should be used with caution for examinees in whom malingering or dissimulation is known or suspected.

SUMMARY AND CONCLUSIONS

In this chapter, nonverbal tests and methodologies intended for the measurement of personality and psychopathology have been described. Some of the techniques date back to the beginning of personality assessment in psychology, whereas others are only a few years old. These techniques demonstrate that nonverbal measures can be constructed to tap constructs not readily assessable with traditional verbal methodologies. It is possible to use nonverbal assessment to span the full range of personality assessment, from objective to projective tests and from structured to unstructured tests. Nonverbal assessments add a potentially valuable set of tools to a psychologist's toolbox.

In addition, nonverbal assessment methodologies are probably somewhat less transparent (or obvious) in their targeted constructs, thereby being less susceptible to the effects of examiner demand, dissimulation, and impression management. With the exception of the visual analog scales, nonverbal measures seem to be less superficially face-valid than verbal self-report or behavior rating scales. Clearly, further research is necessary before nonverbal tests can be proposed as a solution to the biases associated with verbal self-report methods.

Nonverbal personality assessment is its infancy. Although there are advances in the validity and reliability of drawing techniques (e.g., Naglieri et al., 1991), their inclusion in a comprehensive test battery remains challenging to justify. Adaptations of the world technique are widely used in play therapy but generally lack psychometric rigor. The newest measures like the FAST, NPQ and FF-NPQ, and the VAMS promise to usher in a new era of instruments that can meet existing professional standards, but all need additional research. In meeting the needs of practitioners, nonverbal assessments must do more than merely match the informational yield of verbal assessments to gain acceptance. They must also expand the diversity of populations that psychologists can serve and the breadth of constructs that can be measured reliably and validly. The next major evolutionary stage in the development of nonverbal personality assessment will be the demonstration of additional incremental validity in the assessment process, relative to standard verbal personality and psychopathology assessment procedures. If nonverbal measures can be demonstrated to add to the ability of psychologists to explain and predict behavior, then these measures can expect widespread use in the future.

ACKNOWLEDGMENTS. This chapter was supported in part by Grant R215K010121 from the U. S. Department of Education. Thanks to Scott P. Merydith, Rochester Institute of Technology, for several ideas that appear in this chapter, especially those concerning the limitations of verbal self-report measures.

REFERENCES

Aitken, R. C. B. (1969). Measurement of feelings using visual analogue scales. *Proceedings of the Royal Society of Medicine, 62*, 989–993.

Aoki, S. (1981). The retest reliability of the Sand Play Technique: II. *British Journal of Projective Psychology & Personality Study, 26*, 25–33.

Arruda, J. E., Stern, R. A., & Legendre, S. A. (1996). Assessment of mood state in patients undergoing electroconvulsive therapy: The utility of Visual Analog Mood Scales developed for cognitively impaired patients. *Convulsive Therapy, 12*, 207–212.

Beck, A. T., & Steer, R. A. (1987). *Beck depression inventory manual.* San Antonio, TX: The Psychological Corporation.

Beck, A. T., Steer, R. A. & Brown, G. K. (1996). *Beck depression inventory manual* (2nd ed.). San Antonio, TX: The Psychological Corporation.

Bell, J. E. (1948). *Projective techniques: A dynamic approach to the study of the personality.* New York: Longmans, Green.

Bender, L. (1938). *A visual motor gestalt test and its clinical use. Research monograph No. 3.* New York: American Orthopsychiatric Association.

Bernreuter, R. G. (1931). *Bernreuter personality inventory.* Stanford, CA: Stanford University Press.

Bernstein, E. M., & Putnam, F. W. (1986). Development, reliability, and validity of a dissociation scale. *Journal of Nervous and Mental Disease, 174*, 727–735.

Briccetti, K. A. (1994). Emotional indicators of deaf children on the Draw-a-Person test. *American Annals of the Deaf, 139*, 500–505.

Buck, J. N. (1948). The H–T–P technique: A qualitative and quantitative scoring manual. *Journal of Clinical Psychology, 4*, 317–396.

Buck, J. N., & Warren, W. L. (1992). *House–Tree–Person projective drawing technique (H–T–P): Manual and interpretive guide.* Los Angeles: Western Psychological Services.

Buckley, P. D. (1978). The Bender Gestalt Test: A review of reported research with school-age subjects, 1966–1977. *Psychology in the Schools, 15*, 327–338.

Buhler, C. (1951a). The World Test: A projective technique. *Journal of Child Psychiatry, 2*, 4–23.

Buhler, C. (1951b). The World Test: Manual of directions. *Journal of Child Psychiatry, 2*, 69–81.

Buhler, C., & Kelly, G. (1941). *The World Test. A measurement of emotional disturbance.* San Antonio, TX: The Psychological Corporation.

Burns, R. C. (1987). *Kinetic–House–Tree–Person drawings (K–H–T–P): An interpretive manual.* New York: Brunner/Mazel.

Burns, R. C., & Kaufman, S. H. (1970). *Kinetic family drawings (K–F–D): An introduction to understanding children through kinetic drawings.* New York: Brunner/Mazel.

Burns, R. C., & Kaufman, S. H. (1972). *Actions, styles, and symbols in kinetic family drawings (K–F–D): An interpretive manual.* New York: Brunner/Mazel.

Butcher, J. N., Dahlstrom, W. G., Graham, J. R., Tellegen, A., & Kaemmer, B. (1989). *Minnesota multiphasic personality inventory—2 (MMPI-2): Manual for administration and scoring.* Minneapolis: University of Minnesota Press.

Camara, W. J., Nathan, J. S., & Puente, A. E. (2000). Psychological test usage: Implications in professional psychology. *Professional psychology: Research & practice, 31*, 141–154.

Cohen, B. M., Hammer, J. S., & Singer, S. (1988). The Diagnostic Drawing Series: A systematic approach to art therapy evaluation and research. *Arts in Psychotherapy, 15*, 11–21.

Cummings, J. A. (1986). Projective drawings. In H. M. Knoff (Ed.), *The assessment of child and adolescent personality* (pp. 199–244). New York: Guilford.

Derogatis, L. R. (1987). The Derogatis Stress Profile (DSP): Quantification of psychological stress. *Advances in Psychosomatic Medicine, 17,* 30–54.

Dixon, J. L. (1998). Concurrent validity of the Koppitz Bender–Gestalt Emotional Indicators among women with mental retardation. *Perceptual & Motor Skills, 86,* 195–197.

Dumont, F., & Smith, D. (1996). Projectives and their infirm research base. *Professional psychology: Research and practice, 27,* 419–421.

Exner, J. E. (1993). *The rorschach: A comprehensive system. Volume 1: Basic foundations* (3rd ed.). New York: Wiley.

Eysenck, H. J. (1990). *The decline and fall of the freudian empire.* Washington, DC: Scott-Townsend.

Fagan, T., & Wilson, P. (1997). Karen Machover (1902–1996): Obituary. *American Psychologist, 52,* 742.

Frank, L. K. (1939). Projective methods for the study of personality. *Journal of Psychology, 8,* 389–413.

Frank, L. K. (1948). *Projective methods.* Springfield, IL: Charles C. Thomas.

Freyd, M. (1923). The graphic rating scale. *Journal of Educational Psychology, 14,* 83–102.

Fuller, G. G., Preuss, M., & Hawkins, W. F. (1970). The validity of the human figure drawings with disturbed and normal children. *Journal of School Psychology, 8,* 54–56.

Gehring, T. M. (1998). *The Family System Test (FAST).* Seattle WA: Hogrefe & Huber.

Gehring, T. M., & Page, J. (2000). Family System Test (FAST): A systemic approach for family evaluation in clinical practice and research. In K. Gitlin-Weiner, A. Sandgrund, & C. Schaefer (Eds.), *Play diagnosis and assessment* (2nd ed., pp. 419–445). New York: Wiley.

Gitlin-Weiner, K., Sandgrund, A., & Schaefer, C. (Eds.). (2000). *Play diagnosis and assessment* (2nd ed.). New York: Wiley.

Goff, A. F., & Parker, A. W. (1969). Reliability of the Koppitz scoring system for the Bender Gestalt Test. *Journal of Clinical Psychology, 25,* 407–409.

Goldberg, L. R. (1993). The structure of phenotypic personality traits. *American Psychologist, 48,* 26–34.

Goodenough, F. L. (1926). *Measurement of intelligence by drawings.* New York: World Book Company.

Gulbro-Leavitt, C., & Schimmel, B. (1991). Assessing depression in children and adolescents using the Diagnostic Drawing Series modified for children (DDS-C). *Arts in Psychotherapy, 18,* 353–356.

Gurycka, A. (Ed.). (1996). *The representation of the world in the human mind: Typology and functions.* Poznan: University of Poznan Press, Humaniora.

Hammer, E. F. (1958). *The clinical application of projective drawings.* Springfield, IL: Charles C. Thomas.

Hammer, E. F. (1986). Graphic techniques with children and adolescents. In A. I. Rabin (Ed.), *Projective techniques for adolescents and children* (pp. 239–263). New York: Springer.

Handler, L., & Habenicht, D. (1994). The Kinetic Family Drawing Technique: A review of the literature. *Journal of Personality Assessment, 62,* 440–464.

Hanes, M. (1997). Utilizing the circus phenomenon as a drawing theme in art therapy. *Arts in Psychotherapy, 24,* 375–384.

Harris, D. B. (1963). *Children's drawings as measures of intellectual maturity.* New York: Harcourt, Brace & World.

Harrower, M. R. (1950). The Most Unpleasant Concept Test; a graphic projective technique. *Journal of Clinical Psychology, 3,* 213–233.

Hartshorne, H., & May, M. (1928). *Tests of honesty and trustworthiness.* New York: Association Press.

Hays, R. E., & Lyons, S. J. (1981). The bridge drawing: A projective technique for assessment in art therapy. *Arts in Psychotherapy, 8,* 207–217.

Holt, R. R. (1992). The contemporary crises of psychoanalysis. *Psychoanalysis & Contemporary Thought, 15,* 375–403.

Homberger, E. [Erikson, E. H.] (1938). Dramatic productions test. In H. A. Murray (Ed.), *Explorations in personality: A clinical and experimental study of fifty men of college age* (pp. 552–582). New York: Oxford University Press.

Hulse, W. (1951). The emotionally disturbed child draws his family. *Quarterly Journal of Child Behavior, 3,* 152–174.

Hutt, M. L. (1985). *The Hutt adaptation of the Bender–Gestalt Test* (4th ed.). New York: Grune & Stratton.

Jackson, D. N. (1971). A sequential system for personality scale development. In C. D. Spielberger (Ed.), *Current topics in clinical and community psychology* (Vol. 2, pp. 61–92). New York: Academic Press.

Jackson, D. N. (1984). *Personality research form manual.* Port Huron, MI: Research Psychologists.

Kahill, S. (1984). Human figure drawing in adults: An update of the empirical evidence, 1967–1982. *Canadian Psychology, 25,* 269–292.

Klein, R. G. (1986). Questioning the clinical usefulness of projective psychological tests for children. *Journal of Developmental and Behavioral Pediatrics, 7,* 378–382.

Klepsch, M., & Logie, L. (1982). *Children draw and tell.* New York: Brunner/Mazel.

Knoff, H., & Prout, H. (1985). The Kinetic Family Drawing System: A review and integration of the Kinetic Family and School Drawing techniques. *Psychology in the Schools, 22,* 50–59.

Knoff, H. M. (1993). The utility of human figure drawings in personality and intellectual assessment: Why ask why? *School Psychology Quarterly, 8,* 191–196.

Koppitz, E. M. (1963). *The Bender Gestalt Test for young children.* New York: Grune & Stratton.

Koppitz, E. M. (1968). *Psychological evaluation of children's human figure drawings.* New York: Grune & Stratton.

Koppitz, E. M. (1975). *The Bender Gestalt Test for young children (vol. II): Research and application.* New York: Grune & Stratton.

Koppitz, E. M. (1984). *Psychological evaluation of human figure drawings by middle school pupils.* New York: Grune & Stratton.

Lacks, P. (1999). *Bender Gestalt screening for brain dysfunction* (2nd ed.). New York: Wiley.

Lee, S., & Oh, S. (1998). Visuoperceptual and constructive ability disturbances of patients with traumatic brain injury in Hutt Adaptation of the Bender Gestalt Test. *Korean Journal of Clinical Psychology, 17,* 311–317.

Lerner, E. A. (1972). *The projective use of the Bender Gestalt.* Springfield, IL: Charles C. Thomas.

Levick, M. F. (2000) *The Levick Emotional and Cognitive Art Therapy Assessment (LECATA; rev. ed.).* Boca Raton, FL: South Florida Art Psychotherapy Institute.

Lindzey, G. (1961). *Projective techniques and cross-cultural research.* New York: Appleton-Century-Crofts.

Lowenfeld, M. (1939) The world pictures of children; A method of recording and studying them (Paper read on March 23rd, 1938 to the Medical Section of the British Psychological Society). *British Journal of Medical Psychology, 18,* 65–101.

Lowenfeld, M. (1979). *The world technique.* London: Allen & Unwin.

Machover, K. (1949). *Personality projection in the drawing of the human figure (A method of personality investigation).* Springfield, IL: Charles C. Thomas.

Martin, R. P. (1983). The ethical issues in the use and interpretation of the Draw-a-Person Test and other similar projective procedures. *School Psychologist, 38,* 6, 8.

Matavich, M. A. (1999). Discriminant validity of the Draw-a-Person Screening Procedure for Emotional Disturbance for incarcerated juvenile delinquents in special education. *Dissertation Abstracts International, 59,* 3736.

Matto, H. C. (2001). Investigating the clinical utility of the Draw-a-Person: Screening Procedure for Emotional Disturbance (DAP:SPED) projective test in assessment of high-risk youth. A measurement validation study. *Dissertation Abstracts International, 61*(2), 2920.

McNair, D. M., Lorr, M., & Droppleman, L. F. (1981). *Profile of mood states.* San Diego, CA: Educational and Industrial Testing Service.

McNeish, T. J., & Naglieri, J. A. (1993). Identification of individuals with serious emotional disturbance using the Draw A Person: Screening Procedure for Emotional Disturbance. *Journal of Special Education, 27,* 115–121.

Michael, J. C., & Buhler, C. (1945). Experiences with personality testing in the neuropsychiatric department of a general hospital. *Diseases of the Nervous System, 6,* 205–211.

Minuchin, S. (1974). *Families & family therapy.* Cambridge, MA: Harvard University Press.

Morgan, C. D., & Murray, H. A. (1935). A method for investigating phantasies: The Thematic Apperception Test. *Archives of Neurology and Psychiatry, 34,* 289–306.

Motta, R. W., Little, S. G., & Tobin, M. I. (1993a). A picture is worth less than a thousand words: Response to reviewers. *School Psychology Quarterly, 8,* 197–199.

Motta, R. W., Little, S. G., & Tobin, M. I. (1993b). The use and abuse of human figure drawings. *School Psychology Quarterly, 8,* 162–169.

Murray, H. A. (1938). *Explorations in personality.* New York: Oxford University Press.

Naglieri, J. A. (1988). *Draw a person: A quantitative scoring system.* San Antonio, TX: The Psychological Corporation.

Naglieri, J. A., McNeish, T. J., & Bardos, A. N. (1991). *Draw a Person: Screening procedure for Emotional Disturbance (DAP: SPED).* Austin, TX: PRO-ED.

Naglieri, J. A., & Pfeiffer, S. I. (1992). Performance of disruptive behavior disordered and normal samples on the Draw A Person: Screening Procedure for Emotional Disturbance. *Psychological Assessment, 4,* 156–159.

Nyenhuis, D. L., Stern, R. A., Yamamoto, C., Luchetta, T., & Arruda, J. E. (1997). Standardization and validation of the Visual Analog Mood Scales. *The Clinical Neuropsychologist, 11,* 407–415.

Oliver, R. A., & Kronenberger, E. J. (1971). Testing the applicability of Koppitz's Bender-Gestalt scores to brain-damaged, emotionally disturbed and normal adolescents. *Psychology in the Schools, 8,* 250–253.

Pascal, G. R., & Suttell, B. J. (1951). *The bender gestalt test.* New York: Grune & Stratton.

Paunonen, S. V., & Ashton, M. C. (in press). The nonverbal assessment of personality: The NPQ and the FF-NPQ. In B. de Raad & M. Perugini (Eds.), *Big five assessment.* Goettingen, Germany: Hogrefe & Huber.

Paunonen, S. V., Ashton, M. C., & Jackson, D. N. (2001). Nonverbal assessment of the big five personality factors. *European Journal of Personality, 15,* 3–18.

Paunonen, S. V., & Jackson, D. N. (1998). *Nonverbal Personality Questionnaire (NPQ).* Port Huron, MI: Sigma Assessment Systems.

Paunonen, S. V., Jackson, D. N., & Keinonen, M. (1990). The structured nonverbal assessment of personality. *Journal of Personality, 58,* 481–502.

Paunonen, S. V., Jackson, D. N., Trzebinski, J., & Forsterling, F. (1992). Personality structure across cultures: A multimethod evaluation. *Journal of Personality and Social Psychology, 62,* 447–456.

Paunonen, S. V., Keinonen, M., Trzebinski, J., Forsterling, F., Grishenko-Roze, N., Kouznetsova, L. et al. (1996). The structure of personality in six cultures. *Journal of Cross-Cultural Psychology, 27,* 339–353.

Paunonen, S. V., Zeidner, M., Engvik, H. A., Oosterveld, P., & Maliphant, R. (2000). The nonverbal assessment of personality in five cultures. *Journal of Cross-Cultural Psychology, 31,* 220–239.

Prout, H. T., & Phillips, P. D. (1974). A clinical note: The Kinetic School Drawing. *Psychology in the Schools, 11,* 303–306.

Reichenberg, N., & Raphael, A. J. (1992). *Advanced psychodiagnostic interpretation of the Bender Gestalt Test: Adults and children.* New York: Praeger.

Remington, M., Tyrer, P. J., Newson-Smith, J., & Cicchetti, D. V. (1979). Comparative reliability of categorical and analog rating scales in the assessment of psychiatric symptomatology. *Psychological Medicine, 9,* 765–770.

Reynolds, C. R. (1978). A quick-scoring guide to the interpretation of children's Kinetic Family Drawings (KFD). *Psychology in the Schools, 15,* 489–492.

Roback, H. B. (1968). Human figure drawings: Their utility in the clinical psychologist's armamentarium for personality assessment. *Psychological Bulletin, 70,* 1–19.

Rorschach, H. (1921). *Psychodiagnostik.* Bern: Ernst Bircher.

Rossini, E. D., & Kaspar, J. C. (1987). The validity of the Bender–Gestalt emotional indicators. *Journal of Personality Assessment, 51,* 254–261.

Sangster, G., Rogers, B. J., & Searight, H. R. (1993). The validity of Hutt's Bender–Gestalt scoring system for hostility: Correlation with the Interpersonal Behavior Survey's aggression scales. *Psychology: A Journal of Human Behavior, 30,* 22–29.

Scott, W. D. (1919). *Personnel system of the U.S. army* (Vol. 2). Washington, DC: U.S. Government Printing Office.

Sharma, T. R. (1972). Measuring intelligence through bicycle drawings. *Indian Educational Review, 7,* 1–30.

Sjolund, M. (1981). Play-diagnosis and therapy in Sweden: The Erica-Method. *Journal of Clinical Psychology, 37,* 322–325.

Sjolund, M. (1993). *The erica method: A technique for play therapy and diagnosis: A training guide.* Greeley, CO: Carron.

Sjolund, M., & Schaefer, C. E. (1994). The Erica Method of sand play diagnosis and assessment. In K. J. O'Connor & C. E. Schaefer (Eds.), *Handbook of play therapy, vol. 2: Advances and innovations* (pp. 231–252). New York: Wiley.

Smith, D., & Dumont, F. (1995). A cautionary study: Unwarranted interpretations of the Draw-a-Person Test. *Professional psychology: Research & practice, 26,* 298–303.

Spielberger, C. D., Gorsuch, R. L., & Lushene, R. E. (1970). *The state-trait anxiety inventory.* Palo Alto, CA: Consulting Psychologists Press.

Stern, R. A. (1997). *Visual analog mood scales professional manual.* Odessa, FL: Psychological Assessment Resources.

Stern, R. A., Arruda, J. E., Hooper, C. R., Wolfner, G. D., & Morey, C. E. (1997). Visual analogue mood scales to measure internal mood state in neurologically impaired patients: Description and initial validity evidence. *Aphasiology, 11,* 59–71.

Stern, R. A., Rosenbaum, J., White, R. F., & Morey, C. E. (1991). Clinical validation of a visual analogue dysphoria scale for neurologic patients [Abstract]. *Journal of Clinical and Experimental Neuropsychology, 13,* 106.

Swenson, C. H. (1968). Empirical evaluations of human figure drawings: 1957–1966. *Psychological Bulletin, 70,* 20–44.

Taylor, E. M. (1959). *The appraisal of children with cerebral deficits.* Cambridge, MA: Harvard University Press.

Tharinger, D. J., & Stark, K. D. (1990). A qualitative versus quantitative approach to evaluating the Draw-a-Person and Kinetic Family Drawing: A study of mood- and anxiety-disorder children. *Psychological Assessment, 2,* 365–375.

Thomas, G. V., & Jolley, R. P. (1998). Drawing conclusions: A re-examination of empirical and conceptual bases for psychological evaluation of children from their drawings. *British Journal of Clinical Psychology, 37,* 127–139.

Urban, W. H. (1963). *The Draw-a-Person catalogue for interpretive analysis.* Los Angeles: Western Psychological Services.

Vass, Z. (1999). *Projektív rajzvizsgálat algoritmusokkal (A számítógépes formai elemzés módszerének bemutatása a szkizofrénia képi kifejezodésének tükrében)* [Analysis of projective drawings with algorithms. The method of computer assisted formal analysis, validated in visual expression of schizophrenia]. Unpublished doctoral dissertation, Budapest: Eötvös Loránd University of Sciences.

Vass, Z. (2001). *Perspectives on objective assessment of projective drawings.* Unpublished manuscript.

Wagner, E. E. (1999). Defining projective techniques: The irrelevancy of "projection." *North American Journal of Psychology, 1,* 35–40.

Wasserman, C. B. (1995). A study of the Perceptual Adience–Abience scale of the Hutt Adaptation of the Bender–Gestalt test. *Dissertation Abstracts International Section A: Humanities & Social Sciences, 55*(12-A), 3752.

Wertheimer, M. (1923). Untersuchungen zur Lehre von der Gestalt II. *Psycologische Forschung, 4,* 301–350.

Woodworth, R. S. (1917). *Personal data sheet.* Chicago: C. H. Stoelting Company.

Wrightson, L., & Saklofske, D. H. (2000). Validity and reliability of the Draw a Person: Screening Procedure for Emotional Disturbance with adolescent students. *Canadian Journal of School Psychology, 16,* 95–102.

Ziffer, R. L., & Shapiro, L. E. (1992). *Children's self-report and projective inventory.* Bala Cynwyd, PA: Psychological Assessment Service.

15

Nonverbal Neuropsychological Assessment

John D. Wasserman and Robin M. Lawhorn

As an integrated neuroscientific discipline, neuropsychology encompasses the study of brain–behavior relationships. Within the scope of clinical practice, neuropsychological assessment involves measurement of higher order dimensions of cognition, principally in the domains of attention and executive functions, learning and memory, language and communication, and spatial cognition. In this chapter, we address nonverbal assessment in these core neuropsychological domains, noting that related areas of testing commonly included in neuropsychological batteries (e.g., appraisal of intelligence, personality, and psychopathology) are described elsewhere in this volume and that testing of lower sensory and motor functions already tends to be somewhat independent of language.

Disorders of language have historically played a central role in the study of brain–behavior relationships. Among the seminal early discoveries were Paul Broca's (1861) association of a syndrome of nonfluent speech expression with anterior left-cerebral-hemisphere lesions and Carl Wernicke's (1874) description of a fluent language comprehension disorder stemming from lesions to the left posterior temporal lobe. These developments laid the groundwork for the distinction of language from other cognitive functions, for the lateralization of most language functions to the left cerebral hemisphere, and for the methodology of associating

John D. Wasserman and Robin M. Lawhorn, Center for Cognitive Development, Department of Psychology, George Mason University, Fairfax, Virginia 22030.

Handbook of Nonverbal Assessment, edited by R. Steve McCallum. Kluwer Academic/Plenum Publishers, 2003.

characteristic brain injuries with functional behavior deficits (e.g., Goodglass, 1993). Indeed, it may be argued that efforts to understand disordered (as well as normal) language have influenced understanding of brain–behavior relationships in all domains of cognitive functioning, including nonverbal areas.

One way to establish the boundaries between verbal and nonverbal neuropsychological functioning is to understand the central aspects of language, language assessment, and language disorders. Beginning in 1863, Hughlings Jackson (1915) studied language disorders and speculated that at the heart of language disorders was a central deficit in the ability to convey meaning or the formulation of propositions. Finkelnburg (1870/1979) described language disorders as an inability to manipulate any symbols for communication (*asymbolia*), making it difficult for affected individuals to use even nonverbal gestures or pantomime for communication. Henry Head (1926) built upon the Jacksonian tradition to argue that impaired symbol formation and expression in any context— language and nonlanguage tasks—is the central processing disorder in aphasia. Contemporary theorists continue to emphasize the integral role of *meaning* in language and communication, irrespective of whether communication is spoken, written, or gestural (e.g., Caplan, 1994).

The mission of the neuropsychologist during the assessment process is typically to document and describe patterns of neurocognitive and emotional functioning at levels beyond those that are visible to the clinical observer; relate findings to expectations based upon a person's history, clinical presentation, and the nature of any known or suspected brain injury; make predictions as to functional implications and prognosis; and provide guidance for remediation and rehabilitation. Use of nonverbal assessment tools in neuropsychology is indicated for specific individuals whose performance on measures tapping nonlanguage functions is compromised by their cultural–linguistic, educational, or medical background: (a) individuals with an acquired or developmental speech and language disorder; (b) individuals with limited English proficiency, for whom translated or adapted tests are not available; (c) individuals who are deaf or hard of hearing; and (d) individuals who, by virtue of their education or cultural experience, cannot be assessed validly with language-based tasks. Nonverbal assessment in an individual with known or suspected language difficulties may provide a truer representation of neuropsychological functioning than can be expected with language-loaded measures, simply because the role of language as an intervening factor in explaining deficient test performance is minimized. Although it is theoretically possible to conduct a relatively comprehensive neuropsychological assessment using nonverbal instruments, best practice will always involve some verbal assessment if only to document the extent, quality, and severity of language impairment.

AN OPERATIONAL "NONVERBAL" DEFINITION

It is debatable whether the verbal–nonverbal dichotomy corresponds to clear distinctions in the structural organization of human neural systems.

The dichotomy cannot be equated with the auditory–visual sensory modality distinction, as there are nonverbal aspects to auditory processing (e.g., processing of environmental and musical sounds) and verbal aspects to visual processing (e.g., identification of meaningful, semantically processed visual details). Efforts to simplify the verbal–nonverbal dichotomy by defining functions in terms of underlying cerebral lateralization (left hemisphere vs. right hemisphere) also represent an oversimplification of reality, since some aspects of language are seated in the right cerebral hemisphere, and some spatial processing is seated in the left cerebral hemisphere. De Renzi (1982) criticized the association of verbal–nonverbal functioning with lateralized left- and right-hemisphere cortical functions: "There is no need to spend time to demonstrate that labeling the right hemisphere specialization as 'non verbal' is heuristically unsatisfactory" (p. 186). In contrast, Benton (1988/2000) concluded that the verbal–nonverbal dichotomy remains a practical albeit flawed way to think about cortical functions. In general, it is important to recognize that behavior always has a multitude of cortical and subcortical underpinnings. Most human behaviors involve a *microgenesis*, or unfolding, of multiple simultaneous complex processes that change over a span of seconds—activating circuits and pathways throughout the entire brain, never just one cerebral hemisphere.

With these considerations in mind, we can only arrive at a working operational definition of *nonverbal tests* that relies upon their objective, observable, and overt performance requirements. The most obvious definition is that nonverbal neuropsychological tests involve no expressive or receptive language requirements from the examinee, but there are so few tests that meet this requirement that it is unduly restrictive. Accordingly, we must arbitrarily define *nonverbal neuropsychological tests* as instruments (a) requiring minimal receptive language of the examinee (usually not more than several sentences to be comprehended as part of the spoken instructions), (b) utilizing stimuli that are not semantic or numerical symbols (e.g., logographs, letters, words, or numbers), (c) requiring no expressive language (i.e., no written or spoken verbal responses) on the part of the examinee, and (d) having a theoretical or empirical relationship with the integrity of functioning in the brain.

Our rationale for permitting brief spoken instructions (requiring a little receptive language/comprehension) in a nonverbal test while excluding expressive language/production is threefold: (a) expressive language deficits, particularly in naming and word-finding ability, are almost universal in language disorders, whereas receptive language deficits are comparatively rarer; (b) receptive language is developmentally acquired before expressive language and tends to be less impaired in developmental disorders than expressive language (e.g., Ballantyne & Sattler, 1991; Clark & Hecht, 1983; Fraser, Bellugi, & Brown, 1963; see also the differential prevalence rates for developmental language disorders in American Psychiatric Association, 2000); and (c) the sparing of language comprehension relative to language expression after acquired brain injury parallels the better-known sparing of recognition memory relative to free recall memory (e.g., Channell & Peek, 1989). All things being equal, the ability to comprehend ideas is more resilient to brain injury than the expression of ideas.

Our rationale for excluding printed stimuli that involve semantic or numerical symbols (e.g., letters, words, logographic characters, and numbers) is that most of these graphic forms tend to be semantically represented and therefore heavily dependent upon linguistic processes. For example, most forms of numerical processing are mediated by some form of semantic representation (McCloskey & Macaruso, 1995), although it is clear that independent nonlinguistic processes are also associated with quantitative operations. The exclusion of test stimuli using letters, numbers, or words excludes from our definition of nonverbal tests some of the best known neuropsychological measures including the Trail Making Test (Army Individual Test Battery, 1944) and the Halstead Category Test (Halstead, 1947) from the Halstead–Reitan Neuropsychological Battery.

It is theoretically possible to conduct an assessment of language-related functions with nonverbal measures, although there is little reason to do so. For example, language functions such as auditory processing and symbolic communication may be measured with nonverbal tools of sound processing (Seashore, Lewis, & Saetveit, 1960; Spreen & Benton, 1969) and pantomime/gesture recognition (Benton, Sivan, Hamsher, Varney, & Spreen, 1994). Several measures of receptive language and comprehension meet our defining criteria for nonverbal neuropsychological tests (e.g., DiSimoni, 1978; Dunn & Dunn, 1997; Spreen & Benton, 1969), because they involve brief verbal directives to point or manipulate objects with no expressive language. As a rule, however, the assessment of language and communication should involve at least some verbal measures.

NONVERBAL TESTS ACROSS NEUROPSYCHOLOGICAL DOMAINS

In this section, we describe applied and theoretical dimensions of assessment within the major neuropsychological domains of attention and executive functions, spatial cognition, and learning and memory. Representative nonverbal measures that tap central neuropsychological functions are described, including information about the constructs they measure, their administration, scoring, and interpretation, and their limitations. These instruments rank among the most widely utilized by practitioners (see Butler, Retzlaff, & Vanderploeg, 1991; Camara, Nathan, & Puente, 2000). In many instances, there may be as many as half a dozen or more adaptations for a given procedure, so only a limited number of representative adaptations can be described in text. For example, there are at least 10 scoring systems for the Rey–Osterrieth Complex Figure (ROCF; Troyer & Wishart, 1997). Nonverbal neuropsychological measures are also listed in Tables 15.1–15.3 including each test's normed age range, distinctive features, receptive language requirements, and expressive language requirements. Receptive language requirements were estimated for measures already considered to be largely nonverbal by counting the number of essential instructional sentences (or independent clauses) typically spoken by the examiner during a representative phase of task administration, excluding elaborations, examples, or other explanations. The graphical distribution of the number of instructional sentences across all tests was visually examined and found to be trimodal, and the number of sentences was then converted to descriptive terms capturing the three peaks of the distribution: *low* (0–3 sentences), *medium* (4–7), or *high* (8 or more), as estimates of receptive language demands. Expressive language requirements were generally negligible, unless the examinee was asked to indicate with single words (e.g., "Yes" or "No") whether a memory stimulus has been previously presented. These estimates of expressive and receptive language requirements are gross approximations, in order to provide an objective basis for comparison among different tests. They do not, however, address additional examiner gestural communications, demonstrations in task administration (given in conjunction with verbal instructions), and the internal language processing utilized by examinees during task performance.

In this volume, the psychometric properties of nonverbal tests have been described in detail. In this chapter, however, the psychometric properties of nonverbal neuropsychological measures are not directly addressed, in part because existing psychometric standards have not been traditionally or rigorously applied to neuropsychological tests. It has only been in more recent years that neuropsychological tests have undergone standardizations with nationally representative normative samples (e.g., Delis, Kaplan, & Kramer, 2001; Korkman, Kirk, & Kemp, 1998). Moreover, many neuropsychological tests yield multiple interpretive indices, with variable psychometric qualities, that are evaluated with reference to a large number of independently published norms varying widely in quality. Accordingly, it is difficult to make brief summary statements about psychometric adequacy for almost any neuropsychological test. Thoughtful discussions concerning the psychometric properties of neuropsychological tests are available in Franzen, Robbins, and Sawicki (1989) and Mitrushina, Boone, and D'Elia (1999).

Attention and Executive Functions

Attention and executive functions are interrelated constructs. At the simplest level of analysis, attention involves the allocation of cognitive resources in a given direction, whereas executive functions control the implementation of behaviors with some intended outcome. Theoretical models of attention include elements from the executive functions (Mirsky, 1996), whereas most models of the executive functions include elements (e.g., inhibition) that are central to attention (Eslinger, 1996). In some test batteries, attention and executive functions are separated (e.g., Naglieri & Das, 1997), whereas in others, they are combined (Korkman, Kirk, & Kemp, 1998). Some new conceptualizations of disorders of attention emphasize underlying deficits in executive functions (Barkley, 1997; Tannock & Schachar, 1996). We find the approach of Stuss and Benson (1986) to be helpful, that is, that attention and executive functions are hierarchically organized mental processes with executive functions at an upper, superordinate level and attention at a lower level, although the picture is undoubtedly more complex. In this section, we distinguish between attention and executive functions with the recognition that measures of each construct may be readily applied to the other.

In neuropsychology, *attention* is used to describe a wide range of behaviors and processes beginning as soon as environmental events are detected by the senses and involving the subsequent and ongoing allocation of cognitive resources. Attention has the net effect of facilitating cognitive and behavioral performance by filtering and managing incoming stimulation, permitting selection and control of behavioral responses, and maintaining performance over time (Cohen, 1993). Although a number of kinds of attention have been described (e.g., Parasuraman, 1998), most cognitive and neuropsychological models tend to include just a few core types (Cohen, 1993; Koelega, 1996; Stankov, 1988; van Zomeren & Brouwer, 1994):

- Selective attention: Ability to preferentially attend to a particular signal while inhibiting attention to competing signals; related to the concept of focus.
- Sustained attention: Ability over time to maintain a response set or readiness to respond to unpredictable events; related to the concept of vigilance.
- Divided attention: Ability to simultaneously attend to multiple events or perform multiple tasks.

In comparison with attention, the *executive functions* refer to a cluster of activating and inhibitory psychological processes that control the formulation, implementation, coordination, and monitoring of sequences of behavioral responses according to short- and long-term goals (Eslinger, 1996). The executive functions tend to be most strongly associated with activity in the prefrontal cortex, as the active force behind voluntary and deliberate behavior (Pribram, 1973; Tranel, Anderson, & Benton, 1995).

There is some variation in the classes of behaviors identified as executive functions, but they generally include (a) planning and organization, (b) productivity and flexibility, (c) response inhibition, and (d) self-monitoring and self-regulation. An informal survey of an expert panel for the National Institute of Child Health and Human Development listed self-regulation, sequencing of behavior, cognitive flexibility, response inhibition, planning, and organization of behavior (Eslinger, 1996). Factor-analytic studies have provided preliminary support for dimensions entitled concept formation/productivity, planning, schema, cluster, and inhibition (e.g., Levin et al., 1996).

Selected nonverbal tests of attention and executive functions appear in Table 15.1, with classes of these tests discussed below.

Table 15.1 Norm-Referenced Nonverbal Measures of Attention and Executive Functions

Test (source)	Appropriate age range	Distinctive features	Receptive language requirements	Expressive language requirements
Tests of Selective and/or Sustained Attention				
NEPSY Visual Attention subtest (Korkman et al., 1998)	3–12 years	Paper-and-pencil cancellation	Medium	None
TEA-Ch Sky Search (Manly, Robertson, Anderson, & Nimmo-Smith, 1999)	6–16 years	Match identical pairs; motor control parsed out	High	None*
TOVA and TOVA-A (Greenberg et al., 1999)	4–80+ years	Computerized CPT	Medium	None
WJ III Decision Speed (Woodcock et al., 2001)	2–90 years	Conceptual matching; paper and pencil	Medium	None
WJ III Pair Cancellation (Woodcock et al., 2001)	2–90 years	Matching sequences; paper and pencil	Medium	None
Tests of Response Inhibition				
Matching Familiar Figures Test (Kagan et al., 1964; Salkind, 1978)	5 to Adult	Reflective-impulsive responding	Low	None
Motor Impersistence Tests (Benton, Sivan et al., 1994)	5–11 years	Motor persistence	Low	None in six of eight items
NEPSY Knock and Tap subtest (Korkman et al., 1998)	5–12 years	Reciprocal motor responding	Medium	None
NEPSY Manual Motor Seq. subtest (Korkman et al., 1998)	3–12 years	Motor programming	Medium	None
NEPSY Statue subtest (Korkman et al., 1998)	3–4 years	Motor persistence	Medium	None
PANESS-R Overflow Items (Denckla, 1985)	5–10 years	Soft signs; counted during movements	No direct instructions	None
PANESS-R Successive Finger Movements (Denckla, 1985)	5–10 years	Motor programming; time to perform 20 sequences	Medium each item	None
PANESS-R Successive & Alternating Movements (Denckla, 1985)	5–10 years	Motor programming; time to perform 20 sequences	Medium each item	None

Table 15.1 *(Continued)*

Test (source)	Appropriate age range	Distinctive features	Receptive language requirements	Expressive language requirements
TEA-Ch Walk, Don't Walk [Manly et al., 1999]	6–16 years	Audiotape Go/No-Go with visual–motor response	High	None*
Tests of Planning and Organization				
BADS Action Program Test [Wilson et al., 1996]	16–80+ years	Planning; five-step practical problem; object manipulation	Medium	None
BADS Key Search Test (Wilson et al., 1996)	16–80+ years	Systematic and efficient planning; graphomotor; visual searching	Medium	None
Maze Tests				
Porteus Maze Test (Krikorian & Bartok, 1998)	7–21 years	Spatial planning	High	None
WISC-III PI Elithorn Mazes subtest [Kaplan et al., 1999]	6–16 years	Planning; paper and pencil	High	None
Self-Ordered Pointing Test (Petrides & Milner, 1982; Spreen & Strauss, 1998)	6–65 years	Planning; self-monitoring	Medium	None
Tinkertoy Test (Lezak, 1995)	Adults (control group)	Planning; complexity; object manipulation	Low	None (optional questions)
Tower of Hanoi/London Tests				
D-KEFS Tower Test (Delis et al., 2001)	8–89 years	Planning; disc transfer	Medium	None
NEPSY Tower subtest (Korkman et al., 1998)	5–12 years	Planning; bead transfer	Medium	None

Test	Age range	Description	Rating	
Tower of London (Shallice, 1982; Krikorian et al., 1994)	7–13 years	Planning; bead transfer	High	None
Tower of London—Drexel University (Culbertson & Zillmer, 1998)	7–12 years	Planning; bead transfer	High	None
Rey-Osterrieth Complex Figure				
Boston Qualitative Scoring System (Stern et al., 1999)	18–90+ years	Indices of planning, fragmentation, organization	High	None
Developmental Scoring System (Waber & Holmes, 1985)	5–14 years	Indices of organization, style, accuracy	Medium	None
WJ III Cog Planning Test (Woodcock et al., 2001)	2–90 years	Planning; nonverbal working memory	Medium	None
Tests of Cognitive Flexibility/Shifting				
Design Fluency (Jones-Gotman & Milner, 1977; Spreen & Strauss, 1998)	5–72 years	Divergent production; perseveration	High	None
D-KEFS Design Fluency Test (Delis et al., 2001)	8–89 years	Divergent production; perseveration; flexibility	Medium	None
NEPSY Design Fluency Subtest (Korkman et al., 1998)	5–12 years	Divergent production; perseveration	Medium	None
Ruff Figural Fluency Test (Ruff, 1988)	16–70 years	Divergent production; perseveration; strategies	Medium	None
Wisconsin Card Sorting Test (Heaton et al., 1993)	6–89 years	Reasoning with verbal feedback; perseveration	Medium	None

*On the TEA-Ch, the child is given instructions and then asked to verbally confirm their understanding of the task.
Notes: BADS = Behavioral Assessment of the Dysexecutive Syndrome; D-KEFS = Delis-Kaplan Executive Function System; PANESS-R = Physical and Neurological Examination for Subtle Signs—Revised; TEA-Ch = Test of Everyday Attention for Children; TOVA = Tests of Variables of Attention; WISC-III PI = Wechsler Intelligence Scale for Children (3rd ed.) as a Process Instrument; WJ III = Woodcock-Johnson III Tests of Cognitive Abilities.

Tests of Selective and/or Sustained Attention

Although there are many measures of selective and sustained attention, the best known tests with nonverbal forms of administration are the continuous performance tests (CPTs). Developed nearly five decades ago (Rosvold, Mirsky, Sarason, Bransome, & Beck, 1956), the CPTs represent a family of measures intended to assess diverse aspects of attention, along with elements of impulsivity. Ranging from about 10 to 25 min in length, the CPTs involve continuous presentation at either regular or variable intervals of low interest stimuli and require the examinee to respond (or *not respond*) to selected stimuli under specific conditions, usually by pressing a button or switch.

Four major continuous performance tests—Conners' Continuous Performance Test, the Integrated Visual and Auditory Continuous Performance Test (IVA), the Gordon Diagnostic System (GDS), and the Tests of Variables of Attention (TOVA)—currently dominate CPT assessment (Riccio, Reynolds, & Lowe, 2001). Of these, only the Tests of Variables of Attention (TOVA; Greenberg & Waldman, 1993) and its auditory version (TOVA-A) utilize nonlanguage stimuli (i.e., neither letters nor numbers). Over a period of 21.6 min, the TOVA visually presents two geometric figures, one of which is the target; the auditory version TOVA-A uses two tones, the higher tone being the target. Both measures are nonsequential with a fixed interstimulus interval.

The instructions for each version are provided verbally and include a 3-min practice test for both the visual and auditory versions to ensure that the examinee understands the testing conditions and instructions. The tests are computer scored and normed for ages 4 years through 80+ years, generating a score and narrative printout (Greenberg, Kindschi, & Corman, 1999). Results are reported as raw scores, percentages, standard scores, and standard deviations. Scoring indices on the TOVA, like most CPTs, include errors of omission (traditionally associated with inattention), errors of commission (impulsivity or disinhibition), correct response time (decision time to respond correctly) and postcommission response time (inhibitory responding after making an error), anticipatory responses (number of guesses), and response sensitivity (the ratio of hit rate to false alarm rate).

In the most comprehensive treatment to date, Riccio, Reynolds, and Lowe (2001) have summarized the strengths and weaknesses of the CPTs:

- Most CPT paradigms are sensitive to most types of central nervous system dysfunction.
- CPT performance is adversely affected by metabolic disorders with cognitive sequelae, by schizophrenic disorders, by pervasive developmental disorders, by most externalizing disorders in children, and by some internalizing disorders.
- CPTs tend not to be sensitive to disorders of mood or affect.
- CPTs have high levels of sensitivity and specificity for all forms of ADHD but only when ADHD or normal are the only two diagnostic possibilities (and differential diagnosis is not involved). Reliance on

CPTs as a primary diagnostic tool in determining the presence of ADHD will result in an unacceptably high number of false-positive errors (i.e., overdiagnosis of ADHD).

Although the CPTs provide norm-referenced information about multiple aspects of attention, the examiner must also consider the testing time investment and examinee motivation relative to the interpretive yield for these unengaging tasks.

Visual search and cancellation tests constitute a second major class of measures thought to tap selective and sustained attention. These tasks typically involve the presentation of a printed stimulus array with instructions to mark (or *cancel*) specified targets with a pencil. For example, an examinee may be asked to make a mark on all of the cats appearing in a semirandomly organized array of printed line drawings of animals. Performance is typically measured according to speed, although errors of commission or omission may be respectively interpreted as indicating difficulty with impulsiveness or inattention, especially if they are concentrated in one hemispatial field. Depending upon specific parameters of the test stimuli, these tasks require selective and sustained visual attention, visual scanning, visual discrimination, access to a full visual field, psychomotor coordination, lower-order (for simple detection) and higher-order (for decision-making) processing speed, and selection and implementation of visual search strategies. Task demands may be varied according to the randomness or structure of the stimulus array, the density and discriminability of the target stimuli relative to distractors, the nature of the decision to be made (e.g., mere detection of a target vs. comparison of multiple targets), the size of the visual field to be searched, and the use of target stimuli from different domains (e.g., letters, digits, pictures, or abstract figures; Cohen, 1993). For example, the tests of directed attention of Mesulam (1985) sometimes show dissociated patterns of performance between detection of the letter "A" (poor performance) and abstract geometric figure detection (adequate performance) in patients with left-hemisphere lesions (Kaplan, 1988), presumably because of the enhanced role of the left cerebral hemisphere in the processing of symbolic semantic stimuli.

Cancellation tasks differ from the CPTs through use of paper-and-pencil materials (vs. computerized presentation of stimuli), a single-frame simultaneous presentation (vs. a multiframe, sequential presentation), self-paced performance (vs. computer-pacing), heightened demands on visual–spatial scanning (vs. stimuli presented within a more limited visual field), and heightened demands for visual search strategies (different strategies are required for CPTs). They are similar to the CPTs insofar as they measured sustained and selective attention, usually under conditions of limited interest.

Several cancellation tasks with nonsymbolic stimuli appear in Table 15.1. Typically, they involve presentation of a printed stimulus array in landscape orientation (horizontally) in front of the examinee, with the center of the paper aligned with the examinee's midline. Instructions are typically brief. In the NEPSY Visual Attention subtest, for example, children are instructed: "Here is a _____. Down here are more _____s. See if you can find all the _____s. When you find a _____, make a mark on it like this. Mark all the _____s as quickly as you can. Tell me when you are finished. Are you ready? Go!" (Korkman et al., 1998, p. 120).

There are two general scores for cancellation measures: *time to completion* and *number of errors*. The time to completion is simply the amount of time in minutes and seconds until the examinee indicates that they have finished. Total errors typically are a sum of errors of omission and errors of commission. Every stimulus not marked constitutes an error of omission, whereas errors of commission occur when the examinee marks an erroneous target. A hemiattentional neglect syndrome is suggested when errors of omission are substantially greater for the examinee's left visual field than right. Profound neglect for the left hemiattentional visual field has been demonstrated in adults with right-cerebral-hemisphere impairment (Heilman, Watson, & Valenstein, 1993). A generalized slowing of performance may be evident, however, in examinees with a variety of diffuse and focal neurological conditions.

When the stimuli are randomly or semirandomly organized in the array, there are two ways of noting the spatial progress of the search over time. The color coding method, recommended by Mesulam (1985), requires that the task be performed with colored pencils, a different color being handed to the patient after the identification of a specified number of targets or after a specified period of time. An alternative method is simply to have the examiner draw a diagram indicating the sequence of targets circled by the patient. Normal adults and adolescents typically conduct a systematic, planful search beginning on the left and proceeding to the right in horizontal or vertical rows even in the random arrays (Kaplan, 1988; Mesulam, 1985). Children younger than 8 or 9 years usually scan and mark shapes in a random, unsystematic sequence. Some assessment procedures ask the examinee to draw their plan of search for an object lost in an open field (e.g., Wilson, Alderman, Burgess, Emslie, & Evans, 1996), permitting easy determination of the efficiency and systematicity of visual searches.

The paper-and-pencil visual search and cancellation tasks offer several important strengths, namely that they are child and adult friendly, simple to administer without computer equipment, and useful for screening visual field deficits. Their chief limitations are short administration duration, thereby limiting their use as measures of sustained attention, and limited prediction to clinical attention-deficit disorders. On the NEPSY Visual Attention subtest, for example, there is only a negligible performance difference between children diagnosed with ADHD and demographically matched standardization participants (Korkman et al., 1998). Normative performance on most of visual search and cancellation tests is dependent on speed, with few errors of omission or commission expected. As a result, children with visual–motor impairments may produce depressed performance, even if there is no attention deficit. Moreover, children, adolescents, and adults with known attention deficits have been shown in general to be prone to fast, inaccurate, impulsive task performance rather than slow, accurate, and reflective performance (Campbell, Endman, & Bernfeld, 1977; Cohen, Weiss, & Minde, 1972; Hopkins, Perlman, Hechtman, & Weiss, 1979), so tests such as the visual cancellation tasks that can be completed easily without errors may suffer from diminished clinical sensitivity.

Tests of Response Inhibition

Assessment of the executive functions may also include tests that require an examinee to suppress a competing response voluntarily, whether it is a highly automatized response or simply an easier, faster, or shorter pathway to task execution. Tests that involve the suppression of an automatic, easier, or preferred response are considered to tap neural processes of response inhibition. Sergeant, Oosterlaan, and van der Meere (1999) have described 12 assessment paradigms operationalizing response inhibition, a few of which are described below.

A classic and largely nonverbal measure of response inhibition is the Matching Familiar Figures Test (MFFT; Kagan, Rosman, Day, Albert, & Phillips, 1964), in which the examinee is asked to identify which of six choices is perfectly identical to a target picture. The test consists of an elementary set of 12 items and an adolescent/adult set of 12 items. All but one of the six choices (or up to eight choices for the adolescent/adult set) differ in some small; detailed respect from the target, and a careful and deliberate comparison of the choices to the target is required for accurate responding. The MFFT involves spoken directions, only two sentences of which are essential, and requires only a pointing response from the examinee. The examiner records time to the first response, total number of errors for each item, and the order in which errors are made. Responses continue to be coded for each item until the examinee makes a maximum of six errors or gets the item correct. In general, the MFFT is intended to detect children and adolescents who do not take sufficient time to examine the response options carefully, thereby demonstrating an impulsive response style (Kagan, 1965). The MFFT generally yields more errors in individuals with impulsivity-attentional problems compared with normal controls (Douglas, Barr, Amin, O'Neill, & Britton, 1988; Milich, Hartung, Martin, & Haigler, 1994), but performance on it may be depressed for reasons other than defective response inhibition including low intelligence, poor search strategies, and inadequate awareness of the need to inhibit responses until all options have been examined (Schachar & Logan, 1990).

Measures of the ability to inhibit motor responding include the motor impersistence tests, the go/no-go tests and their variants, motor programming, and graphic pattern generation tests (e.g., Cohen, 1993; Denckla, 1985; Goldberg, Podell, Bilder, & Jaeger, 2001). For the most part, these tests are mastered with perfect performance expected at adolescent or preadolescent ages and have very low ceilings.

Motor impersistence refers to the inability to sustain a directed act or intention and can be demonstrated using a variety of body parts including the limbs, eyes, eyelids, jaw, and tongue (Denckla, 1985; Heilman et al., 1993). In the Benton–Iowa neuropsychological battery, motor impersistence is assessed with eight tests requiring the maintenance of a movement or posture (e.g., keeping eyes closed, protruding tongue; Benton, Sivan, et al., 1994). Norms are provided for ages 5–11, as most adolescents and adults perform these tests without error.

The go/no-go paradigm described by Drewe (1975) and other forms of reciprocal responding (Luria, 1966) involve presentation of a series of stimuli (either verbal or nonverbal) to which the examinee must respond according to specified rules, usually inhibiting the inclination to reciprocate with a response identical to the stimulus or to perseverate to previously given responses. A simple nonverbal version of this task involves instructing the examinee to raise a finger ("go") when the examiner taps once on the table but to refrain from any movement ("no-go") when the examiner taps twice (Trommer, Hoeppner, & Zecker, 1991). The children's game of Simon Says may be considered a go/no-go task of behavioral inhibition in which the directed action is to be performed if "Simon says" ("go"), but the action should not be performed if the prefatory phrase "Simon says" is omitted from the directive ("no-go"). The simplest nonverbal form of the reciprocal programming task appears in the NEPSY Knock and Tap subtest, in which the examiner tells the examinee, "When I do this (knock lightly on the table with your knuckles), you do this (tap lightly on the table with your palm). But if I do this (tap lightly), you do this (knock lightly)" (Korkman et al., 1998, p. 171). The task, which is normed for ages 5–12, requires the examinee to respond to a series of knocks and taps with responses that require suppression of the natural inclination to be stimulus bound and echopraxic. There are innumerable variations on these these clinical paradigms, but relatively few of them are norm referenced.

Measures of motor alternation, sequencing, and programming can be utilized to examine diverse aspects of executive functions, including motor inhibition. Assessment of the formulation, execution, coordination, and maintenance of intentional motor action programs can include varied motor sequences, such as repetitive sequences touching each of the four fingers to the thumb (a fingers–thumb sequence); sequentially shifting the position of one hand from closed fist to open palm down to open palm held vertically (a fist–palm–side sequence); or alternating simultaneous bilateral hand movements from left palm—right fist to left fist—right palm to left palm—right fist and so on, each program maintained for a specified period of time. The regulation and maintenance of motor tone during execution of these programs with smooth, fluid, and coordinated movements constitutes what Luria (1973) termed a "kinetic melody" that heavily involves activity in the premotor cortex as well as other cortical and subcortical regions. The phenomenon of motor overflow, in which another part of the body moves involuntarily in conjunction with the intentional execution of motor sequences, is considered to be a neurological soft sign that reflects selective motor disinhibition (Denckla, 1985, 1994). Various test batteries including most adaptations of Luria's neuropsychological examination measure motor programming at graded levels of complexity for children and/or adults (e.g., Denckla, 1985; Goldberg et al., 2001; Korkman et al., 1998).

Graphic pattern generation tests typically involve the motor reproduction and continuation of recurring alternating figures, with the expectation that examinees with executive dysfunction may experience difficulty alternating between figures. Examinees are typically asked to reproduce and continue a pattern with either semantic stimuli (e.g., alternating m's and n's: $mnmnmnm$) or figural stimuli (e.g., alternating peaks and plateaus: $\Lambda\Pi\Pi\Lambda$). Luria (1966) described the reproduction of a series of alternating patterns from a written model, and Goldberg et al. (2001) have included a Graphical Sequences Test in their Executive Control Battery for adults.

Unfortunately, leading measures of behavioral inhibition such as the Stroop task (Stroop, 1935), in which an examinee must selectively attend to and name the color of ink a word is printed in while suppressing the more automatic response of reading the word, are unavailable in nonverbal adaptations. Other inhibition paradigms such as the "stop-signal" task (Logan & Cowan, 1984), designed to provide a pure and reliable measure of defective inhibition during information processing, remain primarily experimental and are not yet available for applied nonverbal use.

Tests of Planning and Organization

Executive functions also include the capacity to formulate and execute an organized sequence of actions with the objective of accomplishing a goal, or *planning*. For complex tasks, planning tends to be hierarchical, so that a task is broken into smaller subtasks, each with its own intermediate goal that can be accomplished in the service of the higher order objective. Because planning involves the generation of divergent response options, sorting through the options, and selecting one for implementation, it necessarily involves behavioral inhibition, sequential processing, and working memory. Lezak (1982) argues that planning is essential for independent, creative, and socially constructive behavior.

Disk-transfer problems, such as the Tower of London (TOL; Shallice, 1982) and Tower of Hanoi (TOH; Simon, 1975), utilize variations of a look-ahead problem-solving assessment paradigm dating back some seven decades (Ewert & Lambert, 1932). These tasks differ in their cognitive demands, with the TOL solution matching some specified final position and the TOH solution involving placement of all disks on one specified peg. At the same time, they share the qualities of being sensitive to sequential planning abilities, with the quality of performance being measured by the number of moves (or trials) required to arrive at the goal state. Problem-solving strategies used to solve the tower tasks include rote approaches, goal recursion strategies, perceptual strategies, and move-pattern strategies, all dependent upon tradeoffs between perceptual and memory functions (Simon, 1975). The TOL and TOH have both been shown to yield impaired performance in individuals with frontal-lobe lesions (Levin et al., 1996; Pennington & Ozonoff, 1996). Adaptations of these paradigms with contemporary norms are available for the Tower of Hanoi (Delis, Kaplan, & Kramer, 2001) and the Tower of London (Culbertson & Zillmer, 1998; Korkman et al., 1998; Krikorian, Bartok, & Gay, 1994). The tower tasks are largely nonverbal, with the examinee response being evident through the sequence of moves. In some ways, these tasks are much like games of chess or checkers, with varying constraints on disk movement but the common requirement of thinking ahead.

One of the oldest available nonverbal measures of spatial planning is the Porteus Maze Test, originally developed by Stanley D. Porteus in 1914 in response to the limitations of the Binet–Simon scales. Mazes in general are thought to measure "the process of choosing, trying, and rejecting or adopting alternative courses of conduct or thought" (Porteus, 1959, p. 7). Initially consisting of 14 mazes for ages 3 through adulthood, the Vineland edition of the Porteus Mazes (12 mazes) has recently been renormed for ages 7–21 years (Krikorian & Bartok, 1998). Administration of the test resembles that of other maze tests with the exception that two or four performance trials are permitted for selected items, the examinee being stopped as soon as an error is made and given a new test sheet to restart. The additional trial(s) may be used to detect perseverative response styles as well as the ability to self-monitor and alter strategy after an error. The Porteus Maze Test ranked among the first psychological tests to have demonstrated sensitivity to frontal-lobe lesions in psychosurgery studies (e.g., Smith, 1960). Porteus (1958) anticipated an increased neuroscientific emphasis on the executive functions, defining intelligence as "the capacity for making planned responses to a wide range of relevant stimuli" (p. 252).

Another largely nonverbal paper and pencil measure of planning is Elithorn's Perceptual Maze Test, originally published in 1965 and now included in the WISC-III as a Process Instrument (Kaplan, Fein, Kramer, Delis, & Morris, 1999). The test consists of a number of maze patterns in which the examinee must find and mark with a pencil a path from the bottom vertex to the top row, passing through as many large black dots as possible. The rules are that the path must run between the vertex and the top, that the path must keep to dotted lines and not jump across spaces, and that at each junction the path may fork left or right but not double back. At the bottom of each maze is a number specifying the largest number of black dots through which a path can pass.

Planning is also thought to be associated with paper and pencil drawing and reproduction of graphic figures, such as the Bender–Gestalt Test and the ROCF. The sequence of placements of the nine Bender–Gestalt figures on a blank sheet of paper has been hypothesized to reveal organization and planning attitudes and skills (Hutt, 1985), and likewise spatial management of elements of other drawings (e.g., person, house, tree, family) within the constraints of an 8.5 × 11 in. (21.59 × 27.9 cm) sheet of paper may also reveal planning deficits. The person with poor planning abilities may leave insufficient space on the page to complete a drawing. Reproduction by direct copy or memory of complex graphic figures such as the ROCF may also be rated according to the planning based on the order in which elements are drawn, the overall placement of the figure on the page, the placement of elements within the figure, and the overall integrity of the structure of the figure (Stern et al., 1999; Waber & Holmes, 1985).

Tests of Cognitive Flexibility and Mental Set Shifting

Cognitive flexibility refers to the ability to establish an attentional focus, mental set, or problem-solving approach, and then to appropriately switch to another set according to environmental demands or task requirements. In its pathological form, impaired cognitive flexibility results in a concrete and perseverative style that can be manifested by repeated execution of the same actions or sequence of actions in unsuccessful attempts to accomplish a goal. The individual with adequate cognitive flexibility can shift fluidly and comfortably from one idea to another.

The test most widely used to measure the ability to shift mental set is the Wisconsin Card Sorting Test (WCST; Grant & Berg, 1948; Heaton, Chelune, Talley, Kay, & Curtiss, 1993). The WCST requires the examinee to sort up to 128 response cards next to one of four stimulus (or key) cards according to a categorical principle, which must be deduced from feedback ("correct" or "incorrect") provided by the examiner after each response. Instructions are fairly nonspecific, requiring examinees to impose organization upon an ambiguous task ("I cannot tell you how to match the cards, but I will tell you each time whether you are right or wrong"; Heaton et al., 1993, p. 5). Sorting principles include matching key card stimuli on several dimensions of the stimuli depicted on each response card. Unknown to the examinee, the examiner will switch the correct sorting principle after the examinee provides 10 consecutive correct responses as a way of eliciting set-shifting abilities. The test continues until six categories have been correctly deduced, all 128 cards have been sorted, or 64 cards have been sorted if not even one category has been deduced.

Scoring on the WCST is challenging even for experienced examiners and should be facilitated with a computer-scoring program. During the test, the examiner indicates on a record form the basis for each card sorted, that is, the identity of the dimensions on which the response card matches the key card. The WCST yields 16 scoring indices, each of which is norm referenced for ages 6 years, 6 months through 89 years, 11 months. Norms are also stratified by education for adults. Percentile ranks, T scores, and standard scores are available.

The degree to which the examinee can respond to the new feedback, deduce that the sorting principle has changed, and alter their actions accordingly are the most important performance dimensions tapped by the WCST. Perseverative responses are defined as persistent responses based upon a stimulus characteristic that is incorrect. Once a perseverated-to principle is established, responses that match that principle are scored as *perseverative*, whereas responses that do not match the perseverated-to principle are *nonperseverative*. We will not address additional scoring indices here, except to note that the WCST provides indices describing the ease with which an individual can formulate a conceptual set, maintain that set when responding, and shift away from that set according to changing task requirements. In general, the WCST is considered to provide a valid measure of executive functions that is sensitive (but not specific) to frontal lobe dysfunction (Heaton et al., 1993).

The strength of the WCST is its largely nonthreatening (and low difficulty) format, as well as its minimally verbal instructions and nonverbal stimuli. The examinee is not required to speak during administration (although it is common for the examiner to ask about the examinee's approach after completion of the test). The fractionation of scores including the index of perseverative responding is useful in understanding and identifying the specific processes that may be impaired. At the same time, the WCST has the significant weakness of sometimes putting the examiner in the position of providing negative verbal feedback over a prolonged period of time. A new generation of sorting tasks (e.g., Delis et al., 2001) is attempting to address this limitation. Several indices on the WCST (e.g., number of correct sorts) have truncated ranges and low ceilings, rendering them most useful only when significant impairment is present.

Spatial Cognition

Spatial cognition has generally been defined to include perception, analyses, and manipulation of stimuli in personal or extrapersonal space. Lohman (1996) emphasizes imagery when he suggests, "Spatial ability may be defined as the ability to generate, retain, retrieve, and transform well-structured visual images" (p. 98). Carroll (1993) includes both perceptual processes and internal operations when he states "Spatial and other visual perceptual abilities have to do with individuals' abilities in searching the visual field, apprehending the forms, shapes, and positions of objects as visually perceived, forming mental representations of those forms, shapes, and positions, and manipulating such representations 'mentally'" (p. 304). In their compendium of measures of spatial cognition over 80 years, Eliot and Smith (1983) note that "measures of psychological space typically entail visual problems or 'tasks' which require individuals to estimate, predict, or judge the relationships among figures or objects in different contexts" (p. iv).

The key dimensions of spatial cognition have proven challenging to identify. Lohman (1996) described three basic spatial ability factors: spatial relations, spatial orientation, and visualization. Spatial relations involve mental rotation of perceived stimuli. Spatial orientation requires an examinee to imagine that they are reoriented in space, thereby changing their perspective to external stimuli. Finally, visualization appears to require complex processing of spatial and figural content, such as is evident in tasks in which a pattern must be perceived and replicated. Carroll (1993) has identified five major factors in the domain of visual perception: visualization, spatial relations, closure speed, flexibility of closure, and perceptual speed. Of these, the first involves unspeeded manipulation of visual patterns, whereas the latter four are all related to speeded aspects of visual pattern processing.

The neural underpinnings of spatial cognition tend to vary according to the quality of the processing and nature of the information being processed, with the abilities to orient in space, reproduce constructions, and recognize objects through visual or tactile cues most strongly associated with the adequacy of right hemisphere processing of spatial information (De Renzi, 1982). Two separate cortical visual systems have been described by Mishkin, Ungerleider, and Macko (1983), one a ventral system specialized for object vision (*what* was seen) and the other a dorsal system specialized for spatial vision (*where* it was seen).

Performance on specialized tasks such as recognition and learning of unfamiliar faces appears to be mediated by different strategic approaches, with an analytical-sequential approach tending to involve more left-hemisphere activity and a global-synthetic approach involving more activity by the right hemisphere (De Renzi, 1982). The global–local visual-processing distinction proposed by Navon (1977) originally reported evidence supporting the hypothesis that perception proceeds from the global, configural aspect of visual objects to the analysis of more local details. More recent investigations have suggested that individuals with focal left-hemisphere damage are more likely to have difficulty reproducing local, meaningful details, whereas individuals with focal right-hemisphere damage appear to experience particular difficulty reproducing global, configural forms (Delis, Kiefner, & Fridlund, 1988). While we consider many aspects of spatial cognition to have neural underpinnings in the right cerebral cortex, it is clear that analysis of meaningful detail in pictorial material may be seated in the left hemisphere.

Beyond these distinctions, it is difficult to identify specialized areas of right-hemisphere functioning (such as those included in several visuospatial test batteries appearing in Table 15.2) that might provide neuroanatomical underpinnings and correlates for differentiation of various aspects of spatial cognition. The right cerebral cortex is considered more diffusely and less focally organized than the left (Semmes, 1968), with a greater ratio of white to gray matter, a greater ratio of long to short association fibers, and fewer neuronal clusters. The right hemisphere's comparatively greater vulnerability to white-matter disorders has been offered as an explanation for the etiology of nonverbal learning disabilities and the association of white matter disorders with spatial cognitive deficits (e.g., Rourke, 1995).

Disorders of spatial cognition may take a variety of forms, including various *agnosias* (disorders of recognition), *apraxias* (disorders of intentional movement), and inattention syndromes (De Renzi, 1982). Benton and Tranel (1993) have provided a more behaviorally defined system of classifying disorders including visuoperceptual disorders, visuospatial disorders, and visuoconstructional disorders. Visuoperceptual disorders include visual object agnosias, defective visual analysis and synthesis, impairment of facial recognition (including the *prosopagnosias*, or loss of ability to identify familiar faces), and impairment in color recognition. Visuospatial disorders include defective localization of points in space, defective judgment of direction and distance, defective topographical orientation, unilateral visual neglect, and Balint's syndrome. Visuoconstructional disorders include defective assembling performance and defective graphomotor performance.

Selected nonverbal measures of spatial cognition appear in Table 15.2 and are described in the following sections.

Tests of Visuospatial Perception

The integrity of visuospatial processes may be assessed with tests that exclude motor responses or with tests that require perceptual–motor integration. In this section, we describe several measures of nonmotor visuospatial perception. Constructs tapped in this domain of functioning include facial discrimination, figure–ground perception, form constancy, perception of position and direction, spatial relations, visual closure, visuospatial discrimination, and visuospatial working memory, among others. As stated above, the degree to which these constructs may be differentiated and specialized remains largely undetermined.

Several test batteries assessing diverse aspects of visual perception and processing have been published. For example, the test battery created by Marianne Frostig in 1964 and recently revised (Hammill, Pearson, & Voress, 1993) specifically focuses on perceptual development in children. The Test of Visual–Perceptual Skills (Gardner, 1996, 1997) also includes multiple subtests to sample diverse spatial functions during the developmental period. In this section, however, we describe three representative and well-researched tests from the Benton–Iowa neuropsychological battery: Facial Recognition, Judgment of Line Orientation (JLO), and Visual Form Discrimination (Benton, Sivan et al., 1994). All three of these tests involve simultaneous presentation (so as to avoid significant memory demands) of the target stimulus and a multiple choice array of responses, succinct verbal instructions, and pointing as an acceptable nonverbal response. Screening for adequate visual acuity is recommended prior to administration of most measures of visuospatial cognition.

The Facial Recognition test (Benton, Sivan, et al., 1994) assesses the capacity to identify and discriminate photographs of unfamiliar human faces and is available in two forms, a 27-item short form and a 54-item long form. Administered in a spiral bound booklet, the test involves matching of front-view photographs with identical photographs, with three-quarter-view photographs, and with varied front-view photographs under different lighting conditions. Instructions are brief (e.g., "You see this young woman? Show me where she is on this picture."), and the test is normed for ages 6 through adult. Age- and education-corrected norms are provided for adults (Benton, Sivan et al., 1994).

The JLO test taps spatial perception and orientation and is available in two 30-item forms. Administered from a spiral bound booklet, it involves

Table 15.2 Norm-Referenced Nonverbal Measures of Spatial Cognition

Test (source)	Appropriate age range	Distinctive features	Receptive language requirements	Expressive language requirements
Nonmotor Visuospatial Perception				
Developmental Test of Visual Perception (2nd ed.) (Hammill et al., 1993)	4–10 years	Measures include figure ground, copying, visual closure, spatial relations, visual motor speed, position in space, form constancy	Medium	None
Judgment of Line Orientation (Benton, Sivan et al., 1994)	7–70+ years	Perception of direction, orientation, and position	Low	None (pointing permitted)
Kent Visual Perceptual Test (Melamed & Rugle, 1989)	5–90+ years	Discrimination, copy, and immediate memory; includes error analyses	Low	None
Motor-Free Visual Perception Test—Revised (Colarusso & Hammill, 1996; vertical format by Mercier, Hebert, Colarusso, & Hammill, 1997)	4–12 years	Measures include spatial relationships; visual discrimination; figure–ground; visual closure, visual memory	Low across tests	None
NEPSY Arrows Subtest (Korkman et al., 1998)	5–12 years	Perception of position and direction	Low	None
NEPSY Route Finding Subtest (Korkman et al., 1998)	5–12 years	Processing of visual-spatial schematics	Medium	None
Stanford–Binet Paper Folding and Cutting (Thorndike et al., 1986)	12–23 years	Spatial sequencing; mental imaging and manipulation; working memory	High	None
Test of Facial Recognition (Benton, Sivan et al., 1994)	16–74 years	Matching of unfamiliar faces with few feature cues	Low	None
Test of Visual–Perceptual Skills—Revised (Gardner, 1996, 1997)	4–13 years 12–18 years	Measures of visual discrimination, visual memory, visual–spatial relationships, visual form constancy, visual figure–ground, visual closure	Low	None

(Continued)

Table 15.2 (*Continued*)

Test (source)	Appropriate age range	Distinctive features	Receptive language requirements	Expressive language requirements
Visual Form Discrimination (Benton, Sivan et al., 1994)	19–74 years	Matching of simple geometric forms	Low	None
WISC-III PI Block Design Multiple Choice Subtest (Kaplan et al., 1999)	6–16 years	Visual discrimination/matching of block patterns	Low	None
WJ III Spatial Relations Test (Woodcock et al., 2001)	2–90+ years	Integrating shapes in separate pieces	Low	None (pointing permitted)
WRAVMA Matching (Visual–Spatial) Test (Adams & Sheslow, 1995)	3–17 years	Matching of pictures or figures to target or missing piece	Medium	None
Paper and Pencil Perceptual–Motor Integration				
Bender Visual–Motor Gestalt Test (Bender, 1938; Hutt, 1985; Lacks, 1999)	7 to Adult	Copying of simple to complex gestalt figures	Low	None
Benton Visual Retention Test (5th ed.) (Sivan, 1992)	5 to Adult	Administration C; direct copying	Low	None
Developmental Test of Visual–Motor Integration (4th ed., rev.) (Beery, 1997)	3–17 years	Copying of simple to complex figures; includes visual perception and motor coordination supplements	Low	None
Embedded Figures Test (Spreen & Benton, 1969; Spreen & Strauss, 1998)	6–79 years	Figure–ground differentiation	Medium	None

	Age range	Description		
Rey–Osterrieth Complex Figure				
Boston Qualitative Scoring System (Stern et al., 1999)	18–90+ years	Direct copy indices based on configural elements, clusters, and details	High	None
Developmental Scoring System (Waber & Holmes, 1985)	5–14 years	Direct copy indices of organization, style, accuracy	Medium	None
Rey Complex Figure & Recognition Trial (Meyers & Meyers, 1995)	18–89 years	Direct copy index based on Rey's criteria for accuracy and placement	Medium	None
Three-Dimensional or Haptic Perceptual–Motor Integration				
NEPSY Block Construction Subtest (Korkman, Kirk, & Kemp, 1998)	3–12 years	3-D constructional ability from model or picture	Low	None
Stanford–Binet Copying Subtest (Thorndike et al., 1986)	2–13 years	Block construction and design copying on one scale	Low	None
Tactual Performance Test (Reitan & Wolfson, 1985; Spreen & Strauss, 1998)	5 to adult	Time for correct placement for right hand, left hand, and both hands; E is blindfolded	Medium	None
Three-Dimensional Block Construction (Benton, Sivan et al., 1994)	6 to adult	29 blocks varying in size; complex constructions; error scores	Medium	None

Notes: WISC-III PI = Wechsler Intelligence Scale for Children (3rd ed.) as a Process Instrument; WJ III = Woodcock–Johnson III Tests of Cognitive Abilities; WRAVMA = Wide Range Assessment of Visual Motor Ability.

matching of a pair of stimulus lines (appearing at full length for easier items and partial length for more difficult items) to a multiple-choice array of lines (including full-length representations of the correct responses) drawn from a common origin. Instructions are brief ("See these two lines? Which two lines down here are in exactly the same position and point in the same direction as the two lines up here?"). Examinees can respond by either saying the numbers of the line corresponding to the choices or pointing to the correct responses. Successful performance is suggestive of adequate visuospatial perception of direction, orientation, and position. The JLO is normed for ages 7 through adult (Benton, Sivan et al., 1994).

The Visual Form Discrimination test involves discrimination between complex geometric configurations differing in minor characteristics. Administered from a spiral bound booklet, it consists of 16 items in which the examinee is asked to match a multiple element stimulus design with the identical design from four multiple choice options ("See this design? Find it among these four designs."). The multiple choices are designed in such a way that one features a rotation of a major part of the stimulus design, one features a major distortion of the stimulus design, and one features a rotation in a small figure peripheral to the central design elements. Scores on Visual Form Discrimination are reported to be particularly sensitive to right-posterior brain lesions, although performance may be compromised by lesions elsewhere in the brain and a variety of functional deficits (e.g., sustained attention). The Visual Form Discrimination test is normed for ages 19–74, but the majority of adults have near-perfect performance (Benton, Sivan et al., 1994).

Tests of Perceptual–Motor Integration

The assessment of visual–motor integration is most commonly accomplished through paper-and-pencil direct reproduction of figural stimuli, with the leading tests including the Bender–Gestalt Test (Bender, 1938), Developmental Test of Visual–Motor Integration (VMI; Beery, 1997), and the ROCF (Osterrieth, 1944; Rey, 1941) according to published surveys of neuropsychological test usage (Butler, Retzlaff, & Vanderploeg, 1991). There are, however, numerous available tests of visual–motor integration with the leading measures appearing in Table 15.2. Measures of visual–motor integration typically require multiple subprocesses: visual–perceptual patterning, visual–perceptual analysis, fine motor abilities, and the transformation and organization of visual–perceptual analyses into coordinated motor programs. Neuropsychological underpinnings of perceptual–motor tasks are relatively nonspecific, involving activity in the motor cortex contralateral to the preferred hand, a variety of right–hemisphere functions (and, to some extent, the left as well as inter-hemispheric connections), and activity in cerebellar and subcortical nuclei, all thought to be operating in a dynamic, parallel fashion (e.g., Grafton, Mazziotta, Woods, & Phelps, 1992). As the organizational demands in figural reproduction increase (e.g., progressing from reproduction of simple to complex geometric figures), the role of the executive/prefrontal functions becomes more prominent in visual–motor integration.

Although the Bender–Gestalt Test (Bender, 1938) offers the richest theoretical underpinnings with regard to perception, the VMI (Beery, 1997) is the simpler, more structured, and more incrementally graded instrument. The VMI is available in two forms (an 18-item version for ages 3–7 and the full 27-item version for ages 3 to adult) and involves copying of geometric figures with paper and pencil. It is supplemented by two tests, one of visual perception and one of motor coordination, intended to parse out the degree to which these narrower abilities contribute to deficient performance. Instructions for the main visual–motor integration test are minimally verbal ("Make one like that. Make yours right here."), and testing ends after three consecutive no-credit reproductions. Each item may be scored as correct or incorrect, according to one or more criteria. Interscorer reliability appears fully adequate ($r = 0.94$ for the VMI). Developmental trends are depicted in the test manual for rapid visual examination of production quality. Beery (1997) has described the developmental progression of visual–motor integration as follows: "First, there is a focus on wholes (little attention to details) through age three. The focus then shifts to parts at ages four and five, to details by age six, and to integration of well-differentiated parts into wholes about age nine. ... Analysis and synthesis of parts and wholes is probably occurring at all ages" (p. 17). Beery (1997) also reports numerous studies of predictive validity in the identification of preschool and school-age children who are at risk for academic difficulties. The VMI is most useful for young children or impaired older children, but its score ceiling is low (its top range drops below +2 SD at about age 12), and near-perfect performance is usually evidence in early adolescence.

Visual–motor reproduction of complex figures offers an assessment methodology with higher test-score ceilings, as well as the opportunity to more closely examine elements of visuospatial analysis and motor reproduction of basic figures that are spatially integrated. The best known of the complex figures was published by Andre Rey in 1941, although alternative complex figures are available (e.g., Spreen & Strauss, 1998). Assessment with the ROCF usually involves three phases (direct copy, immediate recall, and 20- to 30-min delayed recall). The direct copy phase administration requires placement of the ROCF stimulus in front of the examinee along with pencil and blank paper, with the essential instructions to "Copy this figure as carefully and as accurately as you can." There is some variation in these instructions, depending upon the specific normative and scoring system utilized. There is no time limit. Some ROCF administrative methods involve switching the examinee's writing tools during the production with colored markers to track the sequential development of the drawing, although a graphical flow chart may also be utilized. When the colored markers are utilized, several sentences are typically added to instructions to explain how the examinee will be handed different colored markers during task performance. Once completed, the overall quality of the reproduction may be scored according to Osterrieth's

1944 criteria using norms and scoring elaborations described by Lezak (1995) or Meyers and Meyers (1995). Alternatively, the reproduction may be scored on a number of normed qualitative dimensions (e.g., Stern et al., 1999; Troyer & Wishart, 1997; Waber & Holmes, 1985) such as accuracy, organization, rotation, perseveration, confabulation, and asymmetry.

A third class of perceptual–motor tests involves performance in three dimensions, unlike the paper-and-pencil reproductions we have described in this section. Manipulation of objects in three-dimensional space may be sensitive to neural impairment that is not evident in paper and pencil constructions and reproductions (e.g., Critchley, 1953; De Renzi, 1982). Block-building tasks to reproduce a model appear in several test batteries of early childhood (Elliott, 1990; Korkman et al., 1998; Thorndike, Hagen, & Sattler, 1986), but some more complex tasks of three-dimensional block construction involving blocks of varying sizes and shapes are also available (e.g., Benton, Sivan, et al., 1994).

Memory and New Learning

The study of nonverbal memory and learning processes may be traced to some of the earliest studies of amnesia and formal memory assessment. Ribot (1882), who formulated the *law of regression* (stating that memory for recent events is more susceptible to disruption than older memories), described modality-specific amnesias and loss of memory for symbols. Binet and Simon (1905/1916), in their first intelligence scales at the beginning of the 20th century, included separate procedures to assess retention of visual and verbal material. Their nonverbal memory tests included memory for pictures and drawing designs from memory, both memory assessment procedures that survive to the present day. In his 1915 manual of psychological tests, Whipple noted that tests of memory could be classified according to sensory modality involved (e.g., visual, auditory, visual–auditory) and form of presentation with visual material (simultaneous or successive). Early memory assessment batteries such as those offered by Wells and Martin (1923) and Babcock (1930) usually included at least one nonverbal or performance measure, such as the Knox Cube Test (Knox, 1914), a picture-recognition test, and a design-reproduction test. By the time that Wechsler published his first memory scale, there were over 80 available measures of learning, memory, and association, including eight tests or batteries with emphases on memory for figural, pictorial, or visual stimuli (Hildreth, 1939). Test-usage surveys have shown that for the second half of the 20th century, the most widely utilized memory test battery was the Wechsler Memory Scale (Wechsler, 1945) which contained only one subtest (Visual Reproduction) that could be considered largely nonverbal.

There are several leading theoretical distinctions in the memory literature, tapping differences between memory systems, the nature of the material to be remembered, and the core processes that appear to be most susceptible to clinical disorders. In the following section, we mention a few of these distinctions while acknowledging the fluidity in research that contrasts with the same core elements of clinical assessment that have been in place for decades.

The Verbal and Nonverbal Distinction

The distinction between verbal and nonverbal assessment in contemporary clinical memory assessment is usually credited to Milner (1971, 1975), who demonstrated its utility in understanding the sequelae of unilateral temporal-lobe injuries. Although the significance of lateralized brain injuries to the cerebral hemispheres is not as differentiated with children as with adults, there is substantial evidence of modality and material-specific sequelae in memory functioning among adolescents and adults, with verbal memory impairment commonly associated with left-hemisphere injury and visual–spatial memory impairment associated with right-hemisphere injury (e.g. Bauer, Tobias, & Valenstein, 1993; Warrington, 1984). Most reviews of clinical memory assessment refer to assessment of memory for both verbal and nonverbal material (e.g., Bauer et al., 1993; Delis, 1989; Erickson & Scott, 1977; Larrabee & Crook, 1995; Williams, 1991).

In this distinction, verbal memory tends to refer to performance on measures of new learning of material that is symbolic, meaningful, and conducive to semantic mediation. It may involve processing of material in the auditory sensory modality, although it is clear that material that is visually presented may be verbally mediated. By contrast, nonverbal memory tends to include learning of material that has been variously described as visual, visual–spatial, perceptual, figural, unfamiliar, difficult to verbalize, and difficult to encode verbally (Moye, 1997).

Acquisition versus Retrieval Processes

Acquisition refers to the processes by which new material is initially encoded and transformed into an accessible and storable mental representation; in contrast, retrieval describes the process of bringing stored information into conscious awareness.

Acquisition is typically assessed through the use of immediate recall methods across a single exposure or successive learning trials, with or without interference techniques to affect internal rehearsal strategies. The amount and nature of the material recalled, including memory strategies and errors, may yield evidence regarding the integrity of acquisition processes. Demonstration of an age-appropriate learning curve across learning trials may also provide important information about memory acquisition.

Retrieval processes are typically measured in clinical memory tests through methods involving free recall, cued recall, or recognition. Free recall involves the unaided retrieval of previously acquired material, such as reproduction of figural material (e.g., drawing a design) from memory. Cued recall typically involves retrieval of material with assistance to aid retrieval processes, such as verbal cues ("it includes two crossed flags").

Recognition usually involves multiple-choice or signal-detection paradigms ("Indicate yes or no, if you have seen the design before") in which
greater accuracy than expected by chance is considered to provide evidence of previously acquired learning.

Tests of recall are usually considered to be more clinically sensitive
than tests of recognition (Haist, Shimamura, & Squire, 1992). When free
recall is depressed, but recognition is relatively intact, a problem of memory retrieval processes is suggested, whereas depressed performance on
measures of free recall and recognition suggests that memory acquisition
processes may have been compromised. Impaired free recall with relatively
intact recognition memory has been associated with injury to the frontal
regions of the brain (Shallice, 1988). This finding has been explained as
occurring because free-recall tasks make greater demands on retrieval
operations (i.e., an organized internal search process) that are largely
mediated by the frontally based executive functions (e.g., Shallice, 1988).

Short-Term Memory, Working Memory, and Long-Term Memory

The distinction between short-term and long-term memory may be
traced back as far as James (1890), who coined the expression "primary
memory" to describe awareness of the "specious present" (a span of time
extending for several seconds), as distinct from the storehouse of
"secondary memory ... [which] is the knowledge of a former state of mind
after it has already once dropped from consciousness; or rather it is the
knowledge of an event, or fact, of which meantime we have not been thinking" (pp. 643–648). James's distinction between primary and secondary
memory set the stage for more contemporary distinctions between
immediate/short-term memory and long-term memory. Because of the
imprecise manner in which short-term and long-term memory are differentiated, practitioners have adopted more functional descriptions of memory tests, that is, those that involve immediate recall (more short-term
memory) versus those that involve delayed recall (more long-term memory), and those that involve presentation within normal short-term memory capacity (memory span tasks) and those that are intended to exceed
normal short-term memory capacity (supraspan tasks). Working memory
is a newer concept, just a few decades old, for which the first
generation of clinical measures has just been developed.

In brief, short-term memory usually refers to "a limited capacity store"
involving uninterrupted sequential recall of material immediately after it
is presented (Miller, 1956; Watkins, 1974) and is usually considered to
last from a few seconds to a few minutes. Usually tapped by digit span or
block span tasks, short-term auditory sequential memory tends norma-
tively to be slightly greater than that of immediate visual sequential
memory (Orsini et al., 1987). For simultaneously presented information,
however, short-term span of visual apprehension is comparatively unlim-
ited. Short-term memory typically involves passive, temporary, static,
and superficial processing of material that is mentally activated and
stimulated by sensory input (e.g., seeing and immediately reproducing
a simple sequence of visual–motor actions).

There are two main classes of nonverbal short-term span tasks, both analogs to auditory digit span tasks: the Knox Cubes paradigm (Arthur, 1943; Knox, 1914; Stone & Wright, 1980) and the Corsi Block Tapping paradigm (Corsi, 1972; Milner, 1971). The Knox Cubes approach involves tapping a sequence of four 1-in. (2.5 cm) cubes, placed along a straight line 4 in. (10.1 cm) apart, with another cube. The examinee is to reproduce the sequence, span, and location of the taps. Stone and Wright (1980) have introduced an updated and Rasch-scaled version of this test that extends from age 2 years through the full range of adulthood. A second approach based upon Corsi's (1972) dissertation increases the spatial demands of block span. Corsi attached nine wooden cubes to a small board, with the cubes numbered on the side facing the examiner for ease of presentation and scoring. Sequences from two to eight cubes are tapped by the examiner at the rate of one block per second, at the completion of which the examinee reproduces the spatial sequence of taps. The Corsi blocks are available near to their original three-dimensional form in the WISC-III PI Block Span subtest (Kaplan et al., 1999) and the WMS-III Spatial Span subtest (Wechsler, 1997), with two-dimensional adaptations available in several other measures (e.g., Adams & Sheslow, 1990; Williams, 1991). These measures are all adequately normed, but they likely involve different neural systems of memory than digit span because of their high visual–spatial demands. A third class of nonverbal short-term tasks has recently been introduced, aimed at tapping short-term visual memory while making minimal demands on spatial processing (Della Sala, Gray, Baddeley, & Wilson, 1997; Krikorian, Bartok, & Gay, 1996). These tasks typically involve recognition or simple reproduction of visual patterns, such as marking previously seen segments in a grid or checkerboard pattern.

Working memory has been defined as the capacity to hold information in mind and perform some active manipulation, operation, or transformation; working memory tends to be more active, flexible, dynamic, and predictive of real-life outcome than short-term memory (e.g., Goldman-Rakic, 1995; Richardson et al., 1996). Moreover, working memory can operate in the presence or absence of direct sensory stimulation (e.g., with images, thoughts, and ideas). Working memory has been implicated as an essential aspect of the higher order intellectual functions of language, perception, and logical reasoning (Baddeley, 1986; Baddeley & Hitch, 1974). The emergent role of working memory as a necessary prerequisite for human thinking abilities has been elegantly described by Goldman-Rakic and Friedman (1991): "... the brain's working memory function, i.e., the ability to bring to mind information and hold it 'on line' in the absence of direct stimulation, may be its inherently most flexible mechanism and its evolutionarily most significant achievement. It confers the ability to guide behavior by representations of the outside world rather than by immediate stimulation and thus to base behavior on ideas and thoughts" (p. 73).

Working memory operates "across a range of tasks involving different processing codes and different input modalities" (Baddeley, 1986, p. 35), and dinstinctive auditory–verbal and visual–spatial subsystems have been hypothesized. The visual–spatial subsystem, which we discuss now because of its association with nonverbal abilities, has been termed the *visuospatial sketchpad* but is now simply described as *visuospatial working memory* (Baddeley, 2000). It probably consists of a system that passively stores visual images along with a companion system that maintains, refreshes, or transforms the images. The mental manipulation or transformation of images associated with working memory is thought to be mediated by prefrontal, executive processes. Visuospatial working memory may be disrupted by irrelevant movement or distracting visual stimuli (e.g., patches of color) and can be dissociated into separate visual and spatial components (Baddeley, 2000). Baddeley (1986, p. 109) emphasized spatial over visual processing by defining the visuospatial working memory as "a system especially well-adapted to the storage of spatial information, much as a pad of paper might be used by someone trying for example to work out a geometric puzzle."

There are few nonverbal working memory tasks (but many nonverbal short-term memory tasks) that are suitable for individually administered assessment. We consider the WJ III Planning subtest (Woodcock, McGrew, & Mather, 2001) to provide a reasonably good measure of nonverbal working memory with a significant executive function component. This measure requires the examinee to trace over as much of simple to complex geometric figures as possible without lifting the pencil from the paper (and without drawing over a line). This planning subtest stresses short-term memory capacity (i.e., how many moves ahead can the examinee think?) while requiring active manipulation of response options (i.e., what is the outcome if the examinee selects a given starting point and direction). It may be argued that in addition to short-term memory, planning is an operation of working memory, so some of the other planning tests that are listed above under executive functions may also be of use in working-memory assessment.

Long-term memory refers to effective consolidation, storage, and retrieval of newly learned material over time. In clinical practice, it is usually assessed through recall or recognition following a 20- or 30-min intervening time interval after initial presentation, although the interval may span minutes, hours, days, or longer. It may be distinguished from short-term memory and working memory through its capacity, which exceeds short-term memory span, and its duration, which exceeds the seconds or minutes during which short-term memory processes can remain active. Long-term memory is considered to constitute a relatively permanent memory store from which elements can be retrieved into active mental working space. As conceptualized by Anderson and Bower (1973), "working memory is not structurally separate from long-term memory, but it is the currently active partition of long-term memory" (p. 216).

Implicit versus Explicit Memory

Memory researchers have distinguished between broad classes of memory processes with the growth of cognitive psychology and the neurosciences, and the distinction between implicit memory and explicit memory may subsume many of these classes. Schacter (1992) provided the following definition: "Implicit memory is an unintentional, nonconscious form of retention that can be contrasted with explicit memory, which involves conscious recollection of previous experiences. Explicit memory is typically assessed with recall and recognition tasks that require intentional retrieval of information from a specific prior study episode, whereas implicit memory is assessed with tasks that do not require conscious recollection of specific episodes" (p. 559). Unfortunately, clinical assessment has lagged behind theory, and most clinical memory tests only assess explicit memory.

It is possible to classify other memory distinctions within the implicit–explicit dichotomy. The *procedural–declarative* dichotomy refers to memory processes dedicated to procedural learning and knowing how to perform skills (*implicit memory*), in contrast to declarative knowledge (*explicit memory*) associated with memory for facts, events, and semantic content (Squire, 1987). Procedural learning includes learning on perceptual and motor tasks that are usually not directly accessible to conscious awareness (e.g., the psychomotor aspects of riding a bicycle). The *episodic–semantic* dichotomy (Tulving, 1983) refers to systems governing somewhat more explicit forms of memory. Episodic memory captures memory for experiential spatial–temporal context (where and when), permitting the individual to mentally travel back into their personal past by associating certain memory with a personal context. In contrast, semantic memory represents more general and context-independent knowledge about the world. Semantic memory encompasses information such as facts, concepts, and vocabulary but may also include nonverbal representations of patterns of visual motion and object use (Schacter, Wagner, & Buckner, 2000).

Representative Nonverbal Memory Tests

A number of nonverbal memory measures appear in Table 15.3, and in this section, we discuss some representative tasks. As with many tests in neuropsychology, once a simple assessment paradigm is understood, it facilitates understanding of many tasks utilizing the same basic measurement paradigms.

Measures of recognition memory for meaningful pictorial content constitute a leading way to use nonverbal methods to assess memory. These measures typically involve the exposure of one or more pictured objects (e.g., flowers) for several seconds in sequence or simultaneously, followed by a recognition trial in which the examinee must point to the matching object from several choices, including foils that are members of the same semantic class (e.g., different types of flowers) in order to minimize the benefits of verbal mediational strategies. One of the most ecologically relevant tests of this type is the Wide Range Assessment of Memory and Learning (WRAML) Picture Memory subtest (Adams & Sheslow, 1990). In Picture Memory, the child is shown a pictorial scene for 10 seconds (s) and is instructed to look at all parts and to "Take a picture of it in your mind."

Table 15.3 Norm-Referenced Nonverbal Measures of Memory and Learning

Test (source)	Appropriate age range	Distinctive features	Receptive language requirements	Expressive language requirements
Working Memory/Short-Term Memory				
Knox Cube Test (Arthur, 1943; Knox, 1914; Stone & Wright, 1980)	2–80 years	Four cubes linear layout; forward only	Low	None
MAS Visual Span Subtest (Williams, 1991)	16–74 years	Array of 15 stars including six distractors; forward only	Low	None
Stanford–Binet Bead Memory (Thorndike et al., 1986)	2–23 years	Retention for sequences of beads varying in color and shape	High	None
Visual Patterns Test (Della Sala et al., 1997)	13–90+ years	Visual short-term memory without spatial demands; two parallel forms	Medium	None
WISC-III PI Spatial Span Subtest (Kaplan et al., 1999)	6–16 years	Corsi paradigm; forward and backward	Low	None
WMS-III Spatial Span Subtest (Wechsler, 1997)	16–89 years	Corsi paradigm; forward and backward	Low	None
WRAML Finger Windows Subtest (Adams & Sheslow, 1990)	5–17 years	Card with holes; forward only	Medium	None
Memory for Meaningful Pictorial Content				
Stanford–Binet Memory for Objects (Thorndike et al., 1986)	5–23 years	1-s exposure of increasingly long sequences of common objects; immediate recall	Low	None
WJ III Picture Recognition (Woodcock et al., 2001)	2–90 years	5-s exposure; immediate recall	Low	None (pointing permitted)
WRAML Picture Memory Subtest (Adams & Sheslow, 1990)	5–17 years	10-s exposure; immediate recall	High	None
Memory Reproduction of Abstract Figural Content				
Benton Visual Retention Test (5th ed.) (Sivan, 1992)	8–69 years	Three administrative options varying exposure of recall interval	Medium	None

Test	Age	Description		
Biber Figure Learning Test and BFLT—Extended (Glosser, Goodglass, & Biber, 1989)	40–79 years	3-s exposure each of 10 designs; immediate free recall after each of five learning trials; multiple-choice immediate recognition; 20-min delayed recall and recognition; copy phase	Medium to High across testing	None
Brief Visuospatial Memory Test—Revised (Benedict, 1997)	18–79 years	Visual and spatial memory; 10-s exposure of six figures; three learning trials with 25-min delayed reproduction and recognition/copy conditions	Medium	Recognition only ("Yes" or "No")
CAS Figure Memory Subtest (Naglieri & Das, 1997)	5–17 years	5-s exposure; reproduction as an embedded figure	Low	None
Rey–Osterrieth Complex Figure				
Boston Qualitative Scoring System (Stern et al., 1999)	18–90+ years	Immediate and 20–30-min delay recall; scoring indices include presence and accuracy of configuration, clusters, details	High	None
Developmental Scoring System (Waber & Holmes, 1986)	5–14 years	Immediate and 15–20-min delayed recall; organization, style, and accuracy scores	Low	None
Rey Complex Figure & Recognition Trial (Meyers & Meyers, 1995)	18–89 years	3-min immediate, 30-min delayed, recall; recognition trial; scores based on accuracy and placement	Low	None
TOMAL Manual Imitation Subtest (Reynolds & Bigler, 1994)	5–19 years	Reproduction of series of hand movements	Low	None
WMS-III Visual Reproduction Subtest (Wechsler, 1997)	16–89 years	10-s exposure; immediate recall; 25–35-min delayed recall; copy and recognition conditions	Medium	Recognition only ("Yes" or "No")
WRAML Design Memory Subtest (Adams & Sheslow, 1990)	5–17 years	5-s exposure and 10-s delay; immediate recall only; copy condition	Medium	None
Recognition Memory for Abstract Figural Content				
Continuous Visual Memory Test (Trahan & Larrabee, 1988)	7–80 years	2-s exposure each of seven complex figural stimuli shown many times with distractors; acquisition and 30-min delayed recognition, with a visual discrimination task	High	Recognition ("New" or "Old")

(Continued)

Table 15.3 *(Continued)*

Test (source)	Appropriate age range	Distinctive features	Receptive language requirements	Expressive language requirements
TOMAL Abstract Visual Memory Subtest (Reynolds & Bigler, 1994)	5–19 years	5-s exposure; immediate recognition	Low	None
TOMAL Visual Sequential Memory Subtest (Reynolds & Bigler, 1994)	5–19 years	5-s exposure of series of two to eight meaningless figures	Low	None
Memory for Faces				
CMS Faces (Cohen, 1997)	5–16 years	12 or 16 faces exposed for 2 s each; immediate recognition and 25–35-min delayed recognition	Low	Recognition only ("Yes" or "No")
K-ABC Face Recognition (Kaufman & Kaufman, 1983)	2–4 years	5-s exposure to one or two faces with subsequent recognition from a group photograph	Low	None
NEPSY Memory for Faces Subtest (Korkman et al., 1998)	5–12 years	16 faces exposed for 5 s each; immediate recognition and 30-min delayed recognition	Low	None
TOMAL Facial Memory Subtest (Reynolds & Bigler, 1994)	5–19 years	Seven cards with two to 12 faces exposed for 5–20 s; immediate and 30-min delayed recognition	Low	None
Recognition Memory Test—Faces (Warrington, 1984)	18–70 years	50 faces presented serially with 3-s exposure each; two-choice recognition	High	Acquisition only ("Yes" or "No")

	Age	Description		Recognition only ("Yes" or "No")
WMS-III Faces (Wechsler, 1997)	16–89 years	24 faces exposed for 2 s each; immediate recognition and 25–35-min delayed recognition	Medium	None
Memory for Spatial Location				
CMS Dot Locations (Cohen, 1997)	5–16 years	Immediate memory for location of dots in box through placement of chips	Low	None
CMS Picture Locations (Cohen, 1997)	5–16 years	Immediate memory for location of pictures in box through placement of chips	Medium	None
K-ABC Spatial Memory Subtest (Kaufman & Kaufman, 1983)	5–12 years	Recall locations of one or more pictures	Low	None
Location Learning Test (Bucks, Willison, & Byrne, 2000)	50–80+ years	Recall locations of 10 pictures over five trials; 15-min delayed recall or recognition option	Medium	None
Tactual Performance Test Memory (Reitan & Wolfson, 1985)	8 to Adult	Timed fitting of pieces into Seguin formboard; recall after three trials of forms and locations	Medium	None
TOMAL Memory for Location Subtest (Reynolds & Bigler, 1994)	5–19 years	5-s exposure of dot configuration	Low	None
TOMAL Visual Selective Reminding Test (Reynolds & Bigler, 1994)	5–19 years	Six to eight dot locations learned over eight trials; 30-min delayed recall	Medium	None
WRAML Visual Learning Subtest (Adams & Sheslow, 1990)	5–17 years	Four learning trials; 20–40-min delayed recall	Medium	None

Notes: CAS = Cognitive Assessment System; CMS = Children's Memory Scale; DAS = Differential Ability Scales; K-ABC = Kaufman Assessment Battery for Children; MAS = Memory Assessment Scales; TOMAL = Test of Memory and Learning, WISC-III PI = Wechsler Intelligence Scale for Children (3rd ed.) as a Process Instrument; WJ III = Woodcock-Johnson III Tests of Cognitive Abilities; WMS-III = Wechsler Memory Scale, Third edition; WRAML = Wide Range Assessment of Memory and Learning.

The initial scene is then removed, and a second, similar scene is presented. The child is asked to mark with an "X" all parts of the picture that have been changed or added. Errors on the first scene are corrected. Four pictorial scenes are presented altogether. Scoring consists of one point for each correctly identified element in the four scenes. There is no penalty for guessing, although subjects are encouraged to "Just mark the things you are sure of." The admonition to "take a picture in your mind" encourages visual processing. However, this instruction also interrupts spontaneous learning processes and imposes a suggested mnemonic strategy upon the child. It is difficult to verbally mediate Picture Memory because of the brief exposure. Some automatic verbal processing (i.e., labeling of individual objects in the pictures) likely occurs. The Picture Memory subtest probably has reasonable ecological validity, because it closely resembles the naturalistic problem of scanning the environment rapidly and remembering salient details, or "taking in a situation at a glance." The Family Pictures subtest from the Wechsler Memory Scale (Wechsler, 1997) represents an effort to provide a similarly ecologically valid procedure but requires high amounts of verbal expression during the recall phase, effectively making it inappropriate for nonverbal assessment.

The inclusion of paper-and-pencil constructional tasks requiring immediate and/or delayed recall of figural material is one of the leading methodologies used clinically to assess visual learning and memory (Larrabee & Crook, 1995). Figural reproduction tasks date at least to Binet and Simon (1905/1916; see also Binet & Henri, 1894), in which two designs were each exposed for 10 seconds followed by immediate reproduction. The most widely utilized design reproduction tests are the Benton Visual Retention Test, the ROCF reproduction from memory, and the Wechsler Memory Scale Visual Reproduction subtest (Butler, Retzlaff, & Vanderploeg, 1991; Rey, 1941; Sivan, 1992; Wechsler, 1997). The Benton Visual Retention Test—Fifth Edition (Sivan, 1992) includes the same basic paradigm introduced by Binet, as well as offering several administrative variants. Developed during World War II, when Arthur L. Benton examined adults with penetrating head injuries at the San Diego Naval Hospital, the test requires that the examinee view each design for 10 seconds and immediately reproduce the designs from memory (administration A). Reproductions are scored by an objective system, including the number of errors and types of errors (omissions, distortions, perseverations, misplacements, and size errors). In order to parse out the effects of visuoconstructional ability without memory demands, the examinee may also reproduce each design while the design remains in view (administration C). The inclusion of a direct copy supplemental procedure to a figure-reproduction memory test permits separation of memory impairment from constructional impairment. This has been a historic criticism of visual memory-testing procedures, that is, that they often are confounded by general visuospatial processing ability (Larrabee & Crook, 1995), an observation made a century ago by Binet and Henri (1894). Measures of figure reproduction from memory as a rule should optimally include separate norms for direct copy figure reproduction to differentiate nonverbal memory impairment from visuospatial constructional impairment. Moye (1997) has reviewed the construct validity and clinical utility for a number of measures of figural memory.

Recognition memory tasks for abstract figural stimuli are another leading methodology used clinically to assess nonverbal learning and memory (Larrabee & Crook, 1995). Stimuli usually involve abstract designs or geometric shapes that are either exposed a single time or recurrently in series. The examinee must then choose the identical stimuli from multiple choices on an immediate and delayed basis. An example of such tasks is the Continuous Visual Memory Test (CVMT; Trahan & Larrabee, 1988), which uses complex ambiguous stimuli that are not conducive to verbal mediation in a signal detection paradigm. The test has small expressive language requirements, as the examinees must indicate whether they have seen the stimuli before. Recognition paradigms are especially useful for fine motor-impaired clinical populations.

Memory for faces is considered to constitute an ecologically relevant form of nonverbal memory, although its clinical utility as part of memory assessment has yet to be fully and convincingly demonstrated. We have previously discussed disorders of prosopagnosia, or processing and recognition of faces. A number of clinical tests have adopted procedures tapping memory for newly presented faces as a naturalistic form of nonverbal assessment. The first generation of contemporary tests utilizing memory for faces included the Kaufman Assessment Battery for Children Face Recognition subtest (Kaufman & Kaufman, 1983), the Denman Neuropsychology Memory Scale (Denman, 1987) and the Recognition Memory Test—Faces test (Warrington, 1984). The newest face memory procedures involve simultaneous or sequential presentation of multiple faces and subsequent recognition, using either multiple-choice or signal-detection paradigms. For example, the NEPSY Memory for Faces subtest (Korkman et al., 1998) involves the serial presentation of 16 faces during which the examine is directed to verbally identify the gender of each picture (in order to facilitate attention and encoding processes); immediately afterwards, the child is asked to recognize the pictures from sets of children with similar gender, hair stylings, and ethnic compositions. A 30-min delayed recognition is also utilized. The faces are balanced across races, ethnicities, and gender for reasons of fairness, because of findings that individuals are most effective at recognizing faces from their own racial and ethnic groups.

Memory for spatial location constitutes another aspects of memory often included in clinical memory tests. As we previously reported, Mishkin et al. (1983) provided evidence for two separate cortical visual systems, one specialized for spatial processing. They posit that reintegration of these pathways in the hippocampal formation may enable the learning of particular locations occupied by particular objects. When this concept is translated into clinical practice, it typically involves memory for stimuli placed in specific locations, usually in a spatially organized grid. On the TOMAL Memory for Location subtest for example, the examinee is shown for 5 seconds a set of dots distributed on a page, whereupon the page is removed, and the child is asked to point to the locations of the dots on a grid (Reynolds & Bigler, 1994). The raw score is the number of items correct. Other spatial memory tasks require the placement of chips on a grid, according to the location of the original stimulus (Cohen, 1997).

Another paradigm for memory for spatial location may be found in the WRAML Visual Learning subtest (Adams & Sheslow, 1990), an innovative associative-learning task presented in a list learning format which appears to assess long-term cued recall of figural and spatial material. It consists of a number of colored figural stimuli (12 for younger children and 14 for older children) appearing in specific locations on a board in a four-by-four configuration. The association to be learned is between the specific figural stimulus and the spatial location of the stimulus. The examinee is initially shown the location and identity of the figural stimuli for a period of 1 second each. The figures are covered when not exposed. In the recall task, the subject is shown each of the figures and is asked to specify the spatial location of the figure on the stimulus board. Feedback consists of exposure of the appropriate figure for both correct and incorrect responses. This procedure continues over four learning trials (with corrective feedback on all but the fourth trial), with each of the figures being presented once per trial. The sequence of stimuli changes from one trial to the next. Delayed recall occurs after a 5- to 10-minute interval when an intervening task is administered. The Visual Learning subtest yields a learning curve across trials and thereby can provide a sample of the ability to learn visual associations with the benefits of feedback and practice. A learning curve is demonstrated by improvement in the number of items correctly answered over consecutive presentations through trials 1–4.

SUMMARY AND FUTURE DIRECTIONS

In this chapter, we have described nonverbal measures of special abilities within the neuropsychological domains of attention and executive functions, spatial cognition, and memory and learning. The clinical approaches, applications, and limitations of representative tests within each domain have been described. Nearly 100 norm-referenced tests are listed along with appropriate age ranges, distinctive features, and expressive and receptive language requirements. Clinical indications for nonverbal neuropsychological assessment have been described, as well as the cognitive processes involved in nonverbal assessment.

The vast array of options available to the practitioner wanting to utilize nonverbal tests suggests that the current state of nonverbal neuropsychological assessment is healthy and vibrant. Nearly every important domain of neuropsychological assessment (with the exception of expressive language) includes tests with reduced language requirements, suggesting that in the future, it may be possible to conduct a reasonably comprehensive neuropsychological assessment without requiring that the examinee speak. This prospect has particular benefits for examinees who may otherwise not be served when there are no psychologists who speak their native language or because they have lost expressive language functions.

It may also be argued that enhancing the nonverbal administration of most neuropsychological tests may improve test validity and reduce the construct irrelevant variance introduced by the high language loads of most neuropsychological measures. Excessive instructional verbiage may tax examinee language comprehension and memory, thus unintentionally tapping extraneous neuropsychological constructs. We recommend that test developers routinely abbreviate instructional sets and provide alternative gestural instructions in test manuals. Assessment paradigms need ultimately to target their intended neuropsychological constructs in the truest and most focused manner possible, and sometimes language may constitute an impediment to assessment. Nonverbal testing provides a good solution when, to borrow a phrase, words get in the way.

ACKNOWLEDGMENT. This chapter was supported in part by Grant R215K010121 from the U. S. Department of Education.

REFERENCES

Adams, W., & Sheslow, D. (1990). *Wide range assessment of memory and learning.* Wilmington, DE: Wide Range.

Adams, W., & Sheslow, D. (1995). *Wide range assessment of visual motor ability.* Wilmington, DE: Wide Range.

American Psychiatric Association. (2000). *Diagnostic and statistical manual of mental disorders* (4th ed., Rev.). Washington, DC: Author.

Anderson, J. R., & Bower, G. H. (1973). *Human associative memory.* Washington, DC: Winston.

Army Individual Test Battery. (1944). *Manual of directions and scoring.* Washington, DC: War Department, Adjutant General's Office.

Arthur, G. (1943). *A point scale of performance tests. Clinical manual* (Vol. 1, 2nd ed., Rev.). New York: The Commonwealth Fund.

Babcock, H. (1930). An experiment in the measurement of mental deterioration. *Archives of Psychology, 117,* 1–105.

Baddeley, A. D. (1986). *Working memory.* New York: Oxford University Press.

Baddeley, A. (2000). Short-term and working memory. In E. Tulving & F. I. M. Craik (Eds.), *The Oxford handbook of memory* (pp. 77–92). New York: Oxford University Press.

Baddeley, A. D., & Hitch, G. J. (1974). Working memory. In G. A. Bower (Ed.), *The psychology of learning and motivation* (pp. 47–89). New York: Academic Press.

Ballantyne, A. O., & Sattler, J. M. (1991). Validity and reliability of the Reporter's Test with normally achieving and learning disabled children. *Psychological Assessment, 3,* 60–67.

Barkley, R. A. (1997). Behavioral inhibition, sustained attention, and executive functions constructing a unifying theory of ADHD. *Psychological Bulletin, 121,* 65–94.

Bauer, R. M., Tobias, B., & Valenstein, E. (1993). Amnesic disorders. In K. M. Heilman & E. Valenstein (Eds.), *Clinical neuropsychology* (3rd ed., pp. 523–602). New York: Oxford University Press.

Beery, K. E. (1997). *The Beery–Buktenica developmental test of visual motor integration with supplemental developmental tests of visual perception and motor coordination* (4th ed., Rev.). Parsippany, NJ: Modern Curriculum Press.

Bender, L. A. (1938). *A visual motor Gestalt Test and its clinical use. Research monograph number 3.* New York: American Orthopsychiatric Association.

Benedict, R. H. B. (1997). *Brief visuospatial memory test—Revised.* Odessa, FL: Psychological Assessment Resources.

Benton, A. L. (1945). A visual retention test for clinical use. *Archives of Neurology and Psychology, 59,* 273–291.

Benton, A. L. (1988/2000). Neuropsychology: Past, present, and future. In F. Boller & J. Grafman (Eds.), *Handbook of neuropsychology* (Vol. 1, pp. 3–27). New York: Elsevier Science. Reprinted in Benton, A. L. (2000). Neuropsychology: Past, present, and future. In A. Benton (Ed.), *Exploring the history of neuropsychology: Selected papers* (pp. 3–40). New York: Oxford University Press.

Benton, A. L., Hamsher, K. de S., & Sivan, A. B. (1994). *Multilingual aphasia examination* (3rd ed.). Iowa City, IA: AJA Associates.

Benton, A. L., Sivan, A. B., Hamsher, K. D., Varney, N. R., & Spreen, O. (1994). *Contributions to neuropsychological assessment: A clinical manual* (2nd ed.). New York: Oxford University Press.

Benton, A., & Tranel, D. (1993). Visuoperceptual, visuospatial, and visuoconstructive disorders. In K. M. Heilman & E. Valenstein (Eds.), *Clinical neuropsychology* (3rd ed., pp. 165–213). New York: Oxford University Press.

Binet, A., & Henri, V. (1894). Recherches sur le développement de la mémoire visuelle des enfants [Investigations on the development of visual memory in children]. *Revue philosophique, 37,* 348–350. Translated in R. H. Pollack & M. J. Brenner (Eds.). (1969), *The experimental psychology of Alfred Binet: Selected papers* (pp. 127–129). New York: Springer.

Binet, A., & Simon, T. (1905/1916). *The development of intelligence in children* (E. Kite, Trans.). Baltimore: Williams & Wilkins (Original work published 1905).

Broca, P. (1861). Perte de la parole. Ramollissement chronique et destruction partielle due lobe antérieur gauche du cerveau. *Bulletin de la société d'anthropologie, 2,* 235.

Butler, M., Retzlaff, P. D., & Vanderploeg, R. (1991). Neuropsychological test usage. *Professional psychology: Research & practice, 22,* 510–512.

Camara, W. J., Nathan, J. S., & Puente, A. E. (2000). Psychological test usage: I mplications in professional psychology. *Professional psychology: Research & practice, 31,* 141–154.

Campbell, S. B., Endman, M. W., & Bernfeld, G. (1977). A three-year follow-up of hyperactive preschoolers into elementary school. *Journal of Child Psychology and Psychiatry, 18,* 239–250.

Caplan, D. (1994). Language and the brain. In M. A. Gernsbacher (Ed.), *Handbook of psycholinguistics* (pp. 1023–1053). San Diego, CA: Academic Press.

Carroll, J. B. (1993). *Human cognitive abilities: a survey of factor-analytic studies.* New York: Cambridge University Press.

Channell, R. W., & Peek, M. S. (1989). Four measures of vocabulary ability compared in older preschool children. *Language, Speech, and Hearing Services in schools, 20,* 407–419.

Clark, E. V., & Hecht, B. F. (1983). Comprehension, production, and language acquisition. *Annual Review of Psychology, 34,* 325–349.

Cohen, M. J. (1997). *Children's memory scale.* San Antonio, TX: The Psychological Corporation.

Cohen, M. J., Prather, A., Town, P. & Hynd, G. W. (1990). Neurodevelopmental differences in emotional prosody in normal children and children with left and right temporal lobe epilepsy. *Brain and Language, 38,* 122–134.

Cohen, N. J., Weiss, G., & Minde, K. (1972). Cognitive styles in adolescents previously diagnosed as hyperactives. *Journal of Child Psychology and Psychiatry, 13,* 203–209.

Cohen, R. A. (1993). Attentional control: Subcortical and frontal lobe influences. In R. A. Cohen (Ed.), *The neuropsychology of attention* (pp. 459–482). New York: Plenum Press.

Colarusso, R. P., & Hammill, D. D. (1996). *Motor-free visual perception test—Revised.* Novato, CA: Academic Therapy.

Corina, D. P., Vaid, J., & Bellugi, U. (1992). The linguistic basis of left hemisphere specialization. *Science, 255,* 1258–1260.

Corsi, P. (1972). *Human memory and the medial temporal region of the brain.* Unpublished doctoral dissertation, McGill University, Montreal, Quebec, Canada.

Critchley, M. M. (1953). *The parietal lobes.* London: Arnold.

Culbertson, W. C., & Zillmer, E. A. (1998). The Tower of London-Dx: A standardized approach to assessing executive functioning in children. *Archives of Clinical Neuropsychology, 13,* 285–301.

Delis, D. C. (1989). Neuropsychological assessment of learning and memory. In F. Boller & J. Grafman (Eds.), *Handbook of neuropsychology* (Vol. 3, pp. 3–33). Amsterdam: Elsevier.

Delis, D. C., Kaplan, E., & Kramer, J. H. (2001). *Delis–Kaplan executive function system.* San Antonio, TX: The Psychological Corporation.

Delis, D. C., Kiefner, M. & Fridlund, A. J. (1988). Visuospatial dysfunction following unilateral brain damage: Dissociations in hierarchical and hemispatial analysis. *Journal of Clinical and Experimental Neuropsychology, 10,* 421–431.

Della Sala, S., Gray, C., Baddeley, A., & Wilson, L. (1997). *Visual patterns test: A test of short-term visual recall.* Bury St. Edmunds, UK: Thames Valley Test Company.

Denckla, M. B. (1985). Revised neurological examination for subtle signs. *Psychopharmacology Bulletin, 21,* 733–800, 1111–1124.

Denckla, M. B. (1994). Measurement of executive function. In G. R. Lyon (Ed.), *Frames of reference for the assessment of learning disabilities: New views on measurement issues* (pp. 117–142). Baltimore, MD: Paul H. Brookes.

Denman, S. B. (1987). *Denman neuropsychology memory scale.* Charleston, SC: Denman.

De Renzi, E. (1982). *Disorders of space exploration and cognition.* New York: Wiley.

De Renzi, E. & Vignolo, L. A. (1962). The Token Test: A sensitive test to detect receptive disturbances in aphasics. *Brain, 85,* 665–678.

DiSimoni, F. (1978). *The token test for children.* Hingham, MA: Teaching Resources Corporation.

Douglas, V. I., Barr, R. G., Amin, K., O'Neill, M. E., & Britton, B. G. (1988). Dosage effects and individual responsivity to methylphenidate in attention deficit disorder. *Journal of Child Psychology and Psychiatry, 29,* 453–475.

Drewe, E. A. (1975). Go–no go learning after frontal lobe lesions in humans. *Cortex, 11,* 8–16.

Dunn, L. M., & Dunn, L. M. (1997). *Examiner's manual for the PPVT-III.* Circle Pines, MN: American Guidance Service.

Eliot, J., & Smith, I. M. (1983). *An international directory of spatial tests.* Windsor, UK: NFER-Nelson.

Erickson, R. C. & Scott, M. L. (1977). Clinical memory testing: A review. *Psychological Bulletin, 84,* 1130–1149.

Eslinger, P. J. (1996). Conceptualizing, describing, and measuring components of executive function. In G. R. Lyon & N. A. Krasnegor (Eds.), *Attention, memory, and executive function* (pp. 367–395). Baltimore: Brookes.

Ewert, P. H., & Lambert, J. F. (1932). Part II: The effect of verbal instructions upon the formation of a concept. *Journal of General Psychology, 6,* 400–413.

Finkelnburg, R. (1870/1979). Vortrag in der niederrheinische Gessellschaft der Aerzte. *Berliner klinische wochenschrift, 7,* 449. In Duffy, R., & Liles, B. Z. (1979). Finkelnburg's 1870 lecture on aphasia with commentary. *Journal of Speech and Hearing Disorders, 44,* 156–168.

Franzen, M. D., Robbins, D. E., & Sawicki, R. F. (1989). *Reliability and validity in neuropsychological assessment.* New York: Plenum.

Fraser, C., Bellugi, U., & Brown, R. (1963). Control of grammar in imitation, comprehension, and production. *Journal of Verbal Learning and Verbal Behavior, 2,* 121–135.

Gardner, M. F. (1996). *Test of visual–perceptual skills (non-motor) revised manual.* Burlingame, CA: Psychological and Educational Publications.

Gardner, M. F. (1997). *Test of visual–perceptual skills (non-motor), upper level—Revised.* Burlingame, CA: Psychological and Educational Publications.

Glosser, G., Goodglass, H., & Biber, C. (1989). Assessing visual memory disorders. *Psychological Assessment, 1,* 82–91.

Goldberg, E., Podell, K., Bilder, R., & Jaeger, J. (2001). *Executive control battery (ECB).* Melbourne: PsychPress.

Goldman-Rakic, P. S. (1995). Architecture of the prefrontal cortex and the central executive. In J. Grafman, K. J. Holyoak, & F. Boller (Eds.), *Annals of the New York academy of sciences* (Vol. 769). *Structure and functions of the human prefrontal cortex* (pp. 71–83). New York: New York Academy of Sciences.

Goldman-Rakic, P. S., & Friedman, H. (1991). The circuitry of working memory revealed by anatomy and metabolic imaging. In H. Levin, H. Eisenberg, & A. Benton (Eds.), *Frontal lobe function and dysfunction* (pp. 72–91). New York: Oxford University Press.

Goodglass, H. (1993). *Understanding aphasia.* New York: Academic Press.

Grafton, S. T., Mazziotta, J. C., Woods, R. P., & Phelps, M. E. (1992). Human functional anatomy of visually guided finger movements. *Brain, 115,* 565–587.

Grant, D. A., & Berg, E. A. (1948). A behavioral analysis of degree of reinforcement and ease of shifting to new responses in a Weigl-type card sorting problem. *Journal of Experimental Psychology, 34,* 404–411.

Greenberg, L. M., Kindschi, C. L., & Corman, C. L. (1999). *Test of variables of attention clinical guide.* Los Alamitos, CA: Universal Attention Disorders.

Greenberg, L. M., & Waldman, I. D. (1993). Developmental normative data on the Test of Variables of Attention (T.O.V.A.). *Journal of Child Psychology and Psychiatry, 34,* 1019–1030.

Haist, F., Shimamura, A. P., & Squire, L. R. (1992). On the relationship between recall and recognition memory. *Journal of Experimental Psychology: Learning, Memory, and Cognition, 18,* 691–702.

Halstead, W. C. (1947). *Brain and intelligence.* Chicago: University of Chicago Press.

Hammill, D. D., Pearson, N. A., & Voress, J. K. (1993). *Developmental test of visual perception* (2nd ed.). Austin, TX: PRO-ED.

Head, H. (1926). *Aphasia and kindred disorders of speech.* New York: Macmillan.

Heaton, R. K., Chelune, G. J., Talley, J. L., Kay, G. G., & Curtiss, G. (1993). *Wisconsin card sorting test manual* (Rev. ed.). Odessa, FL: Psychological Assessment Resources.

Heilman, K. M., Watson, R. T., & Valenstein, E. (1993). Neglect and related disorders. In K. M. Heilman & E. Valenstein (Eds.), *Clinical neuropsychology* (3rd ed., pp. 279–336). New York: Oxford University Press.

Hildreth, G. H. (1939). *A bibliography of mental tests and rating scales* (2nd ed.). New York: The Psychological Corporation.

Hopkins, J., Perlman, T., Hechtman, L., & Weiss, G. (1979). Cognitive style in adults originally diagnosed as hyperactives. *Journal of Child Psychology and Psychiatry, 20,* 209–216.

Hutt, M. L. (1985). *The Hutt adaptation of the Bender–Gestalt Test* (4th ed.). New York: Grune & Stratton.

Jackson, J. H. (1915). Reprints of some of Hughlings Jackson's papers on affections of speech. *Brain, 38,* 28–190.

James, W. (1890). *The principles of psychology.* New York: Henry Holt.

Jones-Gotman, M., & Milner, B. (1977). Design fluency: The invention of nonsense drawings after focal cortical lesions. *Neuropsychologia, 15,* 653–674.

Kagan, J. (1965). Reflection-impulsivity and reading ability in primary grade children. *Child Development, 36,* 609–628.

Kagan, J., Rosman, B. L., Day, L., Albert, J., & Phillips, W. (1964). Information processing in the child: Significance of analytic and reflective attitudes. *Psychological Monographs, 78,* Whole No. 578.

Kaplan, E. (1988). A process approach to neuropsychological assessment. In T. Boll & B. K. Bryant (Eds.), *Clinical neuropsychology and brain function: Research, measurement, and practice* (pp. 129–167). Washington, DC: American Psychological Association.

Kaplan, E., Fein, D., Kramer, J., Delis, D., & Morris, R. (1999). *WISC-III as a process instrument manual.* San Antonio, TX: The Psychological Corporation.

Kaufman, A. S., & Kaufman, N. L. (1983). *Kaufman Assessment Battery for Children (K-ABC) administration and scoring manual.* Circle Pines, MN: American Guidance Service.

Knox, H. A. (1914). A scale, based on the work at Ellis Island, for estimating mental defect. *Journal of the American Medical Association, 62,* 741–747.

Koelega, H. S. (1996). Sustained attention. In O. Neumann & A. F. Sanders (Eds.), *Handbook of perception and action* (Vol. 3, pp. 277–331). San Diego, CA: Academic Press.

Korkman, M., Kirk, U., & Kemp, S. (1998). *NEPSY: A developmental neuropsychological assessment.* San Antonio, TX: The Psychological Corporation.

Krikorian, R., & Bartok, J. (1998). Developmental data for the Porteus Maze Test. *The Clinical Neuropsychologist, 12*, 305–310.

Krikorian, R., Bartok, J., & Gay, N. (1994). Tower of London procedure: A standard method and developmental data. *Journal of Clinical & Experimental Neuropsychology, 16*, 840–850.

Krikorian, R., Bartok, J. A., & Gay, N. (1996). Immediate memory capacity for nonsequential information: The configural attention test. *Neuropsychology, 10*, 352–356.

Lacks, P. (1999). *Bender Gestalt screening for brain dysfunction* (2nd ed.). New York: Wiley.

Larrabee, G. J., & Crook, T. H. (1995). Assessment of learning and memory. In R. L. Mapou & J. Spector (Eds.), *Clinical neuropsychological assessment: A cognitive approach* (pp. 185–213). New York: Plenum.

Levin, H. S., Fletcher, J. M., Kufera, J. A., Harward, H., Lilly, M. A., Mendelsohn, D., Bruce, et al. D., & Eisenberg, H. M. (1996). Dimensions of cognition measured by the Tower of London and other cognitive tasks in head-injured children and adolescents. *Developmental Neuropsychology, 12*, 17–34.

Lezak, M. D. (1982). The problem of assessing executive functions. *International Journal of Psychology, 17*, 281–297.

Lezak, M. D. (1995). *Neuropsychological assessment* (3rd ed.). New York: Oxford University Press.

Logan, G. D., & Cowan, W. B. (1984). On the ability to inhibit thought and action: A theory of an act of control. *Psychological Review, 91*, 295–327.

Lohman, D. (1996). Spatial ability and g. In I. Dennis & P. Tapsfield (Eds.), *Human abilities: Their nature and measurement* (pp. 97–116). Hillsdale, NJ: Lawrence Erlbaum.

Luria, A. R. (1966). *Higher cortical functions in man.* New York: Basic Books.

Luria, A. R. (1973). *The working brain: An introduction to neuropsychology.* New York: Basic Books.

Manly, T., Robertson, I. H., Anderson, V., & Nimmo-Smith, I. (1999). *The test of everyday attention for children (TEA-Ch).* Bury St. Edmunds, UK: Thames Valley Test Company.

McCloskey, M., & Macaruso, P. (1995). Representing and using numerical information. *American Psychologist, 50*, 351–363.

Melamed, L. E., & Rugle, L. (1989). Neuropsychological correlates of school achievement in young children: Longitudinal findings with a construct valid perceptual processing instrument. *Journal of Clinical & Experimental Neuropsychology, 11*, 745–762.

Mercier, L., Hebert, R., Colarusso, R. P., & Hamill, D. D. (1997) *Motor-free visual perception test—Vertical format.* Novato, CA: Academic Therapy Publications.

Mesulam, M. M. (1985). *Principles of behavioral neurology.* Philadelphia: Davis.

Meyers, J. E., & Meyers, K. R. (1995). *Rey complex figure and recognition trial.* Odessa, FL: Psychological Assessment Resources.

Milich, R., Hartung, C. M., Martin, C. M., & Haigler, E. D. (1994). Behavioral disinhibition and underlying processes in adolescents with disruptive behavior disorders. In D. K. Routh (Ed.), *Disruptive behavior disorders in childhood: Essays honoring Herbert C. Quay* (pp. 109–138). New York: Plenum.

Miller, G. A. (1956). The magic number seven, plus or minus two: Some limits on our capacity for processing information. *Psychological Review, 63*, 81–93.

Milner, B. (1971). Interhemispheric differences in the localization of psychological processes in man. *British Medical Bulletin, 27*, 272–277.

Milner, B. (1975). Psychological aspects of focal epilepsy and its neurological management. In D. P. Purpura, J. K. Penry, & R. D. Walter (Eds.), *Advances in neurology* (Vol. 8, pp. 299–321). New York: Raven Press.

Mirsky, A. F. (1996). Disorders of attention: A neuropsychological perspective. In G. R. Lyon & N. A. Krasnegor (Eds.), *Attention, memory, and executive function* (pp. 71–95). Baltimore, MD: Brookes.

Mishkin, M., Ungerleider, L. G., & Macko, K. A. (1983). Object vision and spatial vision: Two cortical pathways. *Trends in Neurosciences, 6*, 414–417.

Mitrushina, M. N., Boone, K. B., & D'Elia, L. F. (1999). *Handbook of normative data for neuropsychological assessment.* New York: Oxford University Press.

Moye, J. (1997). Nonverbal memory assessment with designs: Construct validity and clinical utility. *Neuropsychology Review, 7*, 157–170.

Naglieri, J. A., & Das, J. P. (1997). *Das–Naglieri cognitive assessment system interpretive handbook.* Itasca, IL: Riverside.

Navon, D. (1977). Forest before the tree: The precedence of global feature in visual perception. *Cognitive Psychology, 9,* 353–383.

Orsini, A., Grossi, D., Capitani, E., Laiacona, M., Papagno, C., & Vallar, G. (1987). Verbal and spatial immediate memory span: Normative data from 1355 adults and 1112 children. *The Italian Journal of Neurological Sciences, 8,* 539–548.

Osterrieth, P. A. (1944). Le test de copie d'une figure complex: Contribution a l'étude de la perception et de la mémoire. *Archives de Psychologie, 30,* 286–356.

Parasuraman, R. (Ed.). (1998). *The attentive brain.* Cambridge, MA: MIT Press.

Pennington, B. F., & Ozonoff, S. (1996). Executive functions and developmental psychopathology. *Journal of Child Psychology & Psychiatry & Allied Disciplines, 37,* 51–87.

Petrides, M., & Milner, B. (1982). Deficits on subject-ordered tasks after frontal- and temporal-lobe lesions in man. *Neuropsychologia, 20,* 249–262.

Porteus, S. D. (1958). What do the maze tests measure? *Australian Journal of Psychology, 10,* 245–256.

Porteus, S. D. (1959). *The maze test and clinical psychology.* Palo Alto, CA: Pacific Books.

Pribram, K. H. (1973). The primate frontal cortex—executive of the brain. In K. H. Pribram & A. R. Luria (Eds.), *Psychophysiology of the frontal lobes* (pp. 293–314). New York: Academic Press.

Reitan, R. M., & Wolfson, D. (1985). *The Halstead–Reitan neuropsychological test battery.* Tucson, AZ: Neuropsychology Press.

Rey, A. (1941). L'examen psychologique dans les cas d'encephalopathie traumatique. *Archives de Psychologie, 28,* 286–340.

Reynolds, C. R., & Bigler, E. D. (1994). *Test of memory and learning.* Austin, TX: PRO-ED.

Ribot, T. (1882). *Diseases of memory.* New York: Appleton.

Riccio, C. A., Reynolds, C. R., & Lowe, P. A. (2001). Clinical applications of continuous performance tests: Measuring attention and impulsive responding in children and adults. New York: Wiley.

Richardson, J. T. E., Engle, R. W., Hasher, L., Logie, R. H., Stoltzfus, E. R., & Zacks, R. T. (1996). *Working memory and human cognition.* New York: Oxford University Press.

Rosvold, H. E., Mirsky, A. F., Sarason, I., Bransome, E. D., & Beck, L. H. (1956). A continuous performance test of brain damage. *Journal of Consulting Psychology, 20,* 343–350.

Rourke, B. P. (Ed.). (1995). *Syndrome of nonverbal learning disabilities: Neurodevelopmental manifestations.* New York: Guilford.

Ruff, R. (1988). *Ruff figural fluency test.* Odessa, FL: Psychological Assessment Resources.

Salkind, N. J. (1978). Development of norms for the Matching Familiar Figures Test. *Catalog of Selected Documents in Psychology, 8,* MS. 1718 61.

Schachar, R., & Logan, G. (1990). Impulsivity and inhibitory control in normal development and childhood psychopathology. *Developmental Psychology, 26,* 710–720.

Schacter, D. L. (1992). Understanding implicit memory: A cognitive neuroscience approach. *American Psychologist, 47,* 559–569.

Schacter, D. L., Wagner, A. D., & Buckner, R. L. (2000). Memory systems of 1999. In E. Tulving & F. I. M. Craik (Eds.), *The Oxford handbook of memory* (pp. 627–643). New York: Oxford University Press.

Seashore, C. E., Lewis, D., & Saetveit, J. G. (1960). *Seashore measures of musical talents.* New York: The Psychological Corporation.

Semmes, J. (1968). Hemispheric specialization: A possible clue to mechanism. *Neuropsychology, 6,* 11–26.

Sergeant, J. A., Oosterlaan, J., & van der Meere, J. (1999). Information processing and energetic factors in attention-deficit/hyperactivity disorder. In H. C. Quay & A. E. Hogan (Eds.), *Handbook of disruptive behavior disorders* (pp. 75–104). New York: Kluwer Academic/Plenum.

Shallice, T. (1982). Specific impairments of planning. *Philosophical Transactions of the Royal Society of London, Series B: Biological Sciences (London), 298,* 199–209.

Shallice, T. (1988). *From neuropsychology to mental structure.* New York: Cambridge University Press.

Simon, H. A. (1975). The functional equivalence of problem solving skills. *Cognitive Psychology, 7*, 268–288.

Sivan, A. B. (1992). *Benton visual retention test* (5th ed.). San Antonio, TX: The Psychological Corporation.

Smith, A. (1960). Changes in Porteus Maze scores of brain-operated schizophrenics after an eight-year old interval. *Journal of Mental Science, 106*, 967–978.

Spreen, O., & Benton, A. L. (1969). *Neurosensory center comprehensive examination for aphasia.* Victoria, British Columbia: University of Victoria Department of Psychology.

Spreen, O., & Strauss, E. (1998). *A compendium of neuropsychological tests: Administration, norms, and commentary* (2nd ed.). New York: Oxford University Press.

Squire, L. (1987). *Memory and brain.* New York: Oxford University Press.

Stankov, L. (1988). Aging, attention, and intelligence. *Psychology & Aging, 3*, 59–74.

Stern, R. A., Javorsky, D. J., Singer, E. A., Harris, N. G. S., Somerville, J. A., Duke, L. M., Thompson, J. A., & Kaplan, E. (1999). *Boston qualitative scoring system for the Rey–Osterrieth complex figure.* Odessa, FL: Psychological Assessment Resources.

Stone, M. H. & Wright, B. D. (1980). *Knox's cube test.* Chicago: Stoelting.

Stroop, J. R. (1935). Studies of interference in serial verbal reactions. *Journal of Experimental Psychology, 18*, 643–662.

Stuss, D. T., & Benson, D. F. (1986). *The frontal lobes.* New York: Raven Press.

Tannock, R. & Schachar, R. (1996) Executive dysfunction as an underlying mechanism in behavior and language problems in ADHD. In J. H. Beitchman et al. (Eds.), *Language, learning and behavior disorders* (pp. 128–155). Cambridge: Cambridge University Press.

Thorndike, R. L., Hagen, E. P., & Sattler, J. M. (1986). *Stanford–Binet intelligence scale: Fourth edition.* Itasca, IL: Riverside Publishing.

Trahan, D. E., & Larrabee, G. J. (1988). *Continuous visual memory test.* Odessa, FL: Psychological Assessment Resources.

Tranel, D., Anderson, S. W., & Benton, A. L. (1995). Development of the concept of executive function and its relationship to the frontal lobes. In F. Boller & J. Grafman (Eds.), *Handbook of neuropsychology* (Vol. 9, pp. 125–148). Amsterdam: Elsevier.

Trommer, B. L., Hoeppner, J. B., & Zecker, S. G. (1991). The Go–No-Go Test in attention deficit hyperactivity disorder is sensitive to methylphenidate. *Journal of Child Neurology, 6*, S128–S131.

Troyer, A. K., & Wishart, H. A. (1997). A comparison of qualitative scoring systems for the Rey–Osterrieth Complex Figure Test. *The Clinical Neuropsychologist, 11*, 381–390.

Tulving, E. (1983). *Elements of episodic memory.* Oxford: Clarendon Press.

van Zomeren, A. H., & Brouwer, W. H. (1994). *Clinical neuropsychology of attention.* New York: Oxford University Press.

Waber, D. P., & Holmes, J. M. (1985). Assessing children's copy productions of the Rey–Osterrieth Complex Figure. *Journal of Clinical & Experimental Neuropsychology, 7*, 264–280.

Waber, D. P., & Holmes, J. M. (1986). Assessing children's memory productions of the Rey–Osterrieth Complex Figure. *Journal of Clinical & Experimental Neuropsychology, 8*, 563–580.

Warrington, E. K. (1984). *Recognition memory test.* Windsor, UK: NFER-Nelson.

Watkins, M. J. (1974). Concept and measurement of primary memory. *Psychological Bulletin, 81*, 695–711.

Wechsler, D. (1945). A standardized memory scale for clinical use. *Journal of Psychology, 19*, 87–95.

Wechsler, D. (1991). *Wechsler intelligence scale for children* (3rd ed.). San Antonio, TX: The Psychological Corporation.

Wechsler, D. (1997). *Wechsler memory scale—Third edition: Administration and scoring manual.* San Antonio, TX: The Psychological Corporation.

Wells, F. L., & Martin, H. A. (1923). A method of memory examination suitable for psychotic cases. *American Journal of Psychiatry, 3*, 243–257.

Whipple, G. M. (1915/1973). *Manual of mental and physical tests* (Part II, 2nd ed.). New York: Arno Press.

Wilson, B. A., Alderman, N., Burgess, P. W., Emslie, H., & Evans, J. J. (1996). *Behavioral Assessment of the Dysexecutive Syndrome (BADS)*. Bury St. Edmunds, UK: Thames Valley Test Company.

Williams, J. M. (1991). *Memory assessment scales professional manual.* Odessa, FL: Psychological Assessment Resources.

Witkin, H. A. (1971). *Embedded figures test.* Palo Alto, CA: Consulting Psychologists Press.

Woodcock, R. W., McGrew, K. S., & Mather, N. (2001). *Woodcock–Johnson III tests of cognitive abilities.* Itasca, IL: Riverside.

Author Index

Subject Index